The Political Climate for Private Foreign Investment

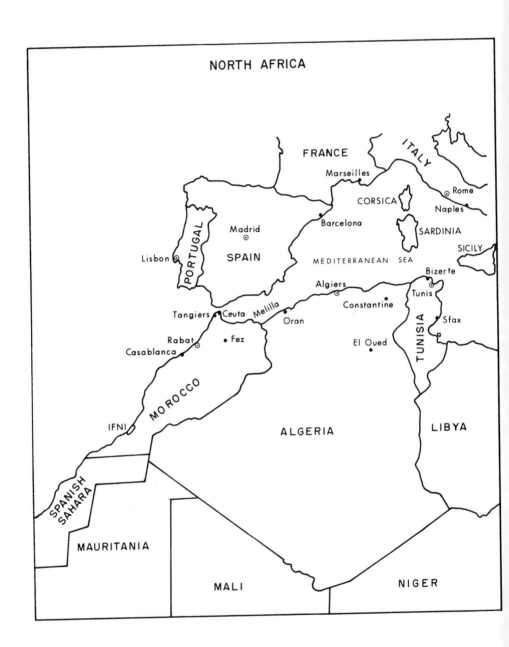

NORTH AFRICA

FRANCE

ITALY

Marseilles

CORSICA

Rome

Naples

PORTUGAL

Madrid

SPAIN

Barcelona

SARDINIA

Lisbon

SICILY

MEDITERRANEAN SEA

Bizerte

Algiers

Tunis

Tangiers Ceuta Melilla

Constantine

Oran

Sfax

Rabat

Fez

TUNISIA

Casablanca

El Oued

MOROCCO

IFNI

ALGERIA

LIBYA

SPANISH SAHARA

MAURITANIA

MALI

NIGER

**PRAEGER SPECIAL STUDIES IN
INTERNATIONAL ECONOMICS AND DEVELOPMENT**

The Political Climate
for Private Foreign
Investment

WITH SPECIAL REFERENCE TO NORTH AFRICA

Lee Charles Nehrt

PRAEGER PUBLISHERS
New York • Washington • London

The purpose of Praeger Special Studies is to make specialized research in U.S. and international economics and politics available to the academic, business, and government communities. For further information, write to the Special Projects Division, Praeger Publishers, Inc., 111 Fourth Avenue, New York, N.Y. 10003.

PRAEGER PUBLISHERS
111 Fourth Avenue, New York, N.Y. 10003, U.S.A.
5, Cromwell Place, London S.W.7, England

Published in the United States of America in 1970
by Praeger Publishers, Inc.

Library of Congress Catalog Card Number: 73-120148

Printed in the United States of America

To my mentor in political economics,

Ahmed Ben Salah

PREFACE

The original research for this book centered on the question of the public-private mix in the industrial sector of the underdeveloped countries and how the specific mix in each came into being. I was aware, at the start, that the relative size of the public sector in the West European economies varied greatly, and that the causes of the growth varied widely from one country to another. It was equally apparent that the relative size of the public sector in the various underdeveloped countries varied even more, and that the causes of this growth (nationalization, expropriation, seizure, direct and indirect government investment, etc.) covered an even greater range than in the developed countries. I was intrigued by the possibility of finding a pattern or a set of determinants to explain the causes of the growth of the public sector in the underdeveloped countries.

The original research on this question was conducted during the summer of 1964 in North Africa and Senegal. The results indicated that far more data were needed. The opportunity to study the problem in depth came when I was invited to go to Tunisia for two years, with the Ford Foundation, to serve as an adviser to the Minister of Planning and Economics. My responsibilities during that two-year period included drafting an investment code and helping to establish an investment promotion center. This brought me into contact with a large number of potential investors, both indigenous and foreign, and also led to conversations with many of the top government officials concerned with the growth of the public sector. This experience added a new dimension to the research problem, namely, the viewpoint of the private investor and the relationship between that viewpoint and the growth of the public sector of the economy. Out of this grew the realization that within the total investment climate of a country is a special portion, which I call the "political climate for private investment;" that the risks associated with it are quite vague in the minds of nearly all potential investors; and that this vagueness leads to fear of the unknown, exaggerates the risk of investing, and

hence acts as a deterrent to private investment, thereby causing the private sector to invest less than anticipated by the
investment plans. The need to develop a model to study this
political climate for private investment became even more
urgent.

The initial step in this book, therefore, is to identify and
define the political climate for private investment and then to
establish a model via which it can be analyzed and which should
be generally applicable for the underdeveloped countries.

The application of this model to Tunisia, Algeria, and
Morocco, in Parts II, III, and IV of this book, is not only a
means of testing the usefulness of the model; it is also an
attempt to fill a void in the literature about the industrialization
process of each of these countries, both during the period of
colonization and since independence.

Finally, Part V (Chapter 15) examines five other countries,
but only in detail sufficient to illustrate the need to apply the
model in order to evaluate the political climate for private
investment.

It should be noted at this point that throughout the book,
all currencies and measures have been converted to dollars,
miles, acres, etc., to facilitate comprehension by the English-
language reader. Currencies have been converted at the exchange rate applicable at the time, so that, for example, if
the value of new investment in Algeria in 1910 was in French
francs, these have been converted into 1910 dollars at the
rate of one dollar to 5.18 French francs.[*]

It should also be stated that all translations are those of
the author, who regrets any errors which may have arisen
in the translation.

There are a great many people to whom I am indebted;
and I regret that most of the key individuals, who were officials
of the governments of Tunisia, Algeria, and Morocco, or
members of the staffs of various embassies in those countries,
have asked to remain anonymous. I do wish, however, to
acknowledge the unfailing moral support of Sir James Hardy;
the helpful substantive comments of Charles Micaud, Richard
Farmer, W. Dickerson Hogue, and Frederick Truitt, each of
whom read parts of the manuscript; and the financial support
of the Advisory Committee on International Studies of Indiana
University, which made possible the original research for
this study.

---

[*]For exchange rates used in text, see "List of
Currency Equivalents."

I wish particularly to express my appreciation to Ardith, Chad, Flip and Dana, who, during the period of Research and writing of this book, accepted with generosity and understanding my absence from the family circle.

Lee Charles Nehrt

CONTENTS

PART I: THE POLITICAL CLIMATE FOR
PRIVATE INVESTMENT

Chapter

xvii

LIST OF TABLES

Page

APPENDIX A

APPENDIX B

xix

LIST OF LISTS

LIST OF MAPS AND FIGURES

xxii

LIST OF ABBREVIATIONS

ALN	Armée de Libération Nationale
AMA	Amis du Manifesto Algérien
BAREM	Bureau Algérien de Recherches et d'Exploitation Minières
BEPI	Bureau d'Études et de Participations Industrielles
BERI	Bureau d'Études et de Réalisations Industrielles
BERIM	Bureau d'Études, de Réalisations et d'Interventions Industrielles et Minières
BMCE	Banque Marocaine pour le Commerce Extérieur
BNA	Banque Nationale Agricole
BNDE	Banque Nationale pour le Développement Économique
BRPM	Bureau de Recherches et de Participations Minières
CAD	Caisse Algérienne de Développement
CAM	Comité d'Action Marocaine
CDG	Caisse de Dépôt et de Gestion
CFM	Compagnie des Chemins de Fer du Maroc
CFT	Compagnie des Chemins de Fer Tunisiens
CGT	Confédération Générale des Travailleurs

CNRA	Conseil National de la Révolution Algérienne
CTET	Compagnie Tunisienne d'Électricité et Transport
FDIC	Front pour la Défense des Institutions Constitutionnelles
FLN	Front de Libération Nationale
GDP	Gross Domestic Product
GNP	Gross National Product
GPRA	Gouvernement Provisoire de la République Algérienne
MP	Mouvement Populaire
OS	Organisation Spéciale
PDC	Parti Démocratique Constitutionnel
PDI	Parti Démocratique de l'Indépendance
PSD	Parti Socialiste Démocratique
SNCFT	Société Nationale des Chemins de Fer Tunisien
SNI	Société Nationale d'Investissement
SONAREM	Société Nationale Algérienne de Recherches et d'Exploitation Minières
STEG	Société Tunisienne d'Électricité et du Gaz
STB	Société Tunisienne de Banque
UGET	Union Générale des Etudiants Tunisiens
UGSCM	Union Générale des Syndicats Confédérés Marocaine

UGTA	Union Générale de Travailleurs Algériens
UGTT	Union Générale des Travailleurs Tunisiens
UMCIA	Union Marocaine de Commerce, Industrie et Artisanat
UMT	Union Marocaine des Travailleurs
UNFP	Union Nationale des Forces Populaires

LIST OF CURRENCY EQUIVALENTS

Algerian Dinar

Pre-Apr. 1964: 1 AF = 1 FF
Apr. 1964: $1 = AD 4.937

French Franc

Pre-1918:	$1 FF = 5.18
1920:	$1 FF = 19.30
1924:	$1 FF = 28.50
1928-34:	$1 FF = 25.51
1937:	$1 FF = 29.50
1939:	$1 FF = 43.83
1945:	$1 FF = 119.
1946:	$1 FF = 186.
1949-57:	$1 FF = 350.
Aug. 1957-Dec. 1958:	$1 FF = 420.
Dec. 1958- Jan. 1960:	$1 FF = 493.70
Jan. 1960-Aug. 1969:	$1 FF = 4.937
Aug. 1969:	$1 FF = 5.559

Moroccan Dirham

Pre-Dec. 1958:	1 MF = 1 FF
Dec. 1958-July 1959:	$1 = MF 420
July 1959-Oct. 1959:	$1 = MF 492.7
Oct. 1959:	$1 = MD 5.06

Tunisian Dinar

Pre-Sept. 1958:	1 TF = 1 FF
Sept. 1958-Sept. 1964:	1 TD = $2.38
Sept. 1964:	1 TD = $1.90

PART   I   THE POLITICAL
CLIMATE FOR
PRIVATE
INVESTMENT

CHAPTER 1   INTRODUCTION

DEFINITIONS

The term "investment climate" has been used by businessmen, government officials, and scholars for many years. It
now has broad, general, and vague meanings which differ, depending upon the individual using it. The subject of this study
is the "political climate" for private investment, which is a
part of the overall investment climate. This term must be
clearly defined to set the limits of this study.

When a manufacturer considers an investment possibility
in a given underdeveloped country, he must be concerned with
the market for his particular product, both short-term and
long-term. In addition, he is concerned with the investment
climate. A company which seeks new sources of raw materials or agricultural products is concerned first with the
availability and costs of extracting or growing these products,
and then must also consider the investment climate. In such
situations, the investment climate for a foreign investor comprises all the aspects of doing business within the country
which will affect the investor's ability to reap a profit, repatriate the profit, and eventually withdraw his capital.

The investment climate, therefore, is made up of a combination of the "economic climate," the "social climate," the
"administrative climate," and the "political climate." The
term "business climate" also is useful and is widely used.
Within this context its meaning is a combination of the "social"
and "administrative" climates, but it also comprises some
aspects of the "economic" climate.

The economic climate consists of two parts. The first
part (Part A in the following figure) relates to the country's
current economic situation and its prospects for future economic growth. To some investors, particularly in the consumer goods industries, this criterion is sufficient in itself.
They feel that if long-term growth prospects are bullish, then

1

FIGURE 1

The Economic Climate

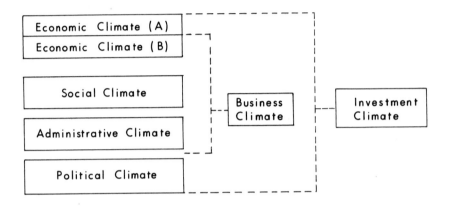

there is a profit to be made, given confidence in the company's managerial ability, because other investors will be
subject to the same business and political climates. The
second part of the economic climate (Part B in the above
figure, classified as belonging also to the business climate)
is the institutional framework for doing business in the country. This would include the availability of marketing channels, transportation, communications, banking facilities,
sources of supply, etc.

Within the social climate one must include the availability
of unskilled and skilled labor and of managerial personnel.
Also to be considered are the existing attitudes toward work,
authority, and material gain, as well as the existence, goals,
and strength of labor unions. The social climate thus includes what has often been referred to as the "labor climate"
but is much broader in content and importance.

The term "administrative climate" is not in common
usage but comprises the most frequent complaints which investors voice when discussing the problems of investing and
doing business in an underdeveloped country. Within the administrative climate are included all of the administrative
actions of government officials which affect business operations. These include exchange controls, import permits,

restrictions on use of foreign personnel, taxation, corruption, and price controls, any of which may be accompanied by administrative delays which may be the result of built-in red tape, the lack of qualified administrators, or both. The "legal climate" is a part of this administrative climate, but the laws themselves are far less important than the society's attitude toward them and the way in which they are administered.

The term "business climate," as noted previously, includes the administrative and social climates, as well as part of the economic climate. If the market potential looks favorable, the prospects for future economic growth look good, and the government is agreeable to the contemplated investment, then what conditions might affect investing and operating within the country? These constitute the "business climate."

Finally we come to the "political climate." It should be made clear at this point that we are not talking about the climate for politics in the country or about the machinations of political parties. The subject is the political climate for private investment. This term is defined as the risk of nationalization or expropriation, the risk of being forced out of business by deliberate government action, the risk of forceful government participation in the capital of a company, and the risk of future direct competition from a publicly owned company. The risk of a revolution or of a change in government which would result in a government with more socialistic or nationalistic tendencies is included within the above definition. Throughout the book, "expropriation" will refer to the compulsory legal transfer of an individual enterprise from private to public ownership; "nationalization" will refer to the compulsory legal transfer of ownership of an entire industry to the public sector.

Governments of all countries of the world follow politico-economic policies which are socialistic to a greater or lesser degree--which provide for public ownership of some of the means of production. The question which must be answered by a study of the political climate is "What is the philosophy of the government of a given country on this point today, and what will the government probably do about it in the future?"

It should be made clear at this point that in the above definition and in future discussion the term "private investment" includes both domestic and foreign private investment. The situation will always arise, of course, where domestic and foreign private investment are treated differently, in which case a differentiation will be made.

OTHERS' VIEWS

As stated above, there has been a confusion in the use of
the term "investment climate" and its various subcategories.
Also, the author has found very little attempt in existing
literature to isolate and study in depth this problem of the
political climate for private investment. The following is a
wide selection of examples showing how various writers have
used these terms and approached the subject of the political
climate for private investment.

In his book Facts and Fallacies in International Business,
John Fayerweather discusses the "investment climate" in
India. Within the term "investment climate" he includes political stability, the meaning of India's "socialistic pattern of
society," selective price controls, and economic planning.[1]

In his earlier book, Management of International Operations, Fayerweather refers to the "economic mix" for foreign
investment, this mix consisting of market size, labor and
management economics, availability of supplies and supporting facilities, competitive conditions, and government policies.[2]
He then refers to the "operating environment" within foreign
countries and divides it into three areas. The first is the area
of governmental control of and interference with management,
the second is the area of governmental assistance and protection, and the third is the political conditions within the country
(this last defined as the risk of Communist take-over, or of
the ascendancy of extreme socialistic or strongly anti-
American political parties).

A. A. Fatouros has noted that underdeveloped countries
receive far less private foreign capital than they need and
that the factors which limit such investment are economic,
legal, social, and psychological.[3] After discussing the economic situation, he then refers to the "investment climate"
as a second obstacle to private foreign investment. He defines
this term as including ". . . all factors affecting foreign investors chiefly in a legal form and neither purely economic
nor purely psychological in character."[4] The term is also
defined as constituting, for foreign investors, "non-business
risks--that is to say, risks far beyond those which the average businessman regards as normal."[5] He then goes on to
discuss the following as the major aspects of this investment
climate: (1) government screening of investments, (2) restrictions on the entry of foreign capital, (3) restrictions on
the employment of aliens, (4) exchange controls, (5) the fear
of expropriations, and (6) the problems of taxation.[6]

A recent study of the business environment of Indonesia by Rossall Johnson, Dale McKeen, and Leon Mears has some of the elements of the political climate for private investment, but very few.[7] It is, rather, a description of the business environment (climate) --the general problems of doing business in the country. In other words, given a set of socio-politico-economic and administrative factors, and given the existence of private enterprise, what problems did the companies have? The study relies heavily on a large number of company case studies and is an interesting approach to the study of the "business climate" as defined earlier.

It is noteworthy that the several pages of this book which deal with Indonesia's attitude toward socialism, private investment, and foreign investment do so under the section "Economic Aspects" rather than under "Political Aspects."

In his Industrial Development, Murray Bryce refers to the investment climate which a government should try to create in order to attract private investment.[8] Within this term he includes (1) guarantees against expropriation, (2) tax incentives, (3) tariff protection, and (4) financial incentives, including low-interest loans and investment subsidies.

In the early 1950's, E. R. Barlow and I. T. Wender carried out a study of the factors which were the major determinants in making decisions on foreign investment, with the aim of defining the role which tax incentives might play in promoting foreign investments.[9] They were, consequently, greatly concerned with the "investment climate" of any given country. They used the term to include government attitudes toward foreign investment, laws and regulations which affect investment, political stability, and economic stability.

One of the most complete studies of the investment climate of a country is a study of India by A. R. Negandhi.[10] It is devoted to private foreign investment and does not include domestic investors. He divides the climate into favorable and unfavorable factors. In the former he includes economic growth and stability, market potential and profitability, socio-political conditions, government attitude toward private foreign investment, and repatriation policies. The unfavorable factors are cumbersome government decision-making apparatus, indecisive policy toward foreign investors, and higher tax rates applied to foreign investors.

As a result of the broad coverage, Negandhi gives little depth to the question of "attitude" toward private foreign investment. Also, the attitude toward private investment per se, by the purpose of the study, is ignored. Thus, the forces and actions which affect the political climate for private investment are only mentioned in passing.

In its study Obstacles and Incentives to Private Foreign Investment, 1962-1964, the National Industrial Conference Board studied the experiences of investors from 12 industrial nations in 88 underdeveloped countries.[11] Referring to the investment climate of these countries, the study identified the following as the major obstacles to foreign private investment: (1) exchange controls, (2) restrictions on foreign companies and persons, (3) import problems, (4) unsatisfactory legal and administrative systems, (5) political uncertainty, (6) labor problems, (7) inflation, (8) unsatisfactory tax conditions, and (9) expropriation and nationalization. Of all these deterrents, only the last belongs within the framework of the political climate for private investment. One subcategory, "alliance with Communist states," listed under "political uncertainty," is an important part of the political climate. The other subcategories listed under "political uncertainty" are basically a part of the administrative climate for private investment, since they determine the difficulty of obtaining government permits and other decisions which affect business operations.

The Board's study's discussion of expropriation and nationalization is basically sound, noting that the fear of expropriation was cited far more often than actual acts of expropriation. Included as subcategories under this obstacle were (1) a government's declaration that it intends to nationalize all industry, (2) a governmental policy of attaining public ownership of certain industries, and (3) uncertainty as to which industries the government may enter. This study also contains a country-by-country review of the obstacles to foreign private investment. The portions on the question of nationalization are, necessarily, quite brief and contain only several representative quotations from industry associations or individual investors regarding governmental policies and actions. These are permeated with vagueness, fears, and doubts rather than specifics.

The American Society of International Law sponsored five studies of the "legal environment for foreign investment," one each in Colombia,[12] India, Japan, Mexico, and Nigeria. The aim of the series was to describe and analyze the legal institutions that affect the participation of foreign capital and technology in economic development and to clarify the factors that impede or facilitate foreign participation. Each study undertakes to indicate how and why laws and policies have

developed as they have in individual countries and their basis
in political attitudes and institutions, social change, and
economic trends.

This series of studies gives much which is of value in
determining the political climate for private investment in
the countries concerned. They tend, however, to deal more
with laws and institutions than with attitudes, actions and results. Nor are they very concerned with the relative movement of the public sector into the sphere of industrial
investment.

Raymond Vernon notes, in the case of Mexico, that if a
foreign investor is investigating the possibility of investing
in Mexico, "his risks will not seem obvious from a reading
of Mexican Law; in fact, on first blush, the law will seem
reassuringly nondiscriminatory in most respects."[13] In
practice, however, the situation is different.

Vernon's description of the development of the current
public-private mix covers most aspects of the political climate for private investment, but the description is implicit
rather than explicit. The emphasis is elsewhere. It is a
comprehensive study rather than an attempt to select those
specific factors which indicate the government's attitude toward the private sector, or to give a historical background
for the evaluation of those factors and thus provide a basis
for evaluating the political climate for private investment.

A study which does deal at length with the general subject of the political climate for private investment is Patterns
of Public Sector in Underdeveloped Economies, by Ignacy
Sachs, Director of the Polish Center of Research on Underdeveloped Economies in Warsaw.[14] It examines the relative
importance of the public and private sectors of the underdeveloped countries, where tendencies and countertendencies
are operating in the midst of a wide variety of socio-economic
institutions and politico-economic policies.

Although much of Sachs' book is devoted to the role which
the public sector can play and has played in the development
of various economies, part of it theoretical and part empirical,
he sets up two models--Japan and India--as approaches to development through different types of use of the public sector.
Emphasis is also given to examination of the public and private sectors in Mexico, Brazil, and Pakistan. Interestingly,
although not intentionally, his study of India is the closest approach to what this author has found as a description of the
political climate for private investment. Most of the elements
are there, though not in great detail and not organized in such
a way as to make evaluation easy.

It is obvious from the above review of the existing literature on the subject of "investment climate" that the term
means different things to different people, and that it has
been broken into a wide variety of subcategories. In addition,
the "political climate for private investment," as defined for
this study, has not been isolated and examined in detail, and
consequently no attempt has been made to understand its
anatomy and measure the risks associated with it.

GOAL AND IMPORTANCE OF THE STUDY

The primary goal of this study is to develop and test a
model by which the political climate for private investment
of a newly independent underdeveloped country can be evaluated. Former colonies have special problems following
political independence. These problems are economic, social, and political in nature and affect the actions of the government, which in turn affect the political climate for private
investment, both domestic and foreign.

According to the experience of the author, the "typical"
investor is aware of the idea of the "political climate for private investment," though he may not call it that. He realizes
that there are risks and, in his way, he sets about evaluating
them in what he feels is a systematic fashion. He stops by
the U.S. embassy or the USAID mission and learns that the
leading political party calls itself (in some way) socialist
(horrors!). He is also bothered (and somewhat confused) to
learn that the government has recently built and is now operating several large factories and that USAID has helped to
finance the construction of some of them. He gets the names
of several U.S. businessmen who have recently invested in
the country and goes to talk with them. Much of the discussion is on the "business climate," but he also learns that the
government expropriated a number of companies some years
ago, although the details and circumstances are vague. The
way to get the straight dope, he feels, is to talk with businessmen who have been operating in the country for many years.
If he is in a country which has recently received its independence, he looks for some former colonialist investors. He
obtains an introduction to several of them and hears a tale of
woe. Things aren't the way they used to be. The government
is taking over everything. Not only have a number of companies been nationalized, but a lot of businessmen have been

forced out of business by the government. The country is
going to the dogs, or to socialism--take your choice.

The investor has, he feels, taken the temperature of the
political climate, and he has found it too hot for his taste.
He decides that it would be very risky, and even foolish, to
invest in a country whose government has engaged in such
activities and has such a reputation.

In 1963 the World Bank, in cooperation with the International Chamber of Commerce, undertook a survey of 400
companies in 21 developed countries to determine what the
investor fears most when considering the possibility of investing in an underdeveloped country. The result was that
61 percent of the companies felt that political risk (defined
in that study as the possibility of governmental action which
would deprive the investor of ownership or would substan-
tially interfere with the control or benefits of the company)
was the main deterrent to investment, while another 30 percent thought that it was one of the principal obstacles.

The problem is that this fear of nationalization or expropriation is usually based on myth and misinformation. For
example, Barlow and Wender found that in 1954 many investors were still shying away from Mexico because they
remembered the nationalization of oil properties in 1938.[15]
They had no clear idea of the extent of the nationalization,
many feeling that it had covered a wide range of industries.
One company which had felt that Mexico would be an advantageous place to invest did not do so because it had heard
that a U.S. company with $14 million invested in Mexico had
recently been expropriated. The authors knew that this was
not true.

In addition to myth and misinformation, the political climate of a country is surrounded by vagueness and uncertainty.
Franklin R. Root did an interesting study which related to the
U.S. investor's attitude toward investment in a given country
to his attitude toward the government of that country.[16] The
attitudinal responses were channeled into five categories:
stability, dynamism, honesty, cooperativeness, and whether
the government was pro- or anti-American. None of these
relates directly to the government's policies vis-à-vis private investment. However, interestingly, one of the major
observations of the study was that there is a high degree of
uncertainty in the minds of executives on these questions.
Yet another conclusion was that every international executive
has images of foreign governments and of the political attitudes of the leaders of those governments, but that such images do not necessarily coincide with reality.

The basic problem in evaluating the political climate for private investment is a lack of mutual understanding. The stated position of the governments of nearly all underdeveloped countries is that private investment (domestic and foreign) is welcome and invited. They claim that their laws and policies are geared toward this goal. Businessmen operating within these countries will claim, however, by recalling certain governmental actions which they have heard about directly or indirectly, that the government is anti-private capital and especially anti-foreign private capital.

It becomes a working hypothesis that the statements of both the businessmen and the host government officials must be discounted by varying amounts, for neither fully understands the viewpoints, constraints, and decision-making framework of the other. The companies are private, seek a profit, and prefer stability, while the government is public, is pursuing development, and must effect change. The government fears that its goals will be thwarted, not necessarily by malice but by conflict of interest. If there is a development plan, the more rigid it is, the more difficult it may be to find a role for private investment which is acceptable to both parties, especially since the development planning may not be simply for development; it may also be to help achieve economic independence--particularly from a former colonial power but also from foreign economic domination per se.

A way must be found to dissipate this mutual misunderstanding. It is important that the potential investor learn, when investigating the political climate, not only what the government did at some time in the past but also why the government took that action--what the circumstances were at the time and what historical events led up to and shaped the government's action.

The author has found that among the newly independent countries, most governmental policies which appear to be anti-private enterprise (or socialistic) and which place dark clouds within the political climate are simply acts of decolonization. To the company affected (the former colonial investor), it does not seem to be a "simple" act at all. It is dastardly, personal, an act of revenge, and a sign of socialism. The investor may feel that the best source of information about a country is the long-time resident businessman. This may be true, but he is also the most biased source. He began operating his business in "the good old days," when the country was run for his benefit. Now things have changed. In almost all cases, they have changed for the worse, for him, since independence.

Even in those underdeveloped countries which have not recently been colonies, many of the residents think of their countries as having been subjected to economic colonialism by the United States or by U.S. companies, and consequently they react in much the same way as citizens of former colonies (or protectorates). They also demand efforts at decolonization. Thus, a long-time U.S. investor in Latin America may be in the same situation as a former colonial investor in Africa or Asia.

These former colonial investors may or may not comprehend the government's need to effect these measures of decolonization, and they may or may not voice such understandings to the potential investor. Thus, it is important that the potential investor learn to distinguish between (1) acts of decolonization, (2) acts which represent a politico-economic philosophy or ideology, and (3) acts which are necessitated by pragmatism--by the need to develop.

Another basic problem is that the governments which have expropriated private companies, forced others out of business, and started publicly owned industries know that such actions serve as a deterrent to further private investment, and hence they try to erase the record. Inquiries regarding such past governmental actions are met with a show of ignorance or with very vague answers. This merely increases the uncertainty of the potential investor. The government's evasiveness regarding such questions does not hide the fact that it once took such actions; it merely means that the potential investor must rely, for his appraisal of the political climate, on rumors and vague memories--usually from highly biased sources.

It is well established that businessmen are not averse to taking risks--that's the name of the game. However, the perceived risk is highly dependent upon the degree of certainty of the inputs of the decision-making process. Consequently, the potential investor is doing himself a disservice if he fails to evaluate the political climate correctly--if he depends upon rumor and hearsay and fails to understand the basis for the seemingly antiprivate enterprise actions of the government.

In addition, the government is failing to act in its own interests if it attempts to hide the facts. No matter how bad the record might be--no matter how many nationalizations and expropriations have taken place, nor how many private companies the government has bought out, nor how many public companies the government has established--it is far better that the government document this and the rationale behind each action, and make this information freely and easily available. Facts are less harmful than rumor. Facts permit an increase in certainty in the decision-making process. Facts, fully understood, result in a more favorable political climate for private investment.

If a government decides that it wants to follow the path of socialism--that it does not wish to have any more private investors, either domestic or foreign--that the private industry which remains will soon be nationalized, the picture is clear and the government will not be able to hide its views from the private sector, both domestic and foreign. But such a situation is extremely rare outside of those countries of Eastern Europe and Asia which are dominated by Communist parties. In almost every other case, the governments want and encourage additional private investment. There usually are limitations on the types of industries in which the private sector may invest and in which foreign investors may invest, but within those limitations the private investment is considered vital to the development of the country. If, however, the private sector does not fulfill the role expected of it--if it fails to invest in those industries which the development plan specifies as needed and as open to private investment, then the government will usually make the investment, if it has the resources available. If it does have the resources and does invest, then potential foreign investors react negatively, interpreting the government investment as a sign of a socialist ideology. Meanwhile, the government finds that the development plan is falling behind because the private sector is failing to play its role. Therefore the government reacts negatively and feels that it must plan more stringently, placing more reliance on the public sector in the next plan. It is a vicious circle which will result in an excess of public investment.

The author believes that the underdeveloped countries can develop most rapidly with a mixed economy. However, the correct mixture of public and private enterprise varies from country to country, depending upon the natural and human resources and upon the level of development. A major problem for the governments of these countries, therefore, is to achieve that correct mixture, which, because of political realities, must also entail an acceptable relationship between domestic investment and foreign investment.

As stated earlier, the primary goal of this study is to develop and test a model by which the political climate for private investment of a former colony can be evaluated.

The utilization of such a model should make it possible for potential investors to improve their evaluation of the entire investment climate by basing it on a more rational approach. It should also illustrate to the top government officials of the underdeveloped countries that their actions and policies project an image which is easily misinterpreted, and that their efforts to encourage private investment will be frustrated unless their actions vis-à-vis the private sector are clearly documented and fully explained. The result should be an increase of private investment in these countries.

The next chapter is devoted to a development of this model of the political climate for private investment. Following it are a series of chapters (Parts II, III, and IV) which test the model on three countries--Tunisia, Algeria, and Morocco. A final chapter (Part V) briefly examines the political climate for private investment in Senegal, Guinea, Ivory Coast, Tanzania, and India, and discusses the general applicability of the model.

NOTES

1. John Fayerweather, Facts and Fallacies in International Business, p. 162.

2. John Fayerweather, Management of International Operations, pp. 495-503.

3. A. A. Fatouros, Government Guarantees to Foreign Investors, pp. 29, 30.

4. Ibid., p. 34.

5. Ibid., p. 37.

6. Ibid., pp. 38-58.

7. Rossall Johnson, Dale McKeen, and Leon Mears, Business Environment in an Emerging Nation.

8. Murray Bryce, Industrial Development, p. 92.

9. E. R. Barlow and Ira T. Wender, Foreign Investment and Taxation, pp. 210-12.

10. Anant R. Negandhi, Private Foreign Investment Climate in India.

11. National Industrial Conference Board, Obstacles and Incentives to Private Foreign Investment, 1962-1964.

12. Seymour Wurfel, Foreign Enterprise in Colombia: Laws and Policies.

13. Raymond Vernon, The Dilemma of Mexico's Development, p. 9.

14. Ignacy Sachs, Patterns of Public Sector in Under-developed Economies.

15. Barlow and Wender, op. cit., pp. 210, 211.

16. Franklin R. Root, "Attitudes of American Executives Toward Foreign Governments and Investment Opportunities."

CHAPTER **2** A MODEL OF THE
POLITICAL CLIMATE
FOR PRIVATE
INVESTMENT

As stated in Chapter 1, the "political" climate for private investment is defined as the risk of nationalization or
expropriation, the risk of being forced out of business by
deliberate government action, the risk of forceful government participation in the capital of a company, and the risk
of future direct competition from a publicly owned company.
Therefore, in the evaluation of the political climate, the laws
of a country are relatively unimportant. The pertinent laws
deal with business operations, and the laws themselves are
not so important as the manner in which they are administered, which is part of the administrative climate or, in a
larger sense, of the business climate. To the extent that the
laws or the constitution deals with the question of nationalization and expropriation, or of government ownership of
means of production, these are almost always recognized as
rights of the government. But whether or not nationalization
or other risks which constitute the political climate will occur, to what extent they will occur, and under what conditions
they will occur are determined by a variety of forces.

What, then, are the tangibles of the political climate
which the potential investor can study and evaluate? What is
the basis for evaluating these tangibles so that the potential
investor can assess the political risk attendant to the contemplated investment?

The elements of the model of the political climate for
private investment are

1. POLICY STATEMENTS of political leaders and the
government

2. ACTIONS of the government, favorable and unfavorable

3. HISTORICAL CONTEXT within which the statements
and actions took place.

The model is very simple. The key to its application is a
systematic study which changes rumors into facts and facts

into understanding. Unfortunately, the potential investor rarely makes sufficient effort and the government officials usually try to foil whatever efforts the investor does make.

POLICY STATEMENTS OF POLITICAL LEADERS AND THE GOVERNMENT

The views of the key individuals in a country are a basic factor in the political climate for private investment. One may attempt to determine their "ideology," but this is a strong term. The use of the term "ideology" usually connotes an attachment to some worldwide economic ideology, such as socialism or capitalism. Rarely are the leaders of the underdeveloped countries committed to one or the other of these ideologies. More often, these individuals have certain personal views on the relative roles of the public and private sectors of the economy. Unfortunately, they feel impelled to attach a label to such views, but great care must be taken not to misinterpret such a label and not to attach too much importance to it.

For example, the term "socialism" is a catchword in many, many developing countries--particularly in Africa. Volumes have been written about African socialism, Middle Eastern socialism, and the socialist political parties in Latin America. This word means different things to different people, and rarely does it mean to the government officials in the underdeveloped countries, what it means to a U.S. businessman. By way of illustration, a U.S. businessman need not feel insulted when his friends call him a capitalist. But when he goes south of the border into Mexico, or into almost any other Latin American country and hears himself referred to as a capitalista, he can tell from the tone of voice that the sense of the meaning has changed.

To the extent that statements and speeches reflect the thinking of the speaker, in whose comments should the potential investor be interested? This must necessarily vary from country to country, depending upon the form and strength of the government, the existence of opposition parties, and the strength of opposition forces. Normally, however, these might include the President, the several key ministers who help determine and administer economic policy, the heads of opposition parties (if such exist), and the leaders of the labor unions (if they have a voice independent of the government).

It is apparent that a political leader can speak out of both sides of his mouth, depending upon the audience. Hence, his pronouncements on the political climate for private invest- ment may differ, depending upon whether he is speaking to the chamber of commerce, to the labor union, to a gathering of the party faithful, or to a reporter from a foreign country which may be a source of aid or investment. Thus, some of what the individual says must be discounted, depending upon the audience. But the fact that the political leader feels im- pelled to skew his comments before a given group indicates that he feels a need to cater to the feelings of that group, and this gives some indication of the strength of that group or audience in the determination of the politico-economic phi- losophy of the government.

Speeches may be biased in one direction or another, but certain documents normally will reflect far more closely the government's views which will determine the political cli- mate. The two key documents for this purpose are develop- ment plans and investment codes. These indicate not only how the private investor is to be treated but also the role that private investment is expected to play in the future growth of the economy.

ACTIONS OF THE GOVERNMENT

However, actions speak louder than words. What has the government of the country in question actually done which seems to indicate a negative attitude toward private enter- prise? And what has the government actually done which shows its desire to encourage private enterprise? What are the facts of the case? Again, a systematic study must be made to build up both sides of the balance, negative and positive.

The significant types of negative governmental actions are nationalizations, expropriations, government take-overs without expropriation, negotiated purchases of private com- panies by the government, establishment of government mo- nopolies in various areas of commerce, establishment of government-owned industries, and reservation of sectors of the economy to public investment.

However, one must look more deeply into some of these actions. For example, were the expropriations truly sei- zures of private property, or cancellations of concessions and licenses, or simply failures to renew the concessions or licenses? If they were expropriations, was compensation promised, was it eventually paid, and was it just? If there were government take-overs of private industry, was the motive political, ideological, or economic? If there were negotiated purchases of private companies (or shares in them), were the former owners under considerable pressure, and was the sale price considered fair by the former owners?

On the positive side, what has the government done to encourage private investment? Such actions would include passing an investment code, signing treaties guaranteeing foreign investments, selling publicly owned companies to the private sector, creation of a stock market, creation of a private development bank, establishment of an investment promotion center, outlawing the Communist party; return of nationalized property to former owners, establishing free-trade zones, repayment by the government of pre-independence debts to foreign private investors, and the creation of a patent office.

Most, though not all, of all the above actions would tend to show that the government is truly attempting to foster private investment and encourage entrepreneurs. In some cases, however, extraneous factors may be the motivating force. For example, the repayment of pre-independence debts may be a quid pro quo for additional foreign aid from the former colonial power. And the signing of treaties guaranteeing investments may be a public relations effort to extract more foreign aid from the Western countries.

Hence, when investigating the governmental actions, both favorable and unfavorable, one must keep in mind that things are not always what they seem to be.

HISTORICAL CONTEXT

The current motivating forces referred to above are relatively obvious. Not so obvious are the internal social and political forces which have their roots in history. The history of most of these underdeveloped countries is dominated by the period of colonialism and a struggle for independence, and this leaves an imprint upon the social and economic structure of the country. This imprint lingers on after political independence. The type and extent of industrialization are usually such that the economy remains highly dependent upon the

former colonial power. Citizens of the former colonial
power, or other non-nationals, have control of much of the
retail trade, most of the wholesale trade, and nearly all of
the import and export trade. The banking system is in the
hands of former colonialists, as is much of the better agricultural land.

Given the above conditions, no government can truly say
that its country is independent. Certain degrees of interdependence are acceptable; others are not. If a government
does not take steps to change this situation, opposition will
soon arise and espouse this popular cause. The answer,
then, is decolonization. This word is the key to understanding most of the acts of the governments of former colonies
(or protectorates) which appeal to be anti-capitalist. The
government must get the key sectors of the economy, mentioned above, into the hands of its own citizens or under its
own control. It must do this for internal political reasons
and, often, to achieve the types of controls it needs to carry
out its development plans.

If the new leader of such a country is strongly private
enterprise-oriented, what possibility does he have of replacing foreign owners and managers with citizens of the
country? This, too, depends upon the historical developments under the former colonial power. Was an indigenous
entrepreneurial class given the chance to develop? Is there
sufficient capital in the hands of private citizens to replace
the foreign capital? How much education was provided for
the "natives" by the former colonial power and, more important, what kind of education? Thus, the social experience
during the colonial period acts as a constraint upon the leaders of the newly independent country. Even if the leader is
a dyed-in-the-wool, 19th-century capitalist, it may be that
decolonization cannot be achieved by substituting a domestic
private sector for the former colonial private sector. The
necessary human and capital resources simply do not exist.
And yet the need to decolonize continues and grows stronger.
What to do? The only answer is that of nationalization and
expropriation, growth of the public sector, and all of those
other measures which frighten potential investors, both foreign and domestic. Only a study of the history of the colonial
period will show the extent to which a newly independent government may have been forced into taking the "anti-capitalist"
steps referred to above in order to achieve economic independence to complement its newly won political independence.
The direction and distance of these steps will vary according

to the type of colonization, the strength of the government,
and the politico-economic philosophy of the leaders.

Regardless of the ideological orientation of a newly independent government, a period of decolonization will take
place. But once a government has passed through this transitional period and achieved its goal of decolonization, its
actions gain more importance as indicators of the future role
of private investment. Unfortunately, the picture is not always clear. Was a significant or predominant role allotted
to the private sector? Did the latter respond? Was a lack
of response followed by a renewed impetus for the public
sector? Or was the lack of response by the private sector
anticipated and used as an excuse by a leftist-oriented government to give additional emphasis to the public sector?

Following the period of decolonization, the situation is
clear in only a few cases. First, if the government says that
it is bent on achieving a socialist economy and that any future
role for private enterprise is limited or non-existent, this
represents a definite position. Second, if the government
begins selling, to the private sector, companies which were
previously nationalized or were established by the government, this also is a clear indicator. Merely announcing that
certain publicly owned companies are for sale is not enough.
This can be a facade accompanied by unacceptable conditions
of sale. A number of actual sales is necessary to show true
intent. Third, the creation of a privately owned investment
bank is a strong indicator; however, governmental administrative discretion can easily negate the operation of such a
bank, so its creation has little meaning. One must wait and
see whether it is given a free hand to invest, and one must
also study the extent of its investments.

The creation of a stock market and a free-trade zone,
the passing of an investment code, and the establishment of
an investment promotion center are all cumulative indicators
of governmental intent, but any one of them may be a facade
which is not intended to be operational.

One other governmental policy may be a clear indicator
of politico-economic philosophy. We have noted that a government may wish to encourage private investment, both
domestic and foreign, but that if this is not forthcoming, the
government may feel that economic growth must be achieved
--that investment must grow--and thus expand its own investment in industry. However, if the government is so strongly
committed to a philosophy of private enterprise that it is willing to wait for the return of confidence of the private sector--

that it is willing to let the economy and the people suffer--one can give credence to its statements of intent. But how long can it wait? Is it strong enough to withstand the popular pressures that such a policy will engender?

This leads us to a final and important variable in the current historical context of the model--the question of social and political stability. A study of the actions and statements of the present and past governments of a country within their historical context will help to predict what the present government will do in the future. However, the firm which is considering investing today is concerned with governmental policies and actions five to 10 or more years in the future. Today's government may not last that long. When the government changes, the transfer may be smooth and constitutional, with the likelihood of a continuation of or only a slight change from today's policies. On the other hand, the change in government may come about through a coup d'état or a revolution. A change of government which is outside of the constitutional framework is more likely to result in a shift of attitude toward private investment, either more or less favorable.

Consequently the potential investor, in assessing the political climate for private investment, must make a judgment as to the probable future changes in government. This is a very complicated question. Some of the elements of the problem are the existence and strength of the opposition leaders and the efforts of the present government to improve the social well-being of the people.

This is a question where the potential investor will probably have to depend upon the judgment of other people who study it continuously. The political officers of each embassy devote most of their efforts to a study of probable future changes in government. Such individuals would be a ready source of information, although the investor still may have to assess the probable attitude of that future government toward private investment in general and toward foreign private investment in particular.

As indicated previously, this model for the study of the political climate for private investment is simple in design. It contains nothing new to the sophisticated investor. It is, rather, a systematic approach to the evaluation of a specific kind of risk. The utilization of the model requires highly subjective judgments. Few of the indicators will be decisive. Its application should, however, cause ignorance to yield to knowledge. An understanding of the facts will avoid excessively high estimates of the risk.

PART **II** TUNISIA

INTRODUCTION TO PART II
TUNISIA TODAY

Tunisia, located between Libya and Algeria and lying just south of Italy, has a population of about 4.5 million and covers an area of 48,000 square miles. Being 475 miles long and about 150 miles wide over much of this length, it resembles the state of Indiana in shape, size, and population. Tunisia also is a land of plains, with half of its area lower than 600 feet and three-fourths lower than 1,200 feet. The good agricultural land is in the northern part of the country, partly because of soil conditions but primarily because of rainfall. The very northwestern corner receives over 40 inches of rain per year; the top third of the country averages 20 inches per year; the central section receives 12 inches in the north and four inches in the south; and the lower third sees less than four inches per year, often having years with no rain whatsoever and being covered almost entirely by the Sahara Desert, with isolated oases.

With 750 miles of Mediterranean coastline, the climate of much of the country is dominated by the sea. However, the mountainous northwest section, bordering on Algeria, has cold winters with appreciable snowfall, and the temperatures in the southern half of the country are determined by the Sahara, although the predominantly northwest winds have a moderating effect in the central region.

The gross national product (GNP) of Tunisia in 1967 was $957 million and had, between 1962 and 1965, been growing at a rate of about 5.5 percent per year. The rate was 6.5 percent in 1965, but poor climatic conditions in 1966 and 1967 caused a poor agricultural harvest and reduced the growth rates to zero, in real terms, each year. Consequently, by 1967 the average per capita income was about $175 per year (about 2.5 times higher than in India). This income is not evenly distributed, however, and a number of people still live at a subsistence level. The government estimates that about 100,000 people are unemployed and another 150,000 are underemployed.

The national budget in 1967 totaled $280 million. Of this
amount, 24.4 percent was spent for education, 9.7 percent for
social welfare programs, and 2.9 percent for military purposes.
This emphasis on investment in education (which has had a
similar share of the budget for many years) resulted in 80 percent of the boys and 42 percent of the girls who reached school
age entering primary school in 1966, whereas the average at
the time of independence, in 1956, was about 33 percent, most
of them boys. As a result of this effort plus a program of
adult education, literacy has now reached a level of 45 percent
of the population.

The economic infrastructure is well advanced. Over 1,200
miles of railroad connect the port cities and most of the major
inland cities with the ports. There are two rail connections
with Algeria, but none with Libya. There are about 7,000 miles
of surfaced roads and 3,600 miles of unsurfaced roads, providing easy access to all cities and villages. There are six
seaports capable of handling ocean-going ships, and two airports. An interconnecting grid provides an adequate supply of
electricity for the major cities. The telephone system is
modern: calls between most of the major cities can now be
dialed automatically, and calls to Algiers, Rome, and Paris
are semi-automatic.

The country's major mineral resources have been phosphates, iron ore, and lead; recent oil discoveries will soon
give petroleum an importance equal to that of phosphates. The
most important agricultural products are olives, citrus fruits,
wine, and alfa grass.

The above mineral and agricultural production is represented in Tunisia's foreign trade. In 1966, olive oil, phosphates,
iron ore, wine, lead, and citrus fruits accounted for 58 percent
of total exports. Still, as industrialization has progressed, the
importance of processed and semi-processed goods in the country's exports has increased rapidly. This is particularly true
of superphosphates, canned fruits and vegetables, and textiles.
Tunisia's imports, on the other hand, are quite diversified.
The major items imported in 1966 were machinery, steel and
steel products, electrical apparatus, vehicles and tractors,
petroleum products, cereal grains, and new cotton. These accounted for 51 percent of total imports.

Tunisia's trade partners have changed significantly in the
past few years, but France still predominates. In 1960, France's
shares of exports and imports were 52 percent and 59 percent,
respectively, while in 1966 these had decreased to 35 percent
and 34 percent, respectively. The other significant movement

has been in Tunisia's trade with the East European countries.
These countries had only 5 percent of Tunisia's exports and 4
percent of her imports in 1960, but these had increased to 14
percent and 12 percent, respectively, by 1966.

In 1967, Tunisia's imports totaled $261 million, while her
exports totaled $149 million. This represented an improve-
ment over 1966, when imports equaled $250 million, while ex-
ports were only $140 million. Tunisia has experienced these
foreign trade deficits every year since 1958. (It has, in fact,
been in deficit each year since World War II, except for 1958,
when it reached equilibrium. Prior to 1959, however, Tunisia
was an integral part of the French Franc Zone and used French
currency.) These annual deficits were partially financed by
using the country's foreign exchange reserves. By 1965 the
net foreign exchange reserves had reached zero.

The major portion of the annual trade deficits were financed
by foreign aid, which has been substantial. (See Appendix A,
Table 1.) Between 1964 and 1968, the United States provided
an average of $45 million per year, and $48 million per year
was received from other sources. This volume of aid is
equivalent to over $20 per person per year. (If India were to
receive foreign aid at the same per capita rate, such aid would
amount to more than $10 billion per year; it currently receives
less than $1 billion.) This level of foreign aid reflects, first
of all, the fact that the United States had chosen Tunisia as one
of the seven countries which was providing a sufficiently high
degree of self-help to qualify for large inputs of foreign aid.
Second, it reflects the confidence of the World Bank, which
organized a consortium of countries to provide aid to Tunisia
and itself allocated $100 million for the years 1965-68, the
period of the last four-year plan. Third, it reflects the astute-
ness of President Bourguiba in maintaining close relations
with the East European countries while at the same time leaning
generally in the direction of the West. This neutrality in international relations, although biased in favor of the West, yielded
a 1966 export market of $20.3 million among the East European
countries, which was 14 percent of total exports. Also, by
June, 1967, Tunisia had received a total of $58 million in bi-
lateral aid from East European countries, compared with a
total of over $800 million from the Western countries.

Tunisia achieved its complete independence from France
in 1956, after a long struggle, which resorted to very little
violence, led primarily by Habib Bourguiba. The binding force
in this struggle for independence was the Neo-Destour party.
The government today is based upon what Clement Moore, in

Tunisia Since Independence, describes as a "permissive, mass-supported, single-party system." This party, while allowing no political opposition, permits differences of opinion and wide-ranging discussion within its own committees and commissions. There are strong party organizations in all parts of the country and at all levels, down to the smallest village. This permits the use of education and persuasion rather than force. It also permits a two-way flow of points of view. The government thus makes every attempt to govern by consensus. This organization, combined with strong party discipline, has resulted in one of the most stable governments in the developing world.

Such a political situation constitutes one of the major factors in the political climate for private investment, but it is only one of the factors. One must also be familiar with the philosophy of the government and the policies which it is following, and particularly the historical basis which generated the philosophy and the policies.

The following chapters constitute an application, to Tunisia, of the model for the evaluation of the political climate for private investment. For a clearer understanding of the statements of the leaders and of the actions of the government, the historical background is presented first, in Chapter 3. The economic, social, and political situations which existed at the time of independence, the manner in which these had developed prior to independence, and their subsequent developments set the stage for the statements and actions discussed in Chapters 4 and 5.

CHAPTER **3** HISTORICAL CONTEXT
OF THE TUNISIAN
POLITICAL CLIMATE
FOR PRIVATE
INVESTMENT

EARLY HISTORY

In North Africa's prehistory, long before the arrival of
the Phoenicians, the area was inhabited by Berbers. The
known history of the area starts with Phoenicians, who began
their penetration in the 12th century B. C. The first important
city was Utica. By the 8th century B. C. they had founded
Carthage (now a residential suburb of Tunis), which soon became the leading city of the Mediterranean basin. Many other
important cities were founded in the area now encompassed by
Tunisia, but Carthage, which reached a population of 800,000,
was without equal. [1] Competition between the Phoenicians and
the growing Roman Empire led to the Punic Wars, which starting in 264 B. C. and ended in 146 B. C. with the destruction of
Carthage and the replacement of the Phoenician civilization by
that of Rome.

Tunisia was first a protectorate, but the territory soon
became a colony, and then a Roman province. This colonization and annexation by Rome brought a renaissance of prosperity; and with its fields of wheat, its vineyards, and its fruit
orchards, Tunisia fulfilled its role of a granary for Rome.
But it was primarily the Romans who prospered. Most of the
land was divided into very large farms which belonged to Roman
aristocrats. Pliny said that at the time he was writing, all of
the farmland of Tunisia belonged to five important Romans.
The Berbers, living in the countryside and the arid regions,
were never integrated; they periodically revolted against Roman
rule and did not participate in the prosperity.

The decline of the Roman Empire led to several centuries
of anarchy in this North African colony. It was not greatly relieved by the rule of the Vandals in the fifth century, nor by

the Byzantine Christians who conquered the area in 533.   Consequently, when the Arabs came from the east in 666, they
met with little resistance.   This Arab occupation quickly removed all vestiges of the old colonial civilizations except for
the structures built of stone.   Christianity disappeared, as
did the Latin language and Roman administrative organization
and education.   Nearly 17 centuries of history were erased.
This historical development is cause for meditation when one
considers the durability of the veneer of French civilization
on the North African countries.

    After several centuries of Arab rule, a new prosperity
arrived.   This was enhanced in the 13th century, under the
rule of the Hafside dynasty, when the Andalusians returned to
North Africa from Spain, bringing with them the technology
and learning of the time.   As a result, civilization was at a
high point in Tunisia at a time when Europe was in the obscur-
ity of the Dark Ages.

    The independence of this kingdom was lost, however,
when the expansion of the Turkish Empire brought about an invasion by the Turks in 1574.   The area remained essentially
a Turkish province until the arrival of the French three centuries later.

ARRIVAL OF THE FRENCH PROTECTORATE

    During the 19th century, Turkish domination was little
felt; the Bey of Tunis exercised essentially complete independence.   In addition, his rule was only nominal outside of the
city of Tunis and its immediate surroundings.   The remainder
of the country was ruled by local tribal leaders; the Bey could
not collect taxes in the countryside.   The economy had greatly
deteriorated, and diseases and emigration had reduced the
population from 5 million in 1828 to 1. 5 million in 1878. [2]   The
government contracted debts in Europe which, by 1870, totaled
$55 million.   With the approbation of the English and the Ger-
mans, and because the greatest percentage of the debt was
owed to them, the French increased their influence in the country.   In 1876, a French railroad company obtained a concession
from the Bey of Tunis to build a railroad from Tunis to the
Algerian border.   This crossed the richest portion of Tunisia
and also placed French troops, in Algeria, in a position to
reach Tunis within several hours.   In 1880, the French consul
wanted a concession to build a railroad from Tunis to Rades,

but the Bey of Tunis was obstinate. A French naval squadron
appeared off La Goulette, and the Bey was given a time limit
in which to make a decision. Under this duress, he gave the
French the right to build a railroad from Tunis to Sousse,
Monastir, and Sfax, as well as from Tunis to Bizerte. In addition, the claims of French citizens to mining concessions
were confirmed. Such claims also gave these French citizens
rights to a large portion of the agricultural land in the country.
Later in the same year, a French company bought nearly 1,000
square miles of rich agricultural land between Tunis and Sousse,
which now constitutes the Enfida Domain. [3]

Diplomatically, the French had prepared to "take over"
Tunisia, and they waited for a good excuse. This appeared in
1881, when a Tunisian tribe crossed the border into Algeria
and killed a number of French civilians and soldiers. One
week later French troops entered Tunisia from Algeria, followed, several days later, by French ships that captured
Bizerte and landed troops, which began a march on Tunis. On
May 12, 1881, the Bey signed the Treaty of Bardo, which established the French protectorate. It was followed, two years
later, by the Treaty of La Marsa, by which France guaranteed
the debts of Tunisia and was authorized to "proceed with such
administrative, judicial, and financial reforms as the French
government might deem useful."

THE FRENCH PROTECTORATE

It is a habit for the newly independent countries to criticize
the colonial powers for having retarded the development of the
country during the period of colonization. (One might disre-
gard the fact that, technically, Tunisia was a protectorate
rather than a colony.) For example, in his book Tunisie
Nouvelle, Salah Tlatli says:

Tunisia, during seventy-five years, saw its economy
systematically crushed and maintained in an infanti-
lism which reduced it to exporting to France, at a
vile price, unprocessed raw materials, to import
in exchange manufactured products at a higher cost
than the world market price. This vassalism prevented the country from advancing beyond the stage
of a primary economy based uniquely on agricultural
and mineral exploitation. French industrialists,
resolute in maintaining their privileged position of an

assured outlet for their factories in their overseas
"hunting preserve, " refused to even think of an industry in North Africa.... Meanwhile, Spain, Italy
and Switzerland were not in a much better position
than we to industrialize, and yet they managed to
do so. [4]

In reality, the French did much to further the development
of Tunisia during the 75 years of the protectorate.

Economic Infrastructure

Considering the extremely low state of the economy in
1880, anything that the French did was bound to be an improvement. The only surfaced road in the country was that from
the Bardo Palace to Tunis and thence to La Goulette, a total
of less than 10 miles. There were no ports and no railroads.
Thus, the entire economic infrastructure, which even by the
time of independence was considerable, was built by the French.

However, since the mines and most of the commerical
agriculture were in the hands of Europeans, mostly French,
this investment in economic infrastructure benefited the
Europeans, not the Tunisians. [5] "The Tunisians were like
guests in their own (modernized) house. " Still, by the time
of independence, the ports of La Goulette, Tunis, Sousse, Sfax,
and Bizerte had been developed; there were 1, 250 miles of
railroad connecting all the port cities, with two lines going
through the interior of the country into Algeria; there were
10, 000 miles of roads, of which 2, 500 were surfaced with
asphalt; a plentiful supply of electricity was available in major
cities; and dams had been built and many deep wells had been
dug for irrigation. [6]

Industrialization

Besides the building of this economic infrastructure, a
fair amount of industrialization did take place, contrary to
Tlatli's statement. Prior to the protectorate, Tunisia was a
country of farmers, artisans, traders, and nomads. The only
industry as such was the lead mine at Djebel Ressas, developed
by an Italian company which received its concession in 1868. [7]
By 1939, however, about 119 relatively large French-owned
companies were functioning in the following sectors: mining,
31; manufacturing, 26; processing, 49; railroads and trucking,
five; ports, docks, and warehouses, eight. [8]

World War II, which interrupted the flow of imports from France, saw the establishment of an additional number of industries, but at the end of the war they could not compete, and many failed. In 1948, the government instituted a program to aid the establishment of new manufacturing and processing companies. The investor could apply for a "letter of guarantee" and a "letter of establishment." The former provided a government guarantee on medium- and long-term loans and thus made it easy to obtain them from commercial banks; the latter provided an exemption from taxes on the new company for a period of up to five years. Between 1948 and 1954, 70 new companies obtained letters of establishment and 24 of these received a letter of guarantee.

In addition, the benefits of the French four-year plans were extended to North Africa. This made funds available to private enterprise through a loan from the French government to the Tunisian government and thence to the investor. During the first four-year plan (1949-52), $11.3 million was thus loaned to private enterprise in Tunisia. If one includes all sources, new private investment between 1947 and 1954 amounted to a total of $162.6 million; this included the creation of new companies and increases of capital of existing companies, and affected a total of 3,907 companies. Of this total, 4 percent went into agriculture, 3 percent into transportation, 5 percent into financial institutions, 11 percent into commerce, and 77 percent into industry.[9] One must realize that a small number of large companies, such as an oil exploration group; a superphosphate plant, and a large cement plant, were responsible for most of the industrial investment. Still, an appreciable effort was also made in such industries as foundries and the manufacture of paper cartons and metal cans.

Appendix A, Table 2, shows the year-by-year status of new private investment for the period 1947-54. The number of new businesses formed gradually decreased over this period, from 403 in 1947 to 315 in 1951 and 170 in 1954.

The same table is also informative insofar as the concentration of these investments. Of the 2,376 new businesses formed, only 203 (less than 10 percent) were sociétés anonymes (corporations); they had a new capital of $21.5 million, which was over 65 percent of the total capital invested in new companies. These totals include both Tunisian and foreign investments, but no breakdown is available as to what percentage was Tunisian-owned. Some interesting insight into the amount of Tunisian-owned industry is available, however, in the 1952 census of companies with more than 50 employees. (See

Appendix A, Table 3.) Of the 254 companies with over 50 employees, 213 were French-owned and only 24 were owned by Tunisians. One also finds that those owned by Tunisians had most of the unskilled and semi-skilled workers, and were in the areas of mining (clay, rock, etc.), construction materials, construction, and transportation.

During the period 1947-54, when $125 million was flowing into private industry, public investment in the economic infrastructure amounted to $390 million, of which 90.3 percent came from the French government and 9.7 percent from Tunisian resources. The majority (65 percent) of this public investment went into energy, communications, transportation, and agriculture. It is noteworthy that only 1.5 percent went into the industrial sector. [10]

Production

As a result of all of this private and public investment in all sectors of the economy, production increased by a fair rate, but very spasmodically. The increase in industrial production was fairly constant, but large variations in agricultural production caused wide swings in GNP and in per capita income. Appendix A, Figure 1, illustrates this point. There was a very significant decline in overall production between 1936 and 1945, and per capita income probably decreased significantly during that decade. However, between 1945 and 1954, production in all sectors increased much more rapidly than population, and this was particularly true of industry.

This rapid growth in industrial production is shown in Appendix A, Table 4. Between 1946 and 1954, such new industries as vegetable oil refining, soap, and glass made their first appearance. Other industries, such as fish canning, cement, superphosphate fertilizer, and lead refining, grew very rapidly; yet others, such as fruit and vegetable canning and construction materials, barely maintained a constant output.

Mining was one of those industries which maintained a more or less constant level of production during the period 1935-55. If 1938 is used as the base year, with an index of 100, we find that production was as low as 75 in 1949, up to 114 in 1952, and back down to 102 in 1954. Phosphate was the most important mineral with a value of $11.3 million in 1956, followed by iron ore ($7.1 million), lead ore ($5.2 million), and zinc ore ($570,000). [11]

Agricultural production, which was approximately 40 percent of GNP in 1954, was dominated by wheat, barley, olives, grapes, citrus fruits, and livestock. [12] The area devoted to wheat grew from 1.10 million acres in 1900 to 2.85 million acres in 1954, while that for barley went from 1.13 million acres in 1900 to 1.79 million acres in 1954. The number of olive trees increased from 7 million in 1881 to 26 million in 1954. The area planted with vineyards grew from essentially zero at the beginning of the protectorate to 90,000 acres in 1954, attaining a production of 20 million gallons of wine in 1954. The number of citrus fruit trees also grew from a relatively small number in 1880 to 350,000 in 1920, 450,000 in 1938, and 1.30 million in 1954.

The export marketing of esparto grass (used to make high-quality paper), which grows wild in the west-central part of the country, was greatly developed during the protectorate, reaching 100,000 tons in the early 1950's; its export value of about $5 million made it one of the leading exports. On the other hand, much of the livestock, which in 1954 was estimated to account for 20 percent of agricultural production, does not even enter the market economy. This agricultural sector grew less, during the protectorate, than any other. In 1954, there were only 3.20 million sheep, 1.90 million goats, and 456,000 cattle--about the same number of each as in 1935.

Foreign Trade

The industrialization policy followed by the French administration in Tunisia naturally had a direct effect upon the foreign trade of the country. In 1949, 98 percent of Tunisia's exports consisted of raw materials and food products; by 1954, this figure was 97 percent. [13] Meanwhile, imports tended to consist primarily of consumable goods. In 1954, for example, 58 percent of imports were consumables, while 7 percent was energy, 21 percent raw materials and semi-processed goods, and only 14 percent machinery. During the several decades prior to independence, Tunisia's foreign trade was in constant deficit. In 1938, for example, exports covered 87 percent of imports. By 1950, this had decreased to 77 percent and in 1954 was 76 percent. [14]

The directions of this trade remained fairly constant over time, with France always very predominant. During the period 1904-13, for example, France bought 47 percent of Tunisia's exports and supplied 55 percent of her imports. In 1938 and

1955, France bought 50 percent and 55 percent, respectively, of Tunisia's exports and supplied 62 percent and 75 percent, respectively, of her imports.[15] Thus, for the half-century preceding independence, France's share of Tunisia's foreign trade continued to increase. The only other trading partner of some importance was the United Kingdom, which took about 15 percent of Tunisia's exports and furnished about 3 percent of her imports.

THE STRUGGLE FOR INDEPENDENCE

The first organized political party, following the protectorate, was the Destour party, founded in 1920. It was made up of many of the older elite, few of whom had benefited from French education. They could mobilize the masses, but they did not attempt to have a mass membership. They were of a conservative nature, and even though they rejected the modernizing influence of the colonial power, they were prone to side with the French rather than with, for example, the new Tunisian trade union movement. Also, they were not imbued with a need to achieve independence from the French. Consequently, there was a vacuum to be filled.

One cannot speak of the struggle for independence in Tunisia without focusing the discussion on its leader, Habib Bourguiba. He began contributing to nationalist newspapers in the late 1920's, after returning from his law studies in France. In 1932 he and several friends began publishing their own newspaper, L'Action Tunisienne. This same group of friends then became the nucleus of the Neo-Destour party. This party was made up of a new elite, mostly French-educated. They were not tradition-bound; they were happy to have Tunisia benefit as much as possible from Western civilization, but at the same time they sought freedom from French rule and resorted to mass membership to build up a truly national party.

Bourguiba and his friends were thrown into jail by the French authorities in 1934, and he spent 10 out of the next 20 years in French prisons, serving three different terms. Each time he was released, however, he would again join in the struggle for independence. This struggle was never to become an open, armed revolt with pitched battles. It was, rather, a combination of armed, individual terrorism plus mass protests which were broken up by French gunfire. The result was a fair number of killings on both sides plus martial law, illegal arrests, and, between 1952 and 1955, hundreds of Tunisians being kept in concentration camps.

The effort of the Neo-Destour party was greatly aided by the labor movement. One of the heroes of the Neo-Destour, Farhat Hached, was also a labor union leader during the early 1940's. However, the only organized labor union was the Confederation Générale des Travailleurs (CGT), a branch of the Communist-dominated French labor union. Farhat Hached split a large number of workers off from this union in 1946 and formed the Union Générale des Travailleurs Tunisiens (UGTT). Thus, strikes and protest marches could be more easily organized by the Neo-Destour leaders.

Bourguiba, when not in jail, was either engaged in clandestine meetings, organizing new moves in the struggle for independence, or on trips abroad, attempting to stir up international support for the Tunisian cause. An increase in the level of terrorism after 1952, resulting in an increase in reprisals and arrests by the French, moved world opinion against the French. The loss of Indochina was, therefore, quickly followed by a desire, by such French premiers as Mendès-France and Faure, to avoid the same type of departure from North Africa. They consequently entered into negotiations to give Tunisia its independence.

The 1955 conventions gave Tunisia self-government, but France maintained responsibility for defense and security. The Bey, who had been put into office by the French, continued as the official ruler; but Bourguiba, as head of the Neo-Destour party, was already the real power of the country.

The party continued to put pressure on France for complete independence, and this was achieved on March 20, 1956. Although Tunisia now had its own army and responsibility for defense and security, the treaty still permitted the continuation of a French military presence in Bizerte and several other bases.

SITUATION AT THE TIME OF INDEPENDENCE

Population

By the time of independence, the foreign population in Tunisia had undergone a significant change. For example, in 1881, when the protectorate started, there were 18,914 Europeans, of whom only 708 were French (the rest were

mostly Italians and Maltese).[16] By 1891, the number of
Italians had increased to 38,000 and the French had increased
to 18,000, of whom 5,000 were merchants, 3,000 were government officials, and 3,000 were in agriculture.[17] In 1936, there
were 108,068 Frenchmen, 94,289 Italians, and 10,848 Maltese
and other foreigners.[18]

In 1956, just prior to independence, the population consisted
of 3,383,944 Tunisian Moslems, 66,845 Algerian Moslems,
19,304 other Moslems, 57,792 Jews, 180,440 French, 66,910
Italians, and 7,974 other Europeans, a total of 3,783,169.[19]

Between 1936 and 1956, the number of French had increased
by about 75 percent, while the number of Italians and other
Europeans had decreased about 30 percent. It should be noted,
however, that most of the decrease in the number of Italians
and other Europeans was a result of their obtaining French
citizenship.

Education

Of the 3,383,944 Tunisian Moslems in 1956, 840,000 were
of primary school age (6-14), yet only 224,000 (27 percent)
were actually attending school. Even this proportion was of
recent origin. In 1950, only 15 percent were in school; in
1940, 7 percent; in 1925, 5 percent; and in 1920, 3 percent.[20]
In addition, only 1 out of 27 Moslems who entered primary
school went on to secondary school. (There were 6,474
Tunisian boys and 872 girls in secondary school in 1956.) The
number who entered higher education was even less, totaling
only 812 in 1956. (The same year, the 254,000 Europeans
and 57,000 Jews who lived in Tunisia had 1,062 students in
higher education.)[21] The result was that only 20 percent of
the population was literate at the time of independence.

Land Distribution

One of the major problems in 1956, remaining from the
time of colonization (the period of the protectorate), was the
proportion of the good land which was owned by the Europeans.
There is a total of about 30 million acres of land in Tunisia,
of which about 7.5 million can be cultivated, 8.75 million is
used for grazing, and 1.75 million is devoted to olive, date,
citrus, and other fruit trees. Of this useful land, Frenchmen
owned about 1.5 million acres, Italians held 125,000, and anothe

50, 000 was in the hands of other foreigners. [22]   The 1.5 million
acres of French-owned land was divided among only 2,000
owners (the 125,000 acres of Italian-owned land was divided
among 2,100 owners).   In fact, four companies owned 23 percent of all of the French-owned land.

Employment and Income Distribution

In 1956, the Italian community was made up mostly of
small farmers, artisans, and skilled workers. Of the 180,000
Frenchmen, 62,500 were active. Of these, about 40,000 were
managers in industry, commerce, or agriculture, or were
lawyers or doctors. In addition, 15,000 were civil servants,
of whom 10,000 worked for the Tunisian government. [23]

Because of the low level of education, few Tunisians could
qualify for entry into the modern economy. Most of them were
agricultural workers, many on a part-time basis. Many others
were small farmers. Some qualified as skilled workers in industry, but most of those in the modern sector were unskilled
workers. Very few, as noted in Appendix A, Table 3, became
owners of industries. They were, however, quite strong in
the artisan trades, in keeping with their tradition. Consequently, at the time of independence, there were about 23,000 "artisan shops," of which about 8,800 were in textiles, 4,800 in
clothing, 2,200 in leather and shoes, 3,300 in wood, 1,800 in
construction, 550 in arts or crafts, and 1,700 in miscellaneous
categories. These provided work for about 90,000 people. In
addition, there were about 35,000 people engaged in artisan
trades in their own homes. [24]

Still, the overall effect of the education levels and the
social structure was such that many Tunisians simply could
not find jobs. In 1956, out of an active Moslem population of
1.06 million, approximately 300,000 were unemployed. [25]
Of these, probably one-third were completely unemployed and
the remainder, while living on the land, were so underemployed
as to be actually unemployed.

Consequently, the income distribution of the country was
highly skewed. Of the 3,383,944 Tunisians, only 14,239 paid
taxes in 1954, whereas among the 254,000 Europeans, 39,702
paid taxes. Appendix A, Table 5, shows the distribution of
income in each of these two groups. It also gives an interesting
breakdown of the professions of the taxpayers in each group.
Of the 14,239 Tunisians who paid taxes, over 10,000 had annual
incomes of less than $1,430. Only 1,020 had incomes greater

than \$2,850. As a result, the average per capita income of Tunisians in 1956 was \$149. [26]

Industrialization

It is true that Tunisian industry may have been underdeveloped at the time of independence, but between 1881 and 1956 it had made significant progress. Appendix A, Table 6, shows the number of industrial companies in existence in 1954, broken down by whether they were located at Tunis or elsewhere, and by whether they employed more or fewer than 50 workers.

We see from this table that there were 8,392 industrial enterprises, of which approximately half were in the region of Tunis and of which only 220 had more than 50 employees. It must be noted, however, that a very high percentage of the 8,000 companies with fewer than 50 workers probably had fewer than five. For example, many of the companies listed under the category "clothing" consisted of a shop with two or three sewing machines. Also, the term "industrial" does not necessarily mean "manufacturing." Thus, most of the companies in the category "mechanical and electrical" were repair shops. Also, included under "food products" were the many small bakeries, and under "construction and public works" were hundreds of small contractors. Table 6 does not show the relative unimportance of the industrial sector of the economy. At the time of independence, industry accounted for only 9 percent of the active population, while the tertiary sector (trade, transport, and services) accounted for 23 percent.

Foreign Trade

As we have seen, at the time of Tunisia's independence 97 percent of her exports were raw materials and food products, whereas 58 percent of her imports were consumable goods and only 14 percent of her imports were machinery. This low percentage of imports devoted to investment, of which a large portion was going to the economic infrastructure, could not result in a rapid industrialization of the country. This composition of exports and imports also resulted in a continual, large deficit in the balance of trade, which was compensated for by French "foreign aid" plus the expenditures of the French government for maintaining a military presence and a large administrative establishment.

France's predominance in Tunisia's foreign trade resulted
from a number of factors. Tunisian government imports were
influenced by French administrators. The major industries
which imported equipment and raw materials were owned by
Frenchmen. Most of the exporters and the importer-whole-
salers were of French nationality. Many of the retail shops
which sold imported goods were owned by Frenchmen or by
Jews, many of whom held French passports. The tariff union
permitted a free exchange of products between the two countries. And, finally, the French government subsidized the
import price of some of Tunisia's exports. Thus, by 1955,
France provided 75 percent of Tunisia's imports and bought
55 percent of her exports. From this exchange, France and
Frenchmen benefited the most. For example, in 1955, of
the total exports, 41 percent was made up of minerals, all of
which came from French-owned companies. If one adds the
portion of agricultural exports which came from French-owned
lands, it is estimated that the proceeds of two-thirds of
Tunisia's exports went directly to Frenchmen. [27] In the other
direction, one example which might be taken is the shoe industry. In 1956, Tunisia exported $1.2 million of raw hides and
imported $2.0 million of shoes--of which $1.9 million came
from France. [28]

Banking and Finance

The first bank to open an office in Tunisia was the Banque
d'Algérie, in 1904. As the economy progressed, additional
banks arrived, so that by the time of independence, there were
14 banks in Tunisia, none of them owned by Tunisians. Of
these, eight were branches of French banks and five were
subsidiaries of French banks. One of these subsidiaries, the
Banque de l'Algérie et de la Tunisie, served as the bank of
issue. Since the parent bank, in France, had been nationalized
after World War II, the French government directly controlled
Tunisia's money supply. This control continued after independence, in accordance with the agreements by which Tunisia
achieved independence.

Also, in 1891, the pre-protectorate Tunisian money, the
piastre, had been changed to the Tunisian franc, which was
fixed at parity with the French franc. This also continued
after independence. Thus, Tunisia could not practice a separate
monetary policy. It was monetarily annexed to France. The
various devaluations of the French franc after World War II

resulted in automatic devaluations of the Tunisian franc. Thus, when the French devalued their currency in 1957, the Tunisian franc was likewise automatically devalued. (This was particularly irritating to the Tunisians, who felt that the devaluation was caused by French expenditures on the Algerian war and that the forced devaluation of the Tunisian franc was, in effect, support of the French cause by Tunisia.)

Finally, there was a complete liberty of transfer between Tunisia and France. Thus, there was no way that the Tunisian government could prevent the flight of capital or restrict trade with France.

THE PRE-PLANNING ERA

Tunisia received its independence on March 20, 1956, but, as noted above, it was a political independence. The Tunisian government was sovereign on its own territory and in its international (political) relations, but the economy was still tied to France. Much of the good land belonged to Frenchmen; a majority of the industrial enterprises, particularly mining and the larger companies, belonged to Frenchmen living in Tunisia or were branches or subsidiaries of companies in France; most of the export products were produced by French companies or farmers; most of the foreign trade was handled by French importers and exporters; a large majority of the foreign trade was with France; the money and the monetary system were controlled by French governmental policy; and the independence agreements permitted French troops to be based in several parts of the country and permitted the French to maintain a powerful military base in Bizerte. Each of these factors was going to be a cause of irritation until it was removed.

In October, 1956, the French seized a plane carrying Ahmed Ben Bella, the exiled leader of the Algerian revolution, who was en route to Tunis for a meeting. The Tunisians reacted by blocking the movement of French troops throughout the country. Incidents with the French troops resulted in 14 people being killed. Tunisia began to assist the Algerian revolution in an open manner and France reacted, in May, 1957, by cutting off foreign aid. Border incidents continued, with raids against the French in Algeria being launched from Tunisian territory. The French retaliated, in February, 1958, by bombing a Tunisian village near the border. The Tunisian authorities again stopped the movement of all French troops in the country and demanded their withdrawal. They also moved more than 400 European farmers (mostly French) from lands near the Algerian border. The tension was eased, after De Gaulle's accession to power, by an agreement which provided for the withdrawal of French troops, although the French military base in Bizerte would remain.

President Bourguiba continued to try to get the French to negotiate the evacuation of the Bizerte military base, but to no avail. A crisis over Bizerte finally erupted in June, 1961, with thousands of civilians crowding around the military base. Some Tunisian military participation resulted in mortar shells being exploded inside the base. Massive retaliation by the French marines and air force resulted in thousands of Tunisian casualties and another rupture of Franco-Tunisian relations. (Chapter 5 describes a number of steps that were taken by the Tunisians against the French-owned business community.) At the same time, a lack of support from the United States and the United Kingdom, in the United Nations, on the matter of Bizerte resulted in a demonstration and the stoning of the U.S. Information Service library in Tunis. It also prompted President Bourguiba to remark, "The American attitude in the Security Council has sounded the knell of the West in North Africa."[29]

Ever since independence, Europeans, who felt that they had no future in North Africa, had been selling out as best they could and leaving the country. In January, 1960, of the original colony of 255,000 Europeans only 98,000 remained. By 1960, the 1.5 million acres of land owned by Frenchmen at the time of independence had been reduced to 1 million. The Bizerte crisis in 1961 and the resultant retaliations and hard feelings resulted in an increased rate of departure.

By that time, however, the Tunisians were in full control of their foreign exchange. On September 19, 1958, a law had established the Central Bank of Tunisia, and one month later, another law substituted the Tunisian dinar, with a value of $2.38, for the Tunisian franc (which had been at par with the French franc). When the French devalued their money in December, 1958, from 420 francs to the dollar to 493.7 francs to the dollar, the Tunisians did not follow suit. This move broke the old ties with the French franc and permitted the Tunisians to follow an independent monetary policy, both internally and internationally.

Consequently, the departure of Europeans after January, 1959, did not result in large withdrawals of capital from the country. It did, however, reduce the number of trained and educated people and also reduced the purchasing power in the economy.

Another step taken by Tunisia to reduce the old colonial ties with France was, on August 20, 1959, to declare the end of the tariff union. Prior to independence there had been complete freedom of trade. The agreements signed at the time of independence permitted each country to restrict the importation of only a certain number of items from the other country. After August, 1959, however, trade with France was put on the same basis as with other countries, with bilateral agreements having a duration of one year. However, via these bilateral agreements, France did continue to subsidize the importation of certain of Tunisia's exports.

The years immediately following independence, however, were the most difficult, because the government was following an economic policy of laissez-faire. The departure of Frenchmen resulted in a flight of capital. The rate of new investment decreased. Some mines and factories ceased operation and industrial production decreased in a number of industries during the first four years of independence. During the period 1956-59, the GNP increased from $760 million to only $795 million-- a total increase of 4.4 percent, while population grew by an estimated 7 percent. At the same time, investments as a percentage of GNP were decreasing. In 1950, investment had equaled 20 percent of GNP. By 1955 this had decreased to 15 percent; from 1956 to 1958 it was 10 percent; and in 1959 it eased up slightly to 12 percent. [30]

The disquieting aspect of the above figures is that it is generally recognized that investment must equal at least 20 percent of GNP if a country wishes to achieve an acceptable rate of economic development. The United States, during the period 1956-63, achieved an average investment rate of 17 percent of GNP, while Italy averaged 23 percent, Germany 25 percent, and Japan 34 percent. During the late 1950's, the East European countries were experiencing investment rates of 25 percent to 35 percent of GNP.

LAUNCHING THE PLANNED ECONOMY

The result of the continuing pattern of insufficient investment rates was that the government made a decision, in 1960, to start a series of economic plans and greatly to increase the rate of public investment. Such investments were to go

primarily into economic infrastructure, as was usual in the
past; in addition, however, the government would invest in industry to make up for the lack of private capital flowing into
that sector.

The decision by President Bourguiba to launch a planned
economy did not come easily. By 1960, however, the dis-
couragingly slow growth of investment and of GNP, a consolidation of the government's political position, and completion of
many of the preparatory steps for planning led President
Bourguiba to announce that planning was necessary and that
the government would take a more active role in the economy.
He noted, however, "We do not like to have ourselves bound
by systems and rigid doctrines. For us, only the result counts.
It is not, therefore, a doctrinal view which has led us to planning. Our objective, with which the nation is in unanimous
agreement, is to conquer underdevelopment. "[31] In January,
1961, President Bourguiba asked Ahmed Ben Salah to take over
the office of Minister of Planning and Finance and to assume
responsibility for economic planning.

The first plan, Perspectives Décennales de Développement:
1962-1971, was not so much a plan as a review of where the
country was in 1961 and where it hoped to be in 1971. It listed
four major objectives to be achieved during the 10-year period:
decolonization, the promotion of man, the reform of the economic and social structures which impede development, and
the achievement of self-development--the ability to continue
on the road of development without foreign assistance. It is
noteworthy that decolonization was stated as the first objective.
The planning document states that this objective "must destroy
the economic aftereffects of colonial domination, " and that this
would be achieved "by the integration of the colonial sector of
the economy and by the Tunisification of the enclaves still remaining in foreign hands. "

To achieve its economic and social goals, the plan foresaw
the need to invest a total of $2.8 billion during the 10-year
period, with $333 million going to industry. It would also be
necessary to increase domestic savings from 11 percent of
gross domestic product (GDP) in 1962 to 26 percent in 1971.
This would result in an annual growth rate of 6 percent and a
near doubling of the GDP from $670 million in 1961 to $1.2
billion in 1972, and an increase in annual per capita income
from $162 to $240.

The Plan Triennal: 1962-1964 was completed and ready
for implementation near the end of 1961, several months after
the 10-year plan had been announced and published. It was

called a "pre-plan," since its aim was to prepare the base
necessary for the launching of the subsequent plans. Just as
in the 10-year plan, the three-year plan announced that its
first objective was decolonization--"rapid and complete decolonization."[32]

The investment and production goals of this three-year
plan were not achieved. They were optimistically conceived
and were far over the average needed to achieve the goals of
the 10-year plan, yet the results were quite impressive. Investment as a percent of GNP grew steadily from 15 percent
in 1961 to 17.7 percent in 1964. During the same period, GNP
itself increased by 1.8 percent in 1962, 5.5 percent in 1963,
and 10.5 percent in 1964.[33] The figures contrast greatly with
the average annual investment of 10 percent of GNP and the
average increase in GNP of less than 2 percent during the
stagnant period 1956-59.

The objectives of the Plan Quadriennal: 1965-1968 stated:
There is no longer a colonial sector in the middle of
the Tunisian economy. The principal activities which
had constituted a foreign impingement into Tunisia
are now integrated and are at the service of the development of the whole of the economy. This is true
of the banking system, mining industries, manufacturing industries, and agriculture. Also, economic relations between Tunisia and the former
colonial power have, in spite of certain vicissitudes,
normalized. France remains the primary trading
partner, but Tunisia no longer has such a strong
dependence on the French economy.

This four-year plan ensured the continuation of the development policies pursued during the three-year plan period and
broadly outlined in the Perspectives Décennales, on which both
plans are based. However, the four-year plan introduced some
modifications in objectives and in the investment program.
Thus, its principal objectives were (1) to effect some wide-
ranging structural reforms, including the progressive integration of the traditional and modern agricultural sectors and the
extension of the cooperative movement in agriculture; (2) to
further the industrialization of the country; and (3) to promote
the development and full use of the country's human resources.
It was planned that during the period 1965-68, the GDP would
increase at an average rate of 6.5 percent per year in real
terms.

In 1965, the first year of that plan, the economy did grow
at a rate of 6.5 percent. But 1966 was a drought year, resulting

in a 29 percent decrease in agricultural production, and 1967
was even worse, with agricultural production falling 10 percent below 1966. These decreases offset increases in industry
and services, resulting in essentially no change in real GDP
(but a 2 percent decline in per capita income in 1966 and in
1967). The details of the components of the GDP are shown
in Appendix A, Table 7.

Although details are not yet available for 1968, the agricultural production increased appreciably. Other positive
factors indicate a significant improvement in economic growth
for that year. Meanwhile, the government has continued to
maintain a high rate of investment (in 1965 gross investment
equaled 27.4 percent of GNP; in 1966 it was 26.4 percent, and
in 1967 25.1 percent). Also, significant increases in oil production and exports and the rapid growth of tourism are serving
to boost the economy and increase foreign exchange earnings.
Lastly, the introduction of new strains of high-yield, drought-
resistant wheat and an extensive effort to increase the area of
land under irrigation will help to insulate the economy from
the effects of future drought years. Consequently, the economic
picture appears favorable for the short as well as for the long
term.

POLITICAL DEVELOPMENTS SINCE INDEPENDENCE

When independence was achieved in 1956, the Bey, who
had been put into power by the French, remained as the traditional head of the government. However, Bourguiba was head
of the Neo-Destour party and the source of power. A constitutional assembly was called by the Bey but was dominated by
the Neo-Destour party. Instead of working on a constitution,
they set out to destroy the power of the Bey. By July, 1957,
he had been deposed and Bourguiba made Chief of State. Not
until 1959 was a constitution published, conferring strong
powers on the presidency, after which Bourguiba was elected
President. Also, by 1959, the party had eliminated all opposition. President Bourguiba, having consolidated his power,
was then prepared to attempt to cure some of the economic
and social ills of the country.

The Neo-Destour party is tightly organized into cells at
the village level, with a very broadly based membership. Its
relationship with the government is such, however, that the
government leaders have control over the party apparatus,

thereby avoiding the possibility that the party might become
the focus of power and impose political decisions on government technicians. [34] Still, most basic policy decisions are
made within party circles, since the government ministers
are also members of the party's ruling body. However, such
decisions are not reached without considerable discussion.
The party does not permit political opposition, but it encourages
participation and expression of a fairly wide range of opinion
within its own circles.

The Neo-Destour party changed its name in 1964, at the
request of President Bourguiba, to the Parti Socialiste Destourian (Destourian Socialist party). However, the change in
name had no policy significance.

In the process of consolidating its power, the party has
also taken under its wing, and dominates, the UGTT, the
Union Générale des Élèves Tunisiens (UGET), the Chamber
of Commerce, and all other organizations which might become
a source of opposition. Also, the army is kept weak and is
apolitical. The result is a constancy of policy which is rare
in the developing countries.

That disagreement does exist is evidenced by the fact that
from time to time (though rarely) a minister resigns in protest over a policy adopted by the government. The latest incident of this type was the resignation in January, 1968, of
Ahmed Mestiri, the Minister of Defense, in protest over the
decision to carry out additional structural reforms in the
commercial and agricultural sectors. Also, Ahmed Ben Salah
was relieved of his responsibility for planning, agriculture,
finance, commerce, and industry, in the fall of 1969, retaining
only the Ministry of Education. However, President Bourguiba
has shown an ability eventually to welcome such dissidents
back into the fold.

While President Bourguiba will undoubtedly remain in office during his lifetime, he suffered a fairly serious heart attack in the spring of 1967, when he was 64 years of age. Although he seems to have recovered completely, one must raise
the question "After Bourguiba, what"? This was foreseen in
1966 by the passage of a succession law to institutionalize the
passing of power. This law was revised in 1968 at the initiative
of President Bourguiba. A Vice-President was elected (Bahi
Ladgham), and the law specifies that upon the death of the
President, the Vice-President shall assume the presidency
for the remainder of the elected term.

It is seen, then, that Tunisia has an elected, single-mass-
party regime which provides channels for the expression of

public opinion. Party members, down to the village level, can express their grievances. Every attempt is made by government leaders to obtain a consensus before announcing important decisions, and this is usually achieved by a broad participation in the decision-making process. Since the party includes members holding a wide range of opinions and free discussion is allowed, the resultant decisions will usually be somewhat "middle of the road." With the UGTT and the UGET subservient to this complex of party-government apparatus, all of the major forces of the society can be channeled into the paths needed to achieve development. Tunisia appears to have the type of political and governmental structure ideally suited to the needs of a developing country.

NOTES

1. Salah Tlatli, Tunisie Nouvelle, p. 41.

2. Dwight L. Ling, Tunisia: From Protectorate to Republique, p. 11.

3. Ibid., pp. 27, 30.

4. Tlatli, op. cit., p. 159.

5. Ling, op. cit., p. 77.

6. Lionel Stoleru, "Tunisie 1956," p. 83.

7. Moncef Guen, La Tunisie Indépendente Face à Son Economie, p. 57.

8. Paul Sebag, La Tunisie, p. 53.

9. Jules Lépidi, L'Économie Tunisienne Depuis la Fin de la Guerre, p. 119.

10. Stoleru, op. cit., p. 116.

11. Government of Tunisia, Annuaire Statistique de la Tunisie 1956, p. 64.

12. Lépidi, op. cit., pp. 36-42.

13. Ibid., p. 76.

14. Ibid., p. 75.

15. Ibid., p. 202.

16. Sebag, op. cit., p. 99.

17. Ling, op. cit., pp. 79, 80.

18. Guen, op. cit., p. 28.

19. Government of Tunisia, op. cit.

20. Tlatli, op. cit., p. 234.

21. Ibid., p. 237.

22. Guen, op. cit., p. 55.

23. Charles Debbasch, La République Tunisienne, p. 98.

24. Lépidi, op. cit., pp. 60, 61.

25. Guen, op. cit., p. 48.

26. Ibid., p. 108.

27. Tlatli, op. cit., p. 199.

28. Guen, op. cit., p. 99.

29. New York Times (July 23, 1961).

30. Government of Tunisia, Perspectives Décennales de Développement: 1962-1971, p. 29.

31. Government of Tunisia, Les Discours du Président Bourguiba, speech of February 7, 1961.

32. Government of Tunisia, Plan Triennal: 1962-1964, p. 13.

33. Banque Centrale de Tunisie, Rapport Annuel, 1964.

34. Clement Moore, Tunisia Since Independence, p. 107.

CHAPTER 4

POLICY STATEMENTS OF TUNISIAN POLITICAL LEADERS AND GOVERNMENT

The political party which runs Tunisia is the Destourian Socialist party. The term "socialist" implies a doctrine and an ideology, but it is a term which means different things to different people. What does it mean to Tunisia's leaders? What is their ideology? What is in the name?

To answer this, we shall go, first, to the origin of the name and see what its author, President Bourguiba, had in mind when he suggested it. Following this will be a clear definition of the term "Destourian socialism," as issued by the party itself.

How did such a concept develop? It is often said that President Bourguiba is conservative in economics but that he was pushed to the left by Ahmed Ben Salah, his Minister of Planning and Economics from 1961 to 1969. Does this fit the facts of the historical development of present governmental policies?

To study this question, we shall review a series of events which took place during the nine months following independence. At the time of independence, Ahmed Ben Salah was the Executive Secretary of the UGTT, the amalgam of all labor unions in Tunisia. He used this as a base from which to try to push the government into rapid action on planning and decolonization. This led to dissension within the UGTT and discontent among government officials, as a result of which Ben Salah was removed from his post in the UGTT.

In 1960 and 1961, President Bourguiba was ready to present a plan to the nation and move into a planned economy. Being committed and prepared to take this step, the President asked Ben Salah to become Minister of Planning and Finance in January, 1961. The plans were, therefore, developed under the direction of Ben Salah; but the introductions to these plans, from which excerpts are quoted, reveal the combined thinking of President Bourguiba and Ben Sahal, as well as other government and party officials.

Having started its planned economy, with public investment going into many spheres of industrial activity, Tunisia
ran the danger of scaring off private investors, both domestic and foreign. Therefore, since 1961 both President Bourguiba and Ben Salah have periodically given talks to assure
private investors by clarifying the role of the government and
emphasizing the continuing, necessary role of private enterprise. Finally, a firm, detailed, and official clarification of
the relative roles of the public and private sectors was presented in 1965 by a committee established by the party for this
purpose.

WHAT IS DESTOURIAN SOCIALISM?

The seventh congress of the Neo-Destour party was held
in Bizerte on October 19-22, 1964. During this congress,
President Bourguiba made a number of speeches, but one of
the most important was on October 21, before the Commission
on Internal Organization of the party. After discussing the
various organisms of the party, the role of the ministers, of
the political bureau, and the governors, he raised the question
of the name of the party. He noted that it began as the Destour
party, but that in 1934 the Neo-Destour spun off from the old
party. After tracing the economic and social situation in
Tunisia and outlining the philosophy which the party had been
following as a result of this, he proposed a new name:
     It will be called, if you wish, the Destourian Socialist
     Party....
          As to its objectives, they are the same as those
     of all socialist parties: raising the level of the disin-
     herited masses, which means social justice, the end
     of exploitation by the abusive exercise of the right
     of property, and the placing of vital sectors of
     production into the hands of the people by means
     of nationalization. However,...
          I am against generalizations. We have nation-
     alized the gas company and we have nationalized
     some land. This does not mean that we are going
     to nationalize everything. It is this which is orig-
     inal in Destourian socialism. We will nationalize
     only that in which there is an interest in national-
     izing; that which the nation is capable of operating

better than individuals, which means in a manner
more advantageous to the entire population.

As to the nationalizations, we will ask ourselves,
in each case, to what extent the action would result
in an increase in production and in an increase in general well-being. And, if it is seen that the action
would be profitable, we will nationalize it, and not be
stopped from doing so by the interest of the individual.
But, if it is apparent that we do not have sufficient
qualified managers to operate the company efficiently,
we will not nationalize for propaganda purposes or for
demagoguery, to show that we are more socialist than
others. [1]

In another speech at the same party congress, President
Bourguiba discussed his conception of Destourian socialism:

Our socialism is distinct from utopian socialism which
is systematically egalitarian and arises from a ro-
mantic vision of life. It is also distant from doctrin-
aire socialism, which is dogmatic and is based on a
hateful class struggle. Our conception of socialism
is something else altogether. It is both objective
and humane; it includes having confidence in man, in
his perfectability and his facility for enthusiasm for
work which is in the general interest. We hope thereby to avoid the arbitrary and tyranny and to save the
people from the terror and the insecurity which accompany denunciations. We feel that if we can
speak with the language of the heart and of reason,
the people will understand the imperatives of our
nation and will not shrink from any sacrifice. Our
actions must first be aimed at the younger generation, in whom we are certain to find a vibrant response.
But the young, being easily carried away by over-
enthusiasm, are sometimes tempted by communism
and other similar doctrines where they think they
will find a remedy for human misery and social
injustice. We must attract them to us and convince
them that this is precisely our objective, and that
our methods are more efficient in achieving those
goals. We must above all make them understand
that revolting against the spectacle of misery is not
the solution, but rather, to look for the proper means
of putting an end to that misery. [2]

Since President Bourguiba is also the head of the party,
there is generally little contrast between what he says and

what the party says. It is of interest, however, to review
the party's position on the meaning of Destourian socialism.

At the conclusion of this same party congress in Bizerte,
a number of motions were passed. One, a motion on the meaning of Destourian socialism, had the following to say about
private property:

The management of private property is a social function, necessarily tied to the general interest and contributing to the realization of national objectives.
This fundamental condition permits the undisturbed
possession of property, with the respect of society
and the protection of the state. Party workers must
not, in the name of any principle, impose their will
on our people, who have so recently left an era of
submission and underdevelopment. [3]

Several months later, the Party issued a sheet which
defined, definitively, the meaning of Destourian socialism. [4]
It is quoted here in its entirety:

The characteristics of Destourian socialism are as
follows:

1. Destourian socialism is not an imported ideology. Its source is the profound aspirations and
historic and sociological conditions of our people.

2. Destourian socialism is not an inflexible
ideology, elaborately set in an ivory tower or immo-
bilized by dogmatism. On the contrary, our socialism
is a continuous creation, a permanent search. In
the underdeveloped countries, socialism is not a process
ripened by the evolution of society and made in-
eluctable by historical determinism; it is an act of
choice, voluntary and rational. In Tunisia, the party
has opted for such a system because it constitutes
the best approach to the problems of development and
the shortest road to the authentic promotion of man.

3. Destourian socialism does not believe in
violent class struggle. Violent class struggle is pernicious and useless. Pernicious because nothing of
value can be constructed on hate and destruction, and
because the evolution of the Tunisian economy does
not generate unshakable social antagonisms. The
nation, so recently formed, cannot, without danger
of disappearance, see its elite and its masses confront and annihilate each other.

4. Destourian socialism is not synonymous with
state socialism. It considers that the essential role
of the state consists not of administering men and
goods under a paralyzing supervision, but rather of
favoring the flourishing of men and the democratic
management of productive activities, and of coor-
dinating, harmonizing, and regulating a coherent
entity, oriented toward the collective well-being and
the functioning of productive enterprises.

5. Destourian socialism is favorable to cooperation. The cooperative, as far as it is authentic (and
the Tunisian state is working towards this end), is a
production unit organized on democratic principles,
making its services and the goods which it produces
available to all and operating in its own interests, as
a small collective, as well as for the general good.
It constitutes a doubly advantageous entity: it is the
crucible in which are forged new productive techniques
and the indispensable elements of modern life, and
it is an effective area of profitable action on economic
and social structures. In this respect, the cooperative,
which is both a productive unit and a school, fits in
perfectly well with our ideological concepts.

6. Destourian socialism is action-oriented. For
an underdeveloped country, doctrines are a luxury
unless they are useful for its rapid development.
Our people, aware of the discrepancy between their
own country and others which are rich, and of the
enormous effort they are called on to make, have
made these principles of action into an ideology which
takes into account the objectives which they periodically identify, which are based on their aspirations
and conditions, and which they must fully achieve.

7. Destourian socialism is responsive to facts.
It is open to the teachings of experience and to necessary corrections, but it is above all aimed at
action, daily and long-term; at efficient action which
draws constantly closer to objectives. Efficiency
is thus one of the principal criteria of our philosophy
of action.

EARLY CONTROVERSY OVER
THE ROLE OF GOVERNMENT

The UGTT had been banned by France until 1954, after which it could operate openly. Its Executive Secretary, Ahmed Ben Salah, worked closely with Bourguiba in the final fight for independence, using union action as necessary and possible to put additional pressure on France. He saw the UGTT as a continuing, potent, and independent economic and political influence after independence.

President Bourguiba, on the other hand, wanted to bring the UGTT into the fold of the party. He did not want to see labor as a separate political force, nor did he think in terms of a class struggle. He felt that there must at all times be unity and consensus. At the same time, he is known for his policy of gradualism. President Bourguiba saw very clearly in 1956 that there was need for governmental action. This is illustrated in the following excerpt from his first speech to the constitutional Assembly, April 17, 1956.

> The country suffers from social immobility and injustice. ... But we do not consider unemployment as inherent in society, nor that the low salaries are inevitable. On the contrary, we believe that there are social phenomena which result from a poor utilization of resources which one can rectify only by appropriate economic policies and by relentless and fruitful work.
>
> That is why the program of the government is to promote prosperity and social justice. We will not improvise from day to day. Our work will be embodied in the framework of a general plan, which will define our economic and social structures and will specify in detail their achievement according to a strict schedule. This plan will correspond to the needs of the country in the various sectors of production: agriculture, fishing, and the artisians.[5]

Thus immediately following independence, President Bourguiba already spoke in terms of the need for economic planning. He also established a planning commission in his first government. He knew, however, that many of the measures he wanted to carry out would meet with resistance among the conservative elements in the society. In addition, he already had the dissension of the Youssefist movement, which crystallized the resistance of the conservative classes.

Furthermore, it was obvious that Tunisia was going to
need considerable foreign aid and foreign investment. Consequently, President Bourguiba did not wish to pursue, immediately after his accession to power, a policy of rapid
nationalization combined with a centrally planned economy.
He wished to present an acceptable appearance to the international community. This is illustrated by the following
excerpt from a speech which he gave in New York on August
17, 1956:

> The position of the government, in economic matters,
> is based on principles which I will try to state
> explicitly, so as to avoid any misunderstanding. The
> first of these principles is respect for private pro-
> perty. In effect, there is no reason for capital to
> feel threatened in our country. We respect private
> property, but it is indispensable that each investor
> feel responsible to manage, in an efficient and
> optimum manner, the source of production which he
> is operating. Without that, this liberty might be
> limited, for liberty is not to be confused with abuse.
> The second principle consists in encouraging foreign
> investment in Tunisia, and I declare, solemnly, that
> there is no reason for foreign capital to feel uneasy.
> On the contrary, we are ready to assist such invest-
> ments by granting them tax reductions, guarantees,
> etc. It is not the intention of the government to
> nationalize companies. In certain sectors, obviously,
> nationalization is justified and sometimes even
> indispensable. [6]

Likewise, in November, 1956, President Bourguiba said:

> Colonialism did not permit us to create technicians
> or the capital which we need today. To apply our
> plan for economic development, we must appeal to
> friendly nations and ask them for technicians and
> capital. In this long-term effort which we are under-
> taking, we will need very large investments. This
> is why we propose to offer the necessary guarantees
> to foreign capital which will be invested in Tunisia
> and to assure them a good return. [7]

But Ben Salah was not so patient. He wanted the government to take immediate action. In July, 1956, he issued a
press release specifying measures which the UGTT felt were
urgent:

> More and more, the country seems to be abandoning
> itself to fear. On the economic and financial planes,

nothing has been announced to give confidence nor
to define the doctrine of this young Tunisia.

Yet we can, ourselves, take certain measures,
which are as urgent as they are effective, and which
are capable of giving the country a strong economic
policy. The measures which we propose should not
make us forget that it is still urgently necessary to
develop an economic plan which responds to the needs
and aspirations of our people.

Therefore, we propose that the government
rapidly commit itself to take the following measures:

... Create free zones to facilitate the establishment of industry in the country and to make
Tunisia, now a poor country, a commercial relay
between the worlds of the Atlantic and the Mediterranean.

... Prepare for the installation of basic industries.

... Reorganize commercial channels and guide
them toward a more moral operation; favor the
creation of large cooperative stores and of state-
owned stores, so as to reduce the cost of living. [8]

The controversy between the UGTT and the government
(between Ben Salah and President Bourguiba) continued. On
September 20-24, 1956, the UGTT held a congress which was
to consolidate its position and was to provide Ben Salah with
an even stronger base from which to push his policies. President Bourguiba, realizing this, canceled a scheduled trip to
Europe so that he could to to the congress and give a speech,
on the opening day, to state his position and that of the government, with the aim of keeping the resolutions of the congress
from being too radical. Among his remarks were the following:

I have often been criticized for not having a doctrine.
I am not a man of doctrines, and do not feel the lack
of one. I prefer to confront my ideas and my actions
with reality.

Certain ideologies pretend that capital is the
result of theft. In considering this question from a
realistic point of view, I think that capital is, rather,
the consequence of privation; a man deprives himself to accumulate money and little by little builds
up capital. To make the masses believe that capitalists are all dishonest exploiters leads to the sowing
of hatred and to disorder. It is a fact that the worker
cannot produce without the help of capital.

Certain regimes, which we all know, have suppressed
capital and dispossessed the capitalists. The result was first a terrible anarchy and, what was more
serious, a decrease in production. To try to remedy
this decrease, the workers were submitted to in-
human disciplines.

The Tunisian government wishes to increase
production. I think that the regime of private
property favors such an effort. [9]

At the end of the UGTT congress, Ben Salah was re-elected
as Executive Director. However, perhaps as a result of
President Bourguiba's opening remarks and his close attention to the proceedings, the resolutions issued by the congress
were relatively mild. One stated that the UGTT continued to
favor the need for economic planning. It stated also that the
economic situation was getting worse and proposed that capital transfers, which were draining investments out of Tunisia,
be blocked; that there be restrictions against the importing of
luxury goods; and that the state begin to control the distribution
of credit. [10]

Meanwhile, Ben Salah had gathered, in the UGTT, a team
of qualified Tunisians and foreign advisers who prepared an
economic plan. This was completed by October, 1956. Not
finding acceptance for his plan in government circles, he decided to use the press as a means of publicizing it. He gave
copies of the plan to the newspapers and was immediately
interviewed by reporters. During this interview, he was
asked to comment on the fact that the government itself had,
for some time, been working on an economic plan. He said:
"The [government] organization charged with the responsibility
of elaborating a plan is insufficient. It does not have the capability of working seriously and could not achieve a workable
plan. [11]

Following this interview, the newspapers began to print,
little by little, each day for over a month, the entire text of
the UGTT-formulated development plan. Since the preface
to this plan was signed by Ben Salah, and the entire effort
was under his direction and close supervision, one can assume
that its philosophy represents his thinking at that time. The
following excerpts were chosen to show the expressed views
of the relative roles of government and of private enterprise:

We believe that our society, which was freed from
a political colonial regime, will not be truly free
until it has destroyed the economic and social
apparatus created by that regime.

We believe that colonialism is the most hideous
form of capitalism.
...We believe also that ... it is not possible to
allow capitalism to follow its usual economic policy,
which is turned exclusively toward immediate and
scandalous profit.

It is true that the instinct for property is
written in the heart of man and that, other than the
desire for private property, there is no incentive to
work; and that, therefore, private property is necessary for the liberty and dignity of man. ...But
it is hypocrisy thus to justify private ownership of
the means of production.

It is necessary to affirm, clearly, the responsibility of the state in the area of the creation and
development of industry, as well as its orientation
for the general good. We must look forward, deliberately, to an ever-increasing role of the public
sector, and we must affirm the incontestable right
of the state to buy any industrial company whenever
the public interest so requires.

The ownership and the right to exploit mineral
resources belongs to the state....

In the domain of industry, as such, new industries producing basic goods and machines must eventually be in the hands of the state. But, in certain
cases, it may be desirable that the state associate
with private capital, although it is more important
that the state have a significant proportion of the
capital than that it makes long-term loans....

The public sector must also encompass transportation....

All other activities can remain in the hands of
the private sector...under two conditions: that
they respect the social contract of the workers...
and that they satisfy the requirements of the plan.

A review of the position taken in this UGTT development
plan shows it to be not too different from that later elaborated
by the government in its Perspectives Décennales. The UGTT
plan, however, was mostly philosophical and descriptive rather
than quantitative.

The publication of this plan in the press (pieces of it
appearing over a six-week period), as well as the UGTT's
continued pressure on the government to undertake active
measures, apparently irritated President Bourguiba. Also,

Ben Salah's policies had caused dissension in union ranks and
a schism in the movement, with a number of unions breaking
off to form a separate federation. This gave Bourguiba the
excuse he was looking for. Consequently, when Ben Salah
made a trip to Morocco late in December, 1956, he returned
to find that the ground had been cut out from under him in the
UGTT; arrangements had been made for his replacement, and
on December 27, 1956, Ahmed Tlili took over as Executive
Director. Ben Salah was without a government post until
July, 1957, when President Bourguiba appointed him Minister
of Public Health.

THE PLANNED ECONOMY

Meanwhile, as noted in Chapter 3, the economic situation
continued to worsen. It became evident that more governmental action was needed. Was there any need to hesitate
further? The Youssefist movement had been crushed and Bourguiba had consolidated his position politically. The old Bey
had been disposed of. The constitution had come into being in
1959, establishing a presidential regime. Although the government had, by 1960 (See Chapter 5), nationalized a number of
gas and electric power companies, Bourguiba had amply demonstrated to the international community that he was not a
hot-headed socialist. In addition, by this time, economic
planning was considered to be de rigueur. In fact, the U.S.
government was encouraging the underdeveloped countries to
develop plans if they wished to receive more foreign aid.
Bourguiba could now proceed with the planned economy which,
in many sectors, Tunisia so badly needed. Although President
Bourguiba had established a National Planning Council as early
as 1956, its initial activities were restricted mostly to building
up a staff and to gathering data. Bourguiba first announced
his intention to issue a development plan on April 1, 1960:

> We decided a short time ago to draw up a general
> development plan into which all our programs would
> be incorporated. In this we are following the example
> of numerous other countries. We are going to study
> this question and learn from the experience of other
> peoples, whether they belong to the Eastern or
> Western blocs, or whether they are neutral. Different
> ideologies and doctrines must not prevent us from
> seeking the most efficient method of production.

The only valid criteria are productivity and the rate
of progress. A ministerial committee was formed.
This will be seconded by a subcommission. We
shall draw up a plan and our efforts, which have so
far been uncoordinated, will thus be rationally
coordinated. We will then be well placed to control
our rate of progress and to avoid projects not
properly thought out. We did not do this at an earlier
stage because we lacked the necessary statistics.
The preliminary studies will soon be terminated.
We have sufficient information to enable us to draw
up the basic outline of a program, which can be
readjusted as we go along. Anyhow, we have now
a definite policy which will take on a more precise
shape later. [12]

For some reason, Bourguiba stated that it was decided
only "a short time ago to draw up a general development plan,"
although the planning commission had been in existence and was
supposedly working on a plan. Perhaps, as Bourguiba stated,
it could not have been done earlier for lack of statistics, but
it is questionable that four years were needed to gather the
necessary statistics.

Having publicly announced his intention to draw up a
development plan and operate a planned economy, Bourguiba
called upon Ben Salah, in January, 1961, to become Minister
of Planning and Finance and assume responsibility for planning.
He did this, according to his own statements, because as
Minister of Health, Ben Salah had demonstrated his ability to
put together a good team and to administer imaginatively, and
because Ben Salah was a long-time advocate of the measures
to be taken.

It is not surprising, therefore, that the Prespectives
Décennales de Développement: 1962-1971 greatly resembles
the UGTT development plan of 1956, except that the Perspectives
is loaded with statistics. Its philosophy is, however, somewhat less radical than that of the UGTT plan.

The philosophy and, if you will, the justification of the
plan are contained in its Introduction, from which the following
is excerpted:

... Planning does not at all envision ruining some
for the profit of others, but must achieve an
equitable distribution of wealth, by eliminating
the scandals existing at the two extremes of the
social pyramid. By raising the national income,
by effecting the economic development of the country,

by searching for and achieving all of its possibilities,
planning must create employment for all and achieve
that which is called the "takeoff" of the Tunisian
economy.

     To achieve this, Tunisia will not bind itself by
any ideology, will not apply any politico-economic
doctrine. It freely seeks its own path and attempts
to find the correct methods which take into account,
above all, the national traditions, the personality of
our people, and the economic and social imperatives.
It can also be said that we do not fear words: if
socialism consists in freeing man from need, in
giving him, through work, the possibility of self-
development; if socialism is this search for equilibrium in the interior of society, through work,
prosperity, and justice, then Tunisia opts resolutely
for socialism. Doing this, she does not particularly
base this on any foreign experiences. Tunisian
planning is socialistic to the extent that by socialism
we mean a society which serves the greatest number,
based on an economy which respects man by assuring
a harmonious development of his needs and his means
with justice and equality; to the extent that socialism
assures maximum efficiency with a maximum of
freedom. Conceived and formulated by Tunisian
officials and technicians, this planning does not model
itself on any other particular method. Basically, it
encourages all efforts, public or private. As a means
of best organizing and utilizing the resources of the
country, so as to obtain maximum advantage for all
the people, this planning encompasses all sectors of
national economic activity. But private companies,
while they will not be suppressed, will be compelled
to act within the framework of the plan. [13]
Having defined the type of socialism which the government
had adopted as a basis for its planned economy, the Perspectives
Décennales became more specific, under the section "Industrial
Development and Reform, " as to the role which the government
was to play and the relationships envisaged between the government and private enterprise.

     It noted that the achievement of many projects included in
the plan presupposes that certain basic industries, which
constitute the infrastructure of industrialization, will be created.
It then goes on to say:

In effect, only by the establishment of these [basic]
industries can small industries be established on a
profitable basis and complementary industries make
their appearance. Toward this end, the state seems
to be the only body capable of playing the role of
entrepreneur because of the magnitude of the investments and because of the financial sacrifices which
will be entailed by these industries. It therefore
follows that (a) investments in the domains of energy,
transportation, and water supply, which determine
the production cost of most other industries, and
which must, therefore, be conceived and managed
on the basis of national policy, must be done by the
state; (b) projects whose undertaking obviously exceeds the potentials of private initiative because of
the importance and variety of factors which must be
combined to achieve them will also be undertaken
by the state; (c) those projects which, to function,
require the granting of a monopoly of a key product
(petroleum products, steel, etc.), or where the
state would have to grant excessive advantages,
must be taken out of the realm of private initiative.

There are generally projects which, by their
nature, do not necessarily call for state control.
The intervention of the state is justified, however,
by the need to promote the undertaking of the project by private enterprise, by providing a portion
of the capital needed. The state has a financial institution whose purpose is to invest in industrial
companies. This organization, the Société Nationale
d'Investissement, is itself a mixed company....
However, the Société Nationale d'Investissement
may, at any time, remove itself from companies
which it has promoted, by selling the shares which
it holds, so as to utilize its funds for other projects. [14]

Lastly, the plan notes that the state will also intervene in
industrial development to encourage private initiative as well
as to orient and control it. After listing the several financial,
fiscal, and economic incentives which the government can
make available to private investors, it notes that any investment must have the prior approval of the government in order
to avoid excess capacity in certain sectors of industry. Then
it goes on to say:

It also appears necessary to induce those Tunisian
companies which in reality are subsidiaries or
branches of foreign companies to make their management and investment decisions in Tunisia on the
basis of the economic realities in Tunisia, rather
than abroad.

Finally, the state should assure the spread of
ownership of industry by encouraging the participation of individuals, with small savings, in subscrip-
tions which are offered by the industrial sector. It
is, moreover, by the active participation of such
small investors that the Tunisification of foreign-
owned companies and the democratization of the
economy can be undertaken. [15]

The last paragraph above sounds more like people's capitalism (a term used in the United States in the 1950's, when efforts were being made to increase the spread of stock ownership) than like any kind of socialism. On the other hand, it is
the most diplomatic and painless way of achieving the eventual
Tunisification of a portion of the foreign investment in the
country.

The Perspectives Décennales was relatively general in
nature, setting the framework within which more specific plans
were to operate. The Plan Triennal: 1962-1964 became very
specific as to which projects were to be undertaken, in what
industries, and what the individual investment costs would be.
It allocated, in totals, the portion which was to be invested by
private Tunisian and private foreign investors. It could have
been specific as to which projects would be left to each sector,
but it chose to be vague, as shown by the following:

The total investments [foreseen by this plan] have
been divided into public investments and private investments according to the criteria given in the
Perspectives Décennales. In effect, there are certain basic sectors which the state must administer
because they condition, in a large measure, the
development of the entire economy. This is true,
for example, of the sectors of energy and transportation. Similarly, the state will intervene in those
sectors which could, in principle, be left to private
initiative, either to stimulate this initiative, when
it fails to arise, or to furnish a portion of the capital
which exceeds the resources of individuals, or...
to offer supplemental guarantees to individuals
against risks which could otherwise inhibit private

initiative. In certain other sectors, the state will
content itself with specific measures aimed at orienting and encouraging private efforts in the directions of the goals of the plan. [16]

The Plan Quadriennal: 1965-1968 differs from the Plan
Triennal in that the latter was aimed at establishing the industrial infrastructure, whereas the former had as its basic
aim the achievement of industrialization. The Plan Triennal
recognized, fairly bluntly, that the state would have to play a
predominant role. On the other hand, the Plan Quadriennal
attempted to take as liberal a position as possible. The following shows a considerable softening of position vis-à-vis the
earlier plan.

From a legal point of view, the industrial sector is
open to all sources of initiative, public, private, or
cooperative. The state... will intervene on three
levels: (a) as promoter and owner in those key
activities which form the basis of Tunisian industry;
(b) as a partner with private investors to create new
industries; (c) as a public authority, through legislation, taxes, and credits, to encourage industrialization according to the provisions of this plan. As
precise a division as possible of industrial activities
between the state and the private sector will be
established so as to reinforce the confidence of the
private sector in determining its responsibilities in
the industrialization of the nation and in mobilizing
all of its resources.

...An important place is reserved, in our industrial development, for the private sector. In a
general manner, this sector can enter into all
activities where public interest does not indicate
that the intervention of the public sector is essential.
The Plan Triennal has already introduced the intervention of the state, or of semi-public organizations,
into such key sectors as energy, transportation, and
basic industries. In addition, the state will intervene more and more in the mining industry, as required, to assure that the mines are operated in a
spirit which is both economic and social in nature.
Other than these situations where the state must
intervene because of considerations of public interest
and social order, industrial activities are wide open
to private initiative, Tunisian or foreign. [17]

CLARIFICATION OF THE ROLE
OF PRIVATE INVESTMENT

The introduction of development plans and the establishment of a number of state-owned companies did cause many
people to wonder how far Tunisian socialism would go, in spite
of the assurances stated in the plans. As a result, President
Bourguiba has, on a number of occasions, attempted to assure
the private sector and the international community that his intentions are middle-of-the-road. In a speech on March 20,
1962, soon after the start of the first plan, he had the following
to say:

Our only aim is to prevent abuses, not to hinder individual initiative when it contributes to progress. We
have never sought to extinguish, among individuals,
that sacred flame which is their liberty, their ability
to create, their initiative, and their judgment. . . .

If to limit the abusive liberty of individuals, one
establishes a governmental regime, one can end up
with all of the evils of statism: seizure by the state
of the entire economic mechanism and an army of
civil servants living off a minority of citizens who
are crushed by taxes. History teaches us that such
societies end up in a catastrophe.

We will not follow this road. [18]

On May 12, 1964, Tunisia nationalized all foreign-owned
farmland. Bourguiba realized that this would upset the international community and act as a deterrent to foreign investment if it were not understood in the Tunisian context. He
therefore made a speech on May 14, 1964, in which he drew
a very interesting and important distinction between investments
which were made prior to independence and those made since.

I wish to note that the Tunisian government has never
failed in its engagements vis-à-vis capital invested
in Tunisia since our independence. For that which
came prior to our independence, decency requires
that I do not speak of it.

Between foreign investments furnished by
friendly countries, and colonial lands obtained during
the colonial period by theft, there cannot possibly be
a confusion. When we decide to recover the latter,
we are only pursuing the effort of decolonization.
As to investments made by foreigners with the aim
of helping us to achieve our development plan, they

are the object of our respect and gratitude, for they
represent a form of cooperation which seems to us
to be the most desirable. [19]

Ahmed Ben Salah, who remained as Minister of Planning
and Economics (as well as of Industry, Commerce, Finance,
and Agriculture) from 1961 until the fall of 1969, frequently
made speeches which were favorable to private investment,
but almost always with the qualification that such investment
must fit in with the plan, or that it must consider the general
good. For example, on June 19, 1964, at the opening of a
private textile company, Ben Salah stated:

> We hope that businessmen follow this example and
> install other factories for the manufacture of other
> essential products, such as toothpaste, towels, etc.
> The government will be on the side of those who
> participate in the industrialization of the country,
> on the condition that they maintain quality in their
> production. [20]

His views on foreign private investment and the treatment
it would receive are most explicitly stated in an interview of
Ben Salah by an editor of Enterprise. Several of the pertinent
questions and answers were as follows:

> Question: What guarantees are offered to foreign
> investors? What, specifically, are the possibilities
> of transferring profits and invested capital?
>
> Answer: Foreign investors receive many guar-
> antees and encouragements. First, we follow the
> principle of nondiscrimination between foreign and
> Tunisian investors. Incentives available to stimu-
> late the private sector to participate in our develop-
> ment are equally available to foreign investors....
> In addition, we follow the principle of complete
> protection against any act which might harm invest-
> ments. Expropriation cannot be justified except in
> the public interest, as is the case in France itself.
> An equitable indemnity is anticipated and its pay-
> ment is immediate. Capital and profits are freely
> transferable. Finally, we follow the principle of
> international arbitration in case of disputes. These
> guarantees are provided for in many agreements
> which exist between Tunisia and a number of other
> countries.
>
> Question: Could you describe your views on the
> cooperation between public and private initiative?

Answer: Destourian socialism does not signify
state ownership and bureaucracy. It aims at the
betterment of the individual through cooperation between the public, private, and cooperative sectors.
The cooperation is coordinated through the development plan. Private initiative is considerably encouraged within the framework of our fundamental
goals, but we consider private ownership of the
means of production in a growing economy, such as
ours, as a social function. The public sector is
limited and interested essentially in such strategic
activities as energy, transportation; the remaining
activities are left to private initiative, which is
continually solicited, by the party and by the government, to carry out its share. In certain strategic
activities, such as mining and credit, the state as-
sociates itself with private initiative, domestic or
foreign. Also, we have always said that the state
is ready to sell its holdings in certain companies
to the private sector. [21]

Perhaps the most authoritative presentation of Tunisia's
socialism and its view on the role of private investment is a
"white paper" issued by the Destourian Socialist party late in
1965. A national seminar was organized by the party, on
September 10 and 11, 1965, to discuss the different sectors
of the economy: public, private, and cooperative. Following
the seminar, the party published a booklet which was a résumé
of the discussions and of the consensus of the participants,
who were from the top echelon of the party and were concerned
with this particular problem. They noted that there was a
fundamental divergence between Tunisia's socialism and
Marxian theory, for that of Marx was based on the concept of
an inevitable class struggle. According to Marx, the dominant
class, which has both political power and the means of production in its possession, uses this power to keep the lower classes
in subjection. It then notes:

The young Tunisian state is not in the hands of a
given class, but in those of an elite which is drawn
from all levels of the population, nourished by the
anti-colonial struggle and by the desire to achieve
justice and the promotion of the individual. . . . In
rejecting the postulate of Marx on the class struggle,
and in affirming the principle of social cohesion, we
cannot do other than to adopt the corollary to our
principle: the development of Tunisia will be

accomplished on a basis of a combining of all creative
forces, without discrimination. There will be neither
unremitting nationalization nor complete liberalism.
We will follow a selective and considered policy oriented toward the use of all creative forces, under the
protection of the party and of the state, both of which
shall guarantee social cohesion and the general interest.

Given the magnitude of the job of constructing
a new society where the well-being and dignity of
the individual are guaranteed, all sources of good
will are necessary and useful. This explains the
maintenance in our system of the development of
three types of enterprises: private enterprise,
public enterprise, and cooperatives. [22]

The publication then proceeds to discuss the role of each
of these sectors. In the discussion of the role of the private
sector, it has the following to say:

Without ambiguity, we say that private enterprise
now disposes of and will, in the future, dispose of
an immense field of action.

However, the immense field of activity which
we leave to private enterprise in Tunisia is not a
guarantee to all private enterprise: the type of
private enterprise which Destourian socialism encourages and supports is that which goes beyond
egoistic and individual interests and deliberately
takes the viewpoint of general interest and social
cohesion.

Having clarified this point, we can state that
private enterprise may enter into any domain of
economic activity except those where the state has
taken charge, either temporarily or finally.

However, the respect of these rules vis-à-vis
the field of action of the private sector rests on the
assumption that the private entrepreneur is able to
overcome his outmoded concepts and can adhere
sincerely and totally to the fundamental principles
of our socialism... justice, equality, solidarity,
social cohesion, etc. This is not a question, simply
of reaffirming these principles, but rather a condition sine qua non of the survival of the private
sector. [23]

NOTES

1. Government of Tunisia, Les Discours du Président Bourguiba.

2. Ibid.

3. From files in the headquarters of the Destourian Socialist party, Tunis.

4. Ibid.

5. Government of Tunisia, op. cit.

6. Ibid.

7. Ibid.

8. La Dépêche Tunisienne (July 28, 1956).

9. Government of Tunisia, op. cit.

10. La Dépêche Tunisienne (September 25, 1956).

11. Ibid. (October 9, 1956).

12. Government of Tunisia, op. cit.

13. Government of Tunisia, Perspectives Décennales de Développement: 1962-1971, pp. 8, 9.

14. Ibid. , pp. 89, 90.

15. Ibid. , p. 93.

16. Government of Tunisia, Plan Triennal: 1962-1964, p. 423.

17. Government of Tunisia, Plan Quadriennal: 1965-1968, Vol. I, pp. 18, 35.

18. Government of Tunisia, Discours du Président Bourguiba.

19. Ibid.

20. La Presse (June 20, 1964).

21. Entreprise (Paris) (July 7, 1966).

22. Commission Économique et Sociale du Parti Socialiste Destourien, Le Séminaire National sur la Coordination des Secteurs Économiques (Tunis, 1965), pp. 17, 18.

23. Ibid. , pp. 34, 35, 37.

CHAPTER **5** TUNISIAN GOVERNMENT
ACTIONS AFFECTING
THE POLITICAL
CLIMATE FOR
PRIVATE INVESTMENT

Tunisia, because of its past history, has done many
things vis-à-vis private enterprise which give businessmen
cause to hesitate before investing in the country. It has, in
fact, done a little of just about everything in the book which
might antagonize businessmen. At the same time, the government has taken many actions to encourage private investment. It has attempted to make the political climate as
attractive as possible, in a positive way, to compensate for
the negative actions which government officials have felt were
necessary, but which they have realized are a blot on the government's reputation vis-à-vis private investors. This chapter reviews the extent to which the Tunisian government has
acted in each of the areas, and presents what the author believes to be a complete compilation of nationalization and government seizure of industrial, agricultural, and commercial
property in Tunisia since independence.

ACTIONS THAT DISCOURAGE
PRIVATE INVESTORS

Nationalization of Industry

The nationalization of a company, even with indemnification, is a disturbing possibility to the potential investor.
What is more disturbing, however, is the knowledge that the
government of a country has resorted to nationalization without indemnification. In Tunisia, there have been some nationalizations of industry without indemnification, and some
with. (Information for this section was obtained from files

of the French embassy, Tunis, from discussions with officials
in the embassy, and from a review of the pertinent governmental decrees and laws.)

When the government took over the railroads in 1956,
immediately after independence, it was looked upon (and still
is, by most people) as the first step in the process of nationalization of basic industries in Tunisia. It may be helpful,
therefore, to clarify the facts in that case.

The French firm, Compagnie des Chemins de Fer
Tunisiens (CFT), was not, in reality, the owner of the railroad. In 1922, the Tunisian government had purchased the
railroad from CFT, which was given a concession to operate
the railroad network. It would be more accurate to say that
CFT had a management contract with a profit incentive arrangement. Since 1922, the land, materials, and rolling
stock had been the property of the government. The 1922
agreement expired in 1948 and was renewed for two years.
This renewal expired on December 31, 1950, and was not
formally renewed. CFT then continued to operate the railroads, but without a legal basis. Between 1945 and 1956 the
government had spent between $4 million and $5 million for
equipment to modernize the railroad and an additional several million in making up deficits in operating costs. The
operating loss in 1955, for example, was $3.5 million.

By decree of February 2, 1956, the government established a management committee to assume control of the railroad. The working capital of the company was immediately
transferred to the government treasury. On December 28,
1956, President Bourguiba issued a decree establishing the
Société Nationale des Chemins de Fer Tunisiens (SNCFT), a
government-owned corporation, to which was transferred all
the property and equipment which had been under the control
of the management committee. The decree did not even mention CFT, which had operated the railroad for about 80 years.

Thus, this did not constitute nationalization of a foreign-
owned railroad. Rather, the Tunisian government formally
assumed responsibility for the operation of a railroad which
had been the property of the government for 34 years and was
being managed by a French company whose concession contract had expired six years earlier.

It is interesting to note that the railroad, which had shown
an operating deficit for many years prior to independence, had
deficits of $3.5 million in 1955, $1.9 million in 1956, $480,000
in 1957, and $120,000 in 1958, but made a profit of $730,000
in 1959.

There were, however, a number of true nationalizations. Appendix A, List 1, is a compilation of the 10 electricity, gas, water, and transportation (truck and bus) companies which were owned by French interests and were nationalized following a period during which the government simply took over the management of the companies. These companies had combined annual sales of approximately $8.5 million in 1956.

Although the decrees which nationalized these 10 companies stated that a later law would provide for methods of indemnification, many years passed without any effort on the part of the government to compensate the former owners. However, late in 1967, the former owners of the seven electric power companies and the Tunisian government asked the World Bank to serve as arbiter in achieving a settlement of the issue. The claims submitted by these companies at the time of nationalization totaled $71 million.

The following is an example of the manner in which the government took control of the management of the above 10 companies. On June 30, 1958, the Minister of Commerce and Industry published a decree in the Journal Officiel indicating that the government would temporarily take over the management of the Compagnie Tunisienne d'Électricité et Transport (CTET). The decree said: "Considering the operating difficulties encountered by the CTET, and seeing the necessity of assuring the continuity and the regularity of this public service, the state is temporarily taking over the management of the company...."

The above 10 companies were nationalized by two sweeping laws, one dealing with electricity and gas, the other with transportation. The following is excerpted from the law of April 3, 1962, which nationalized the gas and electrical industries:

> The production, transportation, distribution, importation, and exportation of electricity and gas are nationalized as of the date of publication of this law. Companies operating in Tunisia which are engaged in these activities and which have previously been put under temporary management of the state, are nationalized as of the original take-over. Excluded from nationalization are (1) the production, transportation, importation, and exportation of natural gas and liquefied gas; and (2) the installations which produce gas and electricity but which are part of companies whose primary activities are other.

The law went on to say that a state-owned corporation, the Société Tunisienne de l'Electricité et du Gaz (STEG), was to take over the management and operation of all the nationalized industries and to receive from the state all property and equipment belonging to the nationalized companies.

A last case of apparent nationalization, which is of interest because it is more recent, is that of the Compagnie des Phosphates et du Chemin de Fer de Sfax-Gafsa. This company had two major activities. It owned and operated one of the major phosphate mines near Gafsa. In addition, it operated a railroad between Sfax and Gafsa. Most of the traffic on this railroad (99 percent) was phosphate rock, mined near Gafsa and shipped to the seaport of Sfax.

According to the convention of August 15, 1896, between the company and the Tunisian government, the former had a concession to operate the line for a period of 70 years. It was expressly stated that the concession would expire on December 31, 1966, at which time the concession to operate this line, as well as all property and equipment associated with its operation, would revert to the government.

The government took control of the railroad on the date specified, and proceeded to integrate it into the rest of the country's railroad network. This action was heralded by some as a "nationalization" of the railroad, but in reality it was an exercise of a contract at the time specified.

Nationalization of Farmland

On May 12, 1964, the Tunisian government passed a law which nationalized all foreign-owned agricultural land in the country. This was the biggest nationalization which has taken place. It led to a rupture in relations between Tunisia and France and to a worsening of the political climate for private investment. It was a political act which, because of the resultant loss of foreign aid and import subsidies from France, had a very negative effect on the Tunisian economy.

It may be helpful, for purposes of perspective, to review step by step the process whereby the Tunisian government nationalized the farmland which formerly belonged to the French. (Information for this section was obtained from files of the French embassy, Tunis, from discussions with officials of that embassy as well as those of Great Britain, Switzerland, Belgium, and Italy, and from the pertinent govermental decrees.)

At the time of independence, about 1.5 million acres of agricultural land (valued at $213 million) was in the hands of French individuals and companies. This represented only about 8 percent of the total arable farmland in the country, but it was a much higher percentage of the more productive land. The first step taken was to enter into an agreement with the French government whereby the Tunisian government would buy those French-owned farms which were located near the Algerian border, where the safety of the owners could not be assured. By an accord dated May 8, 1957, the French loaned $13.2 million to Tunisia to pay for 305,000 acres of land. In addition, the Tunisian government recognized that the equipment which came with the land was worth an additional $1.1 million and that the owners would be reimbursed in four equal payments over a period of four years. The first such payment was made in November, 1963, and subsequent payments were made on schedule.

The agrarian reform law of June 11, 1958, was prompted by a major government irrigation project in the low valley of the Medjerda. The law stated that the irrigation greatly increased the value of the land and that, in return, the property owners who profited from the irrigation would cede to the government 25-70 percent of the area of their land, the percent varying according to the value added by the irrigation. On July 26, 1960, the original law was extended to a much wider area around the Medjerda valley and affected a considerable amount of land which did not profit from the irrigation. Although a high proportion of the lands in this valley were French-owned, there was also considerable Tunisian-owned land, which was equally affected.

On May 7, 1959, the government passed a law permitting it to sequester all lands which were being neglected or insufficiently exploited. In a speech several days before the law was announced, President Bourguiba noted that the country's economy could not afford to have idle land and that steps would be taken by the state to make such land productive. The law affected Tunisian as well as foreign landowners. During the following two years 100,000 acres, of which 75,000 acres belonged to companies and 25,000 acres to individual owners, were sequestered. French embassy officials felt that the definition of "insufficiently exploited" was sometimes stretched.

The next major step was a French-Tunisian protocol dated October 13, 1960, which stated that the French landowners would sell a total of 250,000 acres of land to the

Tunisian government. The list of such lands was to be made
up with the agreement of both governments. This program
proceeded satisfactorily. The Tunisian government gave $24
per acre to the French government to give to the landowners.
The French government realized that this was well below the
value of most of the land and therefore had a commission
make its own appraisal. If, for a given piece of land, the
value was estimated at $60 per acre, the French government
would add $36 to the $24 received from the Tunisian government. This extra $36 was considered as resettlement aid to
the returning French landowners.

The October, 1960, arrangements were proceeding satisfactorily when the military crises at Bizerte occurred, following which the Tunisian government sequestered 200,000
acres of French farmlands "due to a state of emergency."

On March 2, 1963, however, after the resumption of
normal relations between the two countries, the protocol of
October 13, 1960, was extended by 125,000 acres, making a
total of 375,000 acres. Included within this total was the
200,000 acres sequestered immediately after the Bizerte
affair. Also included were the lands in the area surrounding
the Medjerda valley, which had to be ceded to the government
even though they had not benefited from the irrigation.

Additional irrigation projects prompted the law of May
27, 1963. It was somewhat like the 1958 law in that it required the landowner who benefited from the irrigation project to cede part of his land to the government. It did,
however, give the landowner the alternative of paying the
government an equivalent amount in cash, over a period of
five to 10 years. On the other hand, this law limited any
individual holding in the irrigated areas to a total of 125
acres. For all holdings greater than 125 acres, the excess
was expropriated by the government, the indemnities being
paid 50 percent in cash and 50 percent in government bonds
(10-year bonds paying 2 percent interest).

By May, 1964, therefore, the Tunisian government had
obtained about 805,000 acres of land from former French
owners. Of this, 692,000 acres had belonged to individual
landowners, for whom indemnification arrangements had
been made, and most of them had been paid. The remaining
113,000 acres had been owned by French companies and, in
general, they had received no indemnification, since all of
the above-mentioned agreements concerned only individual
holdings.

At the beginning of May, 1964, there remained about 500,000 acres of land owned by individual Frenchmen (about 1,000 individuals, of whom 600 lived in Tunisia) and 150,000 acres owned by companies (about 100 firms, three of which owned about 50,000 acres). The law of May 12, 1964, nationalized all of these lands. The law stated that "ownership of agricultural lands can be only by individuals who have Tunisian nationality, or by cooperative societies."

The French embassy in Tunis estimated that the value of the land, equipment, cattle, and crops thus expropriated from French owners was $163 million. The law stated, however, that the former owners would have the ". . . right to an indemnification, the amount to be determined by a commission. . . . In this determination, the commission will take into account the nature of the land, the origin of the property, the period of exploitation, the amortization effected, and the condition in which the property is found at the time the government takes possession. . . . The method of indemnification will be determined by decree." In private conversations, the Tunisian government had indicated to French embassy officials that much of this indemnification would have to be token.

For the purposes of prospective, one should note that prior to the negotiation of the protocol of March 2, 1963, which extended the number of acres which the Tunisian government would buy from French owners at $24 per acre, a letter from the Tunisian Minister of Foreign Affairs to the French Ambassador to Tunisia stated in part:

I have the honor of advising you that the government of Tunisia, wishing to harmonize the program of purchase of lands with the country's plan for social and economic development, intends to resolve all the problems which might arise in the pursuit of this objective by friendly agreement, respecting the different interests at stake.

Consequently, the French landowners who are not included in the land-purchasing program will be assured of peace and quiet, within the framework of the laws and regulations in effect, for a period of five years from the date of signing of this protocol.

The Tunisian government wishes, however, to note that it has the intention to study, beginning in 1964, with the French government, the conditions and methods for ceding the lands not yet included in the purchase programs covered by the protocol of 13 October 1960, and [that of 2 March 1963].

The French landowners were not, of course, the only ones who lost property during the May, 1964, nationalizations. A number of Swiss farmers and companies lost a total of about 3,000 acres of land, plus associated equipment and buildings. British (Maltese) farmers lost over 5,000 acres of land which was devoted primarily to the growing of esparto grass, plus storage and commercial facilities associated with this agricultural export industry. Belgians were also involved in the growing and exporting of esparto grass. Approximately 2,500 acres of land, plus wholesaling and warehousing facilities, belonging to Belgian citizens were nationalized. Finally, next to the French, the Italian farmers suffered the greatest loss. The nationalizations hit about 1,200 Italian farmers, who owned 68,000 acres of land, most of which was in the rich Cap Bon area. The land was valued by the Italians at a total of $16 million.

The nationalization law of May 12, 1964, stated that a later decree would determine the method of indemnification. Such a decree has not been issued. Instead, the Tunisian government began a series of discussions, with each of the governments concerned, to arrange a settlement. These discussions began early in 1965, when the Swiss government was requested to submit dossiers on the nationalized farms. This was accomplished very quickly, and by July 27, 1965, the two governments had signed an agreement whereby the Tunisian government would pay an agreed-upon indemnification over a period of three years. There were also discussions with the Belgian government, during which the Tunisian government agreed to pay compensation. But by mid-1967 the amount had not been settled, nor had the means of payment. The major difficulty was that most of the former landowners had left Tunisia and would have to be paid in foreign exchange, which Tunisia could not (and cannot) spare. Discussions with the British government are at the same stage as those with the Belgians, agreement in principle having been reached by late 1966. Within several months after the nationalizations, the Italian government passed a law permitting the treasury to make an advance to the Italian farmers of an amount equal to 50 percent of their losses. This law, however, was never implemented. In March, 1967, the two governments reached an agreement whereby the Italian farmers would receive compensation as part of a broad bilateral aid program. The Tunisian government agreed to pay $14.4 million to the Italian farmers, the funds to be disbursed immediately by the Italian government. This was linked to an Italian government loan of $16 million to Tunisia.

Finally, there is the problem of reimbursing the French landowners, which is a much greater problem. Here, also, discussions have been under way since early 1965, but no general agreement has been reached. A partial agreement was reached in July, 1966, whereby France imported 2.6 million gallons of Tunisian wine, valued at $12 million, under very favorable conditions but with the proviso that of this sum, $5.4 million would be placed in an "indemnification fund" kept in France. This fund is being used to compensate the French landowners. No agreement has yet been reached between the French and Tunisian governments as to the total amount due the former landowners.

Management Take-Overs

(Information for this section was obtained from files and from discussions with officials of the French embassy and the company El Bouniane, in Tunis, as well as from the pertinent governmental decrees.)

Besides the 10 utility companies referred to earlier, which were actually nationalized by law, four others had the government take over their management and also take possession of their property, without legal expropriation. These four companies are listed and the situations described in Appendix A, List 2. They were, in effect, sequestered, and remain under government control. The former owners have outstanding claims against the government totaling $1.92 million. In addition to the above four companies, the government sequestered a number of drugstores and two medical clinics following the military action at Bizerte in 1961. These have not been returned, and the owners claim losses which total over $960,000.

There were also three companies which were placed under the control of a government committee but later returned to their rightful owners. (See Appendix A, List 3.) It is interesting to note that the government used these cases to illustrate its attitude toward private investment. An editorial in the January, 1962, issue of the Bulletin of the Chamber of Commerce of Tunis, which to a certain extent spoke with the same voice as the government, noted that the firms were placed under the direction of a governmentally appointed board only because they were operated in a way which was not in the public interest. "The government," it said, "does not want to take over the control of industries which are in the sectors that can be and are properly carried out by private enterprise. The cancellation of this decree and the return of the management of these companies to the private sector was meant to be a manifestation of this intent by the government."

Finally, there is the situation where companies were placed under government committees and, at a much later date, negotiations between the owners and the government resulted in the purchase of company property by the government. The five such cases described in Appendix A, List 4, were not, therefore, expropriations as such. They were sequestrations followed by negotiated purchase. It is important to note that four of the five cases resulted from the Bizerte crisis.

The most important and most interesting case was that of Ets. Schwich et Baizeau (now known as El Bouniane). This major industrial complex contributed to the industrial growth of Tunisia. It was founded in 1902 by Lucien Schwich and Jean Baizeau, who put their fortunes in Tunisia; it continued to grow over the years, and profits were always plowed back into the company. By the time of independence, Ets. Schwich et Baizeau was a holding company which included some of the most important manufacturing companies in the country, as well as large-scale holdings in real estate and commerce.

Negotiated Purchases

(Information for this section was obtained from the files and from discussions with an official of the Compagnie des Phosphates et du Chemin de Fer de Sfax-Gafsa, from the Belgian embassy, and from the pertinent governmental decrees.)

As indicated above, the government has nationalized a number of companies, usually preceding the nationalization with a management take-over. There have also been management take-overs without formal expropriation, amounting, in effect, to sequestration. Several of these companies have been returned to their original owners. Finally, there were several cases where the government simply bought participation in a company sufficient to give it control.

The most important of these cases is that of the Compagnie des Phosphates et du Chemin de Fer de Sfax-Gafsa, important because of the size of the company and its role in export earnings for the country. This is the same company referred to earlier, whose concession for the operation of the Sfax-Gafsa railroad expired on December 31, 1966.

The present case, however, concerns the portion of the company which owned and operated the large phosphate mines. The details are given in Appendix A, List 5.

In addition to this phosphate company, the government also negotiated the purchase of another phosphate company and a lead and zinc mining company. (See Appendix A, List 5.)

Tunisification of the Banking System

(Information for this section was obtained from annual reports of the Société Tunisienne de Banque and of the Banque Centrale.)

At the time of independence there were 14 commercial banks in Tunisia, all them branches or subsidiaries of French banks or owned by French citizens in Tunisia. This sort of situation might have given rise to a policy of nationalization, but the Tunisian government chose to follow another path.

The government's first move was to establish a Tunisian bank, the Société Tunisienne de Banque (STB). It was organized in 1956 with a capital of $960,000. The government itself subscribed 52.4 percent of the capital, and the remainder was offered to the public for purchase by Tunisian citizens or companies. The distribution of the 47.6% was as follows: shareholders with more than 800 shares, 6.2 percent; shareholders with 200-800 shares, 18 percent; shareholders with less than 200 shares, 23.4 percent.

The bank did not actually begin operations until March, 1958. In 1960, the government decided to increase the capital to $2.4 million, although the increase did not take place until 1962. The government share remained essentially the same, decreasing to 52.2 percent of the total, while the distribution of the remainder showed slight movement toward the larger shareholders: shareholders with more than 800 shares, 10.5 percent; shareholders with 200-800 shares, 19.8 percent; shareholders with less than 200 shares, 17.5 percent.

The bank was to be a combination investment bank and commercial bank. It would be able to establish companies, to take equity participation in companies which were being established by others, to provide long- and medium-term credits to assist in the creation of new companies or the growth of existing ones, and to provide short-term credits as required by industry and commerce in the same manner as a commercial bank.

The bank's growth was phenomenal. In 1959 it had out-standing credits of over $33.6 million, which was 14 percent of total bank credits in Tunisia. This grew to 24 percent in 1960, 40 percent in 1961, 41 percent in 1962, and 42 percent in 1963. It has since stayed near this figure.

Not only has the bank grown, but it has been a profitable venture. The profits in 1958, the first year of operation, were $122,400. Profits increased to $600,000 in 1959, and were $1.365 million in 1965. Considering that the equity capital was only $960,000 up to 1962, and has been only $2.4 million since then, this represents an extremely good return. As a result, the bank has followed a policy of declaring an annual dividend of 8 percent.

At about the same time that the government established the STB to serve in the areas of commerce and industry, it also, in 1958, created an agricultural bank, the Banque Nationale Agricole (BNA). This bank has a broad charter, however, and so it also acts as a savings bank and a commer-cial bank, and has even begun making medium-term loans and equity investments in industrial ventures, not all of which are related to agriculture. By December 31, 1965, the STB had 40 percent of total bank assets in Tunisia, and the BNA had 17 percent.

Such activity was certain to have an effect on the banks which were in Tunisia at independence. Two small banks were going bankrupt and were purchased by the STB, at the request of the Central Bank, to avoid an international scandal and to protect the depositors. In addition, four mergers took place, with fresh capital coming from U.S. and Italian banks.

Although the Tunisian government has urged those banks which at independence were branches of French banks to in-corporate in Tunisia, three have not yet done so. Also, two new banks, the British Bank of the Middle East and the Arab Bank, obtained permission from the government to open branches in Tunis, in 1957 and 1959, respectively.

Establishment of State-Owned Enterprises

We have already seen that through nationalization and the purchase of participation in existing companies, the Tunisian government has expanded rather rapidly into the ownership of industry. Much of it, of course, is in the basic industries, which most governments feel rightfully belong in

the public sector. But, as has been noted, the Tunisian government also feels that industries which are critical to the
economy should be in the public sector, or at least controlled
by the government. This explains the movement of the government into most of the mining companies through the purchase of participation.

The government established the STB, the Société Nationale d'Investissement (SNI), and the BNA in the late 1950's
to foster the growth of industry. In addition, the government
has a controlling interest in the Société Tunisienne d'Assurance
et de Réassurance. Through these four quasi-governmental
financial institutions, as well as directly, the government,
especially since the beginning of the three-year plan, has
started a number of new industries. Some of them are owned
100 percent by the government; some are held partially by the
government and partially by the quasi-governmental institutions, and some have only a majority or minority interest by
the quasi-governmental institutions.

These organizations are an important part of the industrial growth of Tunisia and certainly represent a projection
of the government into the economy, especially in the most
important industries. However, the SNI and the STB have an
expressed policy of fostering industries which can later be
sold to the private sector, which could greatly temper the
present significant involvement of the government in new industrial enterprises.

The STB began investing in new companies in 1958, total
direct investment that year being only $67,000. This grad-
ually increased to a total of $3.33 million by mid-1966,[1] at
which time it held stock in 45 companies.[2] Of these, however, it held less than 10 percent of the shares of 25 companies; between 10 percent and 30 percent of the shares of
12 companies; 30-50 percent of four companies; and over 50
percent of four companies. The four in which it had a majority interest were two banks (which it had rescued from
bankruptcy), a boat building company, and a company which
engages in economic feasibility and marketing studies.

The bank's medium- and long-term loan activity was,
however, far more important than direct investments. By
the end of 1966, outstanding medium- and long-term loans
totaled over $13 million.

The SNI was a governmentally controlled institution at
the time that it acquired its present investment portfolio.
Most of its investments were made in projects called for by
the three-year plan. By the end of 1963, it had invested a

total of $3.75 million in 33 companies and had a majority interest in five of them; by the end of 1964 it had invested $4.60 million in 43 companies, but had a controlling interest in only three.[3] Its portfolio changed very little after that year.

The BNA, by the end of 1966, had invested $522,000 in a total of 22 companies. In general its investments have been in food-processing industries, but not all of them have been. It has a majority interest in only one of them.

The Société Tunisienne d'Assurance et de Réassurance had, by the end of 1966, used its financial resources to invest a total of $1.04 million in various branches of industry, most of it in about 20 different companies.[4] Essentially all of these investments were in companies in which either the STB or the SNI, or both, had also invested. It has generally avoided having a majority interest, but often its investment in a given company, along with those of the STB, the SNI, and the BNA in the same company, have added up to a majority interest, and thus given control of the company to quasi-public institutions which are under the authority of the Ministry of Planning and Economics.

Direct investment by the government has not been extensive except in the service industries and mining, which did not entail establishing new companies. It nationalized a number of electricity, gas, water, and transportation companies. Also, it purchased a 55 percent or greater interest in most of the existing mining companies and also in several industrial companies. Beyond this, since independence the government as such has started few new companies in which it has a controlling interest. These are limited to two banks, the insurance company, an oil refinery, a steel mill, a cellulose plant, a number of textile plants, and several other types of plants.[5] The cellulose plant is in the public sector because its operation controls the life of a whole region of the country. Thus, the only plants established and controlled directly by the government which one might have expected to be in the private sector are the textile plants and the several other types of plants.

Most of the government-owned plants were started during the three-year plan, 1962-64. Since 1964, except for several additional textile plants, virtually no new government-owned industries have been established.

Tunisification of Commerce

The decree of August 30, 1961, established the concept
of Tunisification of commerce. The law applied only to com-
merce--importing, exporting, wholesaling, and retailing--
excluding the importation and distribution of petroleum
products.

This law stated that companies engaged in commerce
must be incorporated in Tunisia and that at least 50 percent
of their capital must be owned by Tunisians. Where this was
not the case, the individuals or companies concerned had,
within one month, to notify the Minister of Planning and Finance. If they wished to continue their activity, they could
ask for a waiver. If such a waiver was not granted, they had
one year to incorporate in Tunisia and to sell at least 50 percent of their capital to Tunisians.

Some individuals (mostly French, and some Italians) did
not receive waivers and could not find buyers, and thus had
to close their businesses. Many could sell the 50 percent interest to Tunisians only at a price considerably below the actual value. A few have continued to receive waivers and to
operate as before.

Reorganization of Channels of Distribution

The Tunisification law attempted to force non-Tunisians
out of the commercial sector or to get them to integrate with
Tunisians. Other steps were taken to compete with them and
to give the state a monopoly in importing and wholesaling
certain products.

For example, an Office of Commerce was established on
April 3, 1962, for the purposes of expanding foreign trade
and intervening in the channels of distribution. This office,
by decree, was given the monopoly for importing sugar,
coffee, pepper, tea, tropical fruits, vegetable oil, and rice.
This law thus eliminated the business of a number of major
importers.

Several months later, the Office of Commerce was in-
strumental in organizing regional wholesale companies
(sociétés régionales de commerce), one in each of the 12
regions of the country. The Office of Commerce furnished
a total of $240,000, an average of 20 percent of the capital
of each of these companies; the other $960,000 came from
the former wholesalers and many retailers, as well as other

individuals in each region. There were a total of 15,000
stockholders. The effect of establishing the regional companies was to force most other wholesalers out of business.
In many regions, no other wholesalers remain.

The following year, the government organized a cooperative sector at the regional level, primarily to supervise
existing local cooperatives but also to compete with the
sociétés régionales de commerce in the field of wholesaling.
The shareholders of these new unions régionales de coopératives were (1) the existing retail cooperatives, (2) private
retailers, and (3) the government (through the Office of
Commerce).

The Office of Commerce was also charged with responsibility for attempting to streamline the retail trade, which was
characterized by many very small shops, which kept no books,
and therefore paid no taxes, and did not invest profits in productive enterprises. To help accomplish this, national seminars on the coordination of the private, public, and cooperative
sectors were organized by the party in September, 1965, and
March, 1966. Following the second of these, the government
announced that it would require groups of three or more shopkeepers to form a company, which would open one larger
shop. Such a unité commerciale would be clean, modern,
carry a larger range of items, keep books, pay taxes, and
perhaps invest some profits in the tourist industry. By the
end of 1967 this transformation had been essentially completed.

Meanwhile, during the latter half of 1967 considerable
discussion took place within the party apparatus for a further
transformation of the commercial sector. A consensus was
reached and announced by Ben Salah on February 15, 1968.
This called for the formation of new retail organizations
known as marketing cooperatives. Each of these would be
larger than a unité commerciale and would have at least 15
sales outlets. All existing unités commerciales and retail
cooperatives, plus most of the remaining individual retailers,
were to become members of the new marketing cooperatives,
their value to become their share capital in the cooperative.
Only a few retailers who were sufficiently large could continue to operate independently.

At the same time, the government required the merger
of the sociétés régionales de commerce with the unions régionales de coopératives to form larger regional cooperatives
whose capital was to be owned 50 percent by the marketing
cooperatives (the clients) and 50 percent by the producers
from which they bought.

Labor-Management Committees

By decree of January 13, 1962, the government authorized the unions to establish labor-management committees
(comités d'enterprise) in any company having more than 50
employees. Either the labor union or the management of the
company can initiate the formation of such a committee. A
government official appoints a commission which investigates
the economic, social, and financial situation of the company
and then makes its recommendation. The labor-management
committee is then established by a decree of the Minister of
Public Health and Social Affairs.

The committee is composed of the managing director of
the company and a workers' committee composed of three
members, if the company has 50 to 100 employees; five members, if the company has 100 to 500 employees; and seven
members, if the company has over 500 employees.

The union is asked to select the members of the workers'
committee. The managing director of the company is always
president of the committee, which must meet at least once a
month. The committee makes recommendations to the company president, but he may reject them. If he rejects them,
however, the committee can transmit its recommendation to
a government inspector. The decree does not state what the
inspector might do in such an event, nor have there been any
appeals to him to test possible government sanctions.

Since the decree was published, only a small number of
such committees have been established. It appears, from
numerous interviews by the author, that the managing director of a company, as president of the committee, is generally
able to control the topics to be considered by the committee
and thus to avoid potential problems. There does not appear
to be any fear among the management of companies that the
establishment of such a committee represents a loss of management rights. To date it seems to be acting more as a desirable channel of communication between workers and
management.

Government Control of Investments

Since 1946, Tunisia has had a law controlling investments
in industry, established as a decree by the French commissioner. That decree established a commission which was to
examine requests and give its recommendations to the

Minister of Finance. That decree remained in effect after independence, until April 3, 1962, when a new law was passed which updated the 1946 decree but maintained essentially the same provisions.

In accordance with the 1962 law, the creation, expansion, reconversion, or change of location of an industrial company is subject to the approval of the Minister of Planning and Economics, who acts upon the advice of an advisory commission. The investor must address a letter to the Minister of Planning and Economics requesting approval of the investment contemplated. Attached to this letter should be five copies of a feasibility study, including a discussion of the contemplated types and sources of financing; a description of the equipment required and the probable equipment suppliers; plans for site location; the effect of the investment on the country's foreign exchange position; and a five-year projection of production, employment, and profits (or losses).

These requests are studied by officials in the ministry to determine that they contain all necessary information and to see whether the investment is economically feasible. It is also studied in the light of its effect on competing industries, on applied industries, and on the economy in general. The dossier is then forwarded to the secretary of the advisory commission.

The advisory commission meets three or four times per year. The investor is not usually notified that a meeting is being held during which his request will be considered. Only on very rare occasions will the investor be asked to appear before the commission. Several weeks after the commission has met and made its recommendation, the investor is officially notified of the approval (or disapproval) of the Minister of Planning and Economics.

If the application is refused, there is no appeals machinery nor formal procedure for appeal. The typical reasons for past rejections have been that (1) the application had insufficient information and the applicant did not respond to requests for additional information; (2) there was already an excess of capacity or production in that particular industry; and (3) approval had recently been given to another investor to produce the same product in sufficient quantity to satisfy the market.

The time period between submission of an investment application and notice of approval (or disapproval) varies widely. The delay may be from two to four months if the investor happens to submit his application several months before the meeting of the commission and if the application is in good order and does not encounter any lengthy delays during its review. The typical delay would be near six months, but some approvals involve a delay of nine months to a year.

However, it is possible for an investor to overcome the effects of this administrative delay. He may, at an early stage of his investment plans, discuss the project with one of the top officials of the Ministry of Planning and Economics and obtain a type of "gentlemen's agreement." This does not bypass the established procedure but gives the investor a clear idea of the government's view of his project. The investor can then proceed with his study and negotiations with some assurance that approval can be obtained at a later date.

The purpose of this approval procedure is to permit the government to consider how the investment fits into the four-year plan; how it might affect existing investments in the same industry and in related industries; what relationship it might have to other applications to invest in the same field; and the probable net cost or saving in foreign exchange as a result of the investment.

ACTIONS DESIGNED TO
ENCOURAGE PRIVATE INVESTMENT

Investment Guarantee Treaties
and Arbitration Agreement

The Tunisian government has negotiated private investment guarantee treaties with the governments of the United States, Switzerland, West Germany, Belgium, the Netherlands, and France.

The agreement with the United States was the first, having taken effect on March 18, 1959. It is called the Agreement on the Guarantee of Private Investment. It states that the two governments will, upon the request of either of them, consult on projects in Tunisia proposed by nationals of the United States, where U.S. investment guarantees are being considered. The U.S. government agreed to issue no guarantees unless such action was approved by the Tunisian government. On the other hand, the Tunisian government agreed that if an investment project had been approved by both governments, and the U.S. government subsequently found it necessary to pay the investor against a claim of loss, the

Tunisian government would recognize the transfer to the U.S. government of the assets of the investor, such transfer being made in dinars within Tunisia. Such currency acquired by the U.S. government is to be accorded the same conditions of conversion into U.S. dollars as is accorded private funds arising from similar transactions of U.S. nationals. The U.S. government may, however, choose to spend such funds locally.

The agreement with Switzerland was signed in December, 1961, but did not become effective until November 4, 1963. It is called the Treaty . . . Relative to the Protection and Encouragement of Private Investment. Among the pertinent aspects of the treaty is that Swiss investments in Tunisia are to receive treatment at least equal to that of Tunisian companies. Tunisia also agrees to authorize the transfer of net profits, dividends, invested capital, and reinvested capital which Swiss firms invest in Tunisia, based on existing legislation or on other, more favorable legislation which might be passed in the future. If Tunisia expropriates or nationalizes the investment of a Swiss company, she must make an adequate and effective indemnity, which must be determined at the time of expropriation and must be settled without an unjustifiable delay. The indemnity must be transferred within a reasonable time. If a difference arises between the two governments as to the interpretation of this treaty, and if the difference is not settled satisfactorily manner through diplomatic channels within six months, it will be submitted to an arbitration board of three members. Each government will select one member, and those two members will select the third from a third country. The treaty is for a period of ten years but remains in effect beyond that time unless renounced by either government. It remains in effect, however, for one year after such renunciation. For any investments made prior to the date of expiration of the treaty, the terms of the treaty remain applicable for 10 years after the date of its expiration.

The treaties with the Netherlands and Belgium are essentially the same as that with Switzerland. The treaty with the Netherlands was signed on May 23, 1963, and went into effect on November 4, 1963, at the same time as the Swiss treaty, while the treaty with Belgium was signed on August 15, 1964, and was ratified on February 22, 1966.

The treaty with West Germany was signed on December 20, 1963, and went into effect on May 28, 1964. It differs from the Swiss treaty in that it is more detailed and more

favorable to the foreign investor. It states, for example, that
if a foreign investment is expropriated, " . . . the indemnity
must correspond to the value of the investment expropriated,
be effectively payable, freely transferable, and paid without
delay. At the time of expropriation, at the latest, the government must specify the amount to be paid and the manner
in which the indemnity will be paid." Another article of the
treaty states that the government guarantees the investors
" . . . the free transfer of capital as well as the free transfer
of profits and, in case of liquidation, of the amount of the
liquidation of the investment." This differs from the Swiss
treaty in that the latter hedges by saying that the transfer of
capital and profits is to be permitted, "based on existing
legislation. . . ." The German treaty also specifies that transfers are to be based on the par value of the dinar, as registered with the International Monetary Fund, at the time of
transfer and/or within the variation permitted by the regulations of the Fund.

The treaty with France, although signed by both parties
and ratified by Tunisia on December 31, 1963, was not ratified by France until September 22, 1965. It specified that
the Tunisian government will authorize, without delay, the
transfer of profits and interest, where the foreign exchange
reserves of the country permit it. As to the transfer of
capital of a company which has been liquidated, if the company is one which existed prior to the effective date of the
treaty, the government guarantees the transfer of a "reasonable portion" of the proceeds of the liquidation, the remainder to be placed in a special account in dinars, which can be
ceded to individuals or companies for use in Tunisia for purposes to be specified by the government. If, however, the
company was created after the effective date of the treaty,
the government agrees to transfer, in the case of liquidation,
"all or part of the capital." Finally, in the case of nationalization, the government agrees to pay the owners an "adequate"
indemnity, the amount of which is to be fixed and announced at
the time of expropriation and transferred "without unjustifiable delay."

Finally, it is important to note that not only did Tunisia
become a signatory of the World Bank-sponsored international
arbitration convention, but it made the special effort to be the
first country to sign that agreement, which came into force on
October 14, 1966. It established an International Center for
the Settlement of Investment Disputes, in the hope that the adherence of underdeveloped countries to the convention would

promote an atmosphere of mutual confidence and stimulate a
larger flow of private capital into those countries.

Establishment of a Private Investment Bank

The idea of SNI was first put forth by President Bourguiba
on January 29, 1959, at which time he declared that his government had opted for free savings rather than forced savings.
Through SNI, individuals would have a chance to invest in an
institution which would accelerate the industrialization of the
country and, thereby, raise the standard of living of the
people.

SNI was organized on April 18, 1959, with an initial capital of $600,000 (50,000 shares with a par value of $12 each),
about 80 percent of which was subscribed by the government
or governmental organizations. A month later, however, it
was decided to increase the capital to $4.8 million by the is-
sue of an additional 350,000 shares. The resultant distribution of share ownership was as follows:

Tunisian Government	$ 1,600,000
Tunisian Central Bank	1,080,000
Société Tunisienne de Banque	50,000
Société Tunisienne d'Assurance et de Réassurance	24,000
Société Tunisienne d'Électricité et du Gaz	24,000
Individuals (Tunisians)	2,160,000
Individuals (foreign)	34,000
	$ 4,972,000

Thus, over 45 percent of the share ownership was in the
private sector. The $2.16 million of private Tunisian parti-
cipation includes over 80,000 individual investors. This was
achieved primarily through the national labor union, UGTT,
which "encouraged" many of its members to have deductions
made from their salaries over a period of several months
for purchase of several shares. Farmers, shopkeepers,
and non-union workers also participated. As a consequence,
SNI has a larger capital than any other company in Tunisia,
and also has more stockholders. The primary mission of
SNI, according to its charter, is to encourage investments
in industry by Tunisians and foreigners and, as needed, to
participate directly in financing such investments by providing

either equity or loan capital. It is to promote private initiative in achieving needed industrial projects.

The first three-year plan acted as the main priority determinant as to the types of industry SNI assisted or promoted. Essentially all of its investments prior to 1965 were called for by the plan.

The resources of SNI, prior to 1966, were almost entirely in its capital. It had not received any long-term loans. The management, consequently, decided to follow a policy of utilizing its resources as investment capital. By 1966, therefore, less than $240,000 was outstanding in the form of medium-term loans: the rest was invested in 43 different companies.

As could be expected, however, very few of the new companies in which SNI had invested were able to make profits and pay dividends during the early years of operation (the first dividends were paid at the end of 1964, by seven companies). Thus, when SNI had fully invested its capital, by 1966, it had no further income and was stuck in its position.

Efforts had been made, during 1964 and 1965, to arrange long-term loans from some Tunisian banking and insurance institutions, as well as from four or five French banks, but the solution did not arrive until the World Bank and the International Finance Corporation stepped into the picture. Negotiations between the World Bank and SNI resulted in a reorganization of the capital structure, the Tunisian government's and the Central Bank's share dropping from 57 percent to 7 percent.

The new capital structure is as follows:

	Percent
Tunisian Government	5
Tunisian Central Bank	2
International Finance Corporation	20
Foreign Banks	10
(includes two French banks, a German bank, the Banca Commerciale Italiana and the Swedish Enskilda Bank)	
Local Commercial Banks	7
Private Individuals (mostly Tunisian)	56
	100

In addition, SNI obtained long-term loans from Tunisian sources totaling $2.465 million and a line of credit from the World Bank of $5 million.

In accordance with its new private character, SNI is beginning a policy of attempting to turn over its investment portfolio every five years, and is now looking for investors to relieve it of the first 20 percent of its portfolio, chosen from among those companies which have begun to show profit and thus are of interest to individual investors.

Creation of an Investment Promotion Center

In December 1966, a number of Tunisia's leading financial institutions, plus the Union of Industry, Commerce and Handicrafts, acted as founding members of an investment promotion center. It was organized as an independent non-profit corporation and cannot, itself, finance investments. Its primary purposes are to stimulate new investments, particularly foreign investments; to serve as a reception center for foreign investors, advising and assisting them as necessary in their search for information and for local partners; and to advise investors on the administrative procedures they should follow to obtain governmental approval and assistance, as efficiently as possible.

Although this Center was formed by a number of semi-public institutions, it was organized with the blessing of the Minister of Planning and Economics, who immediately appointed a member of his cabinet to serve as liason between the Center and the government.

Investment Code

Since 1946 the French and then the Tunisian government made an effort to encourage investments by according tax, financial and economic incentives. The basic laws dated back to 1946; the more recent were in 1958 and 1962. This multiplicity of laws was confusing to potential investors and their pre-independence origin gave rise to some doubts about the intention of the government. As a result, the government passed a new Investment Code on June 26, 1969, replacing all of the previous laws and containing a number of innovations in the determination of the types of assistance available.

The new Code still requires that each investor apply for and obtain the approval of the Minister of Planning and Economics before an investment can be made. An Investment

Commission considers all such applications and gives its
advice to the Minister.

All investments are divided into three categories and
each receives a different set of investment incentives. Category A investments are those where the invested capital is
less than $95,000. They receive merely a reduction in
taxes. Category B is where the invested capital is between
$95,000 and $475,000 and which has at least ten permanent
employees. These receive a three-year tax holiday (with a
possible extension to five years) on corporate income and
on dividends. They also receive government guarantees
which facilitate inventory financing plus medium and long-
term loans. And, the equipment imported to make the investment need not pay import duties and taxes. Category
C must have an invested capital greater than $475,000 and
at least fifty permanent employees. Such investments receive the same advantages as Category B, except that the
tax holiday is for five years, renewable for another five
years.

In addition to these automatic features, additional incentives are available, based on the development priority
of the investment, its location, number of employees,
amount of foreign exchange imported, the value added in
the manufacturing process and the percentage of production
which is exported. The kinds of additional advantages which
can be accorded, by negotiation and separate agreement,
are: adoption of a more favorable depreciation schedule;
a guarantee on the level of taxation up to twenty years in
the future; free land for construction of the factory or other
buildings; free site preparation by the government; a monopoly position for a given period of time; and partial or
total prohibition of imports of competing products.

Finally, foreign investors are given a guarantee of
transfer, in foreign exchange, of invested capital and of
profits, without delay, after justification to the central
Bank.

Creation of a Stock Exchange

A most important indicator of the government's thinking
has been the creation, on February 28, 1969, of a stock exchange. It operates as a state enterprise under the direction
of the Ministry of Planning & Economics. Any stocks or
bonds which are issued to the general public, whether from

privately-owned or from State enterprises, must be offered
this exchange. The exchange will accept all issues where
the capital of the company is over $95,000, and where the
company has been in existence at least three years and has
distributed at least one dividend. New companies may also
have their issues handled by this exchange if their shares
have a dividend guarantee by the government or by a bank.
It may be seen therefore, that the exchange also fills the
role of an underwriter, for many cases.

Members of the exchange can be individuals (who have
the proper training and experience and who are citizens of
Tunisia) or banks. These members have a monopoly to
carry out trading transactions but may not trade on their
own account. Their appointment as members must be approved by the Minister of Planning and Economics.

It is apparent that 19th century capitalism is not being
introduced into Tunisia with the creation of this stock exchange. Not only is it closely regulated, it is closely controlled by the government. Yet, it does serve the purpose
of permitting the development banks to sell off shares in
the companies which they own, to the general public. It
also permits the private investor to seek wider sources of
capital. And, it permits the spread of stock ownership to
a much larger percentage of the population.

NOTES

1. Société Tunisienne de Banque, Rapport Annuel.

2. Société Tunisienne de Banque, unpublished report.

3. Société Nationale d'Investissement, unpublished report.

4. La Presse (February 1, 1967).

5. Ministry of Planning and Economics, unpublished papers.

CHAPTER **6** APPLICATION OF THE
MODEL TO TUNISIA

As defined in Chapter 1, the political climate for private
investment consists of "the risk of nationalization, the risk
of being forced out of business by deliberate government
action, the risk of forceful government participation in the
capital of the company, and the risk of future direct competition from a publicly owned company."

The model, described in Chapter 2, to assess these
risks has as its elements (a) the policy statements of key
individuals and documents; (b) the actions taken by the
government; and (c) the historical context within which the
statements and actions took place. For Tunisia, these
elements have been elaborated in Chapters 4, 5, and 3,
respectively. What picture do we receive of Tunisia? What
risks appear to exist? What is the overall evaluation of the
political climate for private investment in Tunisia?

A quick reading of the first section of Chapter 5 is not
very encouraging. We find that the Tunisian government
has, during the period since independence, formally nationalized a number of companies--mostly without compensation;
sequestered some other companies, without legal expropriation;
purchased from 50 per cent to 100 per cent of the shares in
other companies (even though the owners may have preferred
to continue in full control); nationalized all foreign-owned
farmland--without early indemnification; established several
state-controlled commerical banks which immediately obtained a dominant position in the banking sector; established
a number of government-owned or government-controlled
companies in the industrial field, some of them in competition with private industry; established a government
monopoly for the importing and exporting of the major goods
in the country's foreign trade; converted the wholesaling
and retailing sector into a system of cooperatives; forced
the French businessmen who stayed in Tunisia to sell at
least 50 per cent of control of their retail outlets and other
commercial ventures to Tunisians; authorized labor unions

100

to form labor-management committees in industrial firms; and maintained strict and sometimes arbitrary controls over new investments.

Thus, the government appears to have done just about everything possible to discourage private investment. A potential investor, arriving in Tunisia for the first time and having such a record recited to him, would be convinced that Tunisia is committed to Marxist socialism and that it is only a matter of time until the private sector disappears.

But the record, in isolation, is a very distorted view of the total situation. It lacks, first of all, a realization of the real efforts which the government has made to encourage private investment, both domestic and foreign. These efforts include entering into private investment guarantee treaties with the governments of the six countries which are the major sources of foreign investment; becoming the first underdeveloped country to ratify the World Bank's international arbitration convention; selling off most of its shares (and giving up control) of its investment bank to private investors, domestic and foreign; passing laws which offer liberal incentives to private investors, domestic and foreign; and creating an investment promotion center.

The juxtaposition of the government's negative actions with these positive actions presents a confusing picture which seems to indicate a schizophrenic attitude toward private investment. One must look further. Do the policy statements and other official documents, quoted in Chapter 4, clarify the situation?

We find there that although Tunisia has only one political party, which is called the Destourian Socialist party, the term "socialism" is used in a very special sense. It is not an ideology, was not borrowed from another country, and rejects the postulates of Marx. It is not synonymous with state socialism but, rather, represents a pragmatic approach to the achievement of social and economic goals. It does aim at the elimination of the abuses of private property, but not of private property per se. It means that vital sectors of the economy should be in the hands of the government, to the extent that this action would increase the general well-being. Nationalizations, the party has said, will take place, but only within the above context--not for ideological reasons.

These statements make it appear that the use of the term "socialism" in Tunisian political economics follows closely the loose usage of that term in many other developing countries as well as in a number of West European countries.

We find also, in Chapter 4, that the government leaders
have, since independence, envisaged a mixed economy. Clear
statements on this subject have been made by President
Bourguiba and by Ben Salah, and others are to be found in
party documents and in the various plans. The consensus of
all of these is that the economic system of Tunisia will rest
upon the combined efforts of private enterprise, public enterprise, and cooperatives. Public enterprise will be responsible
for energy, transportation, water, and certain key industries which are basic to the economic development of the country.
The remaining industries are left to private initiative. If,
however, private enterprise fails to invest in those areas where
it is needed, then the state will intervene. Meanwhile, the
state will make every effort to stimulate private investment
to play the important role expected of it.

Those companies which have been nationalized are all in
the sector of energy, transportation, and water--industries
which the French government had nationalized in its own territory many years prior to Tunisian independence.

The government leaders have also expressed the opinion
that mining should be in the public sector, or at least have
government participation. This also had been a policy in
France for many years, but had not been extended to her
colonies. This explains the negotiated purchase, by the
Tunisian government, of part or full interest in most of the
mining companies.

Finally, government leaders have frequently stressed the
social function of private enterprise, noting that if it fails to
conform to the needs of the country or fails to function properly,
the government will take action. This explains the seizure of
seven companies in diverse industries. These companies either
had ceased operation or were in danger of going bankrupt because of poor management. Three of the seven companies
were returned to the original owners after a period of time;
two others have not resumed operations. Only two of these
companies, therefore, have continued to operate under governmental control, without formal expropriation, when they might
have been returned to their owners.

The heavy governmental investment in industry is partially
explained by the statements in Chapter 4 that the public-private
mix envisaged government ownership or partial ownership of
basic industries and of those industries which, by their nature,
would within one company have a monopoly position in the
country. Also, although certain industries would clearly be
within the province of private investment, if the private sector

failed to fulfill its role, the government would step in and make
the investment in order to accomplish those investments called for by the development plan.

As a consequence, most of such investment took place,
or at least was initiated, during the three-year plan (1962-64),
and nearly all of it was in the basic industries, the exceptions
being textile plants and several miscellaneous plants. We
find also, in Appendix A, Table 8, that public expenditure
in business enterprises reached a maximum of $115 million
in 1965, with a significant drop to $79.3 million in 1967. It
is not clear, however, whether this cutback was the result of
the government's desire to reduce its relative role in industry,
or whether it was the result of the monetary situation. The
government had been asked by both the International Monetary
Fund and the World Bank, in 1966 and 1967, to reduce its
expenditures. Deficit spending was causing inflationary pressures, and the rapid rate of investment also led to balance of
payments deficits and the disappearance of the foreign exchange
reserves. One cannot be certain how much public investment
in business enterprise might have taken place in 1966 and 1967
if the above pressures, and hence constraints, had not existed.

Appendix A, list 6, is a list of public enterprises, showing
the extent of the public sector in which the government participates directly. In addition, of course, there are the companies which are controlled by the STB and the BNA. Thus,
the public sector is not small, but it is not overwhelming,
except in the key industries.

However, one must ask, why the government found it
necessary to invest in areas which could have been left to the
private sector. Why did the private sector not fulfill its role?
Part of the answer is that many individuals who had the necessary capital and initiative did not have confidence in the
government. In the early 1960's the future of private enterprise in Tunisia still was not clear. The nationalizations
and sequestrations were still to recent. Government planning
and heavy public investment were just beginning. In addition,
one must go back to the historical developments. During the
entire colonial period, the education of Tunisians was limited,
their savings were limited, industrial opportunities were reserved for Frenchmen, and the mentality of the Tunisians
continued to favor short-term commercial ventures. These
factors did not change quickly.

One must also turn to the historical development of the
Tunisian economy to realize the extent to which all aspects
of it were in the hands of French companies or individuals.

Consequently, decolonization was a very vivid fact of life in
Tunisia. In the draft development plan drawn up by the UGTT
under Ben Salah is the statement, "We believe that our society,
which was freed from a political colonial regime, will not be
truly free until it has destroyed the economic and social apparatus created by that regime." This mentality remained prevalent through the early 1960's and was the basis for many of
the government's actions during those years.

For example, all of the banks in Tunisia at the time of
independence were owned by French banks. One would have
expected a political reaction to this situation--a need to decolonize in an abrupt manner--by nationalization. However,
the government did not follow such a course. Rather, it
extáblished one bank (the STB) to service industry and commerce
and another bank (the BNA) to service agriculture. These
two banks grew to the point where they controlled more than
50 per cent of the banking business in the country. Some of
the former French banks have been merged and other foreign
(non-French) banks have been established. This, along with
the establishment of the Central Bank in 1958, has satisfied
the need for financial decolonization and has permitted the
government to maintain a hands-off attitude vis-à-vis the
private banks, which, with the several healthy mergers and
fresh foreign capital, have prospered in spite of the rapid
growth of the government-controlled banks.

To most observers, the nationalization of foreign-owned
farmland seemed an irrational act. To be sure, foreigners,
mostly French, owned 1.67 million acres of Tunisia's most
productive land at the time of independence. Since this was
obtained during the period of colonization, it was to be expected
that efforts would be made to return most of this to Tunisian
ownership. Between 1956 and 1964, Tunisia did manage,
through various programs, to reduce the foreign-owned land
to 730,000 acres. In addition, the government had entered
into an agreement with the French government, in March, 1963,
to purchase, at a very nominal cost, most of the remainder of
the French-owned land over a period of five years.

Why, then, in May, 1964, did President Bourguiba decide
to nationalize the remaining foreign-owned land? It could not
have been for economic reasons, for he could have anticipated
a reaction from the French which resulted in a cutoff of foreign
aid and of trade preferences far in excess of the price which
Tunisia would have had to pay for the land. Nor does the action
seem to have been ideologically based. The only logical explanation relates the action to the nationalization of foreign-owned

farmland, in Algeria, in October, 1963. There was apparently
sufficient internal pressure, from a combination of left-wing
and Arab nationalist forces, to cause President Bourguiba to
take that step in spite of the agreement which he had signed
with the French 14 months earlier. The nationalization of the
farmland is best explained, however, as one of the steps of
decolonization which a newly independent country will take if
a sufficiently large portion of its productive land is under
foreign ownership.

To understand the government's policies on the Tunisification of commerce, it is once more necessary to turn to historical developments. When one notes, in Chapter 3, the
extent of French control of commerce at the time of independence,
one realizes the sense of frustration which a government must
feel. One realizes also that the elimination of the foreign
economic control must be accomplished by one means or another.
The elimination of French interests in the commercial sector
had a great impact on many people, but still it was not a
nationalization. It was, rather, a series of steps which established public or publicly controlled organizations and gave
them monopolies on the importing, exporting, and wholesaling
of the major items of trade, and obliged the remaining companies
to sell at least 50 per cent of their ownership to Tunisian nationals.

So far we have noted the actions which the government
has taken, and the rationale for these actions, but what tendency
is identifiable? What might today's investor expect in the
future?

First, all of the nationalizations of industry took place prior
to 1960 and were legalized in 1962 and 1963. The sequestrations
of industry took place between 1958 and 1962, most of them
in 1961,. immediately following the Bizerte crisis. The negotiated purchases of the various companies took place in 1962
and 1963. The law on the Tunisification of commerce was
passed in 1961 and was essentially implemented by 1963.
The government-controlled regional wholesale companies were
established in 1962 and 1963. And, finally, the foreign-owned
farmland was nationalized in 1964.

Thus, by 1964 the process of decolonization was essentially
completed. The commercial, banking, and agricultural sectors were under the control of Tunisians. The government
had control of the electricity, gas, water, transportation, and
mining, in accordance with the philosophy of its leaders. And
the country's foreign trade had been reoriented so that France
no longer played such a predominant role.

One is consequently concerned by the speech which President Bourguiba made on May 14, 1964, wherein he noted that his government had never failed in its engagements vis-à-vis capital invested since independence but, as for that which came prior to independence, "decency requires that I not speak of it. ... When we decide to take back [foreign investments furnished by former colonial lands], we are only pursuing the effort of decolonization." This was a very strong speech, and threatened with nationalization all French investments made prior to 1956. It must be noted, however, that this talk was given "in the heat of battle," only two days after President Bourguiba had nationalized the foreign-owned farmland.

It was clarified two weeks later, on May 28, 1964, when President Bourguiba recognized that Tunisia had finished with decolonization. He said that eight years had passed since independence and that it had taken that long "to get rid of the aftereffects, of all the vestiges and consequences, of all those things which are the concomitants of the implantation of the colonial domination. ... I believe that we have come full circle and that nothing more remains to cause friction between France and Tunisia." Then, referring again to the recent nationalizations of foreign-owned farmland, President Bourguiba said that "... it is a question of the last vestiges, the last show of anger in the process of decolonization."

Since 1964, there have been no more nationalizations, expropriations, or sequestrations. Nor have any laws been passed which are injurious to foreign private investment. French-owned industry which existed prior to independence continues to be operated unmolested and is able to repatriate profits, although the delay on approval of transfer is usually two years.

In addition, since 1964 the SNI has been changed from a public to a private bank, and an investment promotion center has been created.

Although the government appears to have satisfied its need for decolonization and seems to be doing everything possible to encourage domestic and foreign private investment, many investors are concerned about the continued growth of the public sector. There is no clear-cut analysis of this situation. We have noted that the rate of public investment in industry decreased in 1966 and 1967. We also find, in Appendix A, Table 8, that private investment increased at a rapid rate during those same years. Given the government's philosophy that it will not invest in most industry unless the private sector fails to do so, and given the fact that the government has already made most of its major investments in the

basic industries, the above trends may continue. The buildup
of private investment is a particularly critical factor and
depends upon the confidence of the private investor in the
government's philosophy. The momentum toward more private
investment has started, and such a movement feeds on its own
momentum.

Another of the indications of investor confidence in the
government is the amount of foreign private investment which
is taking place. Appendix A, list 7, is a compilation of the
private foreign investment which has entered Tunisia since
independence. It shows that 30 new companies have been
established since 1956, nearly all of them, however, having
arrived since 1963. This is not a large number per se, but
it is interesting to note that the companies are in a wide variety
of industries and come from a broad range of countries.

As stated earlier, some of the government's actions to
encourage private investment come cheap. It is easy for a
government to establish an investment promotion center and
to sign investment guarantee treaties--and still pursue an
investment policy which encroaches upon and competes with
the private sector. The investor cannot have complete confidence in this area unless and until the government implements
its stated philosophy that it will sell to private investors its
holdings in companies which are not in the category of "basic
and key industries reserved for the public sector."

It has been noted that the government did sell its controlling interest in SNI to the private sector, but this action took
place under very special circumstances, as part of the package deal for obtaining additional capital from the World Bank,
and at the request of the World Bank. Thus, it did not necessarily represent the desire of the government.

To make its policy in this area very clear, the government
must actually select a number of state-owned companies and
announce that these are for sale and that the government is
ready to enter immediately into negotiations with potential
investors, domestic or foreign.

One problem in implementing such a philosophy is that
many of these companies are losing money, and hence are
not attractive investments. Government officials state that
they wish to wait until these companies are profitable before
putting them on the auction block. The problem here is that
they may not become profitable--for several reasons. Some
have inadequate management; others were badly conceived
initially; and others have very unbalanced capital structures;

To solve this, the government must be willing to sell at a loss--
sometimes at a significant loss--so that with a lower capital
burden, a revised capital structure, and an injection of new
technological and management know-how, the firm can become profitable to a new investor, and hence be salable.

Should such a program be implemented, then, in spite of
the past record, it would be clear to potential investors that
the government does plan to restrict its role in industry to
certain well-defined areas.

There remains, then, only the question of a possible
radical change in the government's attitude when President
Bourguiba dies. What is the possibility of this? The Neo
Destourian party is the only party; it has little or no effective
opposition; and there is a divergence of opinions and strong
discussion within the party's ranks. However, it does operate
on the basis of consensus. There are both right-wing and left-
wing tendencies, but the party follows a middle-of-the-road
policy. There is little reason to believe that this would change,
given the system for replacing the President and given the
leading contenders, none of whom are ideologues.

One of the contenders most criticized by private interests
is Ben Salah. Many critics feel that he was a radical socialist
in 1956 but has been kept in rein by President Bourguiba so
that his middle-of-the-road policies do not reflect his true
views. However, if we review his statements, we find that
in 1956, as head of the UGTT (at which time he did not feel
subject to the policy of consensus), he said that new industry
which produces basic goods should be in the hands of the state,
although joint ventures with the private sector were a possibility.
In addition, he stated that mining and transportation should
belong to the state. But, he indicated all other activities
could remain in the private sector if the latter respected the
social contract of the workers and did not operate in a way
which would jeopardize a development plan. The quotations
in Chapter 4 indicate that this continues to be his philosophy
today.

There are also critics who claim that the question of
economic planning demonstrates a difference in philosophy
between Ben Salah and President Bourguiba. They claim that
President Bourguiba was ideologically opposed to planning in
the years immediately following independence, and that only
after the nation's economy grew more and more ill, with a
continual low level of investment, did he change his mind,
under pressure from "left-wingers such as Ben Salah," and
direct the preparation of a plan. We find, however, that

following independence, both President Bourguiba and Ben Salah saw the need for planning and prepared for it. Ben Salah, however, was in more of a hurry and, utilizing the talents available to him as the leader of the labor union, he had a plan prepared and attempted to push the government into immediate planning. President Bourguiba, on the other hand, stated in his first speech before the Constitutional Assembly, in April, 1956, his intention to draw up a development plan within whose framework a schedule would be elaborated to redress the country's economic and social ills. Immediately thereafter, he established a planning commission. However, partly for political reasons and partly for technical reasons, he did not attempt to implement the planning process until late 1960. Thus, between 1956 and 1960, President Bourguiba and Ben Salah were in agreement on the need for planning, but the latter's desire for immediate planning was based on economic reality, while the former, as President, followed a delaying policy based on political reality.

In the fall of 1969, Ben Salah was asked by President Bourguiba to resign as Minister of Planning and Economics (and Industry, Commerce, Finance, and Agriculture). He came under pressure primarily because of his policy of pushing the commercial and agricultural sectors of the economy into the formation of cooperatives. In addition, Bahi Ladgham was elected Vice-President, and it was reconfirmed that the Vice-President would succeed the President. Hence, Ben Salah is not now a leading contender to succeed President Bourguiba.

However, Ben Salah is young, ambitious, and aggressive. His political career is not finished. What policies would he follow if, at some time in the future, he were to become President? The preceding discussion makes it appear that a constancy of policy vis-à-vis private investment is most probable, with either Ladgham or Ben Salah, and this is the most attractive prediction for the political climate for private investment.

PART **III** ALGERIA

INTRODUCTION TO PART III
ALGERIA TODAY

Algeria lies between Tunisia and Morocco and has about 620 miles of coastline on the Mediterranean, directly south of France. Its southern borders, in the middle of the Sahara, touch on Mauritania, Mali, and Niger. Its shape is similar to that of Texas and its population of about 12 million is also roughly equivalent to that of Texas, but its area of 919,591 square miles is nearly four times that of Texas and nearly twice the area of Alaska.

Algeria is divided into two distinct parts. To the north, along the Mediterranean, a strip of land about 150 to 250 miles wide, lying between the Saharan Atlas Mountains and the sea, contains essentially all of the country's arable land and over 95 percent of its population.

The southern portion, containing nearly 90 percent of the land area and covered almost entirely by the Sahara, is part of the Republic of Algeria but, under the Evian Agreement of 1962, France retains certain economic and military concessions. This is the portion which contains the oil and gas fields so important to Algeria's economy.

Climatically, Algeria may be divided into three regions. A strip lying within 40 miles of the coast and containing all of the major cities (and 70 percent of the population) has a temperate climate throughout the year and receives an average annual rainfall of about 30 inches. South of the coastal strip, between the Tellian Atlas and the Saharan Atlas Mountains, lie the high plateaus, which have a continental climate and a rainfall of six to 10 inches per year. Finally, south of the Saharan Atlas Mountains lies the Sahara, with essentially no rainfall but with a series of oases fed by an underground river that brings water from the Atlas Mountains.

About 80 percent of the population is a racial mixture of Arab and Berber and uses Arabic as the major spoken language, while about 20 percent are pure Berber and continue to speak one of the ancient Berber dialects among themselves. Most of the business and government leaders are French-educated and use French for technical discussions. The official language is Arabic, but French is provisionally of equal importance in government documents. Fewer than 50,000 of the 1 million Europeans living in Algeria prior to independence remain today. Islam is the religion of 99 percent of the population and is also the state religion.

The Algerian government does not yet gather sufficiently accurate data and hence does not publish GNP figures. The U.S. Department of State estimated, however, that Algeria's GNP in 1966 was approximately $2.66 billion, and her per capita income was $178.

Education has been given an important place in the government's efforts. In 1966 nearly 20 percent of the operating budget was devoted to education, permitting the teaching of 135 million children in primary school, 120,000 in secondary school, and 6,500 in higher education. In the same year, 55 percent of the children reaching school age actually entered school (70 percent of the boys and 40 percent of the girls). Although the government plans to offer more and more of the education in Arabic, not enough teachers are now available. Consequently, in 1966, 8,000 French teachers and professors were employed in Algerian schools and colleges; two-thirds of the secondary schoolteachers and most of the college teachers were French. Now 10 - 15 percent of the population above 10 years of age is literate.

Since Algeria was considered to be an integral part of France prior to independence in 1962 and over 1 million Frenchmen lived there, every effort was made to have a modern economic infrastructure, and this was inherited by the new nation. Railroads and good highways connect all of the cities and towns of any importance. The nine ports exceed the needs of the country. Airports are scattered throughout the territory. The electricity supply is quite adequate and the telephone system is modern.

The outstanding feature of Algeria's mineral resources is the oil and gas fields which were discovered in the Sahara in 1956. Production increased rapidly and in 1962, the year of independence, reached 20.7 million tons of petroleum and 353 million cubic meters of gas. By 1965 these had increased to 26.5 million tons and 1,743 million cubic meters.

Algeria's other mineral deposits are very modest, and many have already been exhausted, following many years of exploitation. In 1965 Algeria produced only 3.1 million tons of iron ore and small amounts of lead, zinc, copper, and phosphates.

Algeria is well endowed with agricultural land (in the northern portion of the country) and was, prior to independence, capable of supporting herself in grains and of being a larger exporter of wine and citrus fruits. Since independence, and particularly during the drought years of 1966 and 1967, she has become highly dependent on grain imports.

This, in fact, is an important aspect of Algeria's foreign trade: 30 percent of her imports are foodstuffs--mainly grains, but also sugar, coffee, tea, meat, and dairy products. The other aspect is the importance of oil and gas in her exports, equaling 60 percent of the total. Wine constitutes another 20 percent and citrus fruits 5 percent. For historical reasons and through preferential trade agreements, France still receives two-thirds of Algeria's exports and furnishes about two-thirds of her imports. This is particularly true for oil, gas, and wine, since France pays more than the world market price for these products.

Such favorable treatment constitutes an important portion of the foreign aid which France furnishes to Algeria. In addition, as noted earlier, France furnishes a large number of professors, teachers, and other types of technical assistance personnel. And, as part of the oil agreement of 1965, France has agreed to provide Algeria with financial assistance of $40 million per year for a five-year period, directed primarily at assisting Algeria's industrialization.

The United States was, for several years after Algeria's independence, providing her with large amounts of surplus grains, under the terms of PL 480, but this has been stopped. The Soviet Union stepped in and began to furnish such grains late in 1966, and has become the major source of foreign aid to Algeria. Most of this aid is military aid, but much of it is also directed toward assisting Algeria's industrial and agricultural development.

Algeria, whose occupation by France began in 1830, began its struggle for independence in 1953. After years of violence and very great suffering, this independence was finally achieved on July 1, 1962. One of the major political forces during the fight for independence was the Front de Libération Nationale (FLN). A provisional government, with little FLN support, ran the country for the three months following independence, but it was replaced when Ahmed Ben Bella, with the support of the army and the FLN, was elected President. Although the FLN continued to be a political force, Ben Bella remained in power more on the basis of the army than through any political machinery. He was subsequently deposed by the army in 1965 and was replaced by Houari Boumediène, the current president. The political party remains of second-ary importance. The regime suppresses opposition, but there is underground opposition within the country as well as in exile. This constitutes an unstable situation, both politically and ideologically.

Algeria's "socialist option" is more ideologically based than Tunisia's socialism. The government has as its stated goal the achievement of a socialist economy based primarily upon the concept of worker management, somewhat similar to the situation in Yugoslavia. Meanwhile, the government has felt a need for private enterprise and has made a sustained effort to encourage private investment, both domestic and foreign. This constitutes a very peculiar political climate for private investment, and it is extremely important to become familiar with the facts and their historical context in order to understand what role private investment might play in Algeria and to be able to weigh the political risk. The following three chapters present the factors determining the political climate for private investment in Algeria and should permit an evalua-tion of the situation.

CHAPTER **7** HISTORICAL CONTEXT
OF THE ALGERIAN
POLITICAL CLIMATE
FOR PRIVATE INVEST-
MENT

EARLY HISTORY

As in Tunisia, Algeria's early inhabitants were the Berbers, to whom the Greeks and Egyptians referred as "Libyans."
Most of them are short, have black eyes and black hair, and
are what might be called the typical Mediterranean type, a
people who must have ruled both sides of the Mediterranean
basin 5,000 or 6,000 years ago. Physically they are quite
similar to a large proportion of the population in southern
Italy, southern France, and Spain. However, some of the
Berbers are taller and resemble the early Egyptians, whom
the "Libyans" had conquered and ruled during the decline of
the Egyptian Empire. And still another portion of the Berbers
are tall, blond, and blue-eyed, showing the results of what
must have been an invasion from northern Europe.

Very soon after the Phoenicians landed at Carthage and
began their civilization in North Africa, they established themselves in what are now the major port cities of Algeria. Although in Tunisia they colonized and exercised direct control
over the whole country, in Algeria they colonized only the
coastal plain, leaving the rest under the administration of the
local chieftains, who collected taxes and furnished soldiers
for the Phoenician armies.

The Roman colonization of Algeria (then known as Numidia)
was similar to that of the Phoenicians, and therefore different
from that of Tunisia. As a result there was far less inter-
marriage between Phoenicians and the Berbers (and later between the Romans and the Berbers) in Algeria than in Tunisia.

The Vandals came from Spain and took over the area of
northern Morocco and Algeria, as far as Bône, in a period of
only three years, from 427 to 430. They destroyed the Roman

117

administration of Numidia but were themselves just an army
which settled in North Africa and gradually lost its power,
blending into the Berber structure. The Berbers ruled their
own lands for a century, until 533, when the Byzantines conquered the area. They also stayed in the port cities, penetrat-
ing the interior even less than had the Romans and Phoenicians,
and thus leaving the Berber tribes to continue to rule their own
areas.

The Arab invasion of 666 included Algeria, as it had Tunisia, and began the Arabization of the land. During the 850
years of their rule, the Arabs imposed their religion on almost
all of the inhabitants, but not enough Arabs arrived in Algeria
to impose their race on the Berbers. Consequently the population is made up primarily of Berbers with varying degrees
of Arab blood, and today it is estimated that about 20 percent
of the population still speak Berber in their homes and maintain many of their old customs and beliefs. (As recently as
1936, this pure Berber population was estimated at 30 percent
of the total.)[1]

The Spanish influence on Algeria was minor. Having pushed
the Arabs out of Spain, the Spanish followed them into North
Africa, but by sea rather than by land. Consequently, the
Spanish took only the coastal cities, conquering them between
1505 and 1510 and holding them for varying periods. They
were replaced by the Turks in the latter part of the 16th century.

The nearly 300 years of domination by the Turks saw even
less penetration of the interior than that by the Phoenicians and
Romans. A total of 3,000 Turks controlled 1.5 million Arabs
and Berbers.[2] Consequently the Berber-Arab population was
left mostly to itself except in and immediately around the major
port cities. The Turks ruled only where they were in force,
and they were satisfied with the ability to travel from city to
city in relative safety and to collect taxes.

A prominent aspect of the three centuries of Turkish rule
was the activity of the Barbary pirates, who operated primarily
out of Algiers. Various nations attempted to subdue them; they
were often defeated and Algiers was sometimes partially destroyed by naval bombardments, but they always recovered,
rebuilt, and resumed their activities. France was bothered
by this piracy as much as any country and often considered
invading the land to subdue the government, led by the Dey of
Algiers. A minor incident was the initiating factor. During
an interview between the Dey and the French Consul in 1827,
the Dey felt that the Consul was insulting and therefore struck
him several times with a fly swatter. The French government

demanded an apology, but the Dey refused. The French instituted a naval blockade, which lasted three years and was not
really effective. Finally, in 1830, the French decided on a
land expedition. An army of 37,000 landed 16 miles from
Algiers and took the city in 20 days.

FRENCH CONQUEST AND SETTLEMENT

The capitulation by the Dey supposedly gave the French
full sovereignty over all the territory under the former rule
of the Turks, which was administered through the Dey. But,
since his rule was not really effective, the land and its people
were not automatically at the disposal of the French, and they
did not conquer the country easily. They were not content with
ruling in the coastal cities, as the Turks had been. They
wanted to settle on the land, and this meant that they had to
subdue the native population throughout the territory. It was
seven years before Constantine was taken, and 20 years more
before the Kabyles submitted officially, although the last revolt in that area was suppressed in 1871. The Touareg tribes
in the Sahara were conquered in 1882.

Europeans, particularly the French, began settling in
Algeria immediately after the fall of Algiers. First, many of
the soldiers decided to settle there, and so land was found and
given to them. French merchants soon arrived, followed by
individual, land-seeking immigrants. By 1836 there were
32,000 Frenchmen in Algeria and 2.2 million Moslems. In
the succeeding years, Italians, Maltese, and Spaniards also
came. In the 1840's, several groups of German immigrants
who were hoping to go to the United States found themselves
in Marseilles with no money for the ocean voyage; they were
shipped to Algeria. In 1871, many of the French who chose
to leave Alsace-Lorraine after it was conquered by Germany
immigrated to Algeria. Also, the French government periodically sent unemployed workers to Algeria so they would not
make trouble in Paris. As a result, the European population
grew to 252,000 by 1866, 578,000 in 1896, 922,000 in 1948,
and 107 million in 1959. The Moslem population also began
increasing rapidly, from 2.7 million in 1866 to 3.8 million
in 1896, 7.7 million in 1948, and 9.6 million in 1959.

Although many Europeans settled on the land, most of
them remained in the larger cities. As a result, in 1930, they
were a majority of the population in the following major cities:

Oran, 80 percent; Algiers, 67 percent; Sidi Bel Abbes, 65 percent; and Bône, 59 percent. In Constantine, the European
population was 48 percent of the total.[3] By 1959, however,
this had changed; only in Oran did the Europeans remain as
a slight majority. In Constantine they constituted only 18 percent of the population, and in Bône only 36 percent.[4]

As indicated earlier, the Europeans in Algeria were a
mixed group. In 1936, for example, out of the non-Moslem
population of 946,400, there were 92,400 Spaniards, 21,200
Italians, 14,200 others, and 818,600 French.[5] Included in
the total number of French were approximately 100,000 Jews,
who had been decreed French citizens by the French government in 1870. It is also noteworthy that by 1911, of the 746,000
Europeans in Algeria, 64 percent had been born there;[6] by
1954, the figure had increased to 79 percent.[7]

Land ownership in Algeria developed in a pattern similar
to that in Tunisia, but with an even larger proportion of the
arable land owned by Europeans. The land owned and effectively cultivated by Europeans increased from 1 million acres
in 1850[8] to 2.25 million in 1856 and over 5.75 million acres
in 1930.[9] The 5.75 million acres of European-owned land was
divided into 26,153 farms, with an average size of 210 acres;
Algerians owned 19 million acres of arable land, divided into
617,544 farms, with an average size of 30 acres (although 70
percent of these farms were less than 10 acres).[10]

This ownership pattern changed very little in the following 30 years, although more land was put under cultivation.
By 1962, 22,000 European farmers owned 6.75 million acres,
while 630,000 Algerians had 18.25 million acres.[11] In addition, as in Tunisia, most of the best land belonged to Europeans.
In fact, it is estimated that only 15 million acres of truly arable
land exist in Algeria.[12]

SOME ECONOMIC AND SOCIAL
EFFECTS OF FRENCH RULE

Educational Levels

The first school for Algerians did not open until 1883.[13]
In 1900, out of a Moslem population of approximately 4 million, of whom about 900,000 were of school age (6-18), only
about 26,000 (3 percent) were in school. By 1930, the number in elementary school was 54,000 boys and 6,000 girls.[14]

This long history of low attendance is reflected in the literacy rate. In 1950, 90 percent of the Algerians were still illiterate, as contrasted with 6.3 percent of the Europeans in Algeria.[15] However, by 1950 the number of Algerians in elementary schools had climbed to a total of 210,000, and it increased to 265,000 by 1956. Then, suddenly, a large effort was made to educate more Algerians. In 1957 the figure climbed to 325,000; 1958, 441,000; 1959, 586,000; 1960, 695,000. By 1959, also, 37 percent were girls.

Insofar as secondary education is concerned, in 1939, Algerian boys represented 11.7 percent of the total number of boys in secondary schools, even though they represented 92 percent of the total number of boys in that age group. By 1958, the Algerian boys in secondary school had increased to 27 percent of the total. During the same period, Algerian girls increased from 2.7 percent to 11.9 percent of the total.[16] Finally, in the universities there were only 267 Algerians in 1956, versus 4,433 Europeans. The number of Algerians rose to 421 in 1957, 814 in 1959, and 1,317 in 1960.[17]

Employment Pattern

A breakdown of the employment and professional activities of the active population in Algeria in 1954, by sex and by nationality, is given in Appendix B, Table 1. As can be seen, 74 percent of the total active population was in agriculture. But 82 percent of the Algerian population was in agriculture, while only 9 percent of the Europeans were. Outside of agriculture, the European population supplied a very high proportion of the technicians and office workers, while the Algerians, as would be expected, supplied most of the unskilled workers. However, the Algerians did supply a high percentage of the skilled and highly skilled workers; this reflects the experience of Algerian workers who had gone to France to work and, having attained certain skills, returned to their homeland.

The real discrimination against Algerians showed up in the civil service, and this was of key importance to the quality of the post-independence government. It was essentially impossible, prior to 1919, for an Algerian to have a career in the civil service. As a result of their loyalty and service in World War I, however, decrees were issued in 1919 and 1922 allowing Algerians to work in lower- and middle-level civil service. After World War II, it became possible for some individual Algerians to become French citizens and thus to enter civil service with less discrimination. However, such citizenship was not hereditary.

Per Capita Income Pattern

A more revealing indication of the disparity of social and economic achievement between the European and Algerian sectors of the population is shown by the average per capita income figures. In 1954, the Europeans in the agricultural sector had an average per capita income of $2,000 and those in the cities had $930, giving an average of $1,030. On the other hand, the rural Algerians had an average per capita income of $57 and the urban dwellers had $132, giving an average of $83.[18]

One of the reasons for the low per capita income among the Algerians was the high unemployment rate and the underemployment. In 1955, 820,000 Algerian men in the rural areas were unemployed or underemployed, and 60,000 living in urban areas were unemployed.[19] In 1960, for example, 25 percent of the Algerian agricultural laborers worked less than 45 days per year, and 50 percent worked less than 100 days per year. Also, in 1960, 32 percent of Algerian families had no member working or earning an income.[20]

Development of the Economic Infrastructure

The development of the economic infrastructure during the 130 years of French rule was impressive. If a similar effort had been made in the social sphere, the territory would have had an entirely different history.

Whereas in 1830 there were almost no all-weather roads, by 1960 there were 15,500 miles of all-weather roads and an additional 4,700 miles of dirt roads. However, this road network represents about 13 percent of the road density of France and does not service all of the towns and villages.[21]

The entire railroad system has, naturally, been built since the arrival of the French. By the end of 1961, it consisted of 2,565 miles of track, of which 1,621 miles were standard gauge and 944 miles were narrow gauge. These tracks connect all of the coastal cities and send spur lines south into the interior. As a result, manufactured goods tend to move south while agricultural and mining products move north. These railroad lines were started by private companies (in 1900 there

were five different companies). They were of a variety of
gauges and were not connected. The government gradually
bought them and nationalized their networks and their operation.[22]

In Roman times there were several prosperous port cities
in Algeria, but by 1830 Algiers was the only usable port, and
even it was insufficient to handle the initial military traffic
after the French invasion. The French immediately began to
improve it and have since constructed 20 other commercial
ports along the Algerian coastline.

The early period of electric power in Algeria was characterized by the construction of a number of fairly small,
privately owned plants, located in the coastal cities and fueled
with imported coal. Power lines transmitted the electricity
for a short way into the interior from each port city. Farther
inland, small diesel plants supplied electricity for some of
the cities and larger towns. The result was high-cost elec-
tricity--twice as high as in France, which in turn is twice
as high as many places in the United States. This was one of
the deterrents to industrialization. Improvement of this situation began in 1947, when the government nationalized the power
companies and constructed an interconnecting grid. By 1953,
the first hydroelectric power plant, located in the interior,
was in operation, and by 1959, one-third of the electricity in
the country was from hydroelectric plants,[23] thus reducing
the cost and decreasing the need to import coal. The need
for coal was finally eliminated with the availability of gas and
oil from the Sahara.

Industrial Development Before 1958

Mines, especially copper, lead, and iron mines, were
being exploited in Algeria during the time of the Romans. They
had been abandoned for centuries when the French arrived, so
that the economy was an agricultural one, with some artisan
trades. During the first half-century of French rule, the
agricultural production consisted mainly of wheat, wine, oats,
olives, tobacco, cotton, sugar beets, and livestock. The
first phosphate mine was developed in the 1880's and iron,
zinc, and lead mining followed.

Small food-processing industries were gradually developed,
particularly in the period following World War I. These consisted, by the late 1920's, of flour mills, distilleries, brew-
eries, 10-15 canning factories for fish and vegetables, and

cigarette factories. In addition, there were a match factory, many small tanneries (of an artisan type, averaging 10 workers each), 15 shoe factories (with a total of 500 workers), tile factories, and some metal fabricating shops which manufactured simple tools and agricultural equipment.[24]

A review of the foreign trade of Algeria in 1938 shows that exports consisted primarily of wine, grains, fresh fruits and vegetables, cattle, minerals, alfa grass, and cork; imports were made up of machinery and other manufactured metal products, chinaware, glass and glassware, paper, clothing, rice, sugar, meat products, wood, wood products, and fuels.[25] As can be seen, many of the most simple products had to be imported. As a consequence, the advent of World War II, which cut off the supply of many goods, caused some serious shortages. Consequently an effort was made, in 1942, to convince some French companies to establish plants in Algeria, but the exigencies of the war made this nearly impossible and the results were minimal. In 1946, however, a decree was issued which offered a number of fiscal and financial incentives to investors.[26] This campaign was much more successful than that of 1942. Between 1946 and 1948, 93 factories were built, and during 1949, another 20. By mid-1950, 9,500 new jobs had been created by these new companies.[27]

Meanwhile, in 1949, the first of France's four-year plans, which applied also to Algeria appeared. The emphasis during the first four-year plan was on investment in infrastructure. Only during the second four-year plan, 1953-56, was emphasis put on industrialization. Between 1946 and the end of 1954, the Algerian government agreed to requests for the establishment of a total of 160 new plants.[28] It is apparent, therefore, that the rate of new starts had considerably decreased after 1950. By that time, the competition from French imports was so great that even with the incentives still available (from the decree of 1946), new local industry had difficulties. A number of those started during and immediately after the war had to close, for the authorities, considering Algeria an integral part of France, could not agree to the erection of tariffs for the protection of infant industries.

By 1954, Algeria had 8,909 industrial enterprises employing 210,000 workers, but most of the companies were very small. In fact, 6,240 companies employed fewer than five workers, 1,547 had between six and 20 workers, 817 companies employed between 20 and 100 workers, 278 companies between 100 and 500 workers, and only 47 companies had more than 500 workers.[29]

A large number of people were also involved in the service industries, particularly in the retail trade. Combining these with the manufacturing industries, we find that in 1957, approximately 300,000 people were working in 25,000 industrial and commercial enterprises owned by Europeans (mostly French), while 23,000 people were working in 7,000 Algerian-owned enterprises, mostly small ones. It was estimated that over 90 percent of commerce and industry was in the hands of the French.[30]

The dominance of France and Frenchmen in the economy was also shown in the field of banking. In 1957, there were 31 banks, of which 17 were branches or agencies of French banks and 14 were incorporated in Algeria but were owned by Europeans located in Algeria or in France.[31]

Constantine Plan

On October 3, 1958, General de Gaulle, who had recently been elected President of France, made a speech in Constantine, during which he stated that it was France's obligation to give all Algerians their share of what modern civilization could contribute in terms of well-being and dignity. His proposals were incorporated into a long-range program known as the Constantine Plan, which was put into operation in 1959.

The initial phase of the Constantine Plan was a five-year plan, to run from 1959 to 1963; but the essential aspect was that its perspectives and goals were stated in terms of 25 years. These long-range goals included a land reform program to restore 32 million acres of impoverished soil, to decentralize the economy, to create 15 large cities and 40 medium-sized towns, and to quadruple the income of the rural sector.

The first five-year portion of the Constantine Plan was not modest in its goals. It planned, among other things, to increase enrollment in elementary school from 40 percent in 1958 to 66 percent in 1963 (to reach 100 percent in 1966) and, by investing $600 million in industry and doubling industrial production, to create 400,000 new jobs in industry. Among the new industries envisioned were four heavy industry complexes: a large steel plant, a petrochemical complex, a petroleum refinery, and the exploitation of a new phosphate deposit. There was also to be the construction of several oil and gas pipelines from the Sahara to the coast. Finally, production was to be started or increased in a number of industries: e.g., an increase of 650 percent in the textile industry,

450 percent in leather and shoes, 250 percent in metal fabrication, 200 percent in construction materials, and 150 percent in food processing.

The initial five-year plan called for investments (in all sectors) totaling $4 billion. About a half of this amount was to come from the private sector. The French government's budget was to contribute much of the rest.

Of the $600 million to be invested in industry, it was planned that $180 million would be private invested capital; the remainder would be in the form of government subsidies, long-term government loans, and medium-term private loans. The subsidies were the main method used to overcome the otherwise higher cost of producing in Algeria, thereby permitting local industry to compete with imports from France without interfering with the free trade between the two areas. Guillot estimates that the total subsidy-tax reduction-low interest package was equivalent to the government's furnishing 40 percent of the total industrial investments in 1959.[32]

The results of this plan were felt very quickly. By the end of 1960, 500 companies had applied, and 417 had received approval, to invest in Algeria. Nearly all of these were process industries (food, chemical, and construction materials), but there were also four heavy industries (tires, cement, phosphate mining, and an ammonia plant). The progress of the Algerian revolution, however, discouraged many investors who had received approval. The actual investments were, therefore, less than hoped for but not unappreciable. Whereas in 1958 only six new manufacturing companies were started, in 1959, the first year of the plan, 76 were created and in 1960 there were 139 new companies, comprising investments of $6 million in 1958, $80 million in 1959, and $115 million in 1960.[33] By 1961, however, the plan began to lose steam because of the increased realization that Algeria would probably become independent. In that year, only 47 new investments were approved (and few of them actually implemented).[34]

A number of foreign (non-French) investments were also made under the terms of the Constantine Plan. In 1958, foreign investment totaled $21 million, almost wholly in oil exploration and related activities.[35] In 1959, British, Italian, Dutch, Swiss, and U.S. investors accounted for $15 million, again mostly in the oil industry. In 1960, foreign investment increased to $37 million, with nearly $1 million going into manufacturing.[36] One of the foreign manufacturing investments, made in 1960, was Varel-Afrique, a wholly-owned subsidiary of Varel Mfg. Co., of Dallas, Texas. It manufactured rock bits for oil-well drilling. The investment of $100,000 obtained the benefits of the investment incentive program, receiving a 30 percent subsidy on capital equipment, a 25 percent payroll subsidy, exemption from the 12 percent local "production tax," a 10-year exemption from income tax, and low-priced land for the plant site.[37]

Still, the government was not successful in achieving the planned decentralization of industries; 43 percent of the new jobs were located in Algiers. Also, the investments were not in conformity with the plan; only 9 percent were in those industries which were to provide 50 percent of new employment.[38] Thus, the government, even when paying dearly, was unable to push private enterprise into making the investments in the industries needed nor in the locations desired.

Development of Oil and Gas Resources

The most successful industry and the one which attracted the greatest amount of foreign investment was that of oil and gas. The French had created the Société Nationale de Recherche et d'Exploitation de Petrole en Algérie (S.N. REPAL) in 1946 to look for oil in Algeria and to handle all financial, technical, and commercial operations connected with any findings. This company was owned 40.5 percent by the French government and 40.5 percent by an Algerian government organization, with the remainder distributed among various semi-public and private interests. This company began prospecting in 1949 and sank its first well in 1952. This well showed promising signs, but it was not until June, 1956, that the well sunk at Hassi Messaoud led to discovery of a very rich oil field covering 640 square miles. The first oil reached the coast in January, 1958, going part of the way by six-inch line and part of the way by railroad. In November, 1959, a 24-inch line, 410 miles long, began delivering oil to the coast. Production reached 9.5 million barrels in 1959, 66.3 million in 1960, 121.4 million in 1961, and 158.8 million in 1962.

Meanwhile, a number of foreign (including U.S.) oil companies became interested (oil exploration cost was one-tenth of that in the United States, though more than twice that in the Middle East) and received exploration and operating permits. Shell came in as early as 1953; British Petroleum, Cities Service, Sinclair, and Esso followed.

Between 1947 and 1956, the year of the big discovery, approximately $1 billion was spent, mostly by French sources.

By the time of independence, over $1.3 billion had been spent
in exploration, development, and pipelines.

Much of the additional expenditure after 1956 came from
the U.S. and British international oil companies. As a result,
by the time of independence, known reserves were estimated
at 4.97 billion barrels, valued at approximately $11.5 billion
(in 1965 prices).[39] Oil companies operating in Algeria in
1966 and their production figures are found in Appendix B,
Table 2.

Economic Growth During the 1950's

The economy of Algeria during the 1950's was very active.
It can be said that even though the country was in full revolt,
it was also in full boom. But this was to be expected, given
the efforts made by the French to develop the country at the
same time that a large army was kept on Algerian soil and
had to be supplied. The situation was not unlike that in South
Vietnam in the 1960's: the country was torn by war, yet the
economy was booming.

We find, as a result, that the GNP increased by 47 percent between 1950 and 1958,[40] and that the per capita income
increased by 50 percent from 1953 to 1959. For the period of
1950 to 1960, industrial production increased by 97 percent
and agricultural production increased by approximately 25
percent, with very large annual fluctuations.[41] This slow
growth of agriculture resulted in its decreasing importance
as a contribution to GNP, falling from 37 percent in 1950 to
only 26 percent in 1958. Industry remained a constant 27 percent of GNP during that period, while services grew from 36
percent to 47 percent.

The rapid growth of industry kept pace with the growth of
GNP, but the increase in services, which is particularly notice-
able in the period 1954-58, was due largely to the support of
the war effort.

By 1959, industry contributed $880 million out of a total
GNP of $3.2 billion. It employed about 225,000 persons.
The distribution, by type of industry, was food, 30 percent;
mechanical, 20 percent; electricity and gas, 10 percent; construction materials, 9 percent; textiles and leather, 9 percent;
mining, 7 percent; chemical and rubber, 5 percent; and miscellaneous, 10 percent.[42]

Foreign Trade

This speeded-up growth of the economy in the 1950's is reflected in the growth of foreign trade. Between 1954 and 1959, imports increased from $440 million to $1.1 billion and exports increased from $280 million to $365 million.[43] Again, this increase in trade was due partly to the rapid rate of investment and partly to the war effort. As would be expected, most of the trade was with France, and became increasingly so. In 1954, France received 73 percent of Algeria's exports and provided 73 percent of her imports. By 1959 these figures had grown to 82 percent and 78 percent, respectively. The United Kingdom was the second largest trader with Algeria but had less than 7 percent of her trade in the 1950's. The United States provided 3 percent of Algeria's imports in 1954 and 1959, but received only a negligible amount of her exports.[44]

The overwhelming position of France is to be expected, inasmuch as Algeria was considered to be an integral part of France. It is interesting to note, however, that as far back as 1784, almost 50 years before colonization by France, Algeria's foreign trade was already predominantly with France: France, 50 percent; Netherlands, 25 percent; England, 12 percent; and Venice, 10 percent.[45]

A SUCCESSFUL REVOLUTION

We have seen that the French waited until the mid-1950's to make a concerted effort to educate the Algerian population and until 1958 to institute the Constantine Plan, a comprehensive effort to develop the country and its people. But these attempts were too late. The seeds for a revolution had been sown during the preceding century, and the revolution itself already had an impetus.

In 1943, Ferhat Abbas wrote a manifesto which called for self-determination by the Algerians, and there sprang into being an organization called Amis du Manifesto Algérien (AMA). Within a year there were 400,000 adherents. However, such observers as Robert Aron, Charles Gallagher, and David C. Gordon feel that the Algerian revolution was born on May 9, 1945, when the AMA staged a demonstration, supposedly celebrating the end of the war in Europe, which turned into a riot, resulting in about 100 Europeans being killed. Martial law

was declared; planes, tanks, and infantry came in, wiping
out villages. Within several days the French had taken the
lives of 5,000-10,000 Moslems. (Various observers give
estimates ranging from a low of 1,500 to a high of 45,000.)

By 1948, an underground movement, the Organisation
Spéciale (OS), had been formed, with vague plans to fight for
independence. One of its leaders was Ahmed Ben Bella. It
began building up an organization with separate cells in each
village, gathering and storing arms. In 1950, Ben Bella was
caught after robbing a post office to obtain money for the organization, and was jailed. Other leaders were soon arrested
or had to go into exile, and the organization fell apart. Ben
Bella escaped from jail and went to Cairo, to remain in exile
until independence.

All was relatively calm until November 1, 1954, when,
in simultaneous attacks at 40 different locations, 12 Frenchmen were killed with bombs, knives, and guns. The active
revolution had started. It was the work of a small group who
called themselves the FLN. According to Rabat Bitat, one of
the leaders, the total rebel army at that time consisted of
about 900 men.[46] Ben Bella and others continued to work for
the FLN from outside the country, both to obtain and ship arms
to the rebel bands and to arouse international opinion against
the French. In October, 1955, a plane carrying Ben Bella
and other leaders of the FLN was forced down, and they were
captured and placed in jail. The military movement was continued under the leadership of Belkacem Krim. The FLN
continued to grow in importance and served as the prime
political and military force fighting for independence within
Algeria. By 1956, it is estimated that half of the population
was behind the FLN.

In March, 1957, Krim reportedly reached an agreement
with President Bourguiba on a plan establishing an FLN army
staging area, with about 10,000 soldiers, inside Tunisia.
Another FLN army of about 2,000 troops, was located just
across the border in Morocco, under the leadership of Houari
Boumediène. These two groups of "external" troops constituted the Armée de Libération Nationale (ALN).

The year 1958 was a turning point. Militarily, the FLN
continued to lose heavily. The French army had cleaned out
the large pockets of armed resistance. However, the Gouvernement Provisoire de la République Algérienne (GPRA), a rebel
government in exile, was formed in Cairo and began to gain
international diplomatic support for the rebel cause. Also,
the ALN forces remained in Tunisia and Morocco and supplied

arms and small numbers of saboteurs to continue terrorist
activities. The death rate stayed over 10 per day, many of
the victims being Algerians who were working for the French
administration.

Meanwhile, both sides had resorted to torture, reprisals,
and indiscriminate killing. Between 1954 and 1960, official
French army records show 13,000 deaths on the French side
and over 100,000 on the Algerian side. The Algerians, however, estimate that over 250,000 of their people were killed,
500,000 wounded, and 300,000 forced to flee to Morocco and
Tunisia during the struggle for independence. [47] In addition,
several million Algerians were kept within "areas of pacification" and several million more were effectively fenced into
rebel-controlled areas. Over 100,000 who were suspected of
rebel activities were held in detention camps. The revolution
touched every family in the country. In addition, the country
suffered over $1 billion in property damage.

Soon after De Gaulle became President in 1958 and introduced the Constantine Plan, he offered a compromise peace
to the Algerians. They refused. The French army had the
upper hand, but the international community was turning
against the French. In September, 1959, De Gaulle offered
the Algerians three choices: integration with France, complete independence, or independence in cooperation with France.
There followed two years of confusion, first the colons and
then parts of the French army rising up against De Gaulle,
but in March, 1962, top French leaders met with leaders of
the GPRA at Evian and reached agreement on conditions for
a cease-fire on March 19, 1962, after eight years of revolution.

THE ÉVIAN AGREEMENT

The Évian Agreement stipulated that the Algerian government would hold an election to determine whether the people
wished Algeria to be independent and, if so, whether this
should be in a cooperative arrangement with France. Then,
assuming that the choice would be independence and cooperation, it spelled out the terms of such a cooperative arrangement. It indicated that all French citizens who were born in
Algeria, or who had lived in Algeria at least 10 years and
whose parents had been born in Algeria, or who had lived in
Algeria at least 20 years, could, at the end of a three-year
period, choose Algerian citizenship. Meanwhile, they would

be able to vote in Algerian elections and hold political office
without discrimination, and their property rights would be
respected. French citizens who wished to leave Algeria could
take their belongings with them and could freely transfer capital. French citizens who wished to stay in Algeria but maintain their French citizenship could freely enter any profession
and establish any business enterprise.

Meanwhile, France would continue to give financial and
technical assistance to Algeria as before, i.e., would continue the Constantine Plan. In addition, Algeria would remain
in the French franc zone and the two countries would give each
other preferential tariff treatment, although Algeria would be
able to raise protective tariffs to facilitate industrialization.
France and Algeria would continue to cooperate in the exploitation of the Saharan oil and gas fields and in the search for
others. Finally, the French army on Algerian soil would be
reduced to 80,000 within one year and would pull out completely
within two years.

This agreement assumed that the French colons who were
living in Algeria would stay there after independence. But,
about two weeks after the Evian Agreement was signed and
the cease-fire instituted, some members of the colon underground group set out to wreck it. They raided an Algerian
hospital in Algiers and massacred 10 patients in their beds.[48]
A month later, a truck loaded with explosives killed 62 Algerians in the dock area of Algiers. Then a terror wave was
begun against Algerian women; 30 were killed in the streets
of Algiers and Oran on one day in May. On another day over
100 Algerians were killed indiscriminately in the streets.

THE TRIPOLI PROGRAM

In late May and early June, 1962, Ben Bella and other
members of the Conseil National de la Révolution Algérienne
(CNRA), a group of leading political exiles formed in 1956,
met in Tripoli to outline a program--a philosophy and a set
of goals--to serve as their "platform." This document, known
as the Tripoli Program, has served as an ideological base
since independence. The signers of this document did not feel
bound by the Évian Agreement, although they did not directly
repudiate it. They noted that the French army had not attempte
to restrain the Organisation de l' Armée Sècrete (OAS) since
the signing of the Evian Agreement and that the French could

therefore be blamed for being the first party not to live up to
the agreement. Whereas the Évian Agreement promised protection and freedom of action to the French who might choose
to stay in Algeria, and also posited a continuation of the free-
enterprise economy, the Tripoli Program indicated an intention to pursue socialist policies, to nationalize many sectors
of the economy, and to eliminate many privileges of the colons.
(The important, relative parts of the Tripoli Program are
quoted in Chapter 8.)

DEPARTURE OF THE FRENCH

During the final bloodbath administered to the Algerians
by the OAS, following the signing of the Évian Agreement, the
Algerians showed admirable restraint. They did not let themselves be goaded into retaliatory action. However, it is little
wonder that thousands of colons left for France each day for
several months prior to July 1, 1962--the day of complete
independence. Whereas the net departure of Frenchmen in
1961 had been 135,000, in 1962 this increased to 651,000.[49]
By January, 1963, out of a former French population of 1 million, only about 200,000 remained. Of these, 59,000 left in
1963 and 50,000 in 1964. Of the 130,000 Jews (nearly all of
whom had French citizenship), only 10,000 remained by the
end of 1963. By March, 1963, 3.75 million acres belonging
to 5,000 farms had been abandoned.[50] Most of the 1,800
doctors had left the country and, of the 250 public works en-
gineers present in 1961, only 80 remained by July, 1962, and
many of them were preparing to leave.[51] Consequently, the
departure of the French resulted in the loss of most of the
skills needed to maintain a modern economic sector. Most
of the important government files had been destroyed or carried abroad. Also, only a very small percentage of the middle and upper levels had been filled by Algerians prior to
independence. Thus, the departure of the French left chaos
in the government apparatus.
By March, 1965, there were only 92,000 French remaining, and many of these had been sent as part of the French
technical assistance programs. The socio-professional distribution of the French at that time was (1) technical assistance,
and families, 35,000; (2) salaried employees in industry, and
families, 21,000; (3) merchants and artisans, 4600; (4) liberal
professions, 2,100; (5) farmers, 1,000; (6) industrialists, 1,000;
(7) unclassified, 19,000.[52]

ECONOMIC AND SOCIAL DEVELOPMENTS
SINCE INDEPENDENCE

Establishment of the Self-Management System

The rapid departure of the French left many farms and
factories without owners or managers, but the workers were
there and wanted to keep producing. In July, 1962, a large
abandoned farm near Blida became the first workers' cooperative, by agreement among the workers.[53] Others followed.
The same phenomenon occurred in a number of factories and
stores. Thus, the concept of abandoned property (biens vacants)
and the growth of self-management were spontaneous reactions
to a situation. Only after the fact did the government adopt
them as policy and promote them as an ideology.
        Chapter 8 contains a number of quotations from Ben Bella
and President Boumediène with regard to the institutionaliza-
tion of self-management, as well as criticisms of its short-
comings. Chapter 9 deals with the legal structure and the
extent to which self-management has spread in the economy.
Several excellent studies on Algeria's self-management also
exist, the best of which is by Jean Teillac.[54] For purposes
of this study, the author wishes at this time simply to state
that because of a number of deficiencies, the system of self-
management in Algeria encountered many difficulties. The
major problem was a lack of qualified people to manage the
enterprises. The next most important problem was the lack
of financing, because the commercial banks generally refused
to provide credit to firms under self-management, either for
ideological reasons or because such firms were considered to
be very poor credit risks. These two problems led to a third,
the problem of obtaining raw materials and parts from abroad
and of selling finished products abroad, since most purchasing
and distribution channels had been disrupted.

Economic Growth (in Reverse)

A decline in economic activity following independence was
entirely to be expected. The departure of over 1 million French
men and Jews, who had an overwhelming share (especially in
proportion to their number) of the country's purchasing power,
resulted in a decreased demand for many, many items. To a
very large extent, therefore, one cannot place the blame for

the economic decline on bad management. Even with the best
management, a decrease in production would have been necessary, except for those items which were produced entirely for
the export market, such as some of the agricultural products.

One of the hardest-hit sectors of the economy was that of
construction. At the end of 1962, for example, only 15,000
workers were active, compared with 120,000 in mid-1961.
At the same time, the textile industry was operating at 50 percent of its previous high, the food industry at 60 percent, the
chemical industry at 50 percent, and the metalworking and
electrical industries at 25 percent.[55] Another important indicator is that bank deposits decreased by 47 percent during
this period.

The year 1963 showed little improvement. At the end of
September, 1963, some sectors of industry were operating at
12 percent of capacity, and most at less than 50 percent, although the food industry was at 60 percent and soap at 80 percent.[56] Another indicator of economic activity, railroad cars
loaded, shows that 1960 had a monthly average of 22,400,
1962 had a monthly average of only 13,557, 1963 had 10,583,
and the first six months of 1964 averaged 9,700.[57]

Electricity production followed a pattern similar to that
of railroad car loadings, decreasing from 1,386 million kilo-
watt-hours in 1961 to 1,155 in 1962, 1,088 in 1963, and 1,123
in 1964.[58] There are no published figures showing the total
value of industrial production each year since 1960, but several
sets of figures can be given. The production of steel ingots
followed the following pattern: 1960, 31,000 tons; 1961, 30,500
tons; 1962, 5,500 tons; 1963, 9,500 tons; 1964, 20,500 tons;
and 1965, 23,000 tons.[59] During the same period, the production of copper and aluminum wire was as follows: 1960,
4,266 tons; 1961, 4,843 tons; 1962, 2,209 tons; 1963, 1,451
tons; 1964, 1,827 tons; and 1965, 2,146 tons. On the other
hand, the production of superphosphates and fertilizers increased from 46,192 tons in 1962 to 99,261 tons in 1964 and
92,000 tons in 1965. Statistics are available on mineral production, through 1965, in Appendix B, Table 3. For example,
the production of iron ore was 2.1 million tons in 1962, 2.0
million in 1963, 2.7 million in 1964, and 3.1 million in 1965.[60]

The brightest spot in Algeria's economy has been the
petroleum industry. Since independence, oil production has
had only a modest increase--from 21 million tons in 1962 to
24 million in 1963 and 26 million in both 1964 and 1965.[61]
Natural gas production, however, which began only in 1961,
has grown very rapidly, reaching 12.5 billion cubic feet in

1962, 14.1 billion in 1963, 30 billion in 1964, and 65.3 billion in 1965. Most of this was for domestic consumption until 1965, when a gas liquefaction plant at Arzew went into operation, permitting the export of liquefied gas. This plant belongs to CAMEL, half of which is owned by Shell and Comstock, the other half by various French and Algerian oil companies. Long-term agreements for the supply of liquefied gas were concluded first with France, the United Kingdom, and Spain. These were followed by agreements with Austria and Yugoslavia.

All of Algeria's oil and gas exploration and operating companies were combined into one organization called SONATRACH in 1967. This organization is rapidly becoming a state within a state, like ENI in Italy, only more important, relatively, because oil constitutes a larger portion of the national economy in Algeria than in Italy. Besides prospecting, production, and pipeline transportation, SONATRACH also owns the oil refinery at Algiers, part of the gas liquefaction plant at Arzew, and all of the local market distribution network. Over 200 Soviet technicians were working for SONATRACH at the end of 1967. (The U.S. management consulting firm of Arthur D. Little Company has also been supplying a large team of experts [technicians and managers] to SONATRACH since 1965.)

Of course, industry accounts for only about 30 percent of Algeria's GNP. Of nearly equal importance is agriculture. Here we find a significant decrease in production, the major reason being not a lack of market but a lack of agricultural skills resulting from the voluntary departure of many of the French and the nationalization of all French-owned farmland.

Within six months after independence, 2.37 million acres had been abandoned by the French and placed under self-management. By May, 1963, this had increased to 3.63 million acres. By the end of 1966, primarily through the nationalizations, the self-managed sector had increased to 6.63 million acres, or one-third of the total land under cultivation. This included most of the best land, however, and prior to independence had accounted for much more than 50 percent of total agricultural production and for nearly 100 percent of agricultural exports, i.e., wine, citrus fruits, and fresh vegetables. Following nationalization, however, this land ended up in the socialist sector, and there was a considerable decrease in production. In 1957 the European-owned lands had produced $310 million of grain, fruits, and vegetables plus $20 million of animals, while the private Algerian sector had produced $126 million and $92 million, respectively. On the other hand, in 1964, the socialist sector (the former European farms) produced only $167 million of grain, fruits, and vegetables plus $8 million of animals, while the private Algerian farms produced $160 million and $58 million, respectively.[62]

Appendix B, Table 4, shows the decreases in production of various agricultural products between 1957 and 1964. The total value of production decreased from $546 million in 1957 to $396 million in 1964. All products except fruits, whose production increased by about 10 percent, showed a decrease.

Although exact figures are not available, it appears that Algeria's GNP in 1964 had decreased by about 20 percent in comparison with 1960. This does not, of course, mean that the average per capita income of the Algerians decreased during this period, because 90 percent of the Europeans, who had nearly 50 percent of national income prior to independence, had departed in the interim. The following two years, 1965 and 1966, were extremely dry years, resulting in decreases of up to 50 percent for some products and a further decrease in GNP and, probably, in per capita income.

Foreign Trade

Algeria continues to be highly dependent on foreign trade. About two-thirds of her imports are final products which go directly to consumers. Also, about one-third of her imports are food products. In export, oil and gas make up 67 percent of her exports, wine constitutes another 15 percent, and citrus fruits 5 percent. Prior to 1961, wine was the leading export. In that year, however, oil exports constituted 45 percent of the total and wine fell to 28 percent of the total. Algeria's oil and gas exports compete directly with those of Libya, whose deposits are much closer to the coast and thus are lower in cost. The agreement with France, however, has assured Algeria of a market for most of these products (France took 75 percent of Algeria's oil and gas exports in 1965).[63]

In its attempt to diversify its trading partners, Algeria has, since independence, entered into a number of trading agreements. For example, between July, 1963, and July, 1965, she became involved in "clearing"-type agreements with a number of East European countries and Mali, Guinea, and the United Arab Republic. In addition she entered into regular trade agreements with Switzerland, Syria, Cameroon, Congo (Brazzaville), Ivory Coast, Mauretania, Niger, and Senegal. The most important trade agreement, however, is still with France, and as a result, two-thirds of her trade remains with France. Although Algeria has not been publishing foreign trade data, it appears that her trade with France is in surplus and that this surplus nearly offsets the deficit of her trade with other countries.

Unemployment in Algeria and Employment in France

There are no official statistics on unemployment in Algeria, but a government minister estimated early in 1967 that of 11.5 million Algerians, 5 million are capable of working; that of these, 3.5 million are unemployed and, of the remaining 1.5 million, 1.0 million are underemployed.[64] This is an indication of the seriousness of the situation and of the importance of the Algerians working in France.

Prior to independence, there was a free movement of Algerians to France, and many took advantage of this opportunity. During the first six months of 1961, one year before independence, there was a net movement of about 4,000 Algerians per month to France. During the third quarter, the movement was in equilibrium, but during the last quarter, a net of 5,000 per month returned to Algeria. During the first half of 1962 the movement was in balance, but the first two months of independence (July and August, 1962) saw the return of 20,000 Algerians. Disenchantment quickly followed, however, and during the following six months, an average of 20,000 per month, net, left for France. In 1963 the movement reversed, and a net average of 1,000 returned to Algeria each month.[65] In March, 1964, however, 60,000 Algerians arrived in France. This caused such concern that France and Algeria reached an agreement whereby in the future France would accept a maximum of 12,000 per year.[66]

An estimated 600,000 Algerians now live in France, and about 300,000 are gainfully employed. The postal money orders which they send back to Algeria provide sustenance for an estimated 3 million Algerian peasants. Some villages receive 80 percent of their income by mail.[67]

Education

Since independence, the government has continued to pour money into education, which accounts for nearly 20 percent of the annual operating budget. As a result, by 1966 the number of boys in primary education had doubled, in comparison with 1962, to a total of 838,000. The number of girls had doubled to 551,000. In secondary education, during the same period, the number of boys tripled to 68,000, and the number of girls also tripled, to 28,000. In higher education, the number of boys tripled to 7,000 and the number of girls quadrupled to 2,000. Approximately 55 percent of the children of primary school age are now attending school, and 70 percent of those who attain school age actually enter school.[68]

One of the goals is to Arabize education, which has resulted in the use of poorly trained teachers. Thus, although the number in school has increased appreciably, the quality of education has diminished.

Another goal has been to decrease the rate of illiteracy, which at independence was nearly 90 percent. The government has organized a program of adult education for this purpose, but its results are not yet appreciable.

Governmental Budget and Planning

As noted above, the government has been devoting about 20 percent of its operating budget to education. This, among other development efforts, has placed a considerable strain on public finances. In 1966, for example, the budget anticipated receipts of $838 million and expenditures of $989 million, with, consequently, a deficit of $151 million. The major receipts were to come from the following sources: business taxes, $160 million; direct taxes, $133 million; indirect taxes, $140 million; petroleum revenues, $150 million; foreign aid, $70 million; customs, $46 million; and profits from the socialist sector, $30 million. The profits from the socialist sector are illusory, however, since the agricultural portion must be subsidized and the industrial portion does not practice amortization of equipment.[69]

The expenditures of the 1966 budget were divided between $640 million for the operating budget and $349 million for the equipment budget. The operating budget provided $98 million for defense and $126 million for education.

In the past, the operating budget has tended to be overspent while the equipment budget is underspent. One of the difficulties in disbursing the equipment budget is the lack of a development plan. Although the Tripoli Program called for a development plan in 1962, the government was unable to draw up a plan until 1966. Even then, it was still a draft plan, drawn up in three parts: a seven-year perspective, a three-year plan (1967-69) and a one-year (1967) equipment program. Only the latter was truly operational, being the government's investment budget for the year. However, because of Algeria's involvement in the Middle East war and its aftermath, even that budget was disregarded after the middle of the year. The three-year plan was not put into effect and is a document closely guarded by the government ministries. As a result, the government talks about the plan but admits that "the planning tradition and practice have still to be acquired and rest on the following methodological principles: planning plus great flexibility of the targets."[70]

Observations on the Algerian Economy

The above sketch of the Algerian economy shows that the country is in great difficulty. The achievement of political independence did not bring about economic independence. The Algerians had placed much hope in their socialism, but no economic system has a magic formula for development, especially in such a short period of time. Less than 10 years of independence is not long, but it seems long to those who are suffering, and many feel disenchanted. It becomes more and more difficult for the government to mobilize people to work harder and harder.

Industrialization is proceeding slowly. A number of new industries (such as textiles and shoes) are being started to meet the needs of local consumers, and these are operating well. But most of the older industries operate far below capacity.

There is no hope of industrializing rapidly enough to provide employment for those who reach working age each year, much less for those millions now unemployed. Algeria's only hope is for the future--for the next generation. Her resources are considerable and, with a literate population and well-conceived development plans, she has the possibility of achieving self-sustaining growth. As noted in the Constantine Plan, "Algeria is not an underdeveloped country, but most of its territory is made up of underdeveloped regions."

Foreign Aid

As is the case with many other countries, Algeria's future development is highly dependent upon foreign aid. Since independence, Algeria has received approximately half of her foreign aid from France. Only 15-20 percent of this aid is in the form of technical assistance, but this is by far the most valuable to Algeria and the least replaceable by any other country. At first, Algerian leaders were somewhat hostile to the presence of so many French technical assistance personnel, especially to the many teachers. But this aid has continued for six years, and the Algerians have found that France can give aid without becoming involved in internal politics.

Why does France give this massive aid to Algeria? The author sees a number of reasons. First, France is desirous of protecting its interests in the Saharan oil and gas fields. These provide her with a sure and close source of fuel which she can pay for in francs. Second, France wishes to protect the interests of the many private French investors who have remained in Algeria. Third, through this generosity and working arrangement with Algeria, France shows that it is possible for a predominantly capitalist developed country to work closely with a predominantly socialist underdeveloped country. She feels that it is important to show the workability of such a combination, for it may be a pattern for the future. Fourth, France feels that if she can give this aid to such a country, without strings, then in the eyes of the rest of the underdeveloped countries France separates herself from the "imperialist" countries.

French financial aid to Algeria has, however, decreased over the years: 1963, $210 million; 1964, $190 million; 1965, $139 million; 1966, $122 million.[71] During the same period, the number of technical assistance personnel supplied by France fell from 24,500 to 10,000 but decreased only slightly in 1967 to 9,990. Among these technical assistance personnel, the number of teachers fell from 10,500 to 6,540. The major decrease, of about 10,000, was of Frenchmen who served as officials in the Algerian government offices.[72]

France has taken advantage of the oil agreement and aid agreements to achieve certain aims. At the same time, Algeria has adhered strictly to the repayment schedules. For example, Algeria borrowed $110 million from France between November, 1962, and March, 1963. This was paid off by January, 1966. The 1966 negotiations resulted in Algeria's agreeing to pay $80 million to French citizens and companies as compensation for losses incurred in Algeria. As part of the 1965 oil agreement, however, the French agreed to provide $40 million per year, for a five-year period, to finance some new industrial projects in Algeria, in addition to other types of aid.[73] These projects included a fish cannery, a factory for construction materials, and a date packaging plant.

The uses of French aid may be illustrated by the 1966 experience, during which year $10 million was allocated to the construction of a steel mill at Annaba, $40 million to miscellaneous industrial projects, $24 million to untied aid--mostly in support of the government's operating budget--and $26 million to technical assistance, a total of $100 million.

Between 1962 and 1966, Algeria received a total of $666 million in aid from other countries. The socialist countries (mainly the Soviet Union, China, and Yugoslavia) gave $318 million, all of it as tied loans. Arab countries (Kuwait and the United Arab Republic) gave $80 million as tied loans and $28 million untied. Western countries (primarily the United States and the United Kingdom) gave $67 million as tied loans and $120 million in grants. Finally, the World Bank provided $20 million in tied loans and $33 million in grants.[74]

The type of aid given by the Soviet Union may be shown by the agreement negotiated in 1966 whereby it agreed to provide credits for the following: (1) a steel mill at Annaba (in cooperation with the French); (2) a lead and zinc ore treatment mill; (3) an electric power plant; (4) a distillery; (5) a professional training center for mining and oil exploration; and (6) experts to help put into operation, with worker management, about 20 factories which had been closed since the French owners left in 1962. In return the Soviet Union agreed to receive repayment by buying cognac and alcohol from the distillery over a period of years.[75]

Most of the U.S. foreign aid to Algeria has been in the form of wheat. The 200,000-300,000 tons per year sent in 1962 and 1963 was sufficient to help feed 2 million to 3 million people. Ben Bella condemned U.S. policy in Cuba and the Congo, and Boumediène strongly criticizes the U.S. position in Vietnam. This is a major source of discord between the two countries. Undoubtedly the U.S. missions attempted to influence Algeria's attitude, and very likely Algeria did not receive financial assistance because of her attitude, but the wheat kept coming. In 1966, however, it was insufficient to meet Algeria's needs during a second consecutive year of drought. Consequently, near the end of 1966 the Soviet Union stepped in and agreed to give Algeria 200,000 tons of wheat. Then, as an aftermath to the June, 1967, Middle East war, the Algerians broke off negotiations with the U.S. government for surplus wheat, whereupon the Soviet Union agreed to increase its contribution.

The World Bank had, in the early years following independence, provided loans to Algeria. The amount of such loans was minimal, however, because of a lack of well-defined projects. In 1967, the World Bank as a source of foreign aid was placed in doubt by Belaid Abdesselem, the Algerian Minister of Industry and Energy. Following his visit to the Bank to negotiate some loans, the official Algerian Press Agency stated:

> The attitude of the Bank's directors vis-à-vis the various projects submitted by the Algerian government was profoundly deceiving and in many respects dangerous. This attitude demonstrates not only a deliberate intention to force underdeveloped countries which have opted for socialism to renounce their choice, but also to accept an economic process which would bring them back to the system which existed under the execrable colonial regime.[76]

POLITICAL DEVELOPMENTS SINCE INDEPENDENCE

As noted above, the economic developments in Algeria since independence have been very unfavorable. The political developments have not been a great deal brighter.

The FLN was formed in 1954, when Ben Bella and other leading revolutionaries were in exile in Cairo. Ben Bella built up his reputation and position in the FLN not only by being an early leader in the OS, but also by buying and supplying arms to the FLN rebels and by establishing a close alliance with President Nasser in Egypt. It will also be recalled that the FLN's external army, the ALN, which was located in Tunisia and Morocco (the latter under the leadership of Houari Boumediène), remained as the only organized fighting force in Algeria by the time of independence. It was not a political force as such, but it served to put Ben Bella in power and, later, to unseat him.

Two other important political organizations were formed in the mid-1950's. The first, the CNRA, was formed in 1956 by the political exiles in Cairo, who did not wish to be left sitting on the sidelines when independence arrived. Also, within Algeria itself, the FLN's leaders were too easily exposed to capture by the French and could function well as an organization only from outside the country. Initially there were 17 members of the CNRA, but later, with 54 members, it served as the ruling body of the revolution. It was this group which met in Tripoli, in May and June, 1962, to draw up the Tripoli Program.

The GPRA was established in Cairo in September, 1958. One of Algeria's moderate nationalist leaders, Ferhat Abbas, who had not been in the FLN movement, joined with the FLN to form the GPRA. Abbas was made Premier, while Krim and Ben Bella (the latter still in jail) were Vice-Premiers. One of the aims of the GPRA was to obtain diplomatic support for the revolution. Thus it was asked by the CNRA to negotiate the Évian Agreement with the French. The GPRA achieved a cease-fire in cooperation with the French and had to work with the French in arranging a transition of governmental functions.

There were also the willaya commanders. During the struggle for independence, Algeria had been divided by the FLN into regions (willayas), each with its own military commander. French tactics effectively prevented them from working with each other and also isolated them from the outside. Thus, they operated fairly independently and recognized no common leader.

All of these forces arrived in Algeriers in July, 1962, and instead of trying to put together an effective government, they began to maneuver for power and privileged positions. Most of the willaya commanders resented the ALN (the external army), which had not fought. They threw their lot in with the GPRA, which, in turn, attempted to demote Houari Boumediène. Another group of willaya commanders remained separate, under the leadership of Belkacem Krim.

Finally Ben Bella, operating from within the CNRA, established the political bureau of the FLN, with himself as leader, proclaiming that this bureau should be the supreme body. Taking advantage of the GPRA's opposition to Boumediène, Ben Bella sided with the ALN. On September 3, 1962, he asked Boumediène to march on Algiers, where he, as head of the political bureau, assumed power. A Constitutent Assembly was elected on September 20 and Ben Bella was elected President on September 27.

Having achieved power on the strength of the external army, Ben Bella created strong antagonism among the willaya

commanders. Also, GPRA leaders had opposed Ben Bella
since before independence. Counterrevolutionary activities
against the Ben Bella regime began to build up in the spring
of 1964. Some opposition was against the dictatorial methods
of the regime; others felt it was too socialist-oriented; others
felt that it was straying too far from an Islamic basis; and
there were those who felt simply that the government's policies
were leading to economic chaos. As a result, Ben Bella had
to use the army to put down open revolution in some areas.
He gradually eliminated from power those who had voiced
opposition to him. Most of his colleagues and supporters
suffered the same fate. Boumediène, however, remained as
Vice-President, Defense Minister, and éminence grise.

The regime thus became essentially a dictatorship. It
operated on the cult of the personality of Ben Bella. Its ideology was based on the Tripoli Program, which, in April, 1964,
was supplemented by the Charter of Algiers. The National
Assembly, elected in September, 1965, was a rubber-stamp
assembly, the election ballot consisting of a single list from
which all those who in the past two years had voiced opposition
to the regime had been eliminated.

Another potential source of opposition to the regime was
the Union Générale des Travailleurs Algériens (UGTA), the
Algerian labor union. It had attempted to follow an independent
line in the period immediately following independence, but
once Ben Bella became President, he began to assert control
over the union. This was achieved at the first national congress of the UGTA, in January, 1963, through the use of
strong-arm methods, and the UGTA has since served as an
arm of the government's policies. The government believed
that in a socialist state, unions work through the one party.
There cannot be an independent outlook. Also, workers' demands which may have been appropriate under a colonial,
capitalist regime are not appropriate under a revolutionary,
socialist one, especially in a country which is still essentially
agricultural. Thus the role of the labor union was to act primarily as a mechanism for communication between the government and the workers.

Thus, Ben Bella seemed securely in power. He had overcome all opposition and undermined all organized bodies,
except the army, upon which he depended. On June 19, 1965,
the army removed him, and Houari Boumediène assumed the
powers of the Presidency.

Having taken over the government (with Ben Bella safely
in jail), President Boumediène accused Ben Bella of financial

mismanagement, of criminal attempts to discredit the army, and of treason, calling him a "diabolical dictator with a morbid love of power." He announced that the new regime would respect all of Algeria's international engagements, and made special mention of a desire to continue a policy of cooperation with France.

Ben Bella was the chief target. Only a few arrests were made. It was a bloodless coup with the full backing of the army. Student demonstrations took place for several days but were kept under control. The new cabinet had 11 new ministers and retained nine from the Ben Bella government.

Very soon after assuming power, President Boumediène gave a speech in which he intimated that he might institute a more liberal economic regime. As a result, the U.S. government and others began to reassess their policies vis-à-vis foreign aid to Algeria. Talks were started, but the situation soon became clear: President Boumediène was not going to change Algeria's "socialist option" in order to get more financial aid from the Western powers.

Meanwhile, the subordination of the UGTA to the FLN (and to the government) was not completely settled. Difficulties continued to arise. Early in 1967, the management of the government-controlled Algiers oil refinery fired an Algerian engineer, whereupon the UGTA called a strike in protest. Management then fired six of the union officials, which led to somewhat of an interministerial crisis. The UGTA charged that the Minister of Industry was replacing the injustices of the private sector with those of national enterprises, and that he had decided to liquidate (nationalize) the self-management sector of industry. The Minister of Industry responded with the charge that "self-management is not an ideology but must be an economic reality. That is to say, the battle of production will be won with results and not with slogans."[77]

According to the UGTA, the revolutionary character of the regime rests in large measure upon the workers and the extent to which they are involved in the economic and political affairs of the country. It now appears, however, that neither the UGTA nor the FLN holds the reins of power in Algeria; rather, they are held by the new technocrats, who have arisen through the six years of administrative experience since independence and operate within a framework established by the ruling Revolutionary Council.

NOTES

1. J. Saint-Germes, Economie Algérienne, p. 34.

2. Marc Lamunière, Histoire de l'Algérie, p. 44.

3. David C. Gordon, The Passing of French Algeria, p. 17.

4. Government of France, Plan de Constantine, 1959-1963.

5. Saint-Germes, op. cit., p. 30.

6. Augustine Bernard, L'Algérie, p. 405.

7. Government of France, Tableaux de l'Economie Algérienne, 1960, p. 19.

8. Mostefa Lachéraf, L'Algérie: Nation et Société, p. 17.

9. Bernard, op. cit., p. 392.

10. Saint-Germes, op. cit., p. 151.

11. Claude Estier, Pour l'Algérie, p. 31.

12. Ibid.

13. Lamunière, op. cit., p. 148.

14. Bernard, op. cit., p. 382.

15. J. Guillot, Le Développement Économique de l'Algérie, p. 104.

16. Government of France, Plan de Constantine, 1959-1963.

17. Francois Perroux, L'Algérie de Demain, p. 53.

18. Raymond Barbe, "Les Classes Sociales en Algérie," Économie et Politique (September-October, 1959), p. 362.

19. "L'Algérie," an unpublished report by the French Resident Minister (dated 1957), pp. 37, 38.

20. Perroux, op. cit., pp. 70, 90.

21. John C. Pawera, Algeria's Infrastructure, p. 13.

22. Ibid., pp. 29, 33.

23. Ibid., p. 144.

24. Bernard, op. cit., pp. 475-87.

25. Guillot, op. cit., p. 63.

26. Ibid., p. 69.

27. Ibid., p. 70.

28. Ibid., p. 85.

29. Government of France, La Micro-Industrie.

30. Le Monde (14 July 1957).

31. Government of France, Guide de l'Industriel en Algérie.

32. Guillot, op. cit., p. 192.

33. Government of France, Plan de Constantine: 2 Ans de Réalisation.

34. Government of France, unpublished papers of the Caisse d'Équipement pour le Développement de l'Algérie (1962).

35. La Dépêche Quotidienne d'Algérie (March 11, 1960).

36. Government of France, Études et Programmes.

37. From discussions with officials of the company (August, 1964).

38. Guillot, op. cit., p. 216.

39. Pawera, op. cit., pp. 163, 169.

40. Government of France, Plan de Constantine, 1959-1963.

41. Government of France, Tableaux de l'Économie Algérienne, 1960.

42. Ibid.

43. Government of France, Plan de Constantine, 1959-1963.

44. Ibid.

45. Saint-Germes, op. cit., p. 10.

46. Gordon, op. cit., p. 57.

47. "Algeria Changes Course," Africa Report (November, 1965), p. 10.

48. Gordon, op. cit., p. 69.

49. Government of Algeria, Bulletin de Statistique Générale: 1961-1965.

50. Estier, op. cit., p. 31.

51. Ibid., p. 172.

52. Algier Ce Soir (August 22, 1965).

53. Estier, op. cit., p. 31.

54. Jean Teillac, Autogestion en Algérie.

55. Government of Algeria, Actualité et Documents, No. 20, p. 16.

56. Banque Industrielle de l'Afrique du Nord, Rapport Trimestriel (October, 1963).

57. Les Echos (July 16, 1964).

58. Government of France, "La Situation Économique de l'Algérie," Notes et Études Documentaires, No. 3406-3407 (July 6, 1967), p. 49.

59. Ibid., p. 65.

60. Ibid., pp. 61, 67, 68.

61. Ibid., p. 53.

62. Ibid., p. 43.

63. Ibid., p. 78.

64. Government of France, "La Situation Économique de l'Algérie en 1966: Premier Aperçu," Problèmes Economiques, No. 1.015 (June 15, 1967), p. 17.

65. Government of Algeria, Bulletin de Statistique Générale, 1961-1965.

66. Jeune Afrique (September 18, 1966), p. 12.

67. Ibid.

68. Government of France, "La Situation Économique de l'Algérie," Notes et Études Documentaires, p. 77.

69. Ibid., p. 80.

70. Government of Algeria, L'Algérie, Cinq Ans Après.

71. Government of France, "La Situation Économique de l'Algérie en 1966: Premier Aperçu," Problemes Économiques, p. 22.

72. Ibid.; Le Monde (October 16, 1965; March 18, 1967).

73. Le Monde (December 12, 1966).

74. "La Situation Économique de l'Algérie: Premier Aperçu," Problemes Économiques, p. 22.

75. El Moudjahid (August 6, 1966).

76. La Presse (April 15, 1967).

77. Le Monde (September 6, 1967).

CHAPTER **8** POLICY STATEMENTS
OF ALGERIAN
POLITICAL LEADERS
AND GOVERNMENT

Algeria has two major ideological documents, the Tripoli
Program and the Charter of Algiers. The former was prepared by leaders of the FLN just prior to independence and
has continued to be referred to as the basis for the government's actions. The Charter of Algiers did not replace the
Tripoli Program but supplemented it. As a result, this chapter begins with extensive quotations from the Tripoli Program.
It will be noted that this document said nothing about the system of self-management, which had to be developed after independence and had to be legitimized.

The section on the Ben Bella regime starts, therefore,
with Ben Bella's defense of the system of self-management,
followed by a warning that if the workers moved too quickly
in socializing the economy (taking over the management of
more and more factories, by using the strike as a weapon),
the results could be very negative in terms of the development of the economy.

The Algerian trade union, the UGTA, is a force in itself.
It has become an arm of the FLN, but it is an arm which
sometime flails without instructions from the brain. Its
leaders tend to be more Marxist-oriented than the governmental officials feel is economically feasible. Hence the
views of the UGTA officials are important because, whether
or not they can carry out their ideology, the force of the
workers, as exerted through the UGTA's leaders, is a continual influence on the government's policies.

The contents of the 1963 investment code were not so important as were the views of Ben Bella regarding the need for
such a law. Consequently, his defense of the code before the
National Assembly is quoted at length.

The section on the Ben Bella regine ends with his defense
of Industrial Expansion Organizations, an institution which

was an innovation of his government. It represented a formula for utilizing private savings and private entrepreneurship without really strengthening the private sector.

The section on the regime of President Boumediène
starts with its foreign policy, as stated by his Foreign Minister and close confidant, Abdelaziz Bouteflika. The remainder of the section is devoted to statements by President
Boumediène on the role of self-management and the need for
agrarian reform, plus the views of his two most important
ministers on the role of self-management and on the need to
stimulate private investment--hence the need for a new investment code. This section also contains quotations from
the 1966 investment code, a legal document which encourages
private investment, both domestic and foreign, and offers it
certain advantages and guarantees.

PRE-INDEPENDENCE IDEOLOGY

The Tripoli Program, prepared during the latter stages
of the struggle for independence, served as the ideological
base for the FLN and continues to be quoted as the basic
charter of the Algerian revolutionary government. The following excerpts were chosen because they demonstrate the
ideological position on existing economic and social structures,
on the role of private enterprise, and on the middle class.

The Principal Tasks of the
People's Democratic Revolution

The People's Democratic Revolution is the deliberate
construction of the nation within the framework of socialist principles and of power in the hands of the
people. . . .

The Democratic Content

. . . The economic conditions of the country determine its social and cultural situation. Algeria's
development, in order to be swift, harmonious, and
aimed at the satisfaction of the needs of all in the

framework of collectivization, should necessarily be
planned in a socialist perspective.

The democratic spirit should not be a purely
theoretical exercise. It should be made concrete in
well-defined state creations and in all sectors of the
country's social life. The sense of responsibility,
the truest manifestation of the democratic spirit,
should everywhere supplant the principle of authority,
feudal in its essence and paternalistic in its nature.

The Popular Content

. . . The experiences of certain newly independent countries teach that a privileged social class can
seize power for its own exclusive profit. In so doing,
it cheats the people of the fruit of their struggle and
deserts them for an alliance with imperialism. In
the name of national unity, which it exploits shrewd-
ly, the middle class pretends to act for the good of
the people and asks their support. But its relatively
recent origin, its weakness as a social class without
deep foundation, and its lack of real traditions of
struggle limit its ability to promote the construction
of a nation and to defend it against imperialistic aims.

The middle class is the bearer of opportunistic
ideologies whose chief characteristics are defeatism,
demagoguery, alarmism, contempt for principles,
and lack of revolutionary conviction, all of which
make the bed of neo-colonialism. Vigilance requires
that these dangers be combated at once and that adequate measures be taken to prevent the middle class
from broadening its economic base in cooperation
with neo-colonial capitalism. . . .

Toward the Accomplishment of the
Social and Economic Tasks of the
People's Democratic Revolution

. . .

Principles of our Economic Policy

**Opposition to Foreign Domination and Economic
Liberalism.** In newly independent countries, resort-
ing to the methods of classic liberalism will prevent

a real transformation of society. Liberalism aggravates anarchy in the market, increases economic dependence on imperialism, turns the state into an instrument for the transfer of wealth to the hands of those already in the best position, and fosters the activity of parasitic social classes allied with imperialism. The local middle class progressively supplants the foreigner in non-productive sectors of the economy and grows rich. As for the people, they remain in misery and ignorance • • • •

The reluctance of foreign private capital to make investments that return less than the average rate of profit, its foreseeable weakness with respect to immediate needs, and the conditions under which it operates should impel us to view foreign help as we would view a collection agency.

A Policy of Planning with the Democratic Participation of the Workers in the Economic Authority. To break the grip of the monopolies by reorganizing our economic ties abroad, first of all with France; to eliminate internal obstacles by radically transforming the institutions of rural life; to industrialize in accord with the needs of the people--these are the imperatives for development of the country.

To reach these goals, economic planning and the control of the economy by the state, with the participation of the workers, are vital necessities. Only planning will make possible the accumulation of the capital required for profitable industrialization in a relatively short time, for centralization of the authority that is to determine the most important investments, and for the elimination of the waste and the false costs arising out of competition among companies.

The Economic Tasks of the People's Democratic Revolution

Agrarian reform. . . In the context of Algeria, the People's Democratic Revolution is primarily an agrarian revolution.

. . . Agrarian reform should be based on the slogan that the land belongs to those who work it and should follow these principles:

1. The immediate prohibition of all dealings in land and agricultural equipment.

2. Restrictions on holdings according to crops and production.

3. Expropriation of holdings in excess of the maximum to be decided.

4. Free grants of such [expropriated] land to landless peasants or those whose land is insufficient.

5. The democratic organization of the peasants into productive cooperatives.

6. The creation of state-owned farms on part of the expropriated land, and the participation of the workers in the management and in the profits of such farms. These farms will expedite marketing and will provide a point of departure for the establishment of technical staffs and agricultural instructors.

7. The prohibition of subsequent sale or rental of redistributed land in order to prevent the revival of large estates.

8. The cancellation of the debts owed by peasants, khammès, and sharecroppers to landowners, moneylenders, and public services.

9. State aid in the form of goods and financing.
. . .

The Development of the Substructure. . . The party's policy should seek to nationalize all forms of transportation; improve and increase the railroad and highway networks; construct road connections between major communications routes and rural markets.

The Nationalization of Credit and Foreign Trade.
The nationalization of credit and foreign trade includes:

The nationalization of insurance companies.

The nationalization of banks; this task must be performed with minimum delay. The numerical strength of the banks makes it possible for them to evade national control. Their recent or imminent conversion to development companies should not conceal their basic character, which is that of an instrument of financial blackmail.

The nationalization of foreign trade. . . . Priority nationalizations of the essential instruments of foreign trade and of wholesaling, and the creation of state corporations based on products or groups of products. Such an organization gives the state real control of imports and exports, assists effective

action with respect to consumption, and reaps commercial profits for investment in productive areas.
The Nationalization of Mineral Resources and
Sources of Energy. This is a long-term goal.
Industrialization. The progress of agriculture and
the mobilization of the masses can help the country
to advance only if the proper technical and economic
foundation is provided by industrial progress.

A state sector already exists in Algeria. It will
be the mission of the Algerian state to extend it to
the mining, quarry, and cement industries. However, the real long-term development of the country
is tied to the establishment of the basic industries
which are necessary to meet the demands of modern
agriculture.

Algeria has great potential for the development
of petroleum and metallurgical industries. It is the
function of the state to create the conditions appropriate to the establishment of such heavy industries.
In the other areas of the economy, private initiative
may be encouraged and directed within the framework of the general goal of industrialization.

At all costs, the state should not contribute, as
it has done in some other countries, to the creation
of an industrial base by which the local middle class
can profit. It is the state's duty to limit the development of this class by appropriate measures.

The contribution of foreign private capital is
desirable within certain limitations: It should be an-
cillary within the system of mixed economy; the withdrawal of profits should be controlled; and provision
should be made for the reinvestment of a part of the
profits.

THE REGIME OF AHMED BEN BELLA

The Tripoli Program contained no mention of self-
management as the means of socializing industry in Algeria.
This system grew out of the situation which developed after
independence, when workers attempted to keep a number of
factories and farm properties operating after the departure
of the owner-managers. This was partially legitimized by
several decrees in October and November, 1962. These

decrees, hastily put together in piecemeal fashion, required a more elaborate law in March, 1963, to provide a legal foundation for worker-management. Ben Bella was always careful to point out that self-management was a spontaneous phenomenon. The following speech by Ben Bella, delivered March 29, 1963, announced the new law and justified the advent and growth of self-management by putting the onus on the French owners and managers who had abandoned their responsibility to the economy of Algeria and to the welfare of the people.

    Workers of Algeria: At this moment, the Journal Officiel [of Algeria] is publishing the text of one of the most, if not the most, important decisions which the government has made since it was formed. This is a decree concerning the organization and management of industrial, mining, and artisanal enterprises, as well as agricultural lands.

    . . . I must say, it was not we who chased the former owners from these vast sections of the Algerian economy which became "abandoned property." It was not we who wished to asphyxiate the Algerian economy. It was the former owners who left, wishing to make their departure serve as sabotage, to compromise the possibility of reconstructing an independent Algeria.

    The government asked those who left to return. How many of them have returned? Before attempting to talk about principles, how many of them responded to the government's call? How many agreed to return and participate in the reconstruction of the country? Could the government, which arose out of the Algerian Revolution, stand still, with its arms crossed, before such a challenge?

    Also, did the decrees of 22 October and 23 November 1962 close the door in the faces of those who had left, neglecting their responsibilities vis-à-vis the land which had nourished them? Not at all! Revolutionary Algeria had a tradition of generosity. The decrees of 22 October and 23 November 1962 left those individuals the possibility of returning and resuming their activity in the enterprises or properties which they had abandoned, but with the condition that they give guarantees to carry out a productive and honest management and that they agree to collaborate with a management committee.

How many of them returned and accepted such
collaboration?

What national government, worthy of its name,
would permit such a situation to deteriorate? It
was necessary that one day the government, which
grew out of the Algerian Revolution, organize the
management of the abandoned enterprises and properties. . . . It was necessary to elaborate a law on
"abandoned property" so that the sector could be
defined, once and for all. It was in such a spirit
that we issued the decree of 18 March 1963. [1]

As noted in Chapter 7, the economy of Algeria declined
rapidly after independence. This was due partially to a severe
decrease in demand, caused by the departure of so many Frenchmen; partially to a disruption of supplies of materials and credits, as traditional channels were broken; and, among other
factors, partially to a lack of competent managers in the many
firms where the workers had taken over from the former owner-
managers. The government recognized this last factor as a
difficulty, as evidenced by the following excerpts from a speech
made by Ben Bella in November, 1963, before a siminar of
leaders of the UGTA. [2]

After one year of independence, . . . our main accomplishment has been the return of our land to our
sovereignty, which permits the land to be worked
according to a new doctrine. . . that of self-management. . . . Already, 6.4 million acres of land are
in the hands of our peasants. In addition, the majority of the industrial enterprises are in the hands
of the workers; the principal riches of the country
are either nationalized or controlled by the Revolution, and we are preparing to do more to consolidate
our political options on the road to socialism.

Ben Bella then went on to talk about the extremely valuable
role which the labor movement had played in the struggle for
independence. But he stated:

. . . when an authentic revolutionary regime exists,
and I think it now exists in Algeria, the labor union
activity must be channeled within the overall policies
of the government. If not, we will fall into the same
sickness that exists in certain labor movements in
Africa in the name of syndicalism. We must not
suffer from such a sickness. Labor union action
must be conceived within a political framework.
This is not simple, for in Algeria there is a

two-headed situation; we have a private sector as
well as a self-management sector.

Ben Bella then discussed the dangers of spontaneous
action by workers in the private sector. Such action, he said:

. . .runs the risk of making us go faster than we
should. We do not want the workers' committee of
a company, because they want the firm to be nationalized, to go on strike again and again so as to cause
the government to nationalize the enterprise. It is
important that each nationalization respond to the
interest of the overall economy. And the economy
is restrained by certain rules which, if they are
not followed, can result in stagnation. . . .

The UGTA was ideologically oriented even prior to the
revolution. Its Marxist leanings were strengthened during
the struggle for independence, during which period over 1,000
UGTA members received training in communist countries.[3]
This may be one reason why the system of self-management
developed without having been anticipated in the Tripoli Program and with the encouragement and planning of the government. It also explains why Ben Bella found it necessary to
ask the workers to refrain from strikes as a weapon for socializing the economy.

On January 20, 1963, when the UGTA was preparing for
its first congress, the FLN found it necessary to remove
some of the members of the UGTA's central committee by
force and replace them with individuals more responsive to
governmental policy.[4] As a result, the report prepared by
this committee, prior to the congress, reflected the government's view that there was a definite role for private enterprise, particularly foreign private investment.[5] The following excerpts from that report show, however, a pronounced
ideological content and end with a quote from Mao Tse-tung.

World capitalism has, in the last few years, chosen
Africa as a new zone of influence. Algeria, an integral part of that continent, becomes a stake for
international capitalism. That is why she is solicited by the West, which plays the role of a seducer.
Algeria is a new zone of influence where the fight
for markets and sources of raw materials has already begun.

Foreign capitalism is not present in our country
for the purpose of encouraging the establishment of
socialism. No one is unaware of its objective, which
consists, in various forms, of slowing down the

revolutionary movement by allying itself with the most reactionary national forces.

The erection of heavy industry is a long-term job. In the initial period, the Algerian socialist government must improve its artisan production and establish small industries which permit the processing of raw materials at their point of origin. During this transitional phase, in which we now find ourselves, Algeria needs foreign private capital. But its contribution must be complementary . . .and the transfer of profits must be regulated so that a part of them is reinvested.

The establishment of socialism during this initial period is impossible because of the weakness of our productive forces and of our working class. For a certain period, the government must follow a policy of compromise with the capitalists; it will be led, by the existing conditions, to seek help from all classes of the population and to adopt capitalistic methods. But this does not include the preparation of the necessary conditions for the establishment of socialism.

The great majority of Algerians will be the builders of socialism. They are all proletarians. Proletarians are not only those people who dirty their hands by working the land or machines, but also those intellectuals who take the side of the workers. As Mao Tse-tung said, "To determine whether any given intellectual is a revolutionary, non-revolutionary, or counterrevolutionary, there is a decisive criterion; one must determine whether he wants to link himself with the peasant and working masses and whether he can effect such a link."

Although the FLN (and hence the government) made an attempt to bring the UGTA under its control, the independence of the trade union was not destroyed. This is shown by the fact that in November, 1963, Ben Bella still found it necessary to ask the workers to refrain from strikes whose goal was worker-management.

However, the strikes continued. In May, 1964, there was another wave of strikes. The UGTA newspaper published an editorial entitled "Unions and Strikes," outlining the goal of strikes:

. . .strikes are a means by which the trade unions can integrate themselves into the management of the

companies. [The unions] wish to extend their activity to join the management in making management
decisions.

    This is in keeping with the party [FLN] thesis
that "In the transitional period the trade union's
essential tasks in regard to the private sector are,
first, to guard against overt or covert attacks by
the private sector against the socialist sector;
second, to defend the workers' interests in this
sector; third, to propagandize for the enlargement
of the socialist sector."

    The workers' struggle is therefore directed
toward the development of management in cooperation with the workers so that management's decisions will be in harmony with the general economic
planning of the country, and the ultimate fusion of
the private with the socialist sector.[6]

The Tripoli Program had stated that private initiative
would be encouraged and that foreign private capital was desirable. However, for a year following independence, private
enterprise had been a whipping boy--there was a rapid spread
of self-management and far more talk of socialism in the industrial sector than had seemed indicated by the Tripoli Program. The government realized that if foreign private investment was to play any role, it had to be encouraged. It had to
have a legal framework; it needed governmental guarantees;
and it had to know the rules of the game. The following speech
by Ben Bella was given on July 11, 1963, before the National
Assembly, in support of the bill then being discussed, to establish an investment code. It shows that Ben Bella at least
partially understood the psychology of the foreign investor
and also that he realized Algeria's need for such investment.

    Before the Assembly votes on this bill, which would
    establish an investment code, I would like to under-
    line the importance of this code. . . .I would first
    like to indicate that formulation and adoption of such
    a code does not indicate any desire to abandon our
    fundamental economic orientation or our wish to
    follow a vogue. It is a conscious political act which
    rests upon an analysis of our situation and the means
    at our disposition.

        . . .Our policy for industrialization continues
    to be the growth of the public sector. . .[but] the
    task is immense and the resources of the country
    certainly do not suffice to satisfy our ambitions for

a rapid industrialization. . . . That is why we envisage the participation of foreign capital, not as
a basic element in our industrial development but
as an accelerator which complements the actions
of the government.

We have already called for the assistance of
foreign public investment, and I should underline
that Algeria receives such aid from all the political
horizons of the world. But this aid, as you know,
is directed mostly to the economic infrastructure
of the country, as well as to agriculture and education. The needs in those areas are still very large.
Only a small part of such aid is directed toward
industrialization.

The only remaining source for financing investment in industry is through the participation of
foreign private capital. We feel that, without being
a traitor to our principles, such a participation is
possible and even desirable, in that it helps to place
Algeria's industrialization in the chain of scientific
and technical research in the modern world.

This bill has as its aim, precisely, to make this
foreign participation possible. If, as we believe,
foreign private capital can aid our industrial development, it remains to create the necessary conditions.
Two conditions are fundamental for any private investment: a profit and a certainty that such profit
can be repatriated to the country of origin. Any
code which ignores these two conditions is completely useless. Capitalists are not philanthropists;
it would be political romanticism to look for disin-
terested private investments.

. . . To conclude. . . I wish to say, while presenting this bill for an investment code, that the
government has attempted to assemble all the conditions necessary to accelerate the rhythm of our resources and other possibilities open to us. In
conformity with the principles of our socialist revolution, this code fixes the limits, establishes a framework, and sets the rules of the game. The guarantees
which it accords do not impede our march toward
socialism. [7]

The most complete statement of the government's views
of the role of domestic and foreign private investment was
given by Bachir Boumaza, the Minister of Economics, on

December 30, 1963, before the National Assembly, while
presenting the government's budget for 1964. By this time
the government had had six months of experience with the
investment code, whose implementation was Boumaza's responsibility. He was a key man not only in the conduct of the
economy but also in determining the FLN's ideological position and the way in which the government interpreted the ideology. The following are major excerpts from that speech.

    Today, the budget which I am presenting cannot be
judged except in relation to the government's economic and financial policies; it is only a translation, into
numbers, of the means by which the government pro-
poses to achieve its goals. Also, it will be useful,
in order that you might understand the interrelation-
ships within the budget, for me to give a general
statement of the political economics of the government. . . .

    The fact is that, today, the socialist sector has
become a predominant sector whose effect is a determining factor in the economic life of the nation. . . .
We have chosen socialism and rejected capitalism
as the method of development. One may say that
capitalism made possible the development of Western
Europe. That is true, but that development was
slow and would be possible only through sacrifice
by the poorer classes. Eight years of war as well
as our contacts with the modern life cause us to
reject that slowness and unjust distribution, which
are incompatible with the conscience of our people.

    Capitalism, besides its slowness and injustice,
would increase our dependence on foreign countries
and aggravate the economic dualism between the
traditional sector and the modern sector, thus increasing the disparities between the different regions
of our country. Thus, economic reason reinforces
the sentiment which comes from the heart of our
people and which chose socialism for ideological
reasons.

    . . . Algerian socialism must create the condi-
tions for an accelerated development by a radical
change of our economic and social organizations,
whether they be colonial or traditional, which constitute an obstacle to our economic progress. . . .

    . . . Our economic policies will resemble, first,
a trait of all socialisms . . . that of planning. . . .

Only by planning can our objectives be made coherent (particularly the priority to be given to the
socialist sector). It will also be possible to avoid
the waste which might result from competition.

Our planning in the area of production in the
private sector will have to be flexible and restricted
to periodic review, with the aim of fitting the policies
and goods of the private sector more and more closely
to the needs of the economy.

. . .At the present time, the socialization of
the means of production must not be considered as
an end in itself but, rather, as the path which
should make possible the acceleration of our development and our freedom. In other words, we
want enterprises which respect the orientation of
our economic goals and discuss their plans with
our national planning offices.

. . .With regard to those who are impatient
to see the government manage everything, we
respond that the government must first have the
means to do so. Before the government and the
people can take over the economy, organizations
must be formed and people trained for such new
responsibilities. In our fight against capitalism
and neo-colonialism, we must never forget that
their principal advantage is our disequilibrium. . . .
Our socialism must reject, without hesitation,
sterile agitation as a method of governing. . . .
In fact, obstacles to the immediate and total installation of socialism require an organizational
phase. . . . The guiding spirit during this organizational phase, consequently, is the maintenance
of order. This will entail, first, the consolidation
of the existing socialist sector. . . .This consolidation necessitates the resolution of financial problems and the rapid determination of an investment
policy. It also requires that the socialist sector
obey the need for increased productivity, which is
common to any regime, be it capitalist or socialist
. . . .

But along with the rapid consolidation of self-
management in the socialist sector must come the
co-management of the private sector. The co-
management, which respects existing authority,
should educate the workers so as to put an end to

private property at the end of the organizational
phase.

. . . To achieve constant progress of our socialism, the spirit of the organizational phase is
the acceptance of an active role, limited in time
and extent, of a domestic and foreign private sector.
It also recognizes the special relations with France,
which likewise are limited in time and extent.

. . . We ask the important [private] enterprises
to help us in our progress toward socialism and, if
they accept, we will give them every encouragement.
They must make every effort to follow policies which
are in accordance with our socialist goals. This
means taking actions which are favorable to our
economy: processing raw materials, seeking new
foreign markets, and reinvesting profits. In such
cases, we encourage them. We have no desire to
nationalize them. To be sure, we intend to create
a public industrial sector. In particular, we want
the industries on which the peasants depend directly,
and with which thousands of peasants must enter
into contracts, such as sugar plants and spinning
mills, to be public. Also, we want the key, heavy
industries to be public. However, we recognize the
existence of a private and a semi-public sector.

We anticipate a semi-public sector, based on an
association of the Algerian government with a foreign
company which is either public, such as Renault, or
private. We want such contracts, providing they
respect our march toward socialism. . . .

. . . We also hope to have a private sector which
brings or keeps the qualified personnel whom we need.
And, if it conforms to our needs, we will encourage
it. We know that a private enterprise seeks a profit, and we know that it needs security and order
before it will invest and thus increase production
and decrease costs, which, in Algeria, are often
too high. Well, we agree that a foreign investor
may repatriate an appreciable portion of his profits;
our exchange controls will not change the regulations
which we have already adopted in our investment code.

As to order, our people aspire to this and will
not permit systematic social agitation. . . . As to
security, we will provide this for a period of time
which will permit the capitalists to follow their

financial and economic policies. In a short time we
will issue the details of such guarantees. And, in
cases where we find that nationalization is indispensable to national interest, formulas for compensation will take into account the firm's recent efforts
to increase production.

    We have shown, I believe, that in doing all this,
we do not in the least renounce socialism. But we
cannot do everything at the same time, and while we
prepare for socialism, economic life cannot stop
. . . . By the end of the organizational phase, which
will take time, the private sector will disappear.
But, meanwhile, we regard it with vigilance, not
with suspicion. It can serve socialism if it prepares,
little by little, the conditions for its own disappearance.[8]

Several weeks later, Bachir Boumaza made a speech before a luncheon sponsored by Le Centre des Jeunes Patrons
d'Alger, the Junior Chamber of Commerce of Algiers.[9] This
speech is remarkable for its frankness, especially considering the audience, which was supposedly the most important
group of entrepreneurs in the country. In the introduction to
their résumé of the speech, the Chamber of Commerce of
Algiers noted that Boumaza presented them with a paradox
and even with illogical reasoning in asking them to volunteer
eventually to do away with their entrepreneurship.

In the speech itself, Boumaza noted that although Algeria
would eventually be an all-socialist state, this could not be
achieved immediately because of a lack of management talent.
Thus, for an interim period there would be a private sector,
a sector of mixed companies (which seemed to be to his liking),
and a public sector.

He noted that all food-processing industries would be
nationalized quickly. Then the "key" industries would move
into the "mixed" group and later become public. Finally, the
private sector would gradually be integrated into the public
sector.

He noted that it was not possible to predict a schedule for
any of these steps. It might be a question of months or years.
"This is not," he said, "different from China, which, even in
1965, will be nationalizing private companies." Meanwhile,
private companies would stay private longer, depending on
their behavior. The criteria were adaptation to governmental
policies, growth, increased exports, training of Algerian
workers and management, degree of technical cooperation

with foreign companies, and willingness to cooperate with the government in preparing for conversion into the public sector.

The company which followed such policies, according to Boumaza, would not be brutally expropriated. During the transition period it could make profits and repatriate them, or at least part of them. It would also receive all possible governmental assistance. Then, at the time of nationalization, such a company would receive indemnification and the foreign parent company could enter into agreements for technical assistance, furnishing supplies and parts, marketing agreements, etc.

Although the Tripoli Program had been written prior to independence, without a realization of what conditions would develop afterward, it remained the basis of dogma and ideology for several years. The constitution, which was ratified on August 28, 1963, was relatively unspecific on the question of political economics. The preamble simply declared that Algeria would be faithful to the Tripoli Program and would be in favor of socialism, and that the management of the economy would be assured by the workers.

There was, thus, a need to update the Tripoli Program. Toward this goal, the FLN held its first congress on April 16-21, 1964. At its opening, Ben Bella gave a talk in which he stated that the main task of the congress was to enrich the Tripoli Program, which was a useful framework but resembled a beautiful bureau with drawers three-fourths empty. It was necessary to fill the drawers.

The result of this first congress of the FLN was the Charter of Algiers, which was a compilation of texts adopted by the congress. The following are excerpts from these texts, which deal with socialism, capitalism, and the role of the public and private sectors.

Capitalism in Algeria is found in two sectors of the economy: the large private agricultural properties and the large commercial enterprises. Political action by these forces is quite limited if it is isolated--if it is not permitted to join with foreign anti-socialist forces . . . .

Besides this Algerian capitalism, there is a presence which is much more menacing--that of foreign capitalism. This poses certain problems, for the indispensable rupture with it cannot be carried out easily; one must take into account the possibilities which are compatible with socialist policies. What must be done, first, is to neutralize the attempts

of foreign capitalism to influence our national
political life, and to think clearly of the relationships which the government can have with foreign
invested capital in line with our fundamental objectives. . . .

The industrial base bequeathed to Algeria by
colonialism is minimal. It consists mostly of shops,
of small food industries, and of several complexes of
medium importance which require supplies from
France. Contrary to what we have accomplished in
agriculture, only a small part of the industrial sector has been placed under self-management. This
factor, plus the means of action of foreign capital,
which is particularly interested in industry, makes
the self-managed sector of industry particularly
vulnerable.

The development of the self-managed industrial
sector requires not only the orientation and progressive transformation of the private industrial sector,
but also the creation of new industrial companies
by the government. . . .

One can envisage several forms of companies,
including mixed companies and state-owned companies. The desire to create a mixed company
must be based on the interests of the country. . .
the government should not associate with foreign
capital except when the investment is too large for
the capabilities of the government. . . .

The channels of distribution, which are indispensable for the development of the socialist sector,
must still be created in Algeria. . . . The take-over
of this essential sector must occur as quickly as possible. The nationalization of foreign trade must be
effected, step by step, and one of the first steps
must be the take-over, by the socialist sector, of
the import and export of those products which it
needs and which it produces. Thus, the reorganization and diversification of trade is an immediate
goal.

Private banks, which were one of the principal
means of action of the colonial economy, still exist
in independent Algeria. These banks still control,
directly or indirectly, the totality of the economy of
the country and exert menacing pressures on the
entire socialist sector. The absorption, by the

socialist sector, of all of these banks, and thus the availability to the socialist sector of savings and credit, must represent a fundamental goal of action by the party and the government. Meanwhile, it is necessary to create organizations which can supply the financial facilities needed by the socialist sector . . . .

Nationalization of the mineral wealth is a long term goal. At present, the priority use of this wealth will determine, to a great extent, the development of the economy. It is principally in this sector that the use of mixed companies, with a majority ownership by the government, will permit training of technicians and the creation of conditions which will be favorable to a future take-over.[10]

At the end of the congress, a number of resolutions were passed. Among the more interesting, from the point of view of this study, were the political resolution and the economic and social resolution. The former had the following to say about Algeria's socialist and revolutionary policies:

The first congress of the FLN . . . demands the confirmation, by action, of our socialist option by (a) systematically favoring the socialist sector to consolidate it vis-à-vis the private sector; (b) integrating into the socialist sector all the economic units necessary for its operation; and (c) enlarging this [socialist] sector through the installation of self-management in more enterprises or through nationalization.

[The FLN] declares that the cornerstone of our foreign policy must attempt to make the Algerian Revolution a pole of revolutionary radiation within the Maghreb, in the Arab world, in Africa, and elsewhere by (a) leading a firm and resolute struggle against imperialism and Zionism and taking the initiative in the formation of a vast anti-imperialist alliance made up of the countries of Asia, Africa, and Latin America; and (b) applying a policy of non-alignment.

The economic and social resolution, which also was adopted by the first congress of the FLN, read, in part:

The first congress of the FLN . . . decides: (1) that socialist planning be rapidly undertaken, democratic in its formulation and imperative in its execution, fixing quantitative goals and specifying the

means for reaching them; (2) that the self-managed
socialist sector be consolidated by the strict application of the decisions of the two congresses on
agricultural and industrial self-management and by
a strong reinforcement of the control of this management, in conformity with the decrees of March, 1963;
. . . (4) that those enterprises which are necessary
for the operation of the socialist sector be placed
under self-management; (5) that the nationalization
of foreign trade, banks, and transportation be prepared and put into practice; (6) that Algerian production be protected from foreign competition; . . .
(14) that a national commission be created to investigate all property which has been obtained under
doubtful circumstances or whose origin has not been
justified since the beginning of the revolution; . . .
and (16) that the work of the commissions created
to examine the appeals of certain small shopkeepers
who were abused by nationalizations be accelerated.

Although the Charter of Algiers says almost nothing of
the domestic private sector and the need to encourage it, the
facts of life dictated otherwise. The government did not have
the personnel required to run many state-owned plants and had
even less entrepreneurial talent for starting the many new
enterprises needed to progress along the road to socialism.

We find, therefore, new types of organizations being
created. Called Industrial Expansion Organizations, they
were a type of small business investment corporation whose
purpose was to attract savings from many small investors
and to use this capital, along with some government capital,
to establish a number of mixed (public-private joint venture)
companies.

On January 21, 1965, Ben Bella gave a speech at the
inauguration of the first such Industrial Expansion Organization. The following are excerpts from that speech.

I wish to underline that certain of our brothers are
perhaps not aware of the decisive character of the
times in which we live. The President of the Republic is aware, however, as is the Minister for
Industry and Energy. The idea which is taking
form today is not the result of an improvisation
or of individual and opportunistic speculation. On
the contrary, it is the result of a thorough study.

First of all, a country without industry can
have no future. This truth is confirmed more each

day. A country which does not industrialize does
not advance. . . . How can we achieve this industrialization which is essential to everyday life?

The idea of using savings, through the means
of joint stock companies, had a great influence on
the growth of industry in the Western countries.
These countries had, of course, chosen the path of
free enterprise, that is to say--the road of capitalism. . . .

That [path], which entails catastrophes and
misery, must be rejected. For us it is a question
of chosing a path which conforms to our socialist
option. We are in favor of cooperation. We reject
financial despotism. But we ask, all the same,
that the service of this cooperation, meanwhile,
guarantee the individuals a reasonable profit. . . .

Without this cooperation, dear brothers, no
progress is possible. In the industrial sphere, one
may ask oneself if the government can achieve this
industrialization by itself. We think that it can,
especially if the orientation of the government is
correct and if the affairs of the government are
well managed. But this takes a long time to achieve.

If we really want to industrialize this country
and see the economy grow, we must apply the method
of today, which consists in not giving the government
sole responsibility for industrialization. To the
government should be allotted those sectors which
the people cannot undertake on their own account.
As to the other sectors, the people must take responsibility. . . .

Money, dear brothers, must be used in the
interest of the country, and not hidden under the
pillow. It must be used to erect factories and be
placed where it will be fruitful. That was the idea
which guided the initiators of this project and that
is why we thought it necessary to encourage them.
By this we wish to demonstrate our agreement and
backing, for the good of the country. . . .

We hope that today's example will be multiplied
like the seeds of pollen which, starting from a small
source, go on to multiply until they become millions
or even billions of seeds. Thus, the country will
know the prosperity and life which are so intimately
bound up with industry.[11]

On February 21, 1965, when inaugurating another Industrial Expansion Organization, Ben Bella called on the people
to invest in $20 subscriptions in such organizations.[12] He
said, "While Algeria has rejected the free enterprise system
and its resultant uneven and unjust division of wealth, she
must put private capital to work on a cooperative basis." He
added, "It is the people's duty to help to execute the government's economic plans. For example, although the government is constructing the steel mill at Bône, which will produce ingots, private initiative must turn the ingots into nails,
machine parts, and other products."

Finally, in his May Day speech of 1965 (one of his last
major speeches), Ben Bella officially launched a national
campaign to promote the establishment of the Industrial Expansion Organizations. He said: "New decrees will determine the nature of the shares and will establish a system in
which investment is not synonymous with profits, in order to
prevent exportation."[13] It is apparent that Ben Bella was
seeking a way to permit industrialization, to utilize whatever
entrepreneurial talent there was, without forming many state-
owned and -operated companies, and without permitting the
growth of many new, small private companies. He sought a
new formula to put private capital to work within the constraints
of some ill-defined Algerian socialism.

THE REGIME OF HOUARI BOUMEDIÈNE

The coup d'état which removed Ben Bella from power
took place on June 19, 1965. Was the new regime going to
shift its orientation? Was it going to be more socialistic and
lean more toward the socialist countries, or was it going to
change direction and establish closer ties with Western Europe
and the United States? On the day of the coup, the Foreign
Minister, Abdelaziz Bouteflika, gave a talk in which he stated
the foreign policy of new government in general terms.

The foreign policy of Algeria rests on the principles
spelled out in the Tripoli Program and the Charter of
Algiers, which translate the fundamental options of
the FLN. Dictated by objective conditions which require a policy of nationalism, its perspectives include non-alignment and friendship with all countries,
especially those which are already our partners.
It attempts to promote a fruitful and sincere

cooperation with all other peoples with mutual respect for sovereignty. Algeria supports, without
reserve, the aspiration of peoples for liberty,
justice, and well-being and gives its assistance to
struggles which they undertake for the independence
of their countries.

The policy of cooperation with France constitutes
a basic and noble experiment which rests on the common desire of the two countries to serve interests of
their people while respecting their origins and independence. Through constant and frank discussions,
this policy will continue and develop in a most happy
and harmonious manner. . . .[14]

This speech indicates essentially no change. It says that
the new regime will rest on the principles of the Tripoli Program and the Charter of Algiers, and it then restates those
principles.

The speech of Bouteflika was on foreign policy. How
about the internal political economy? Did President Boumediène
plan to foster private enterprise? In his July 5, 1965, dictum,
President Boumediène stated: "Algeria must inspire confidence so that domestic and foreign capital will be encouraged
to invest in the country's progress." At the same time he
called for the "co-existence in Algeria of private and socialized
capital."[15]

Was President Boumediène committed to the system of
self-management to the same extent that Ben Bella had been?
He certainly had been critical of its operation and some of its
abuses. At a press conference on October 20, 1965, he spoke
of self-management in the following terms:

We are for self-management, but not for disorder;
we are for self-management which is profitable for
the worker and for the economy of the country, but
not for self-management which is financed by the
population. . . .We are for self-management, but
not at any price. It must not become synonymous
with bad management.[16]

About a week later, President Boumediène was interviewed
by a reporter from Le Nouvel Observateur on a wide range of
topics. At one point the reporter asked a question about the
reorganization of the socialist sector. President Boumediène
responded:

The reorganization of the self-management sector
does not signify a backward step. It is not a question of renouncing the revolutionary gains of the

people. No, no one has the right to touch that.
Our people suffered too much, courageously maintained an atrocious struggle, and accepted immense
sacrifices. No one can fool them and deter them
from their goal. Also, they wanted not only political
independence but also the return of the wealth of
their country to their hands. This desire is completely legitimate. Our socialist option is irreversible because it rests upon fact and upon a given
historical evolution. Having said this, there obviously are different paths to socialism. We have
chosen the system of self-management; and, like
all systems, it has its weaknesses. . . . But I
believe that it is too early to make an objective
judgment of self-management. The experience cannot be clearly appreciated until it has functioned
under normal conditions and over a long enough
period of time. Before all else, let's start by re-
dressing its ills. . . .

One does not carry out half of a revolution. I
believe that a revolution is a global option. So why
not do it seriously? It takes time to transform a
society. In addition, too much haste goes against
arriving at the goal one seeks. Look where we are
in the economic sphere: for three years, in this
country, we have not, as one says in Arabic, placed
one stone on top of another. No one invests; no one
has entered into any truly constructive activity.
Yet Algeria is a rich country--it is a country where
tens of millions are sleeping. The problem is one
of confidence. I go even farther by saying that it
is a moral problem. First and foremost, we must
moralize our actions by restoring their value in the
area of right and justice. The government can
nationalize, but not confiscate. . . . To renew this
moral solidarity, which alone can engender confidence, it does not suffice to issue laws or undertake
spectacular measures. One must go more deeply
than that to restore, little by little, certain essential ideas, so as to reascend a slope which one
descended so rapidly. One must moralize the
government.
Finally, on March 28, 1966, in his closing speech at the
Self-Management Week Seminars, President Boumediène took
an even stronger position vis-à-vis self-management as it
was operating in Algeria at the time.

To assure the success and continuity of self-management, we must be made aware of those organizations
which have succeeded and made large profits and in
which the workers have shown willingness to sacrifice. We must also be informed of those which
have failed. . . .Only thus will we have the facts,
positive and negative, of our success or failure
and so pass a decisive stage in the construction of
our national economy.

We have many times reaffirmed our faith in
socialism, and in self-management as the path
leading to such a political economy. . . .To be sincere, we must prove to ourselves that our system
is the true path which translates the aspirations of
the industrial and agricultural workers. This proof
must be administered solely in the consideration of
the general interest, which must come before individual interests.[17]

One of the major problems of the self-managed sector,
from its inception, had been a lack of trust in the self-managed factories by the commercial banks. A lack of credit
continuously plagued the management of these organizations.
In early 1966, therefore, the government established a national bank, one of whose major purposes was to provide
credit for the self-managed sector. At that time, Belaid
Abdessellam, Minister of Industry and the governmental official most directly concerned with the success of the self-
managed sector, was interviewed by El Moudjahid. His views
on the relationship between the government and these socialist
enterprises is of great interest. The reporter asked:

Mr. Minister, you know that the director of a self-
managed factory was interviewed by El Moudjahid
and complained of having difficulty in competing
with some private companies because his company
was not authorized to develop its activities along
the lines that the management committee thought
necessary. As this case is probably not unique,
could you comment on it so as to dissipate some
of the ill feeling caused by its publicity?

Abdessellam responded as follows:

I do not wish to speak in detail of any particular
case, but my collaborators are at your disposal
to give you any necessary additional details with
regard to the particular case of which you spoke.
I wish only to say that it would be a gross

misrepresentation to have anyone conclude that there could be any favoritism of any kind, by the government, vis-à-vis the private sector.

Having said that, it is certain that when a self-managed factory is in competition with private enterprises and is not able to win the battle, the temptation for the managers is to put the blame on the government. They feel that the solution would be to suppress the competition by nationalizing the entire industry. That would be too simple! And also, that would simply mask the difficulty. Instead of that, we must make every effort to see that the socialist enterprises are able to fend for themselves. That is what we are trying to accomplish. But there are limits. The self-managed factories must, first of all, face up to their responsibilities and not ask us for an artificial subsidy, whose cost would be borne by the nation. We are attempting to shelter the self-managed sector from aggression. After that, it is up to them to do what they can. [18]

Meanwhile, the investment code of 1963, passed during the Ben Bella regime, had failed to attract any significant amount of investment. President Boumediène's Minister of Planning and Finance, Ahmed Kaid, felt that this could be corrected by writing a new code. (A comparison of these two investment codes may be found in Chapter 9.) To explain and discuss the new code, Kaid chose, as his audience, the members of the Chamber of Commerce of Algiers. This meeting, which took place on August 30, 1966, received very complete press coverage. [19] He began by presenting his views on the roles of public and private enterprise in Algeria.

In Algeria today, socialism has been founded in an irreversible manner, under diverse forms--self-management, governmental ownership, and the mixed company, in which the government has a majority ownership. Alongside the public sector, which covers the key sectors of the economy, Algerian socialism tolerates the existence of a semi-public and a purely private sector, for objective reasons which affect its rapid development.

As to the private sector, the government has the right to expect the spirit of creative initiative in those areas where private enterprise is more efficient than public management; the ability to organize and to improve productivity; and the

ability to take risks, applied in the national
interest.

The Minister deplored the fact that the above is not always
the case for domestic and foreign investments. He then criticized the actions of many companies which did not follow the
rules of the game and whose only aim was to transfer the
maximum amount of funds abroad. Kaid cited the example of

. . .a foreign investor who had a very small invested
capital and had large debts with the local banks, and
who repatriated his amortization funds to pay his bills
abroad. This same company showed no profits on
its tax return in order to avoid paying taxes. Tomorrow, this firm will leave Algeria, leaving behind
its useless machines and [its] debts.

Such companies are not in a position to say that
Algeria does not keep its promises, considering
that they were the first to break the moral and legal
contract which ties them to the nation. If the rules
of the game are followed by both sides, a sure and
stable harmony can and must exist between private
initiative and the public sector.

Kaid then went on to paraphrase several parts of the
investment code. Rather than quote him, it may be best to
go directly to the pertinent passages of the code which relate
to the respective roles of the public and private sectors.[20]
Under Title I, "Principles," the code states:

This law defines the framework in which private
enterprise can operate in the economic development
of the country.

. . .The initiative for the establishment of
projects in the vital sectors of the economy rests
with the government and its organizations. However, the government can decide to ask for private capital to carry out such projects. The government will determine, on a case-by-case basis, the
method by which domestic or foreign capital might
intervene in such investments. . . .

When the government enters into a joint venture
with private investors, whether domestic or foreign,
the statutes of such a company must be approved by
governmental decree and must contain the following
provisions: (a) the right of the government to buy
shares owned by the private investors, and the conditions under which such right might be exercised;
and (b) the right of the government to a first option

to buy the shares of the private investors, should
the latter decide to sell.

Individuals or companies, domestic or foreign,
may . . . invest in any other industrial or tourist
ventures which augment the productive capacity of
the nation, and they will receive the benefits of all
or part of the guarantees or advantages noted in
Title II of this code.

When the implementation of national economic
plans so requires, in no matter what sector of the
economy, the government can issue bid requests to
private investors for the creation of specific companies whose production plans, geographic location,
and other operating conditions are well defined.
The government can in such cases, make its economic feasibility studies available to interested
parties.

Finally, there is the question of agrarian reform. Is
President Boumediène going to follow the path started by Ben
Bella, which itself followed the initiative of the peasants who
took over the land abandoned by the French? Ben Bella had
also nationalized the rest of the foreign-owned (mostly French)
farmland and turned some of it into farming cooperatives and
some of it into self-managed state farms. But there still was
considerable land, in large estates, owned by Algerians.
Does President Boumediène plan to take the step which Ben
Bella hesitated to take, and which is called for in both the
Tripoli Program and the Charter of Algiers: expropriation
of private farmland above a certain maximum holding?

On October 21, 1966, President Boumediène gave a speech
in which he took a strong position on the need for agarian reform.

Everyone is aware, today, that in revolutionary and
socialistic Algeria, four years after independence,
there still are people who own not hundreds, but
thousands, of acres. Is this permissible?

Ask our people, 80 percent of whom are poor.
Their answer will be "No."

Algeria is for all the people. It is intolerable
that a fraction of her population lives in opulence
and the rest lives in poverty. All religions reject
such a thing. Our religion does not fail to do so.

For all these reasons, we have decided to suppress large landholdings. . . .It is indispensable
that we take away the excess land held by the large

landholders. We recovered the colonial lands, and
we will make no differentiation between those and
the land held by Algerians. We must give these
lands to the farm workers who have none and who
have waited for four years for the government,
which represents them, to satisfy their needs and
leave behind them their poverty and misery . . . .
We have also decided that 1966 will be devoted to
the study of such an agrarian reform. Its application will require time, and the end of the agricultural season, in 1967, will be the beginning of the
execution of this project.[21]

On May 22, 1967, the President gave another speech
when inaugurating the Week of Arab Socialists. During this
speech, he again discussed the question of agrarian reform
and followed somewhat the same vein as in his October 21,
1966, speech.

In spite of the difficulties which surround this stage
[of socialism], Algeria is determined to put an end
to the large landholdings in order to honor the debt
which she contracted vis-à-vis the rural working
class, which supported the heaviest burden during
the armed struggle [for independence].

In this same vein, Algeria has taken up the
struggle of industrialization, which she ties directly
to the battle for the recovery of her national wealth,
with the aim of liquidating all of the foundations of
neo-colonialism. The latter does not fail to mobilize all its forces and to employ all possible exped-
ients to try to turn our country from the path she
has chosen. But Algeria did not consent to sacrifice
one and one-half million of its sons to favor the
establishment, on its soil, of the same exploitation
under a new form.

We can affirm, today, that our socialist ediface
has reached the point of no return. [Difficulties remain, but] the only way to overcome these difficulties is to adopt a revolutionary theory which arises
from the reality of the situation and which achieves
a perfect harmony between ideology and practice.[22]

NOTES

1. Government of Algeria, Discours de Ben Bella--1963, pp. 38, 39.

2. Ibid., pp. 223-226.

3. Edward Behr, The Algerian Problem, pp. 232-233.

4. Gerard Chaliand, L'Algérie Est-Elle Socialiste?, pp. 123-132.

5. New York Times (January 22, 1963).

6. Révolution et Travail (May 28, 1964).

7. Government of Algeria, op. cit., pp. 121-124.

8. Government of Algeria, Actualité et Documents, No. 28 (January 1-15, 1964).

9. A résumé of this speech, given on January 13, 1964, was provided by the Chamber of Commerce in Algiers.

10. Government of Algeria, La Charte d'Alger.

11. Government of Algeria, Actualité et Documents, No. 53, (January 16-31, 1965), 15-18.

12. Le Peuple (March 8, 1965).

13. Le Monde (May 4, 1965).

14. El Moudjahid (June 20, 1965).

15. "Algeria Changes Course," Africa Report (November, 1965), 10.

16. El Moudjahid (October 22, 1965).

17. Front de Libération Nationale, Thèses, Résolutions et Declarations se Rapportant à l'Autogestion (Algiers, 1966), p. 31.

18. El Moudjahid (March 26, 1966).

19. El Moudjahid (August 31, 1966; September 1, 1966).

20. Government of Algeria, Journal Officiel (September 17, 1966).

21. El Moudjahid (October 22, 1966).

22. Ibid. (May 23, 1967).

CHAPTER **9** ALGERIAN GOVERNMENT
ACTIONS AFFECTING THE
POLITICAL CLIMATE FOR
PRIVATE INVESTMENT

The FLN will follow the Tripoli Program and the Charter
of Algiers. But it is demagogic and irresponsible to pose
problems of the building of socialism in terms outside the
realities of our country. Henceforth verbal socialism is
dead and the construction of a socialist economy will
begin. Future generations will judge not from speeches,
but from acts. [1]

ACTIONS THAT DISCOURAGE PRIVATE INVESTORS

"Abandoned Property"

Just prior to and following Algerian independence, a very
large number of Frenchmen left Algeria. Most of them simply
abandoned whatever property they could not carry with them,
including houses, apartments, shops, cafes, restaurants,
hotels, offices, factories, and farms. This abandonment by
the owner-manager usually meant that the enterprise ceased
to function, which caused a decrease in production of goods
and services and a loss of jobs. Many of these properties
were being taken over illegally by the workers. It soon became apparent that the situation could not be continued indefinitely, so on August 24, 1962, the government issued an
ordinance concerning the protection and management of abandoned property. [2] This law gave the local prefect the authority,
within his territory and under the Ministry of Economics, to
take possession of abandoned property, afford it his protection,
and appoint a manager who would be responsible for resuming
normal operation. In those cases where there were a number
of workers, they would choose a manager, who would then
be confirmed by the prefect.

Another ordinance, of September 21, 1962, authorized the establishment of a National Bureau for the Protection and Management of Abandoned Property, but this was never implemented. In fact, rarely did the prefect make an inventory of goods belonging to each property and, frequently, the workers took possession and continued operation of the property prior to any action by the prefect.

The above laws were completed by a decree of March 18, 1963, which added to the class of "abandoned property" any property which was not being "operated in a normal manner," even though the owner had not abandoned it. [3] This opened the door to any type of arbitrary action on the part of the workers or the prefect. Subsequently, a decrease in inventory or a reduction in production became sufficient reason for declaring the property subject to the decree of March 18, 1963. In addition, according to the terms of this decree, the management committee which took over the property took possession only of the assets--not the liabilities. The former owner was still subject to legal action by his former creditors.

By May, 1963, out of 2,000 industrial companies of some importance, 822 had been declared "abandoned property." (Of these, 655 had actually been abandoned, and 12 had been placed under a management committee even though the owners were actually there; for the remaining 155, whether or not the property had been abandoned was not clear.) Of the 1,382 companies still belonging to their former owners, 265 had closed, 408 operated well below capacity, and 709 were operating normally. [4]

Retail shops, restaurants, bars, etc., owned by Europeans totaled approximately 30,000 at the time of independence. By May, 1963, about 25,000 had been abandoned, but few of them were placed under an official management committee by the prefect; usually someone other than the departed owner merely moved in and resumed operation. [5]

"Self-Management"

Chapter 7 discussed the way in which the system of "self-management" (autogestion) arrived in Algeria. It first occurred as a natural reaction of the workers, given the sudden departure of the French owners and managers. It was then encouraged by some of the Marxist-trained union leaders, and finally was sanctioned by law. Chapter 8 contains quotations from Ben Bella which attempt to justify the institution of

self-management, and several quotations from President
Boumediène which criticize the way in which self-management
was operating but at the same time defend it and indicate a
need to improve it.

The laws which instituted and regulated self-management
were décret No. 63-95, dated March 22, 1963, and décret
No. 63-98, dated March 28, 1963, both of which appeared in
the Journal Officiel de la République Algérienne of March 29,
1963. The first is concerned with the organization and management aspects, and latter deals with the distribution of the
profits of such a company.

There were two ways in which a company could come
under self-management. The first way was for the former
owner and manager to abandon the company, with the workers
taking over. The second was for the workers to claim that
the company was being badly managed. In the latter case,
the workers might ask the government to expropriate the
company, and then institute self-management (the legal method),
or the workers might take over the company (locking out the
manager), present the government with a fait accompli, and
ask the government to expropriate the company and thus legal-
ize the self-management ex post facto.

The workers' voice in management is expressed through
the following organizations and procedures:

(a) A general assembly consisting of all the workers. If
the company has more than 30 employees, the general assembly
elects a workers' council, whose term of office is three years.
The number of members on the council may vary from 10 to
100, depending upon the number of workers. (If there are
fewer than 30 workers, the general assembly elects a management committee, of from three to 11 members, directly.)

(b) The workers' council, if the company has more than
30 workers, elects the management committee. This management committee serves as a board of directors and elects
its own chairman.

(c) The manager of the company (similar to the president
of a U.S. firm) is selected and assigned to the company by
the government. A special city council (of the city in which
the company is located) must approve the appointment of a
company manager and can also request his removal.

The system, as described, is quite similar to the system
in Yugoslavia. In operation, it is much less effective because
(1) so many workers are illiterate; (2) there are very few
qualified managers; (3) financial resources are less readily
available or are nonexistent; (4) the supply and marketing

system if operating badly; and (5) the self-managed firms must operate side by side with state-owned companies and with a strong private sector. Consequently, salaries have often been months behind; taxes have rarely been paid; the companies do not set aside reserves for amortization of equipment; and workers are disappointed because there have been no profits to distribute to themselves.

Within nine months after independence, 167 companies had been placed under self-management. During the following five months (by October, 1963) another 94 companies, of which 30 had not been "abandoned" by the owners, had been put under self-management. [6] By the end of 1965, self-management was operating in 507 companies employing 14,935 workers. [7] (Appendix B, Table 5, breaks down the self-management sector by type of industry.) It accounted, however, for less than 15 percent of total industry, since most of the companies were small. The larger companies either were in the private sector or had been nationalized and were state-owned and -operated.

Is the government going to continue the spread of the self-managed sector? It appears not. The tempo has slowed greatly since 1965. The difficulties encountered by this sector are all too apparent, and the solutions to its problems are elusive. It would be politically difficult for the government to reverse direction and try to eliminate this sector. Such critical observers as Teillac feel that the government will have to keep up appearances for the 15,000-20,000 workers involved, but the application of the system has probably passed its zenith. [8] Most future expropriations will probably place the companies under the direct control of the government.

Nationalization of Farmland

At the time of independence there were 17,991 French farmers with land totaling 4.98 million acres. One year later, by June 12, 1963, a census by the French Embassy showed only 9,277 farmers, with 2.16 million acres; 8,408 farmers had returned to France, abandoning 2.45 million acres. [9] (This would seem to indicate that 306 farmers had quickly sold 370,000 acres to Algerians.) By October 11, 1963, when Ben Bella announced the nationalization of all agricultural land not belonging to Algerians, 6,500 French farmers, with 1.76 million acres were affected. [10]

The nationalization was effected by decree No. 63-388, dated October 1, 1963, [11] and was announced by Ben Bella during a speech before a crowd of 200,000 people. The decree said nothing about compensation, but in his speech Ben Bella stated that the owners would be reimbursed for the value of the harvest they were losing, but not for the value of the land. Such reimbursement has not taken place.

The amount of agricultural land owned by non-French foreigners was very small. For example, there were only four U.S. citizens who had their land nationalized, representing a claimed loss of $450,000.

Other Nationalizations and Expropriations

The nationalization of foreign-owned agricultural land took place, essentially, with one stroke of the pen. This has not been true of industry. Nationalization in the industrial sector has been piecemeal, sometimes one enterprise at a time, sometimes in large blocks.

The usual pattern for individual enterprises, until recently, was that the company decreased production because of a decline in demand and a lack of credit from the banks. As a result, it laid off some of its workers, who then went on strike in protest. While on strike they asked the government to expropriate the company because the management was not operating in the interests of the economy. Although such a pattern was frequent, there were a wide variety of situations under which the expropriations took place.

In the case of EMBALBOIS (a fairly large furniture factory which had employed 200 workers prior to independence), for example, the government issued a press notice in November, 1963, announcing the expropriation, stating that the owners were sabotaging the factory. The sabotage, it said, consisted of laying off 50 workers out of the 60 who still remained, and in transferring most of the capital and better machines back to France.

In the case of Les Papeteries et Cartonneries Modernes d'El Harrach, which produces 40 tons of paper and boxes per day, the prefect of Algiers visited the factory in February, 1964, and announced to the assembled 85 workers that it had been expropriated and placed in their hands. He justified the expropriation by stating that the former owner was in the process of destroying the company and hence was not producing sufficiently to supply the demand, which was causing difficulties for other companies because they did not have enough cartons to package their goods and ship them to market.

On July 31, 1963, the cement works of El Harrach was expropriated and placed under self-management, with the following justification: The former owner had apparently abandoned it, and another man had appropriated the property and set himself up as owner. Later, claiming that the business was bad, he closed the factory and refused to pay back wages, where upon the workers appealed to the government.

A last example is a fish canning factory employing 200 workers to take care of the catch of 800 fishermen. It was expropriated in August, 1963. The local prefect gave a simple verbal notification to the owners, offering no justification.

On a larger scale, in April, 1963, the government nationalized 69 hotels and 21 restaurants which had been sold to Algerians at cut-rate prices by French nationals just before the latter fled the country.

On September 18, 1963, the government nationalized the remaining French-owned newspapers, claiming that their operation was a carry-over from the colonial days and contrary to the welfare of the people.

In a similar vein, on August 19, 1964, Ben Bella, during a speech in Oran, announced the nationalization of 380 movie theaters. He said, in justification, that "the films which we see in these theaters are not in conformity with our option. From now on, a better selection will be made so that the theater will assist our education and our socialist option."[12]

The types of nationalizations and expropriations described above did not call for indemnification to the owners. There were, however, a number where the government announced its intention to do so. For example, when the government nationalized the importation, manufacture, and sale of tobacco and matches, in November, 1963, the law promised indemnification to the shareholders or owners of the companies affected.[13] (Such indemnification had not been paid by the end of 1968.) This industry was sizable, for Algeria, employing a total of 13,000 workers.

In the case of the mining industry, government officials toured all of the mining concessions during January, 1965, and found 76 out of the 87 to be inactive. Some concessions had been given as early as 1846; some were virgin lodes which had never been worked; and others had been closed for economic reasons. The government gave a formal notice to the owners that all concessions which were not in operation within two months would be seized.[14] These concessions were

duly canceled and taken over by the government on May 31,
1965, leaving 11 mines in operation and in the hands of foreign
companies. The annual sales of these 11 mines in 1965 was
about $30 million. [15] Most of these mines were owned by
French and Belgian interests, but U.S. companies (Newmont
Mining Corporation and St. Joseph Lead Company) had a
20 percent interest in two of them.

On May 8, 1966, President Boumediène announced the
nationalization of these 11 mines. He said that such mineral
resources must belong to the state, for it was an anachronism
and it was intolerable that the new government-owned steel
mill being constructed at Annaba would have to negotiate with
a foreign company in order to utilize Algerian iron ore. [16]
The decree effecting these nationalizations specified the manner in which the owners of the major iron ore mines would
be indemnified, and President Boumediène announced that
the former owners of all the mines would receive "full indemnification. "[17] These constitute virtually the totality of major
nationalizations made prior to the spring of 1967. Any not
mentioned were small, individual companies.

It should also be noted that most of the nationalizations
and expropriations during the Ben Bella regime took place
between mid-1963 and mid-1964. In late September, 1963,
a number of nationalizations were without rationale. The
evening before the nationalization of the foreign-owned farmland, Ben Bella expropriated the large Huileries Tamzali.
Three days later he expropriated three large transport companies, and the following day he nationalized the tobacco and
match industry. These apparently were moves to head off
the growing opposition from some far-left socialists. By
mid-1964, however, the government was more hesitant to
nationalize. It realized its need for the private sector and
did not necessarily wish to burden itself with enterprises
which it could not manage. They became a liability rather
than an asset.

This new policy confused and frustrated a number of the
ardent socialist union leaders. They were convinced that the
FLN slogan "The factory for the workers" was a labor union
objective and that any excuse to achieve this goal was good.
As a result, another wave of strikes took place in December,
1964, and January, 1965. In the December 9 edition of Alger
Républicain, an editorial stated that most of the strikes were
undertaken without even notifying the top union officials (who,
by the way, were appointed by the government). It denounced
the gap between workers and top union officials and called

upon the latter to explain to the workers the complex problems of the country's economy "so that they will realize that Algeria is passing through a period of transition where capitalism and socialism must exist side by side...."

As a result, very few nationalizations took place during the last six months of Ben Bella's regime. After President Boumediène took over, nearly a year passed without any nationalization, the pattern being broken only by the nationalization of the mines. Then another year passed without nationalizations until the Middle East war of June 1967.

At a meeting of the Council of Ministers, on June 5, 1967, a set of principles was drawn up for the liquidation of U.S. and British economic interests in Algeria.[18] The first implementation of this decision took place on August 29, when the government announced the expropriation of refining and distributing facilities of the Esso and Mobil petroleum companies. This included 200 Esso service stations and 170 Mobil service stations, plus Esso's 17.6 percent and Mobil's 6 percent interest in the Algiers oil refinery. The research and producing subsidiaries and interests of the same two companies were not touched, and the decree provided for compensation. All of the expropriated property was placed in the custody of SONATRACH.[19]

In fact, direct U.S. and British investment in Algeria, outside of the oil industry, was practically nil. In the heat of its reaction to the Middle East situation, therefore, the government expropriated Detersav-Algérie, which is a subsidiary of Procter and Gamble of France, which in turn is a subsidiary of the U.S. firm Procter and Gamble. Ordinance No. 67-182, dated September 7, 1967, stated that the state would pay an indemnification.[20] An official explanation of this expropriation did not mention the Middle East crisis. It gave as reason for the action: "The company's unique concern was to pay the minimum taxes possible and to transfer as much capital as possible out of Algeria....This company had...a definite neo-colonialist attitude: its objective was to maximize repatriated profits with a minimum financial investment. Thus, it refused to reinvest profits...: it also rejected any suggestion to use Algerian personnel in its management."[21]

In September, 1967, besides the Procter and Gamble subsidiary, the government expropriated two French companies: ETAT, which makes electric lamps, and SEXEMA, which bottles mineral water. There seemed to be no connection with the Middle East war; the author is not aware of the rationale for these take-overs.

For many months, it appeared that these expropriations of U.S. and British companies were strictly a reaction to the 1967 Middle East war, and that it would stop there. But a new round of nationalizations came in May, 1968.

It began on May 13 with the nationalization of all of the channels of distribution of petroleum products and natural gas which remained in the private sector. This included not only all of the chains of service stations, but also transportation and storage facilities. The nine companies nationalized were Shell and eight French companies. These companies had been asked by the government, in January, 1968, to cede their properties to the government. Most of the companies had submitted proposals to the government for the sale of their assets, but the government, through the official press agency, said that the assets, which the companies said had a total value of $50 million, had been fully amortized for many years. Consequently, no indemnification was promised.[22]

On May 20, 1968, 27 industrial companies--all owned by Frenchmen or by parent companies in France--were nationalized. These companies were in three industrial sectors: engineering, fertilizer, and construction materials. They employed 4,600 workers and had annual sales of about $32 million. The government stated, as reason for these nationalizations (which make provision for indemnification), that this was necessary to permit balanced planning and development. French circles in Algeria remarked that these firms employed mostly Algerian personnel and operated smoothly and without social difficulties.[23] All of these companies were established in Algeria prior to independence, and in some cases under the Constantine Plan. Some of them, had according to Le Monde, recently made new investments to increase production in the wake of orders resulting from the industrial development of Algeria.[24] Interestingly, at the same time, the government nationalized four Algerian companies which were under worker-management. (The nationalization of companies under worker-management is discussed later in this chapter.)

During the same week, the government announced that it would absorb two French banks, the Banque de Paris and the Crédit du Nord, into the state-owned Banque Exteriéur de l'Algérie. The head office of the Banque de Paris (in Paris) had previously decided to close the Algerian branch within several months, but was surprised by the rapidity of the nationalization. On May 28, 1968, the Algerian branch of the French-owned Banque Industrielle de l'Algérie was also

absorbed by the Banque Exteriéur de l'Algérie. This left
only two private, French-owned banks--the Compagnie
Française du Crédit and the Société Marseillaise de Crédit.
and they expected to be absorbed in the near future.[25]

The government described the absorption of these banks
as necessary to the Algerianization of the economy and to the
streamlining of the banking sector, thereby making the trained
personnel of the nationalized banks available to the government banks.

Finally (?), on June 14, 1968, the government nationalized
18 more companies, representing four sectors of the economy:
metal construction, cement, chemical products, and food products. These companies had a total of 2,888 employees and annual sales of $60 million. All were French-owned except Uni-
lever, whose ownership was two-thirds Dutch and one-third
French. In justifying these nationalizations, the government
said that the firms continued to import semi-manufactured
products at high prices and refused to invest in new equipment
or to train Algerians for staff positions. It also indicated that
this would give the government control over plants in sectors
considered essential to the economy, so as to carry out plans
for modernization and concentration. It also permitted the
government to reinforce its struggle against imperialism and
to construct socialism on a solid base.[26]

Government Insurance Monopoly

Prior to independence, a number of foreign insurance
companies, including over 100 French insurance companies,
were operating in Algeria, all of them through branch offices.
Consequently, the capital of the companies was located abroad
and premiums were sent out of the country.

The government started to move against this situation
in April, 1963, by forming a company in which the state owned
50 percent of the capital, the Caisse Algeriénne d'Assurances
et de Réassurances owned 11 percent, and the Compagnie
Arabe d'Assurances (from the United Arab Republic) owned
39 percent. The latter helped train the personnel and supplied part of the management.

In mid-1966 the Minister of Finance claimed that the
insurance companies which were still in operation in Algeria
were draining $40 million per year (2 percent of the GNP)
from Algeria.[27] In May, 1966, a number of newspapers
carried dispatches indicating that Algeria had nationalized

all insurance companies. In reality, it was not a nationalization. No assets were lost, and the government indicated that
existing policies could continue until expiration. All new
policies would have to be placed with the state-owned company.

Eleven foreign companies were affected by the move. Their
home offices were located as follows: Morocco, one; United
States, one; Switzerland, one; Italy, one; India, one; Tunisia,
one; United Kingdom, two; and France, four.[28] The largest
operation was the Société Tunisienne d'Assurance et de Réassurance, which had been established in Tunisia by the French
and had since been taken over by the Tunisian government.

Government Monopoly of Publication and
Distribution of Printed Matter

One of the major publishers and distributors of books and
magazines in France is the Société Hachette. They established
themselves in Algeria at an early date and had a monopoly
position, with stores in most of the cities and towns of any
importance.

In mid-1965 the manager of Hachette fired five workers,
and the union decided to make an issue of it. The manager
was brought before a people's court, where the prosecution
was represented by the General Counsel of the UGTA. The
manager was found guilty of firing the employees without first
having consulted the labor inspector and was ordered to rehire
them.[29] He refused. On January 27, 1966, the Minister of
Information announced the creation of a government-owned
company with a monopoly on the publication and distribution
of printed matter. It would, he said, replace Hachette. He
also stated that it was not a nationalization as such; the government was merely organizaing the new company on Hachette
premises and with Hachette personnel.[30]

Government Monopoly of Transporation

The Council of Ministers adopted an ordinance on July 6,
1967, defining a new legal status for trucking. As a result
the government has, technically, a monopoly of all means of
land transportation. It will take effect only gradually, however. At that time, 90 percent of the trucks were in the private sector, some of them belonging to industrial companies
for the transportation of their own finished products or of raw

materials and the rest belonging to private trucking companies.
A first step in moving toward a government monopoly was to
limit the percentage of its total annual tonnage which a factory
might transport in its own vehicles; the remainder had to be
carried by vehicles from the Société Nationale de Transport
Routier.

Import-Export Companies and Syndicates

Following the nationalization of the mines, the government
had great difficulty in exporting iron ore. At the same time,
there were about 20 private importer-distributors handling
iron and steel products. Consequently, in May, 1967, the
government announced the establishment of the Société Nationale
de Sidérurgie, which would have a monopoly on the importation
of iron and steel products. It was to use this monopoly position
as a bargaining power, buying only from those foreign steel
companies which bought Algeria's iron ore. [31]

As for the rest of the foreign trade, the Minister of Commerce, Nourredine Delleci, when testifying before the FLN's
commission for the new development plan, stated, "There
is no doubt that Algeria will nationalize foreign commerce,
but it will take time to carry this out. We have already grouped
most imports into a small number of syndicates." [32]

These foreign trade syndicates were established in August,
1964, by governmental decree. [33] The members of each syndicate are the importers of the products handled by the syndicate, and the capital of the syndicate is contributed by them.
However, of the seven members of the board of directors of
each syndicate, the government appoints four and also selects
the president and the treasurer.

The major rationale behind this move was that the government did not have qualified people to run government-owned
trading companies--it needed the cooperation (and even the
capital) of the private sector. At the same time, however,
the government had entered into trade agreements with many
countries (particularly East European countries) which obligated Algeria to import certain amounts of materials from
those countries.

Six syndicates were established: one each for textiles,
shoes, leather, wood, clothing, and dairy products. They
did not initially assume a complete monopoly position, leaving
some room for individual importers. For example, in 1965,
the textile syndicate imported only 40 percent of total textile

imports. By 1966, however, this had increased to 95 percent. The countries from which the syndicate imported textiles in 1966 were Poland, Yugoslavia, the Soviet Union, Hungary, the United Arab Republic, Czechoslovakia, China, and France. [34]

Government-Owned Retail Stores

Many larger stores and smaller shops had been abandoned by their French owners at the time of independence, and many of them were taken over by the workers and ended up in the self-management sector. The private sector still predominated, however. At the end of 1963 the Minister of Economics announced that the government was going to establish 15 "pilot" stores in Algiers. [35] He stated that the private sector was increasing prices very rapidly when goods were in short supply, increasing prices beyond the reach of the poorer classes, and causing inflation. The "pilot" stores were to combat these price movements. At the same time he said that the prefects of the other regions would be urged to create similar stores in the cities in their areas.

Government-Owned Banks

Prior to independence, there was a Banque d'Algérie which served as a central bank, in that it was a bank of issue and served as a discount bank. It did not act independently, however, because Algeria was part of France and its monetary policies came under the control of the Banque de France.

Seventeen foreign banks had branches in Algeria. All were French except for Barclay's Bank of the United Kingdom. These branches represented all of the major banks in France, including the French government's medium - and long-term banks. Some had many branches, scattered throughout the territory. Thus, any financial service available in France could also be had in Algeria. In addition, there were 14 local banks, opened by French settlers in Algeria. None were owned by Algerian Moslems. [36]

Following independence, the departure of most of the French community and the closing of many businesses caused the banks to encounter great difficulty. Most of their qualified people left and their deposits greatly diminished, as follows: end of 1960, $591 million; end of 1961, $510 million; end of 1962, $300 million; and end of 1963, $270 million. By the end

of 1963, most of the local banks had closed, and several of
the branches of the French banks had also ceased operation. [37]
Two new banks opened their doors during 1963, however:
Banque Populaire Arabe, whose head office is in Geneva, and
Banque Algerie-Misr., based in Cairo.

The situation of the banks continued to deteriorate as
some clients were nationalized or put under self-management
and others fell into financial difficulty and could not repay
debts.

Meanwhile, there were many ominous warnings of nation-
ization of the banking sector. Initially, however, the Algerian
government chose a path other than nationalization: competition and exclusion. Thus, on August 10, 1964 a law created
the Caisse Nationale d'Épargne, which is really a postal
savings institution. Its resources can, however, be lent for
local housing construction. (A new program of the Caisse
Nationale d'Épargne, starting January 1, 1967, permits home
construction loans to individuals, providing 80 percent of the
cost of the house, up to $10,000, repayable over up to 20 years.)

The next institution created by the government (on July 1,
1966) was the Banque Nationale d'Algérie. In the process of
creation, it took over the operations and offices of a former
French bank, the Crédit Foncier d'Algérie et de Tunisie,
apparently under terms agreeable to the owners. This bank
has 60 branches scattered throughout the country. Its main
purpose is to provide credit to the self-managed and public
sectors of industry. It is, thus, a commercial bank. The
government furnished some of the initial capital but also
made provision for the sale of shares to the general public,
with required annual dividends of at least 5 percent. [38]

On December 30, 1966, the Crédit Populaire d'Algérie,
a regrouping of former private and semi-public banks, was
inaugurated. Its primary purpose is to provide credit to the
self-managed sector of agriculture, but it may also make
loans to artisans and small shopkeepers. [39]

Finally, on October 1, 1967, the government created the
Banque Extérieure d'Algérie. [40] Its primary purposes are,
of course, to finance Algeria's foreign trade and to administer
the government's foreign exchange controls. On November 1,
1967, the government revoked authorization for private commercial banks to deal in foreign exchange. After that date,
only the Algerian government banks (and, of course, the
Banque Extérieure d'Algérie) were permitted to handle foreign
exchange transactions.

During the inauguration ceremony of the Banque Éxterieure d'Algérie, Ahmed Kaid, Minister of Finance, stated (President Boumediène being present), "With the creation of the Banque Éxterieure d'Algérie, you can, Mister President, consider that we have achieved the Algerianization of the banking system and have adapted it to the needs of financing and controlling of our economic planning.... It [the Banque Éxterieure d'Algérie] will permit the banking system to be almost entirely coordinated by the government and to be integrated into our financial policies...."[41]

It appeared, therefore, that the government would not attempt to nationalize the foreign banks in Algeria. There was little need for it to do so, and it had only to be patient. Since many of the private banks earned nearly all of their profits from foreign trade transactions, and since they were forbidden to deal in this area, their life expectancy was greatly shortened. In addition, many businesses which had to use the government banks to finance their foreign trade transactions would also have shifted their deposits to the government banks. As a result, more of the private banks would disappear and private business would be at the mercy of the government banks. The French Embassy in Algiers predicted that there would then be many voluntary shutdowns by French businessmen, followed by another wave of declarations of "abandoned property" and the installation of "self-management," or by nationalization.[42] As a result, the nationalization of the remaining private banks in May, 1968, came as a complete surprise.

Government Commissioners

Another governmental action irritating to many businessmen was the decree which permitted the government to assign commissioners to certain private companies "which are operating in an economically abnormal manner."[43] Considering the times, just about every company in Algeria would fit this description.

The commissioner is appointed by the Minister of Economics for a period of six months to a year, after which time he is to submit a report on the management of the company. The Minister may then cancel the assignment of a commissioner to that company, renew his assignment, or nationalize the company. While assigned to the company, such a commissioner has the title of chief of personnel, and may

hire or fire any employee. He is a member of the board of
directors, reviews all major decisions of the company, and
has a veto power.

Obviously, the assignment of a commissioner is extremely
repugnant to the owner or manager of a company, and on a
number of occasions it has provoked the owner into closing
immediately. In other cases the reaction can be more subtle
and indirect. For example, there was a chain of 13 Monoprix
department stores, a subsidiary of the large French department store chain. After the government has assigned a commissioner to this company, the local commercial banks
(according to the owner) lost confidence in the future of the
company and refused to grant credits to it. [44] The company
directors went to Paris to try to negotiate a loan. During
their absence, the government took direct action to keep the
stores operating. Upon their return, the directors announced
that management authority had been undermined and that they
were therefore closing.

State-Owned Industries

The system of self-management grew rapidly during the
first several years following independence, but its growth rate
diminished greatly after 1965, at which time the self-managed
sector accounted for less than 15 percent of industrial activity.
On the other hand, the establishment of state-owned companies
started slowly, based first on the nationalization of several
large industries, such as the tobacco and match industry,
mining, and flour mills, and then increased in tempo as new
industries, created by the government, came into operation.

State-owned industries have come from five different
sources. First, there are those, such as the huge Algerian
Electricity and Gas Company, the railroad, and the port
authorities, which were already public companies prior to independence. Second, there are a number which originally
were under self-management but, because of poor self-management, were taken over by the government (the steel foundry
and rolling mill, ACILOR, and the North African Glass Company are two outstanding examples). Third, there are the
former private companies which the government has nationalized. Fourth, there are the companies established by the
state and owned 100 percent by the government. Finally, there
are mixed companies, which result from foreign private investment joining with the government to form semi-public
companies.

Focusing upon the latter two categories, we find that the principal instrument serving as originator of the new state-owned companies is the Bureau d'Études et de Réalisations Industrielles (BERI). It originated by decree in February, 1963, as the Bureau d'Études, de Réalisations et d'Interventions Industrielles et Minières (BERIM). [45] As BERIM's activities expanded, it was separated into two organizations, the Bureau Algérien de Recherches et d'Exploitation Minières (BAREM), which now operates the country's mining sector, and BERI. In May, 1967, BAREM was renamed Société Nationale Algeriénne de Recherches et d'Exploitation Minières (SONAREM).

During its first year of operation, BERIM instituted a program for the establishment of about 30 new companies, most of which were textile, ceramic, and shoe factories, tanneries, and fruit juice canneries. These gradually reached fruition so that in 1966 BERI's investment program amounted to $110 million and saw the start-up of three textile plants, three tanneries, four shoe factories, a fruit juice cannery, a mineral water bottling plant, and a sugar refinery. [46]

Although its statutes provide for the possibility that BERI will help private companies to invest in projects whose studies were originated by BERI, or will join with private companies to form semi-public joint ventures, this has very rarely occurred. The result has been that BERI is an instrument for the expansion of the public sector of the economy. Thus, the public sector is growing rapidly in certain types of industry, particularly in heavy industry, with the construction of the steel mill at Annaba ($30 million), and in heavy chemicals, with the construction of the chemical complex of Arzew ($60 million). Private investment is growing only in the petroleum and gas fields, and there the growth has slowed considerably.

At the present time, the private sector is still predominant in manufacturing, but its margin decreases every month.

ACTIONS DESIGNED TO ENCOURAGE
PRIVATE INVESTORS

While the Algerian government has done many things which have frightened and deterred private investors, there is no doubt that it does need and want them.

France has shown that, for a number of reasons (noted near the end of Chapter 7), she is going to keep giving foreign aid to Algeria, no matter how many times Algeria kicks her in the teeth. Algeria has already told off the World Bank and the U.S. government, so there is little reason for the government to pay lip service to private enterprise in the hope that this will gain her some additional foreign aid. No, she genuinely wants private investment and doesn't understand why it is not forthcoming. She is like an ill-mannered child who wants to make friends with the children next door, but when they come to play with her, she pulls their hair, kicks them in the shins, threatens to throw them out of the house, and then wonders why they don't want to come back to play with her. She really needs them for playmates--at least until she grows up--so she makes overtures to the neighbor children and sends over more invitations.

Outlawing the Communist Party

One of the first acts of the Ben Bella regime which was a positive factor to private investors (although that was not a motivating factor) was the outlawing of the Algerian Communist party on November 29, 1962. The Minister of Information announced this decision and stated that the party's newspaper, al Hourriya, was burned, since "there is no place in Algeria for the Communist party."

Caisse Algeriénne de Développement

When the French were instituting the Constantine Plan, they organized a Caisse d'Équipment pour le Développement de l'Algérie, whose primary purpose was to help finance industrial investment in Algeria. Its primary source of financing was the French government, but it also received a small percentage of the revenues from Saharan oil and an annual subsidy from the government in Algeria. It became apparent to the Algerians, after independence, that they would need a similar institution if they were going to continue with the Constantine Plan (in the absence of any other plan). Thus, on May 7, 1963, they established the Caisse Algérienne de Développement (CAD).

The CAD was to help finance industrial projects, in contrast with infrastructure projects. It could buy shares or bonds and could make medium- and long-term loans to private, semi-public, or public companies. It was, essentially, an industrial development bank.

Although the government's intentions were good, so few private investment projects materialized that the CAD became primarily a means of channeling public funds into public projects. This was obviously an unnecessary function, and CAD was disbanded in 1967.

Investment Code of 1963

Within a year after its independence, Algeria had passed its first investment code. [47] Its passage through the National Assembly is an amusing incident in Algeria's legislative history. As presented to the National Assembly (after having been examined by five legislative committees), the code authorized foreign investors to repatriate "at least 50 percent of profits." The deputies showed little interest in the bill, many of the meetings having fewer than 40 out of 196 deputies present. Just prior to the final vote, one of the deputies (Ali Yayia) suggested that the bill be amended to read that foreign investors would be authorized to repatriate "at most 50 percent of profits." He argued that "to read 'at least' is being negative: the new Algeria likes to take a positive approach, so it is preferable to replace 'least' by 'most.'" The amendment carried. The final vote on the code was unanimous, following a speech by Ben Bella on the necessity to offer private investors certain guarantees.

This 1963 code guaranteed that the government would not expropriate new foreign investment without due process of law and, in any case, not before the sum of accumulated net profits was equal to invested capital brought into the country. In addition, any expropriation would give rise to just compensation.

One of the toughest provisions of the code was that if a foreign investor borrowed money in Algeria from the CAD or some other governmental institution, the government would have the right, in the future, to buy a part interest in the company.

The 1963 code applied only to "foreign" private investors. There was little thought, at that time, of encouraging local private investment, self-management being very much in vogue.

An Investment Commission was established to examine investment applications and rule on their acceptability. It was unfortunately, not flooded with applications. At the end of its first year of existence it had approved only about 10 investments, and only a few of these were actually implemented after approval. The several foreign investments which did take place between 1963 and 1966 were on the basis of separate agreements between investors and the government, so that one can say that the 1963 code was never really implemented. There was too great a distance between the desire of the investor and the flexibility of the government.

For example, Armour & Company had applied to the Algerian government on December 17, 1962, for permission to build a $26 million nitrogen fertilizer plant, a project which had been studied prior to independence as part of the Constantine Plan. Armour requested the following terms, which were inspired by the Constantine Plan: (1) exemption from income tax and other taxes for 10 years after start of commercial operations; (2) a 40 percent subsidy on capital equipment purchases; (3) a long-term loan of $20 million at 4 percent interest; (4) a medium-term loan of $2.2 million at 4 percent interest; (5) permission for the company to retain and utilize, without restriction, any foreign exchange generated by exports from the plant, sufficient to service debts, pay dividends, and purchase supplies and spare parts; (6) a guarantee against any kind of expropriation for 20 years; (7) a refund of 75 percent of the cost of a domestic market study of fertilizer needs; and (8) protection from imported nitrogen fertilizers as long as Armour's local production was sufficient for Algeria's needs.[48]

After the passage of the investment code and the formation of the Investment Commission, Armour resubmitted its application. Needless to say, there was never a meeting of the minds.

Creation of a Patent Office

Although few investors would plan to carry out research and development in Algeria, and hence the existence of a patent office was not a terribly significant factor, it is indicative of the mood at the time, in mid-1963, that the authorities thought it advisable to establish the Patent Office.[49] On the other hand, officials of the office, in discussing its operation, noted, "In free enterprise countries, the protection

of patents is total and their use is exclusive. In socialist
countries, the protection as well as the benefits received
[by the inventor] are more of a moral character, and such
property rights are limited because of the predominance of
the general interest. " It then goes on to say that Algeria will
find a middle ground between these two, to fit its own realities.

Return of Nationalized Property

In Chapter 7 it was noted that President Boumediène had,
soon after his take-over of the presidency, announced the
return of several companies which had been put under self-
management to their "rightful" owners. This led a number
of Western countries to think that the new regime was going
to reverse the socialist direction of the economy. However,
it will be recalled that Ben Bella had previously taken similar
actions.

On October 6 and 7, 1964, for example, 10 stores, 14
hotels, and two restaurants which had been officially put under
self-management a year earlier were returned to their former
owners. No secret was made of the fact that the restitutions
were meant to encourage businessmen who had fled to France
to return and invest their capital. [50]

Unfortunately, such restitutions were not carried out
systematically or as a matter of policy, although a commission
had been appointed to investigate all allegedly illegal nationalizations. Also, only a few of these restitutions were of
factories, where a fair number of workers would be affected.

Repayment of Foreign Debts

The pre-independence Algerian government (under French
control) had contracted a series of debts to French citizens,
banks, and other financial organizations. Most of these were
bonds issued by various Algerian city governments, by the
Electricity and Gas Company, and by the forerunner, of the
CAD. These are the kinds of debts one might expect a newly
independent country to repudiate.

During 1966, however, French and Algerian officials negotiated an arrangement whereby all of these debts were consolidated, amounting to a total of about $80 million. Algeria
was to repay them at the rate of $6 million-$8 million per
year (representing about 1 percent of the government's
operating budget) over a period of 25 years. [51]

Creation of Industrial Expansion Organizations

Chapter 8 contains a quotation from Ben Bella when he inaugurated the first Industrial Fxpansion Organization on February 22, 1965. The discussion explained that this was a sort of small business investment corporation. It developed to get individual Algerians to invest their money in industry. A share in such a company cost $20, and an individual could buy up to (but not more than) 100 shares. However, each investor had only one vote, regardless of the number of shares he owned. On the other hand, the shares were shares and not bonds, so that the profits of industrial companies established by such an investment corporation would be divided among the shareholders. (Actually, the statutes provide that 60 percent of net profits be reinvested and 40 percent be distributed as dividends.) The stockholders elect the board of directors, but the government appoints a committee which effectively controls the actions of the board of directors.

It would appear that whereas with self-management Algeria was trying to find her own brand of "Algerian socialism, " with its Industrial Expansion Organizations she was attempting to develop her own style of "Algerian capitalism. "

Investment Code of 1966

The most important, and one of the most recent, efforts of the government to attract private investors was the investment code of 1966.[52] Its necessity was made obvious by the failure of the 1963 code. Not only were the guarantees of the 1963 code vague and its incentives insufficient, but local investors were not included in either its guarantees or its incentives.

The 1966 code suffered the same fate as the 1963 code, in that one of its most important provisions was changed just before it was promulgated. Whereas the draft law stated that in no case would the government nationalize a company during the first 10 years of its existence, the final text states simply that a company will not be nationalized except where the public interest requires it "imperatively"; that such nationalization can be effected only by legislative action; and that a just indemnity will be paid automatically within a period of nine months. (The 1963 code had said that a company would not be nationalized until the accumulated net profits were greater than the invested capital imported into the country.)

Also, while the 1963 code restricted repatriation of profits to not more than 50 percent of net profit each year, the 1966 code restricts annual repatriation to not more than 15 percent of the invested capital imported into Algeria. To the foreign investor, therefore, the new code is really no improvement.

However, for the local investor it is a great improvement. First of all, it does apply to local investors, offering them fairly liberal financial and tax advantages. Second, its administrative procedures for investments of less than $100,000 are greatly simplified.

On April 14, 1967, the National Investment Commission met, under the chairmanship of the Finance Minister, Ahmed Kaid, to examine the first specific investment applications to be considered under the new code. The commission announced that it would judge proposals on the basis of compatibility with Algeria's politico-economic goals, particularly with regard to whether the new investment would compete with existing socialist companies. In addition, the commission would use such criteria as (1) integration with domestic production; (2) creation of employment; (3) satisfaction of market demand of low-income groups; (4) amount of saving or earning of foreign exchange; and (5) location within Algeria.

During its first session, the commission rejected an application of a chewing gum firm which had already made the investment. It also rejected applications to manufacture soap and assemble bicycles, because the government had plans to do both of these. It approved, in principle, applications for the manufacture of cigarette filters and for a metal packing plant, provided these investors would enter into joint ventures with related state-owned companies or self-managed companies. A project for the manufacture of plastic household articles was accepted, as was one for school notebooks-- provided the factories were located outside of Algiers. A foreign private investor's project for the manufacture of suitcases and trunks was accepted without condition, as were projects for fabricating ball point pens and shoe heels and soles. Returned for further study were applications to make cardboard packing and dry cell batteries. [53]

Within one year after the new code had appeared, over 40 projects had been approved. Also, the Chamber of Commerce and Industry of Algiers took a survey of its members and found that there were tentative plans to apply for permission to invest in 275 different projects representing a total value of $24 million. [54] One must wait and see how

many of these plans are translated into applications, how
many applications are approved, and how many approvals are
implemented. It would appear, however, that the Algerian
middle class is gaining confidence in the regime of President
Boumediène.

NOTES

1. Excerpt from a speech by Houari Boumediène, on
July 5, 1965; "Algeria Changes Course, " Africa Report
(November, 1965), 10.

2. Journal Officiel de l'État Algérien, September 7, 1962.

3. Journal Officiel de la République Algérienne,
March 22, 1963.

4. Obtained from unpublished reports from the files of
the Chamber of Commerce of Algiers.

5. Ibid.

6. Obtained from unpublished reports of the French
Embassy in Algiers.

7. Government of France, "La Situation Économique
de l'Algérie, "Notes et Études Documentaires, No. 3406-
3407 (July 6, 1967), 46.

8. Jean Teillac, Autogestion en Algérie, pp. 46, 65-68.

9. Obtained from unpublished reports of the French
Embassy in Algiers.

10. Ibid.

11. Journal Officiel de la République Algénienne
(October 4, 1963).

12. Government of Algeria, Actualité et Documents,
No. 43 (August 15-31, 1964), 9.

13. Journal Officiel (November 5, 1963), Ordinance No. 63-427, dated November 4, 1963.

14. Alger Ce Soir (January 24, 1965).

15. Le Monde (May 17, 1966).

16. El Moudjahid (May 21, 1966).

17. Ibid.

18. Ibid. (August 30 and 31, 1967); New York Times (August 31, 1967).

19. Ibid.

20. Journal Officiel (September 12, 1967).

21. El Moudjahid (September 16, 1967).

22. Le Monde (May 16, 1968).

23. Ibid. (May 28, 1968).

24. Ibid.

25. Ibid.

26. Ibid. (June 16, 1968).

27. Wall Street Journal (May 31, 1966).

28. Le Monde (May 30 and 31, 1966).

29. Ibid. (January 24, 1966).

30. Ibid. (January 1, 1966).

31. CEDIES Information, (May 13, 1967).

32. El Moudjahid (May 30, 1967).

33. Journal Officiel (August 13, 1964), decree No. 64-233 (August 10, 1964).

34. Obtained from unpublished documents of the Chamber of Commerce of Algiers.

35. Government of Algeria, Actualité et Documents, No. 28 (January 1-15, 1964), 7.

36. Government of France, "Crédit et Banque, "Guide de l'Industriel en Algérie, pp. 7-9.

37. Chambre de Commerce et de l'Industrie d'Alger, Flash, No. 1 (1964), 22.

38. El Moudjahid (July 2-4, 1966).

39. Ibid. (December 29, 1966).

40. Journal Officiel (October 6, 1967), Ordinance No. 67-204 (October 1, 1967).

41. Chambre de Commerce et de l'Industrie d'Alger, Flash, No. 11, (October 15, 1967), 2-7.

42. From discussions with personnel of the French Embassy in Algiers.

43. Journal Officiel (April 18, 1964), decree No. 64-128 (April 15, 1964).

44. Le Monde (January 2, 1965).

45. Journal Officiel (February 22, 1963), decree No. 63-56 (February 11, 1963).

46. El Moudjahid (October 8, 1966).

47. Journal Officiel (August 2, 1963), decree No. 63-277 (July 26, 1963).

48. From a file of the Investment Commission (August, 1964).

49. Journal Officiel (July 16, 1963), decree No. 63-248 (July 10, 1963).

50. Le Monde (October 9, 1964).

51. Ibid. (December 24-26, 1966).

52. Journal Officiel (September 17, 1966), Ordinance No. 66-284 (September 15, 1966).

53. Information on the first meeting came from reports in the U.S. Embassy in Algiers.

54. Chambre de Commerce et de l'Industrie d'Alger, Flash, No. 12 (October 30, 1967), 2-4.

CHAPTER **10** APPLICATION OF THE
MODEL TO ALGERIA

The first section of Chapter 9 gave a fairly dismal view
of the future of private enterprise in Algeria. The workers
have taken over a significant number of factories; all foreign-
owned farmland has been nationalized; many companies in a
broad range of industrial sectors, not just the basic industries,
have been nationalized; the government has established monopolies in transportation, insurance, publishing, and many
sectors of foreign trade; some state-owned retail stores have
been created; banking is in the public sector, as a result not
only of the establishment of state-owned banks but also of
the nationalization of those private, French-owned banks
which had not voluntarily ceased operation; and the government has begun the establishment of many state-owned manufacturing companies in both basic and secondary industries.
The record of the first six years of independence would indicate a definite movement toward an orthodox socialist
economy.

Why, then, has the government also taken measures aimed
at encouraging private investors, both domestic and foreign?
It has outlawed the Communist party; established an industrial
development bank to help finance private investors; created
a patent office; created Industrial Expansion Organizations
(a type of small business investment corporation); passed
two investment codes which offer incentives and guarantees
to private investors; and returned some companies, which
had been nationalized "without cause," to their former owners.

Do the policy statements contained in Chapter 8 help us
to understand the above actions and indicate future trends?
We find, first of all, that the basic Tripoli Program pointed
to the Algerian middle class as being antagonistic to the goals
of the people and hence to be combated. This differs from
the situation in Tunisia, where the government took care not
to create class distinctions and antagonisms. Second, the
Tripoli Program advocated economic planning, state control

of the economy, and the elimination of wasteful competition.
Consequently, it called for the nationalization of all forms of
transportation, insurance companies, banks, foreign trade,
and mineral resources, and for the establishment by the state
of basic heavy industries. This has been followed in its entirety, except for petroleum production. "In other areas of
the economy, " it said, "private initiative may be encouraged
and directed within the framework of the general goal of industrialization. " And "the contribution of foreign private capital
is desirable within certain limitations. "

The Tripoli Program was, of course, written just prior
to independence, in the heat of battle, and might, therefore,
be suspected of having more of an emotional than a rational
approach. The follow-up document, coming nearly two years
after independence and hence representing a considered formula based on experience, was the Charter of Algiers, which
appeared in April, 1964. It is supposed to be the ideological
basis for governmental policies in the economic and social
spheres. This document also calls for the eventual nationalization of the mineral wealth of the country, with an interim
transition state consisting of the formation of joint ventures
between the government and foreign private investors, permitting the training of Algerian technicians and managers.
This long-term development is now in progress and proceeding
fairly rapidly. The Charter of Algiers also calls for the absorption by the public sector of all the existing private banks,
thereby making available to the socialist sector all of these
sources of savings and credit. This process has now been
essentially completed.

The Charter of Algiers also indicates the need to nationalize foreign trade on a step-by-step basis and to diversify
Algeria's foreign trading partners. This nationalization effort
has been accomplished for a number of product classifications
and can be expected to proceed with others. The diversification of trade is proceeding slowly, but trade is still oriented
predominantly toward France.

The Charter of Algiers further notes the menacing presence of foreign capitalism and emphasizes the need to neutralize this potential influence on the country's political and
economic life. Such neutralization, it indicates, can be accomplished by the gradual absorption of the private industrial
sector and by the establishment of state-owned companies.
Again, as seen in Chapter 9, this process has been gradual
but has tended to move in spurts. The Charter has nothing
to say about the role of the domestic private industrial sector.

Thus, the ideological documents of the regime provide an explanation of most of the policies followed by the regimes of Ben Bella and of President Boumediène, but not of all of them. The rise of the self-management sector immediately after independence, for example, was not foreseen by the Tripoli Program but arose as a result of the situation and of the Marxist tendency of the UGTA. The existence and importance of the self-managed sector is recognized by the Charter of Algiers, but it is not given a key role to play in the economy.

The Ben Bella regime appeared to try to achieve a co-existence of the self-managed sector, the public sector, the private domestic sector, and the foreign private sector. His July 11, 1963, speech before the National Assembly, arguing for passage of the first investment code, was a strong statement in support of foreign private investment, and his January 21, 1965, speech inaugurating the first Industrial Expansion Organization was quite a pitch for the utilization of Algeria's private entrepreneurship.

The regime of President Boumediène has made similar policy statements. It also has stated that a clear role exists for the private sector, both domestic and foreign. At the same time, this regime has confirmed the "socialist option" of Algeria. Although the self-managed sector is lauded and called the basis of the economic revolution, ever since his inauguration President Boumediène and his ministers have left some question mark in their comments on the future of self-management. There seems to be some consensus that the sector must prove itself. Meanwhile, as was indicated in Chapter 7, a number of self-managed firms have been converted into public companies, managed by the government rather than by the workers. None have moved from the public to the self-managed sector. Over time, therefore, one can foresee a gradual diminution of the self-managed sector, as poorly managed firms are "nationalized." But, for the sake of appearance and to prevent an open break with the UGTA, the government will probably permit the continued existence of a self-managed sector which is not so large as to be too significant to the economy or too much of a drag on economic growth.

What of the future of domestic private investment? We have seen in Chapter 9 that many Algerians were responding to the second investment code. There appeared, in 1967, to be a renaissance of private investment, or at least of interest in investing, as evidenced by applications to invest. How

many of the approved investments are actually being implemented is unknown. In any case, as shown by the decisions of
the National Investment Commission, the types of permissible
private investments are highly circumscribed.

Another factor limiting the possibilities for domestic
private investment is the heritage of the colonial period. As
was shown in Chapter 7, prior to independence over 90 percent
of industrial and commercial enterprise was in the hands of
Frenchmen. Thus, few Algerians had the possibility of ex-
ercising entrepreneurship or practicing management. In
addition, the small number of Algerians who were given
secondary or higher education during the colonial period, plus
the very high rate of adult illiteracy (still nearly 90 percent),
another inheritance from the pre-independence days, means
that there is a very small number of individuals who might
develop management talents or be capable of founding industrial
companies. The few who have such capabilities are drawn to
government service, which is the seat of power in today's
Algeria. And there is great need for them in government, for,
as indicated in Chapter 7, French policy excluded Algerians
from responsible positions in the civil service. Thus, few
gained administrative experience; and those who did were
tainted and therefore are excluded from responsible positions
today.

Thus, entrepreneurial talent is drawn into the government
instead of being free to express itself in the private sector.
But it is not suppressed; it springs forth as governmental
entrepreneurship. As a result, the government has already
taken over most of the service industries and, through its
annual equipment budget, is investing in a broad range of
manufacturing industry, much of which is not in the category
of basic industry and hence could be left to the private sector.
Consequently, while attempting to encourage private entrepreneurship, the government, through its investment policy,
stifles this entrepreneurship.

But the government is not closing the door completely.
Domestic private investment is still encouraged, and the
nationalization measures have hit primarily the U.S., British,
and French investments. It is significant that the May 20,
1968, nationalizations finally affected several domestic private investors.

Is Algerian socialism really orthodox? What has
really motivated the various anti-private enterprise measures of
of the government? One must note that the private Algerian
agricultural holdings have not been touched--the agricultural

reform promised by the Tripoli Program and the Charter of Algiers has not appeared. Nor, as noted above, have the Algerian shops been expropriated, and only a few Algerian-owned factories have been nationalized. The government has, in general, catered to them. It appears, therefore, that if the government is in fact ideologically committed to orthodox socialism, it is not yet prepared to alienate its own middle class completely.

On the other hand, the government has undermined, attacked, and decimated foreign private investment. This was to be expected, considering that nearly all such investment was in the hands of Frenchmen or French companies. But, strangely enough, the government did not undertake these measures in the name of "decolonization." Whereas this term was very common in the parlance of government officials in Tunisia in the first eight years following independence, it has hardly been mentioned in Algeria. The government is, rather, carrying out these actions in the name of "socialism." This is an indication of the strength of the socialist forces in the power structure.

This is also shown by the nationalization of the private banks in May, 1968. As noted in Chapter 9, one would have expected these banks to close as a matter of course, as a result of other measures that the government had taken. These nationalizations were contrary to the advice of M. Simon, a highly capable Belgian banker who had turned communist, gone to Algeria, been attached to the office of the President, and become a close adviser to President Boumediène. His advice resulted in giving the Banque Extérieure d'Algérie a monopoly on the financing of foreign trade. He felt that this would result in a voluntary shutdown of the remaining private banks and the eventual abandonment of many more French-owned manufacturing firms. Simon advised that, in the international picture, this was preferable to nationalization. But the government chose nationalization, in the name of socialism.

Thus, as in most other countries, the Algerian government is doing a balancing act between competing internal forces. One of these forces is the mass of unemployed. As noted in Chapter 7, about 70 percent of the employable population is without work, and many of those who have work are under-employed. Their main ideology is a full stomach, and their existence acts as a time fuse, forcing the government to take every step possible to speed up development. Unfortunately, many of the socialist measures taken to satisfy the socialist forces result in decreased production in agriculture and

industry, making the satisfaction of the hungry unemployed
that much more difficult.

If the growth of the domestic private sector is still possible, what of foreign private investment? One factor involved
is Algeria's current wave of nationalism, following the 1967
Middle East war. This has increased suspicion of all things
foreign, but especially of the Anglo-Saxon world. The timing
of the May-June, 1968, nationalizations of French oil distributing companies, banks, and many industrial firms probably
sprang from a hasty decision that President De Gaulle's regime was about to tumble and be replaced by a leftist government. Thus, these nationalizations were probably conceived
not only to satisfy the internal socialist forces but also to
appeal to the future French government. The latter aim back-
fired, however. In addition, the co-existence of the French
private sector and the public sector of industry in Algeria has
been seriously compromised.

There is now little likelihood that the remaining French
companies in Algeria will expand their investments, and even
less possibility that new French investment will come. When
the government's actions vis-à-vis the foreign private sector
are seen to follow the vagaries of internal pressures and external events, there is also little likelihood of private investors
arriving from other countries, particularly since the Algerian
government has not entered into bilateral investment guarantee
agreements with any foreign governments and has refused to
sign the World Bank's multilateral arbitration agreement.

It seems possible, therefore, that Algeria may be destined
(if not determined) to follow the pattern which the East European countries followed in 1946-47, which China followed in
1949-53, and which the United Arab Republic followed in the
early 1960's. Even though communist parties were in power
in East Europe and China, all private investment was not
immediately nationalized, nor was such a once-and-for-all
step taken in the United Arab Republic. Rather, the pattern
progressed step by step, beginning with some foreign investors,
then others, then some of the local private sector, then more,
until finally, over several years, all had disappeared.

Each step taken so far had been previously spelled out by
the Tripoli Program and the Charter of Algiers. These are
the ideological documents of the Algerian regime. They have
been followed so far. Unless there is a counter-revolution
(as contrasted with a coup d'état, which only changes faces),
we should expect that these documents will continue to be
followed, particularly when leading personalities in the regime

reiterate their ideological policies. What can we say about
the future on the basis of these documents and statements?
Is Algerian socialism to be "total"? Will the entire private
sector of industry disappear?

The Tripoli Program speaks of the "construction of the
nation within the framework of socialist principles." But,
as we know, there are all degrees and types of socialism.
The Tripoli Program also states that the middle class must
be controlled, but it does not call for the elimination of that
class. It calls for the nationalization of many sectors of the
economy, but not for the eventual elimination of the private
sector.

The Charter of Algiers confirms the "socialist option"
and calls for the nationalization of several sectors of the
economy. In addition, it specifies that the way must be prepared for the future nationalization of all of the country's
mineral wealth. But, again, it appears to leave the way open
for an indefinite continuation of the private sector in some
areas of the economy.

On the other hand, the UGTA continues to call for the
ultimate fusion of the private and the socialist sectors.
Bachir Boumaza, the Minister of Economics under Ben Bella,
specified, when testifying before the National Assembly, that
Algeria was in "an organizational stage" permitting the consolidation of the existing socialist sector and requiring a tem-
porary co-existence with the private sector. But, he stated,
the co-management experience "should educate the workers
so as to put an end to private property at the end of the organizational phase." This same Bachir Boumaza, when speaking
to the Junior Chamber of Commerce of Algiers, stated that
"the private sector would gradually be integrated into the
public sector."

However, since 1965, these specific statements indicating
that the private sector will eventually disappear have been
avoided, both by President Boumediène and by his ministers.
They state that the socialist option is irreversible, but as
President Boumediène indicated in his May 22, 1967, speech,
Algeria has adopted a "revolutionary theory which comes out
of the reality of the situation and which achieves a perfect
harmony between ideology and practice." It appears, therefore, that the technocrats who are now running Algeria are at
least as much pragmatists as they are ideologists, and that
pragmatism may require the co-existence of a private sector
with the semi-public, public, and socialist sectors for an
indefinite period.

PART **IV** MOROCCO

INTRODUCTION TO PART IV
MOROCCO TODAY

Morocco lies on the northwestern tip of Africa, just south of Spain and separated from Gibraltar by the nine-mile-wide Strait of Gibraltar. Its northern coast, consequently, is on the Mediterranean, while the western coast is on the Atlantic. It greatly resembles the state of California. Its length of 850 miles and width of 300 miles are both similar to those of California, while its area of 174,471 square miles is only 10 percent greater and its population of about 14 million is only 10 percent smaller than California's. Also like California, it has a temperate coastal climate. Portions of the interior are very cold in the winter and very hot in the summer. Also, similarly, Morocco has several inland mountain ranges (the High Atlas, the Middle Atlas, the Anti-Atlas, and the Rif Massif--some reaching over 13,000 feet) and also has desert in its southern reaches.

The northwestern portion of the country consists of a coastal plain and low plateau area known as "inner Morocco." It is a rich, open agricultural area with usually adequate rainfall. It is the most economically advanced and heavily populated portion of the country and contains almost all of the major cities. The mountain ranges cover the central part of the country. To the east of them is the continuation of the Algerian high plateau, with only four to 10 inches of rain per year, while to the southeast and south are the semi-arid and arid desert regions with less than four inches of rain.

The population is Moslem, except for about 100,000 Jews and 190,000 Europeans (1965 estimate). The nearly 14 million Moslems are predominantly of Berber origin, but the majority of them speak Arabic. About 35 percent of the population, however (primarily those living outside the coastal plain and plateau of "inner Morocco"), speak Berber in their homes. While the official language is Arabic, the use of French is prevalent in government documents and has replaced Spanish in the northern (formerly Spanish-held) zone, although attempts are being made to utilize Arabic in official circles.

Prices and wages have been relatively stable in recent years and, in fact, fell in 1966. However, the annual increase in GNP has not, since independence, quite kept up with the

2.3 percent population increase. In 1967 GNP reached $2.66 billion. In 1966 the very poor agricultural production, due primarily to drought conditions, resulted in a slight decrease in GNP, but in 1967, in spite of a poor agricultural yield, there was a 4.3 percent increase in GNP. With an estimated gross national income in 1967 of $2.35 billion, and a population of 14 million, the average per capita annual income was approximately $168. There were, however, wide variations in income. On the one hand there was a fairly large wealthy class of landowners, merchants, and industrialists. On the other hand, in 1966, unemployment was very high, estimated to equal 40 percent of the active urban population and approximately 50 percent in the rural areas.

Illiteracy is very high. A 1960 census indicated a rate of 89 percent for Moroccan Moslems (82 percent for men and 96 percent for women). The literacy rate was only 7 percent in the rural areas, but 23 percent in the cities. Literacy campaigns and large increases in the percent of school-age children attending school have, since 1960, resulted in a near doubling of the literacy of the population between the ages of five and 14, to a rate of nearly 30 percent.

This educational effort is evident in the government's operating budget. The largest item is education, which was 21 percent of the total in 1965 (as compared with 15 percent of the total for the military--the second largest item).

The economic infrastructure of Morocco is advanced. There are six well-equipped ports (Casablanca, Agadir, Safi, Port Lyautey, Tangier, and Mohammedia) which can receive ocean-going vessels. Casablanca is by far the largest, and ranks third, in terms of tons of freight handled, in all of Africa. In 1965 there were over 10,000 miles of primary and secondary highways, of which about 7,000 miles were paved. There were also about 1,200 miles of railroad, all standard gauge, one-third electrified and the rest using diesel locomotives. As in Tunisia and Algeria, there are a widespread, modern telephone system and a plentiful supply of electricity.

Agriculture is the mainstay of the economy, with 70 percent of the active population engaged directly in farming, livestock raising, and forestry. The principal crops are barley, wheat, corn, and citrus fruits. Of the country's total area, in 1965 about 19 percent was in cropland, 24 percent in grazing land, 15 percent in forest, and the remaining 42 percent in wasteland or urban areas. Of the 13 million acres in cropland, about 40 percent is in the modern sector. The remainder is highly fragmented and is farmed by traditional methods. The result of this situation is that Morocco is about self-sufficient in cereals.

Morocco is not very well endowed with mineral resources. The outstanding mineral, by far, is phosphates, of which Morocco is the world's largest exporter and second largest producer. There are coal and iron ore deposits, but these are low-quality and high-cost. Extensive exploration for oil and gas have resulted in the discovery of only two small oil fields and one small gas field.

Manufacturing contributes only about 15 percent of the GNP and employs about 130,000 people. The most important area is that of food processing, but textile manufacturing is expanding rapidly. Leather working, construction materials, and some metalworking are also important.

The above production picture shows up in Morocco's foreign trade, where her major exports are phosphates and citrus fruits. She exports some cereals and imports others. During a good agricultural year she is a net exporter of cereals, but she often becomes a net importer. Her major imports are consumer goods (led by textiles), foodstuffs (led by sugar), and semi-finished products (led by iron and steel). This trade picture does not differ greatly from that in the year of independence. Nor has Morocco been able to change significantly the direction of its trade. Trade with France has fallen by only 10 percent from 50 percent of total trade at the time of independence to about 40 percent in recent years. Imports from the United States have increased appreciably, reaching about 11 percent of total imports in 1967, but this was due primarily to U.S. foreign aid. Meanwhile, exports to the United States remain at the very low level of about 2 percent of total exports. The most significant change in Morocco's trade picture is the growth of trade with East Europe, Cuba, and China, which has grown from nearly zero at the time of independence to exports of 6-14 percent between 1964 and 1966; imports from them have stayed at about 20 percent of the total.

Morocco's balance of payments has been traditionally in deficit and has continued to be so since independence. She sometimes has surpluses in the balance of trade, but these have been offset by transfers of profits out of Morocco by French companies and by expenditures of Moroccan residents of European origin who travel abroad. The deficits in the balance of payments in 1966 and 1967 drew net foreign exchange reserves down to a low level of $35 million at the end of 1967.

These current account deficits have necessitated a considerable amount of foreign aid, although this aid has not been sufficient to achieve high investment rates or to prevent decreases in the foreign exchange reserves. Because of a crisis in diplomatic relations, French financial aid to Morocco was suspended between 1957 and 1962, during which time the United States stepped in, eventually providing a total of over $500 million between 1957 and 1966. In 1962, French aid resumed and became much more important than U.S. aid, which has recently been restricted to surplus agricultural products and project aid. Then, in 1966, French-Moroccan relations again deteriorated (because of the Ben Barka affair), and French financial aid came to a halt. As a result, foreign aid receipts were down to $121 million, 12 percent lower than in 1965, even though Germany, Kuwait, and the World Bank became contributors, as had Russia, Czechoslovakia, and Poland.

Morocco achieved her independence from France in 1956, mainly by force, after two and a half years of revolt. The French occupation (protectorate) began in 1912 but did not achieve a final pacification of the country until 1934. By 1955, nearly 250,000 French troops were in Morocco but could not stabilize the situation. The Sultan, one of the leaders of the fight for independence, who had been in exile, was brought back to Morocco and resumed his traditional powers at independence. His powers were not wholly traditional, however, since there were three political parties in existence; their strengths were based upon their roles in the struggle for independence. More parties were formed. In 1961, the Sultan (Mohammed V) died and was succeeded by his son, King Hassan II. The latter promulgated a constitution in 1962 and held parliamentary elections in May, 1963. Unfortunately, the bickering between the numerous parties made the Parliament unworkable, as happened in France during 1946-58. The King dismissed the Parliament in June, 1965, and personally assumed the office of Prime Minister. Ministers of the government are now appointed by the King with little regard to party labels, and laws are passed by royal decree.

As a result, the government is made up of close friends of the King. Most of them are large landowners, and several are related to the royal family. Consequently they reflect a conservative attitude. While political parties exist, they have little or no raison d'être. Several of them are left-wing socialist and constitute an underground current of opposition to the government. The army is loyal, well organized, and

well equipped, so there is little chance of a successful up-
rising, even if opposition to the regime could organize itself.

The above constitutes a situation which is generally favorable to private enterprise, yet there have been nationalizations of farmlands, a growth of government participation in
industry and commerce, and some nationalistic reactions
which have called for measures of decolonization. Under
what circumstances have these acts taken place? What are
the views of the government officials? How rapid is the
growth of the public sector? What is the probable future role
of private enterprise? Such are the answers to be sought in
the following chapters.

11

HISTORICAL CONTEXT OF THE MOROCCAN POLITICAL CLIMATE FOR PRIVATE INVESTMENT

EARLY HISTORY

The Phoenicians first established a trading post in Morocco about 1100 B.C., on the Atlantic coast near the present city of Lukkus. This was followed by similar posts at locations which correspond to present-day Melilla, Tangier, and Salé. Over time, as more and more Phoenicians arrived, their influence spread inland--they intermarried with the Berbers and gave them a more efficient administrative system. The Phoenician language became the official language. By 200 B.C., the Kingdom of Mauritania coincided with the northern half of present-day Morocco (just as the Kingdom of Numidia approximately coincided with present-day Algeria). These two kingdoms were really Berber, since there were so few Phoenicians, but the names of the rulers were Phoenicians (Punic). They existed independently of Carthage, although there is some reason to believe that the rulers of Carthage, Numidia, and Mauritania were related.

Carthage fell to the Romans in 146 B.C., but Numidia and Mauritania remained independent for nearly another century. In 82 B.C., a Roman general came down from Spain and seized Tangier. It received the rights and privileges of a Roman city in 38 B.C. King Juba I of Numidia had sided with Pompey, and after Pompey's defeat he committed suicide. Numidia was placed under Roman administration and Juba's son was given a Greco-Roman education, the best available. He was made King of Mauritania (Morocco) and married Cleopatra Silene, daughter of Antony and Cleopatra. The Romans ruled through him and his successor but, near the middle of the first century, transformed the area into a Roman province.

As a province, it was left somewhat underdeveloped. Few archaeological remains have been found, nor has a system of paved Roman roads been discovered, such as existed in Algeria and Tunisia. Probably as a result of this, Morocco was not greatly disturbed by either the Vandals or the Byzantines, both of whom occupied Ceuta but left the rest of the country to itself. As a consequence, the Romanized Mauritanians were able to carry on with some sort of Roman life and administration until the seventh century. (Latin inscriptions have been found dating from the sixth and seventh centuries.)

The Arab invasion of Mauritania took place in 680 and was launched from Tunisia. The army returned to Tunisia after having subdued a number of cities in Mauritania and left a number of converts. Within 30 years, however, Arab rule was so well established in Mauritania that it was used as a base for the invasion of Spain, using mostly Berber soldiers who had been converted to Islam. As in the other North African countries, the Moslem religion spread very rapidly; but because of the greater distance from the Middle East, because of fewer Arabs arriving in the area, and because of the remoteness of many regions of the country (due to its mountainous terrain), the Berber language remained predominant for a much longer period.

From approximately 700, the Arabs and the Berbers alternated in ruling most of what is present-day Morocco. Soon after the Arab conquest, Berber rulers dominated large parts of the area. They were subdued, however, by Moulay Idris, the most famous member of the Alid (Idrisid) dynasty, which ruled in the late eighth and the ninth centuries. This was followed by three great Berber dynasties, which rules from the 10th to the 15th centuries. There was, thus, a long history of rivalry between the Arabs and the Berbers, although the rivalry usually became evident only when there was a question of succession. Once the ruler was established, he tended to be accepted by both sides, and the rivalry greatly diminished. The greatest difficulty, however, was the anarchic character of the Berbers living in the mountainous regions and in the southern desert. Their allegiance was more to the tribe than to any central ruler, be he Berber or Arab.

The Almohades dynasty (1147-1296) gained control over the area from Castile to Tripoli, thus uniting the Maghreb for the first time. This intrusion into the Iberian peninsula later provoked raids from Portugal and parts of Spain on the Moroccan coast towns, particularly in the 13th century.

Meanwhile, the Moroccan rule of much of Spain resulted in an interchange of peoples, so that there were also colonies of Spaniards in Morocco. In addition, Spain captured the city of Melilla in 1497 and the city of Ceuta at the end of the 16th century (taking it from the Portuguese, who had held it since 1415). Spain has held these cities since then. A constant flow of people and ideas between Spain and Morocco over the centuries and the return of Arabs to Morocco after having been expelled from Spain resulted in a special relationship between the two countries.

Although the Portuguese and Spaniards intruded into Moroccan territory, they never ruled the country. Nor did the Turks establish themselves in Morocco, as they had in Algeria and Tunisia.

The French became directly involved in Morocco in 1844, when the Moroccans aided the Algerian rebel leader, Abd al-Zadir. A war between the two resulted in a defeat of the Moroccan army. During the remainder of the 19th century, it became increasingly clear to the Moroccan rulers that they were at the mercy of any incident which gave a European power the excuse to intervene. European influence grew and, during the reign of Sultan Moulay Abd al-Aziz, which began in 1902, many Europeans were attached to the court as advisers. The Sultan's penchant for pleasure and his lack of administrative abilities, however, led to economic difficulties.

Disagreement among the European powers had maintained the independence of Morocco for so long. Finally, in 1904, in exchange for a free hand in Egypt, England offered to leave France free to act in Morocco. Several months later, the French and Spanish reached agreement on zones of influence in Morocco. In 1907, attacks by Moslems on some European workmen in Casablanca led to French occupation of the city and its surrounding area. French influence grew and, by 1912, the Treaty of Fez had been signed, making Morocco a protectorate of France, of Spain, and of international interests.

ARRIVAL OF THE PROTECTORATE

The agreement signed on March 30, 1912, between the French government and the Sultan indicated that the two agreed to work together "to institute in Morocco a new regime for reforms of administration, of justice, of education, of economics, of finances, and of the military, as the French government might judge useful to introduce on Moroccan territory." It also said that the Sultan recognized "that the French government, after having so advised the Sultan, may proceed with the military occupation of the Moroccan territory as necessary to maintain order and security . . . and that it will exercise police power on Moroccan territory, on land and on sea."

It further stated that the French government would come to an agreement with the Spanish government with regard to the latter's geographical interests and possessions, and that Tangier was to retain its special international status.

France considered itself as the only protectorate power. The Spanish zone was considered to be a portion of Moroccan territory, under the influence of the Sultan, in which the French permitted the Spaniards to carry out necessary administrative reforms and maintain internal order and security.[1] The French considered it to be the Zone of Spanish Influence, while the Spanish called it the Protectorate of Spain in Morocco. The Sultan appointed a Viceroy to the Spanish zone and delegated to him all of the Sultan's powers for that area. This Viceroy therefore had the same relationship to the Spanish High Commissioner as the Sultan to the French High Commissioner.

Tangier, meanwhile, was administered by a commission appointed by diplomats from the countries which were signatories of the Algeciras Treaty of 1904.

Although the Treaty of Fez was presented as an "agreement" between the French government and the Sultan, it was in reality a unilateral act by which the French imposed their law and will on Morocco, meanwhile satisfying their commitments to Spain and to the countries interested in the status of Tangier. There was a facade of "rule" by the Sultan, in that his signature had to be affixed to all decrees.

The signing of the treaty did not automatically give the French control of the country. Much of the country was in revolt against the Sultan for having signed the Treaty of Fez. In addition, the mountainous regions had not really been under the control of the Sultan prior to the arrival of the French.

But the French did not hesitate; they immediately undertook to pacify the entire territory. They were interrupted in 1914 by World War I and recommenced in 1919. Not until 1926 was the northern part of the country, inhabited by the Berber tribes of the Rif, conquered. The efforts to subdue the pockets of resistance in the south began in 1929 and were completed in 1934.

ECONOMIC DEVELOPMENT UNDER
THE PROTECTORATE

The French did not wait for pacification before proceeding with their efforts to develop the potential of the country. They had, in fact, been quite busy prior to the start of the protectorate. French capitalists had decided, prior to the end of the 19th century, that Morocco was to be conquered by France. An informal committee created for this purpose included the presidents of the West Algerian Railroad Company, the Banque de Paris et des Pays Bas, the Société Marseillaise de Crédit, and Schneider et Cie. They were, according to newspaper reports, willing to go to war to achieve this conquest because they felt that France's presence in Algeria gave it a greater right to Morocco than that of other European countries.[2]

In 1900, one-third of Morocco's foreign trade was with France. (England also had one-third, the remainder being primarily with Spain and Germany.)[3] At the same time, French investments in Morocco, primarily in commerce and in urban real estate, amounted to about $1.2 million. (The fact that German interests amounted to about $1.6 million bothered the French.)[4]

In 1904, the Banque de Paris et des Pays Bas arrived in Morocco as head of a consortium of French banks and made a large loan to the Sultan, with customs duties as security. Within several years, this bank was in charge of collecting customs for the Sultan to assure servicing of the loan.[5] However, other international creditors were suffering and were looking for a way to assure a regularization of Morocco's finances. As a result, in 1907 a group of foreign banks, mostly central banks, formed a consortium and, with the approval of the Sultan, established a Moroccan Central Bank (Banque d'État Marocain). The French had a larger share of ownership than any of the other countries, and the Banque de Paris et des Pays Bas, one of the shareholders, dominated this Moroccan Central Bank. (By 1947, French banks owned 57.2 percent of the Moroccan Central Bank, and the Banque de Paris et des Pays Bas owned 61.5 percent of that.)[6]

In 1912 the Banque de Paris et des Pays Bas formed the Cie. Générale du Maroc and the Omnium Nord Africain as investment subsidiaries and worked through them in the establishment of many industrial companies.

Other French interests (many of them members of the
"committee" for the conquest of Morocco), such as Schneider
et Cie. and the Société Marseillaise de Crédit, joined in
1902 to form the Cie. Marocaine. In 1912 this company was
given charge of the construction of the port of Casablanca.
Soon thereafter it organized and financed railroad, electric
power, and mining companies. [7]

The actions of these companies, from one point of view,
represent the quick results which private enterprise can
achieve in the economic development of a country when the
conditions are right. Another point of view sees such actions
quite differently. Ayache describes this experience in the
following manner:

Their [the French financial and industrial interests]
seizure of Morocco did not hesitate, as it had during
the colonization of Algeria and Tunisia. Knowing their
objectives, masters of a colonial technique forged in
Algeria and corrected and perfected in Tunisia, Indochina, and Madagascar, they acted with method and vigor.

All their tasks were conducted simultaneously: the
organization of a political administrative regime; the
establishment of modern financial institutions to assure
and direct capital investments; the seizure of lands and
the planting of rural and urban colonies; the execution
of public works; the creation of commercial organizations to collect local products and to distribute imported goods; and the development of mining industries
and of light manufacturing. [8]

However, regardless of one's viewpoint, the development
of Morocco's economy started from a very low base. Not
having been conquered by the Turks was not, in the long run,
a blessing to Morocco. Because of the absence of the Turks,
Morocco missed the influences of the Crusades. This left
her free to pursue conquests to the south and made her more
ingrown and less receptive to the modernizing influences from
Western Europe in the 18th and 19th centuries.

For example, in 1912, there were no roads in Morocco.
This doesn't mean that there were simply no highways: there
were no roads--even for carts. All goods had to be moved
on the backs of donkeys and camels. The French immediately
set out to remedy this, and by 1955 there were 7,000 miles of
all-weather road and 34,000 miles of local roads.

In 1912, also, there were no railroads, but by 1955 there
were 1,100 miles, of which 450 miles had been electrified.
In 1912, there was essentially no effort at irrigation, but by

1935, 38,000 acres had been irrigated and by 1955, 650,000 acres. In 1912 there were no ports where ocean-going vessels could load or unload at a dock; they had to anchor and load or unload by lighter. In 1956 Casablanca had become a very important port in world commerce and Safi, Agadir, and Port Lyautey could also receive ocean-going vessels.

Under the Sultan, prior to 1912, the government had very few revenues and thus could have done little, even it if had been so inclined. However, under the French, the government's budget grew very rapidly. The following shows the pattern of growth: 1910, $4 million; 1920, $16 million; 1930, $34 million; 1946, $40 million; 1951, $152 million; 1954, $190 million. [9]

Industry

In 1903, 95 percent of the population depended on agriculture and livestock for a living. The only Moroccan industry was artisanal, producing such products as rugs, tapestries, blankets, woolen cloth, muskets, pistols, jewelry, and chinaware. [10] It was rare that more than three or four workers were found in one shop. Production methods showed no evidence of European technology; motors were not used, all work being done by hand.

Not only was Moroccan industry far behind European and other North African industry; it was becoming more decadent. For example, the Moroccan sword industry was once well-known (in the late 18th century there were 200 artisan shops in one city), but by 1903 only 20 artisans could be found in this field and swords were imported from Europe for use by the court. [11]

Consequently, the field of industrial investment was wide open. World War I broke out soon after the opening of the protectorate and delayed French investment, but the fever of the period following the war is illustrated by Dugard in his book, Le Maroc de 1919, when he asks, as the title to a chapter, "Is It Possible to Go to Morocco and Make a Fortune?"[12] In his answer to this question he says, "Yes, but it takes energy and, above all, capital." The industries in which he indicated investments would be interesting were brewing, tanning, sugar refining, distilling, furniture, cork products, brick and tile, salt, sawmills, chinaware, flour mills, and soap.

However, the French had not been entirely idle. By 1918, there were already 157 industrial investments employing a total of 2,666 workers. The growth following that year was very rapid, with 509 factories and 6,488 workers by 1922, 800 factories and 10,990 workers in 1926, and 1,932 factories with 45,032 workers in 1930.[13] The types of industries into which these investments were flowing are shown in Appendix C, Table 1.

In 1930, out of the total number of companies, 51 were in the mining industry; these tended to employ large numbers of workers. Out of the 1,932 companies, only seven employed more than 500 workers and 49 employed between 100 and 500 workers. Of the remainder, 457 companies had between 20 and 100 workers and 1,419 had fewer than 20 employees.[14]

The period of most rapid capital flow into industrial investment in Morocco was from 1926 to 1931. During each of these years, approximately $10 million flowed into the country. The apex was in 1928, when capital inflow going into industry reached $24 million.[15]

A great deal more French capital flowed into Morocco for investment in commerce, housing, and agriculture, and for government expenditures of various kinds. Ayache estimates that during the period 1912-39, there was a capital inflow of $204 million, representing an average of $7.3 million per year.[16]

Most, but not all, of the capital inflow came from France. Looking again at investment in industry and taking 1929, when $1.8 million entered Morocco for investment solely in industry, we find that 86 percent came from France, 11 percent from Belgium, and 3 percent from other countries. That this pattern was typical is illustrated by the fact that in 1930, 80 percent of the companies were subsidiaries of French firms.[17]

In 1929, only 14 percent of new investment in industry came from local sources. Since most of this would have come from the French colons, it is obvious that Moroccans participated very little in the industrialization process, except as unskilled workers. There were very few entrepreneurs and the artisans continued to practice their trades, though with more and more difficulty, as tastes changed and as competition from local manufacture increased.

However, even local manufacturing began having difficulties in the early 1930's. This was due partially to increased competition from Western Europe, partially to a slump in

demand for Morocco's exports and hence a decline in the
Moroccan economy, and partially a question of running into
a limiting factor on industrial investment deriving from a
pre-protectorate treaty.

In 1906, an international conference was held at Algeciras, resulting in a treaty signed by the Sultan and by
representatives of France, Spain, England, Germany, and
seven other countries. This treaty, the Act of Algeciras,
internationalized Tangier. It also tied the hands of the Sultan
insofar as customs duties were concerned, and its provisions
were embodied in the protectorate regime. In effect, all imports were subjected to a duty of 12.5 percent and Morocco
could not offer most-favored-nation treatment to any country;
consequently, she did not receive most-favored treatment
from other countries. The result of this was that all industrial
investment had to pay a 12.5 percent duty on imported capital
equipment, that infant industries could not have tariff protection greater than 12.5 percent, and that exported manufactured products encountered high tariff barriers because
of a lack of most-favored-nation treatment.

Consequently, new industrial investment was at a very
low level during the 1930's and during the war. In the late
1940's however, new investment was stimulated by a lack of
competition from abroad, by increased demand at home, and
by the encouragement and aid from France, as France began
its own five-year plans and included its overseas territories
in the planning effort. During the five-year equipment plan,
1949-53, France gave $423 million to Morocco as foreign
aid, of which $235 million was in loans (25 years at 1.5 per-
cent interest) and the rest in grants.[18] Although the second
plan (1954-57) overlapped with the independence of Morocco,
the conditions of "independence with interdependence" (with
France) resulted in France's continuing the investment plan,
through its foreign aid program, until 1957. Both of these
plans were devoted to improving agriculture and the general
economic infrastructure, leaving industrial investment primarily to the private sector.

Ayache estimates that French capital flowing into Morocco
reached a rate of $137 million per year during the period
1940-45 and increased to a rate of $185 million per year
from 1946 to 1953, making a total inflow of $4.3 billion be-
tween 1912 and 1953.[19] Most of this was public capital to
defray the military expenditures, governmental operating
expenses, port development, and other government investments.
Ayache also estimates that $930 million represented direct

private investment and $285 million was capital obtained from the sale of bonds, primarily in France.

One aspect of both development plans was an active encouragement, through guarantees and subsidies, of private French investment in Morocco. A capsule view of the investments carried out during the two plans is shown in Appendix C, Table 2, and the resultant growth in industrial production is presented in Appendix C, Table 3.

Table 3 shows, first of all, a considerable number of products being manufactured in 1948 which were not being manufactured in 1938, as a result of loss of supplies from Western Europe during 1939-47. Second, it shows a decrease in production of some items between 1948 and 1953, such as treated vegetable oils, fruit juice, canned vegetables, wool cloth, and rayon cloth, as competitive products arrived from abroad. Third, it shows a considerable increase in the production of most products during 1948-53, when the economy was booming.

Gross investment in the Moroccan economy reached its peak in 1952. The influx was rapid from 1945 to 1951 because of a flight of capital from France after World War II and because of the idea of an Eldorado marocain. During that period the capital inflow was accompanied by 110,000 Europeans. A 1952 study by the Banque du Maroc showed that of the $1.93 billion in private capital invested in Morocco, 68.7 percent came from France; most of the remainder was from Frenchmen who were Moroccan residents.[20] During the period 1949-52, Swiss, Belgian, and Dutch private investment in mining and industry averaged a total of $6 million per year. But most (70-80 percent) of the private investment was going into real estate and most (60 percent) of the public investment was going into construction.

After 1952, private investment grew at a slower pace. If the index of private investment in 1952 is 100, we find that it grew to 113 in 1953, 118 in 1954, and 122 in 1955.

By 1955, there were 200,000 workers employed in industry, of whom 150,000 were Moslems (compared with 45,000 workers in 1930, of whom 35,000 were Moslems).[21] These figures do not include artisan workers but do include workers in the mining industry.

Mining

Although Morocco was relatively rich in mineral resources, at the end of the 19th century mining was practically unknown.

The Sultan had forbidden his subjects to engage in it, and his government had done nothing.[22] He had given several foreign companies permission to explore and exploit certain mineral deposits, which were known and exploited in Roman times, but they had done little. Only several salt mines and a copper mine were in operation in 1903.[23]

Subsequently, the mining industry of Morocco developed more slowly and in a context different from that of manufacturing. First of all, it was difficult to undertake thorough mineral exploration in an area which was not pacified, and once deposits were found, it was not wise to invest in equipment and attempt to mine the minerals unless the security of the area could be assured. We have seen that the pacification lasted until the mid-1930's, although large areas of the interior were secure by the mid-1920's. Consequently, the mining of phosphates did not begin until 1921, and the development of other mineral resources followed slowly.

Meanwhile, the Sultan's edict and then Moroccan law stated that mineral rights belong to the state rather than to the individual who owns the surface. This gave the government control over all mineral development. Also, in 1919, France passed a new law, representing a new concept, whereby the government was to assume operating as well as ownership responsibilities in such areas as mining, electricity, and transportation. This concept was partially borrowed by the French Resident General in Morocco in 1920, when he established the Governmental Phosphate Office and gave it a monopoly for the exploitation of all of Morocco's phosphate deposits. Thus the largest mining operation in the country (phosphates represent about half of the value of all mineral production) belonged, and continues to belong, to the government. It was an extremely successful venture. Production grew rapidly: 1921, 8,232 tons; 1924, 429,958 tons; 1926, 885,720 tons; 1929, 1,608,249 tons.[24] From an original investment of $7 million and a reinvestment of some of the profits, by 1930 this Office provided the government with an annual income of $6 million.[25] It also has always had a monopoly on the exportation of the phosphates.

In the mining of other minerals, the government took a somewhat similar step in 1928, establishing the Bureau de Recherches et de Participations Minières--(BRPM), a public corporation which participates with private enterprise in the exploration for and exploitation of mineral resources. It owns shares in many of the private mining companies, generally between 20 and 50 percent of the outstanding shares.

The private interests which were most important in the development of the mining industry were the Omnium Nord
Africain, the Groupe Walter, and the Cie. Royale Asturienne
des Mines (a Belgian company).[26] Most of the iron deposits
were in the Spanish zone and had Spanish investment. There
were also small mining investments by British and American
interests.

The Moroccan tendency toward mixed enterprises in the
mining sector has also been very evident in the fields of
electricity and transport. For example, the railroads were
developed primarily by a combination of the government and
the Banque de Paris et des Pays Bas. The government and
this same bank were, for example, the major owners of the
Compagnie des Chemins de Fer du Maroc (CFM). Morocco's
largest trucking company was having difficulties in the 1930's
and for some years was subsidized by the government. It
swallowed up most of its competition, but was then itself
swallowed by the CFM, making the government and the Banque
de Paris et des Pays Bas the major owners of transport.[27]

Foreign Trade

The development of the foreign trade of Morocco has
three aspects of interest to this study. The first is the
rapidity of its growth; the second is the constant deficit position; and the third is the predominance of France as a trading
partner.

At the beginning of the 20th century, Morocco's foreign
trade was at an extremely low level, imports and exports each
equalling about $1 million.[28] Nearly all of the people lived
outside the money economy; the artisanal trade produced goods
to satisfy the simple needs of most of the rest; no development
was taking place and thus capital goods were not needed for
investment purposes; only the needs of the court, of a few
wealthy families, and of the small European community had
to be satisfied. In addition, Morocco produced very little
which could be exported to pay for its imports. The trade
was in deficit, but by relatively small amounts, and these
deficits were financed by foreign loans to the Sultan. The need
for additional imports, as development began to take place
and as consumption by a growing European community grew,
is evidenced by a large increase of imports in 1913, to $7
million. Exports, however, increased to only $2 million in
1913, and this was the beginning of very large deficits in the

trade balance. By 1930, imports equalled $86 million, while
exports reached only $28 million. From 1900 to 1956, the
only year in which there was a surplus in the balance of trade
was in 1941, a year in which import sources had suddenly
dried up. Most of these deficits were covered by advances
from the French treasury.

As could be expected, the presence of the French in
Morocco and the covering of the trade deficit by the French
treasury resulted in a majority of Morocco's trade being with
France. As was noted earlier, a third of her trade was already with France at the turn of the century. This percentage
increased greatly, and by 1926, for example, France took 46
percent of Morocco's exports and provided 65 percent of her
imports. By 1953, these figures had changed relatively little,
to 47 percent and 56 percent, respectively.

SOCIAL DEVELOPMENT UNDER
THE PROTECTORATE

Population

A major factor determining the effect of the protectorate
on the economy and on the social development of Morocco
was the influx of Europeans. The immigration came very
quickly after the beginning of the protectorate. In the first
year (1912) 9,000 entered Morocco, and during 1914, 27,000
entered the country.[29] The number of Europeans grew from
81,000 in 1921 to 172,000 in 1931, to 363,000 in 1951. At
the same time, the number of Jews grew from 91,000 in 1921
to 125,000 in 1931, to 199,000 in 1951. The Moslem population nearly doubled during this period, from 4.2 million in
1921 to 7.4 million in 1951.[30]

The breakdown of the 172,000 European population in
1931 shows French, 128,000; Spanish, 22,000; Italians,
11,000; and other, 11,000. By 1951 the percentage of Frenchmen had increased so that out of a European population of
363,000, there were: French, 304,000; Spanish, 26,000;
Italian, 13,550; Portuguese, 5,200; British, 1,900; Swiss,
1,750; American, 1,060; Russian, 1,060; Greek, 1,040; and
Belgian, 940.[31] By this same year, 36 percent of the Europeans had been born in Morocco.

The occupation distribution of these Europeans, plus the
Jewish and Moslem communities, is of interest in showing the

effects of the colonization on the citizens of the country.
Appendix C, Table 4, shows this distribution for 1951. A
notable feature of this table is that even after 40 years of development under the protectorate, 70.8 percent of the Moslem
population remained engaged in agriculture. Still, this is a
considerable improvement over the 95 percent in agriculture
at the beginning of the protectorate.

The Jews received almost as much education as the
Europeans, and thus are found in occupational categories far
different from the Moslems. The almost total absence of the
Jews from agriculture and from the police is remarkable.
The large percentage in commerce results from their traditional pre-protectorate role in Moroccan society, while the
very large percentage under "Handicraft and Manufacturing"
would result primarily from the "Handicraft" and would,
again, reflect one of their traditional occupations.

There were 8,382 Europeans and 2,055,155 Moslems
engaged in agriculture. What was the land ownership pattern
and how did it develop?

Land Ownership

Since the mid-19th century, foreigners could own property
in Morocco (with the Sultan's permission), but until 1900 it
was essentially city real estate. A treaty in 1904, however,
permitted Europeans to acquire property within a radius of
10 kilometers from the port cities, without the permission
of the Sultan. This started the movement of Europeans into
agriculture.

By 1913, Europeans owned over 188,000 acres, all of
which had been bought privately. By 1935, they had a total
2.1 million acres divided into 3,822 farms. Of this total,
1.42 million had been purchased privately and 680,000 acquired
"officially" from the protectorate government. In 1953,
Europeans had approximately 2.5 million acres, of which
about one-fourth had been acquired as "official land" from
the government. [32]

Morocco has a total area of 100 million acres, so the
European portion does not, at first glance, seem to be terribly
out of proportion, considering that Europeans made up 4.5
percent of the population. However, only about 37 million
acres can be considered as agricultural land suitable for
farming or grazing; and only 6 percent of the Europeans live
on the land. In addition, the European-owned land is nearer

the coast and is of better quality. As a result of this and modern production methods, European farming accounted for approximately 25 percent of the gross value of all crops produced in the modern agricultural sector in 1956.[33]

The most pertinent aspect of the story, however, is the manner in which much of this land was obtained. At the beginning of the protectorate, only a small portion of the land was privately owned by individual Moroccans. The rest belonged either to the government, to tribes--as collective land, and therefore not for sale--or to habous, as religious land which could not be sold. After several years, the privately owned land was getting in short supply and the protectorate government began to sell land owned by the state to keep the price down and encourage immigration. But soon the better state-owned land was also running short, and steps had to be taken to make available some of the collectively owned land and some of the religious lands. Through a series of decrees, the protectorate government abrogated the customs and ancient laws so that some of these lands could be bought by the government at very low prices and sold to Europeans, while other of these lands were legally identified as belonging to private individuals, who could then sell them. Over a period of 40 years, it was thus possible for Europeans to acquire approximately 2.5 million acres of good land.

Education

Prior to the beginning of the protectorate, the government paid very little attention to education. There were a few Koranic schools, but the population was mostly illiterate. The arrival of the French in large numbers necessitated the establishment of a French school system: primary, secondary, and higher education. These schools admitted very few Moslems or Jews. A separate school system was set up for each of these groups. These separate systems, at the primary level, badly prepared the Moslems, so that very few of them could enter the French secondary schools. And if they could not finish a French secondary school, they had almost no hope of higher education.

The number of Moslems in government schools reached 3,728 in 1919 and grew slowly until the end of World War II: 1926, 6,451; 1931, 12,400; 1939, 25,000; 1944, 52,000. In 1944, there were about 1 million Moroccans of school age, but only 52,000 were in modern schools. (There were, in the

same year, about 100,000 in Koranic schools.)[34] The French
then realized their error and began allocating a larger budget
for education. By 1952, with 15 percent of the government
budget going to education, there were 160,000 Moslems in
school and by 1953, 230,000.

Although the numbers grew, very few of the Moroccan
girls were being educated. In 1926, for example, there were
only 1,041 Moslem girls in school. By 1931 this had increased
to 2,816, and the upward progression continued: 1945, 10,320;
1952, 33,372. Yet very few of these girls entered secondary
schools. In 1945, only 15 successfully completed primary
school, and in 1952 only 150 did so.[35]

The number of Moroccans who entered higher education
was even lower. In 1952, for example, only 509 Moroccans
signed up to take the baccalaureate examination (for completion of secondary education), compared with 2,381 French
children, even though the Moslems outnumbered the French
by 20 to 1. The following is a breakdown of young men and
women, in 1952, who were enrolled in higher education:
French, 755; Moslem, 233; Jewish, 67.[36]

MOVEMENT FOR INDEPENDENCE

How did the Moroccans react to the economic and social
development which occurred under the French? Why did the
Moroccans demand independence? Did they appreciate all that
was being done for them?

Although the consumption of electricity in Morocco grew
by leaps and bounds (tripling during the period 1925-30, and
tripling again between 1938 and 1953), Ayache estimates
that non-European Moroccans (95 percent of the population)
accounted for less than 12 percent of the electrical consumption in 1954, owned less than 20 percent of the cars and
trucks, and used about 20 percent of the railroad ton-miles.[37]
From 1914 to 1938, 75 percent of the government's expenditures went into conquering the Berber tribes and building the
economic infrastructure, while 20 percent went into administration and 5 percent into hygiene and education. Of this 5
percent, the Moroccans received the benefit of about one-fifth.

Another factor involved in the independence movement
was that the French protectorate government kept Morocco
in a state of siege (martial law) until 1939. This was considered necessary until 1934 to support the efforts to pacify the
interior tribes, but was continued after that because of custom.

Lorna Hahn traces the beginning of the nationalistic movement back to 1930, when the French, attempting to use the old system of "divide and rule, " passed the Berber Decree. [38] This made the Berbers subject to French law rather than to Islamic law. The French, however, found that Islam was deeply accepted by the Berbers, and so this decree was interpreted as an attack on the Islamic religion, a point around which all Moroccans could rally.

A Comité d'Action Marocain (CAM) was organized in 1934 and published a 134-page document containing specific demands. They did not ask for independence--only for modification of the protectorate into a sort of mandate. The two major leaders of the CAM were el-Ouazzani and al-Fassi, who were later leaders of the Istiqlal party.

The Istiqlal (Independence) party was formed in 1943, with al-Fassi as head. Its first move, in 1944, was to present a manifesto announcing that its goal was the independence of Morocco. Its leaders were soon arrested. The formation of a Moroccan Communist party in 1944 provided the French with an excuse to taint other nationalist movements.

But the Istiqlal continued to grow and, of even greater importance, it gained the favor of the Sultan, who began to refuse to cooperate with the French. In 1951, the French Resident General, General Juin, threatened the Sultan, Mohammed V: "Sign these decrees or be deposed. " He signed them, but let it be known that it was under duress and that he did not consider them to be legal.

In 1953, a petition was circulated by anti-Istiqlal Moroccans, at the instigation of the French, asking that the Sultan be deposed. Signatures were obtained from some important Moroccan leaders and the Sultan was exiled, to be replaced by weak-minded, 76-year-old Moulay ben Arafa, a man willing to sign anything the French placed before him. However, the conditions under which Mohammed V was deposed became widely known, and his popularity quickly increased. His exile became a rallying point for the nationalist movement.

Meanwhile, Spain, anxious to undermine France's position in Morocco and hoping to oust the French while maintaining their own position, granted amnesty to a number of Moroccan nationalists whom they had imprisoned and appointed some Morrocans to ministerial posts (Justice and Education-Culture). Such action gave impetus to the nationalist movement in the French zone and terrorist activities became more frequent. In addition, the Berber tribesmen rose up against the French. By the summer of 1955, the French were willing to look for

a way out. The 250,000 French army troops in Morocco
could not pacify the country, but they could greatly help in
the effort to save Algeria. The French brought Mohammed
V back as Sultan and negotiations were undertaken for Moroccan "independence within interdependence with France."
France, recognizing the relative moderation of the Sultan and
realizing that he would be a better friend of France than such
radicals as the Istiqlal party, quickly agreed to the terms
requested by the Sultan. Morocco received its independence
from the French on March 2, 1956. By April 6, the Spanish
had done likewise for their zone.

ECONOMIC AND SOCIAL DEVELOPMENT
SINCE INDEPENDENCE

Integration of the Three Zones

At the time of independence, Morocco was still split into
three parts, with Tangier maintaining fairly complete autonomy
and with the Spanish zone operating separately; there were no
administrative liaisons and no connecting economic infrastructure. Also, Tangier was an international city with a
free money market, no tariffs, and no internal taxes. Soon
after independence, the Sultan weighed the political advantages
of completely integrating Tangier into the Moroccan economy
versus retaining its economic advantages as a free zone.
The latter policy prevailed, and the city was given a royal
charter in August, 1957, confirming its status as a free money
market and free trade area and providing for tax schedules
much lower than those in the rest of the country. It did,
however, put the city under royal control, and the new tax
schedules scared away many financial interests. Nationalistic
pressures from the Union Marocaine des Travailleurs (UMT)
and the Istiqlal for the "Moroccanization" of Tangier continued
to be felt, and in the fall of 1959 the king announced the complete integration of Tangier into the Moroccan economy. This
caused a deep slump in the economy of the city and the surrounding area.

Although political unity of the former French and Spanish
zones had been achieved by April, 1956, economic unity of
the two areas was more difficult. The Spanish peseta continued in use in the north, and a separate budget was needed
until 1958. There was also a lack of communication and

transportation between the two areas. The industries established in the north could not compete with those in the
south once the border had been removed. As a result, a
large portion of the Moroccan national budget had to be devoted to these problems in the late 1950's.

French Investment and Emigration

In 1955, the French owned about 48 percent of the productive resources of the Moroccan economy. More specifi-
cally, they owned 22 percent of total investment in agriculture,
80 percent of investments in commerce, industry, and mines,
and 40 percent of the investment in the construction industry.[39]
In the area of consumption, the French represented only 4
percent of the population, but their annual per capita income
was about $850, compared with about $150 for the Moroccans,
a ratio of about six to one. In addition, considering the
manner in which consumption varies with income, most of
the Moroccans' income was consumed in food, so that the
average Frenchman consumed far more than six times as
much in manufactured goods as the average Moroccan.
    Independence naturally affected the outlook of the French
community upon their future in the country, but not nearly to
the extent that it did in Tunisia and later in Algeria. Various
attempts have been made to assess the outflow of capital,
and while no accurate figures are available, it appears that
flight capital amounted to approximately $60 million in 1955
and $285 million in 1956.[40] On the other hand, much of this
was liquid funds or the proceeds of businesses and properties
sold by French residents who returned to France. However,
the exodus of Frenchmen was relatively small, roughly
100,000 between 1955 and 1958. (The European population of
Morocco decreased in the following pattern following independence: 1956, 555,000; 1957, 500,000; 1958, 455,000;
1959, 420,000; 1960, 396,000; 1962, 335,000; 1965, 190,000.
By 1967, the number of Frenchmen had decreased to about
97,600 and the number of Italians to about 12,000. The Jewish
population followed a somewhat different pattern: 1956,
170,000; 1957, 150,000; 1958, 155,000; 1960, 162,000; 1962,
155,000; 1965, 100,000.) Although this represents a decrease
of about 20 percent, there was not a rush out of the country
and an abandonment of property, as happened later in Algeria.
Most of the businesses sold were quite small and mostly in
the retail and service areas. The King made every effort to

impress the French community that they were needed and wanted, and should stay in Morocco. There was far less animosity between the French and Moslem communities in Morocco than in Algeria. There was also more appreciation of the work which the French had done to organize and modernize the country.

Consequently, much of the French capital which left during the several years following independence was risk capital which was not wedded to the long-term future of Morocco, even though its departure did have immediate consequences. To the extent that it greatly decreased bank balances, it reduced, in particular, the amount of new construction. The departure of a portion of the purchasing power also reduced plans to expand production. But French investment in basic industries, mining, petroleum, agriculture, manufacturing, and processing industries was not greatly disturbed.

As a result, the French have retained a predominant position in Moroccan industry. A survey was taken by the French Embassy in Morocco in 1963, to determine the position of French industry. [41] It included all industrial firms which were owned or controlled (more than 50 percent ownership) by Frenchmen or French companies, and which employed more than 10 people or used more than 10 horsepower of machinery. These firms numbered 445, employed 57,654 workers (of whom 88 percent were Moroccans), and had annual sales of $330 million. This annual sales figure represented 57 percent of the total for Moroccan industry. It is somewhat surprising to find that non-French companies had 43 percent of industrial production, but this figure is somewhat distorted by the mining industry, which is about 10 percent of the total and in which non-French (mostly Moroccan government) interests represent up to 66 percent of the total. For the rest, one finds, for example, that French companies are responsible for 100 percent of the production of agricultural equipment, pharmaceutical products, paints, soap, and fertilizer; 98 percent of the leather tanning; 95 percent of the sheet metal firms; and 86 percent of the construction materials, glass products, and foundries. The only areas (other than mines) where French production was less than 50 percent were clothing and wood products.

Foreign Trade

In 1956, Morocco's foreign trade was fairly closely tied to France, though not so closely as was the case for Tunisia

and Algeria. The Act of Algeciras had prevented France
from eliminating Moroccan import duties vis-à-vis France's
products, but France did, unilaterally, eliminate her own
import duties on certain Moroccan products, such as citrus
fruits, wine, cereals, canned vegetables, and canned fish.
This, plus the fact that most of the importers and retailers
as well as a large proportion of the effective consumers or
purchasers of equipment were French, resulted in a majority
of Morocco's foreign trade being with France. At the time
of independence, France bought 53 percent of Morocco's exports and furnished 49 percent of her imports. This proportion has not changed greatly since then. In 1960, France had
40 percent of Morocco's exports and 49 percent of her imports; by 1965 the trade balance had shifted so that France
had 42 percent of Morocco's exports and provided 39 percent
of her imports.

Among the rest of the countries, West Germany has been
the next biggest importer of Moroccan products, purchasing
an average of 8-10 percent of Morocco's exports between 1958
and 1966, whereas the United States received between 1 percent and 3 percent of Morocco's exports during the same
period. On the other hand, the United States is the second
most important supplier of Morocco's imports, furnishing
between 7 percent and 13 percent of her imports each year
between 1958 and 1966. This is due almost entirely to U.S.
foreign aid.

The role of the East European countries as a group has
grown in importance in Morocco's foreign trade. In 1957,
the value of Moroccan imports from these countries was only
$3.6 million; this increased to $28.8 million in 1964, growing
from 1.2 percent of total imports to 6.2 percent. Meanwhile,
Moroccan exports to these countries increased from $4.6
million in 1957 to $29.4 million in 1964, or from 1.9 percent
of total exports to 6.7 percent. [42] These increases have been
fairly constant over the period in question, with Poland and
Czechoslovakia being the most important in the early years
but being surpassed by Russia since 1960.

Monetary System

At the time of independence, the central bank of Morocco
was an internationally owned institution controlled by private
French banks (essentially by the Banque de Paris et des Pays

Bas). The Moroccan franc was defined in terms of the French franc. Since Morocco remained a member of the French franc zone after independence and maintained the terms of free transfer between member countries, the pre-independence situation continued; the French treasury kept an operating account for Morocco's Banque d'État and there was no limit to the credit which the French treasury could grant to the Moroccan institution. Meanwhile, of course, the Moroccan Banque d'État had to deposit all of its foreign exchange earnings with the French treasury.

On December 28, 1958, France devalued its currency by 17.5 percent without consulting Morocco, which heard the news at the last minute. A decision was made not to follow the devaluation but, rather, to levy a tax of 10 percent on all transfers to the French franc area. But transfers were still not controlled, and between January and July, 1959, more than $100 million in Moroccan francs left the country.

In July, 1959, Morocco obtained the agreement of the foreign countries who owned shares in the Banque d'État for Morocco to set up its own central bank, the Banque du Maroc. By the end of that month, the Banque du Maroc instituted exchange controls on transfers to other countries in the French franc zone (including France), thus cutting off the flow of flight capital. And in October, 1959, the new Moroccan currency, the dirham, was introduced and the money devalued to about the equivalent of the French franc (10 French francs = 10.25 Moroccan dirhams = U.S. $2.00).

Deficits in Morocco's balance of payments had always been covered by overdraft facilities with the French treasury. This was stopped in July, 1959, with the establishment of the Banque du Maroc. At that time Morocco's gold and foreign exchange reserves were not adequate, but through trade and foreign aid, they grew to the comfortable level (equivalent to six months of imports of goods and services) of $257 million by the end of 1960.

Each year since then, however, there has been a drain on these reserves, which, by October, 1964, were down to $28 million, representing only three weeks of imports. Austerity measures and import restrictions which have since been applied have resulted in some improvement in this situation, so that by June, 1968, net reserves were up to $60 million, representing six weeks of imports. Crop failures and a relaxation of import restrictions have resulted in subsequent decreases of the reserve level.

Banking System

(Information on the development of the banking system
since independence was obtained from officials of the Banque
du Maroc.)

In 1956 there were 22 different banks operating in the
French zone of Morocco. Some of them, such as the Compagnie Algérienne de Crédit et de Banque, had as many as 50
offices scattered around the country. None of these banks
were incorporated in Morocco. They were branches of French
banks. In the Spanish zone there were seven banks, all of
them branches of Spanish banks.

Within several months after independence, the Banque
Marocaine pour l'Expansion Économique was created in the
former French zone as a subsidiary of one of the Spanish
banks in the Spanish zone. In 1957 the various banks in the
Spanish zone merged into two banks, the Banca Imobiliano y
Mercantil de Marruecos and the Unión Bancaria Hispano
Maroque. They became a part of the Moroccan system, but
as branches of the Spanish parents. In 1958 the government
established the Banque Marocaine pour le Commerce Extérieur
(BMCE). This was the first bank in Morocco where a majority
of the capital was Moroccan, but the capital had to be provided by the government. There was also an appreciable
amount of foreign capital. The BMCE absorbed the branch
of the Banca Commerciale Italiana, which had been in Morocco
before independence and had been a branch of the French subsidiary of the Italian parent bank. In addition, the Bank of
America and a German bank invested in the capital of the BMCE.

In 1959 a Spanish bank, the Banco Salvador Hassan y
Hijos, and a Dutch bank, the Société Hollandaise de Banque et
de Gestion, both of which had been operating in Tangier, were
given permission to operate as Moroccan banks, since Tangier
was then being integrated into Morocco. The following year
saw the opening of a branch of the Arab Bank (whose head
office is in Jordan) and the purchase, by the British Bank of
the Middle East, of a bank which had been in Morocco prior
to independence. In 1966 the Continental Bank of Illinois
bought a 33 percent interest in the Banque Franco-Suisse,
changing its name to the Banque Americano-Franco-Suisse du
Maroc. In 1967 the First National City Bank established a
subsidiary bank in Casablanca.

Meanwhile, several of the smaller banks closed, and beginning in 1960, the government asked the banks to plan to

change their legal status from that of a branch to that of a
subsidiary incorporated in Morocco. This Moroccanization
of the branches took place gradually, and by 1967, only two
banks, the Arab Bank and the Banque de Paris et des Pays
Bas, remained as branches of foreign parent banks. At the
same time that Moroccanization was taking place, a number
of mergers occurred, so that by 1967, only 17 banks remained.

Thus, the 11 years following independence saw some
important changes. Whereas in 1956, all banks were branches
of French and Spanish (and one Dutch) banks, by 1967 all banks
except two were incorporated in Morocco. Also 15 other non-
French foreign banks (four American, four German, one
British, three Italian, one Belgian, one Jordanian, and the
International Finance Corporation) had investments in Morocco.

The desire of the Moroccan government to have more
Moroccan capital in the banking system has not, however, met
with success. The only bank to have the majority of its capital owned by Moroccans is the BMCE, and in that case the
Moroccan ownership is in the hands of the government. There
is very little private Moroccan capital in any of the banks.

Two other banking organisms are not included in the
above discussion. One is the Banque Nationale pour le Développement Économique (BNDE), which was created in 1959.
It offers only medium- and long-term credit and also invests
directly in companies. As such, it is a development bank
rather than a commercial bank. Its shareholders include a
large number of foreign banks, among them the Morgan
Guaranty Bank of New York. Its organization and operation
are discussed in Chapter 13.

The other organism is the system of banques populaires.
Each of these banks is organized as a cooperative with a
variable capital owned by private individuals and companies;
their purpose is to make small loans to small and medium-
sized businesses. There are seven such banques populaires
and they have combined, at the request of the government, to
organize the Banque Centrale Populaire, which capital also
includes a contribution from the government. Its purpose is
to regulate the activities of the individual banques populaires
and to provide a financial cushion for the system.

Planning

After independence the planning function, which had been
a part of the office of the General Secretary of the government,

was made a separate division under the Minister of Economics
and Finance. This division had a staff of 60, of whom about
15 were top-level technicians. They were mostly Frenchmen; there were only two Moroccans, one Algerian, and
several U.N. advisers. [43]

In June, 1957, a decree indicated that a two-year plan,
for 1958-59, would be put into effect and that a five-year plan
(1960-64) would be promulgated by October, 1959.

The objectives of the two-year plan were (1) to increase
agricultural productivity; (2) to educate and train more Moroccans; and (3) to stimulate industrial investment and production.
As a plan it had specific goals, but it was essentially a public
investment budget. It fell far short of its goals, primarily
because the departure of many French technicians delayed
the implementation of projects and funds allocated were not
spent. Also, capital flight reduced credit and the general
possibilities of economic expansion. Investment equaled only
14 percent of GNP in 1958 and only 10 percent in 1959, most
of this being in the public sector, since new investment in the
private sector barely equaled disinvestments. [44]

Although the two-year plan fell short of its objectives, a
number of institutions were created which were important to
the future industrialization of the country. These included
the Bureau d'Études et de Participations Industrielles (BEPI),
the BNDE, and the Banque du Maroc, the country's central
bank. (More will be said of these organizations later.) In
addition, the first law to stimulate private investment was
passed in 1958. (This will be discussed in Chapter 13.)

The five-year plan (1960-64) was to have been promulgated by October, 1959, but its preparation was delayed. It
still had not been issued in May, 1960, when the King took
over as Premier of the government and changed the ministers.
As a result, much of the previous work was discarded or
changed by the time the plan finally appeared, in November,
1960. This plan was not complete and not very workable, so
a revised plan was issued in February, 1962, this plan being
concerned primarily with industrial expansion and specific
investments in industry.

For all practical purposes, the five-year plan (1960-64)
was abandoned by 1963. Although public investments took
place somewhat along the lines forecast by the plan, their
impact on the economy was less than expected.

The three-year plan (1965-67) was put into effect early
in 1965 and, in its first chapter, blamed the private sector,
which had not invested as much as forecast by the five-year

plan, for a major share of the failure of that plan. The
priorities of the three-year plan, according to the King's discussion, were agriculture, tourism, and education. However, the plan presented a detailed elaboration of the investments to be made in industry and projected a significant
investment in that sector. Appendix C, Table 5 shows the
projected investments for the three-year period.

Although the plan did not purport to emphasize industrialization, 38 percent of the expected investment was in that
sector--more, in fact, than in the three priority sectors combined. Also, although the plan stated that the private sector
was to play a major role in industrial investment, only 34 percent of the projected investment in industry was allocated to
the private sector. This percentage is distorted, however,
by the inclusion of mining in the industry sector, because 57
percent of the public and semi-public investment in industry
was in the mining sector. If one discounts this sector (which
also projected $12 million in private investment), for the rest
of industry the plan anticipated that the private sector would
contribute 44.5 percent of the investment. The public investment, however, was concentrated in several major projects:
a sugar refinery, a chemical complex, and a steel mill.

The three-year plan was not really a plan as such; it was
more of an investment program. It merely projected the investments which the government planned to make and which it
hoped the private sector would make during the three-year
period. It did not consider the effect which such investments
would have on the economy, nor on the public finances, foreign
trade, etc. The result was that, according to statistics published by the Moroccan government, only 60-70 percent of the
three-year plan's objectives for industrial investment were
achieved.[45]

Meanwhile, another five-year plan (1968-72) has been developed and made operational. It is a more "complete" plan
than the preceding ones. One of its primary goals is to increase the rate of industrialization to 6 percent per year (in
contrast with the 2-3 percent which had been the pattern in
the preceding several years).

This plan calls for total industrial investment of $2.71
billion during the five-year period. The government plans to
invest about $28 million directly in wholly government-owned
factories (sugar refineries and metal foundries). In addition,
the government plans to enter into joint ventures with the
private sector for the establishment of a textile company and
another sugar refinery and to invest $32 million in these projects.

The remainder of the industrial investment is to be left to the private sector.

Government Budget

At the time of independence, Morocco was in the middle of the second modernization and investment plan (1954-57), which was being administered by the French. In 1954, the government's operating budget was approximately $200 million. Following independence, this increased appreciably, reaching $255 million in 1959 and $400 million in 1964.

The investment budget expenditures, however, were much higher during the French administration than they have been since. The average investment expenditures during the period 1954-57 were $160 million per year, whereas the government investment expenditures in 1959 equaled $72 million and increased to $137 million by 1964.

The breakdown of investment expenditures, by sector, has not exhibited any startling changes. This breakdown, for several key sectors, is shown in Appendix C, Table 6. The only important shift in emphasis has been a new and very important increase in public investment in manufacturing industry.

Education

During the last years of the protectorate, the number of Moroccans being educated was increasing very rapidly. Out of the 1 million children of school age in 1944, only 52,000 were in schools, but this number had increased to 230,000 by 1953 and 317,000 by 1956. In that period, between 15 percent and 20 percent were girls.

The independent Moroccan government did not increase the rate of investment in education; in fact, the amount invested has, since 1956, stayed below the average annual investment in education during the period 1954-57. The number of children in school has, however, continued to increase significantly.

In 1958, 631,000 Moroccan children were in primary school and 34,000 in secondary, whereas by 1967 almost 1.09 million were in primary school (of whom 30 percent were girls) and 240,000 in secondary schools (of whom 23 percent were girls). By 1967 also, nearly 10,000 Moroccans were

receiving higher education. Of these, slightly over 1,000
were studying outside Morocco.

The major difficulties are not only a shortage of schools,
but more important, a shortage of qualified teachers. Consequently, classes are very large and the quality of the education has declined. In 1965, the French were still supplying
2,796 teachers (9 percent of the total) for the primary schools,
5,158 teachers (60 percent of the total) for secondary schools,
and 279 professors (60 percent of the total) for Morocco's
universities and colleges.

Efforts are being made to increase the use of Arabic in
the modern schools. Complete Arabization and the elimination of French teachers in primary schools were achieved in
1967. French is now being taught as a foreign language. In
secondary schools Arabic is now used for nearly all courses
except for scientific studies.[46]

Foreign Aid

Prior to independence and until 1959, when Morocco imposed exchange controls on transfers to France, the means
by which French foreign aid fed foreign exchange into Morocco
were (1) maintenance of military bases in Morocco; (2)
technical assistance--payments of salaries of professors,
teachers, and other types of technical assistance; (3) loans to
the government for equipment and investment projects; and
(4) loans from the French treasury for Morocco's operating
budget. These reached a peak annual total of $300 million
in 1956.[47]

The construction and operation of U.S. military bases in
Morocco in the mid-1950's were also a source of foreign exchange, reaching a peak of about $28 million in 1956. In
addition, U.S. foreign aid, as such, began to flow into Morocco
in 1957, amounting to $20 million that year, $29.5 million in
1958, and averaging $40 million per year from 1959 to 1964.
Some of the U.S. aid was for budgetary support and some for
project financing; over half came in as food, in support of the
public works program. In 1965, however, the U.S. government announced an end to budgetary support assistance; all
future aid was to be in the form of food or project financing.

French financial assistance to Morocco, particularly in
the field of budgetary support, has varied with political relations. In general, however, France has been quite constant
in providing teachers and other technical assistance, and

fairly constant in project assistance. In 1964, for example, France agreed to provide $78 million, much of which was for budgetary support, and a slightly lower amount in 1965. But in 1966 she stopped budgetary support because of the Ben Barka affair.

Until 1962, France and the United States were the only countries providing foreign aid to Morocco. That year, however, Poland offered $12 million in long-term trade credits and agreed to $18 million more in 1965. (Only about $1 million of this Polish aid has actually been utilized by Morocco.)[48]

The World Bank became a regular contributor to Morocco in 1964, with a loan of $3 million, and increased the level to $7.7 million in 1965. Probably as a result of the World Bank's entry into the field, other donors showed up in 1965: Germany provided $10.5 million that year; Kuwait, $16.9 million; and Saudi Arabia, $3 million.

In 1966, which saw a reduction in aid from France and the United States (the former sustaining donors), Germany greatly increased her aid to $25 million, and Kuwait signed an agreement for an additional $28 million.

In 1965, the Soviet Union began discussions with the Moroccan government and concluded an agreement late in 1966 to provide $42 million in aid, of which $10 million was as long-term trade credits and the remainder as project financing, primarily in the field of irrigation.

Rate of Investment

Gross investment in the Moroccan economy had reached its peak in 1952. Immigration into Morocco was continuing; the Korean War caused an increased demand for goods and services; and both the French and U.S. governments were building military bases in Morocco. The French four-year plans were providing a basic flow and a framework for other investments. There was general optimism and gross investment reached 20 percent of GNP. But 1953 began the long slide down. It saw the end of the Korean War and the outbreak of revolution in Algeria; investment decreased to only 17.5 percent of the GNP.[49] This decline continued through independence and reached a low point in 1957, when it equaled 9 percent of GNP.

Consequently, an investment code was promulgated on September 13, 1958, and an investment commission was created simultaneously to administer the incentives offered

by the code. In 1959, the commission approved private industrial projects whose investment totaled $9 million. In
1960, 1961, and 1962, approved projects averaged $20 million
per year.[50] By 1963 this increased to $24 million and in 1964
to $30 million.[51] In 1965, it decreased to $22 million but
went up to $36 million in 1966.[52] Of course, not all of the
projects which were submitted and approved were finally implemented. As a result, and because of lower rates of public
investment, gross investment in the years since 1957 has remained at 9-12 percent of GNP.

Foreign investment has been coming to Morocco at an
uneven rate since independence. Most of it appeared in the
period 1958-60, as joint ventures with BEPI in relatively
large projects. The rate slowed during the early 1960's but
is again increasing, primarily in the tourist industry. In
fact, in 1967, private foreign investment doubled over the
1966 rate. Appendix C, Table 7, is a compilation of the
specific foreign investments which have been made since independence.

Industrial Production

During the 10 years following independence, industrial
production has increased a total of 30 percent. This growth,
by sector, is shown in Appendix C, Table 8. The great
growth industry has been textiles, increasing by 85 percent
between 1959 and 1965. But the brightest spot in the picture,
because of its much greater contribution to the economy, is
phosphate production. In 1964, phosphate exports reached
10 million tons, an increase of 100 percent over 1955, the
last year of the protectorate. The production of all other
minerals, however, has decreased, in some cases considerably.

Because of the low rate of investment, and because of the
very small increase in industrial production (an average of 3
percent per year), the World Bank, in its 1966 study, The
Economic Development of Morocco, recommended a continuation of the policy which the government has been following:
encouraging a mixed industrial economy with a healthy private
sector supported by direct public investment in industry itself.
The Bank recommended, in fact, that the government itself
plan to make direct investments totaling $86 million in the
following types of industries during the six-year period 1965-70:

a.   Large-scale enterprises beyond the capability of
domestic private investors and in which the national interests
preclude a predominantly foreign participation.

    b.   Pioneer enterprises in which government support can
help establish further investment opportunities.
    c.   Joint enterprises with private investors otherwise
unable to supply sufficient capital.[53]

Agricultural Production

    Since approximately 70 percent of the population is still
engaged in agriculture, the development of the agricultural
sector is vital to the economy of Morocco. Because of the
traditional methods employed by most of the peasants,
productivity is very low and agriculture contributes less than
one-third of the GNP. Consequently, a high proportion of the
peasants live in a subsistence economy and very close to the
subsistence level. The traditional agricultural sector encompasses 65-70 percent of the rural population and 60 percent of the cultivated land. Consequently, the development of
the Moroccan economy depends upon the development of the
agricultural sector, including land reforms.
    Unfortunately, all too little has been done to effect change,
and the lack of progress in agriculture has tended to drag
down the rest of the economy. The value of agricultural production during the period 1951-55 averaged $510 million.[54]
The 1965 agricultural production was about equivalent to that
of 1964--an average year. But 1966 and 1967 were drought
years, resulting in crop failures. In 1966, wheat production
was down by 36 percent, corn by 45 percent, and barley by
57 percent. This alone represented a loss of $65 million and
a drop of 4 percent in the GNP. The 1967 crop was slightly
better than 1966. However, good climatic conditions in 1968,
plus the introduction of more fertilizer and new high-yield
seeds, resulted in yields of cereals of about 44 percent greater
than in the preceding year. Still, the long-range trend has
been for agricultural production to increase an average of
0.4 percent per year over the past 15 years.

GNP, Unemployment, and the Standard of Living

    Given the above trends in industrial and agricultural pro-
duction, it is evident that little progress has been made in
GNP. The 1951-55 average for GNP was $1.65 billion. This
decreased to $1.60 billion in 1957 and rose to $2.66 billion
(in current dollars) in 1967. The average real growth of GNP

for the past 15 years has been 2.2 percent per year, and the
rate during the 10 years following independence has been
about 2.3 percent per year. [55]

Considering that industrial production has been growing
at an average of 3 percent per year, agricultural production
at 0.4 percent per year, and GNP at 2.3 percent per year,
it is not surprising to find that, with population growing at a
rate of 3-3.5 percent per year, the standard of living is decreasing. The gross national income in 1965 was $2.35
billion for a population of 14 million, representing an average
annual per capita income of $168. This is, however, a de-
ceptive figure, for a large portion of the national income is in
the hands, first, of the European population and a small number of wealthy Moroccans and, second, of the urban population,
leaving two-thirds of the population living at a subsistence
level of $50-$70 per year.

According to figures cited by the Deputy Minister of
Agriculture, only 33 percent of the peasants own land, and 98
percent of these own less than 2.5 acres. [56] Rural unemployment is 50 percent and illiteracy rate is 93 percent. Also,
there are 350,000 births each year, and usable land is decreasing due to erosion.

In 1966, urban unemployment was estimated at 700,000--
about 40 percent of the active urban population. [57] At the same
time, a total of 150,000 new workers arrive on the labor market each year. Even if the optimistic hopes of the industrialization plans are realized, it will be difficult to create more
than 50,000 new jobs per year in the cities. Thus, 100,000
new jobs will have to be found each year in the rural areas.

One major effort of the government to alleviate the unemployment situation has been its program of promotion
nationale. It was started in 1961 to carry out public works
projects, primarily in the rural areas, using labor-intensive
methods for such projects as reforestation, land terracing,
small dams, and small irrigation schemes. At its peak,
however, it provided jobs for only about 60,000 workers,
paying them $0.40 per day in cash (supplied by the government)
and an equivalent value in cereal grain (usually wheat) supplied
by the United States under its surplus food program.

No solution to the unemployment problem is in sight.

POLITICAL DEVELOPMENTS
SINCE INDEPENDENCE

Political developments in Morocco since independence are interesting because of their diversity and peculiarities and because, more recently, they have been more apparent than real.

When independence arrived, there were three political parties in existence: the Istiqlal, the Democrats, and the Liberal Independents. The last two did not have nearly as much popular backing as the Istiqlal. Still, in the first Council of Government the Sultan gave the Democrats a number of important ministries and gave several to the Liberal Independents. The Istiqlal strongly objected to this and, by the time the King formed the third government (May, 1958), the Istiqlal was given all ministries except for a few independent (non-party) appointments.

Meanwhile, in August, 1957, the Sultan began calling himself "King," to indicate his desire for modernity and progress. He announced his plan to call a constitutional assembly to define his role as a constitutional monarch. Since there had never been elections in Morocco, there was no electoral machinery for the constitutional assembly. The 600 representatives were to be appointed by the King, from a wide variety of groups.

The Liberal Independent party began with a small group of intellectuals, under the leadership of Reda Guedira, who had worked for the King during the protectorate. They had found neither the Istiqlal nor the Democratic party compatible and formed a small intellectual elite after the war. Their close association with the palace and their freedom of action during the last years of the protectorate made it possible for them to play an important role in the negotiations for independence. The Liberal Independents continued to exist as a party until 1963 (when Guedira disbanded it to form a new party), but it is unlikely that it ever had more than 50,000 members. [58]

The Democratic party, or Parti Démocratique de l'Indépendance (PDI), was formed in 1946 under the leadership of Mohammed al-Ouazzani, one of the outstanding nationalists under the protectorate. It was a splinter party from the Istiqlal. Its approach to obtaining independence was more moderate than the Istiqlal's, and thus it escaped the

suppression of the nationalist movement in 1952. It gained
considerably more support in the Spanish zone than did the
Istiqlal, but it is still doubtful that the PDI ever had more
than 150,000 members (one-tenth the strength of the Istiqlal
at its peak).[59] The Democratic party's strength gradually
withered away after 1958, and it ceased to exist after 1961.

The strength of the Istiqlal lay in its backing by the UMT,
which within a year after independence claimed 600,000 members. The UMT, as such, did not come into existence until
1955, since union activities by Moroccan workers had been
illegal for a number of years.

A brief view of the history of the Moroccan labor movement shows that the first labor union organized in Morocco
was the Confédération Générale de Travail (CGT), a
communist-dominated French labor union formed in 1943.
It was solely for European workers but soon afterward established an affiliate, the Union Générale des Syndicats Confédérés
Marocaine (UGSCM) to organize Moroccan workers. By 1948
the UGSCM had 100,000 members and continued to grow. In
1952, however, it went on a general strike and was declared
illegal by the protectorate government.

The formation of the UMT in 1955 naturally absorbed the
remnants of the UGSCM. The leaders of the latter who had
been communists were excluded from the leadership of the
UMT, so the UMT appears to be relatively free from the
possibility of becoming communist-dominated.

Thus, the strength of the Istiqlal rested upon its reputation of having led the struggle for independence and upon the
membership of the UMT, whose members and leaders had
cooperated with the Istiqlal in the pre-independence struggle.
In addition, however, this Istiqlal gathered many of the conservative elements of the population, including the Arab and
religious traditionalists, the middle-class merchants, and
some of the wealthy class.

Another organization which was originally tied to the
Istiqlal party was the Union Marocaine de Commerce, Industrie
et Artisanat (UMCIA). Since the Chambers of Commerce,
prior to independence, essentially represented the French
business community, the UMCIA was formed, one month after
independence, to give the Moroccan business community a
voice. Its leaders had, prior to independence, given substantial donations to the Istiqlal to help finance the struggle
for independence. This, plus the fact that the membership
of the UMCIA soon grew to 120,000, meant that it was not
without influence.[60] It was represented on the various

economic commissions of the government and had a voice in
the drafting of the initial two-year plan and the following five-
year plan. Within several years, however, the leaders of
UMCIA decided that its best interests lay in not being too
closely identified with any given party, so all formal connection with the Istiqlal was discontinued. By 1962, the organization itself was disbanded, the members by this time feeling
that they could adequately present their views via their local
Chambers of Commerce, which by then were dominated by
the Moroccan rather than the French business community.

A new party, the Mouvement Populaire (MP), made its
appearance in 1957 under the leadership of Mahjoub Ahardine,
Governor of the province of Rabat. Its strength was based on
the Berber tribes in the Middle Atlas and on the former Berber tribesmen in the Rif who had made up the resistance
army which fought for independence. It was immediately declared illegal by the Istiqlal but continued to function clandes-
tinely until it was finally recognized as a new political party
in February, 1959.

Meanwhile, in December, 1958, the Istiqlal split into
right-wing and left-wing elements and the King asked a leader
of the left wing, Abdallah Ibrahim, to take over as Prime
Minister. Some of the former right-wing Istiqlal ministers
quit and were replaced by left-wing ministers. This left-
wing Istiqlal group was in power in 1959 when additional
dissension caused another split. Many of the far-left elements
formed the Union Nationale des Forces Populaires (UNFP) in
July, 1959, under the leadership of Ben Barka, with the support of the far-left wing of the UMT. The Istiqlal leaders
were disturbed; there were attacks on individual members of
the Istiqlal and of the UNFP, followed by street rioting between these two parties' supporters. The King refused to
send troops to keep order, fearing that action would favor
one side or the other, and he wished to remain above the
parties. The situation was slowly drifting toward chaos until
May, 1960, when the King decided to abandon his above-
politics position and lead the government himself. He dismissed the Prime Minister; made his son, Prince Hassan II,
the Deputy Prime Minister; and selected the various ministers
to suit his own tastes, without regard to their party affili-
ations (if any). All of the parties except the UNFP, which
wanted a more democratic rather than a more monarchic
regime, accepted this approach.

King Mohammed V died quite suddenly, following minor
surgery, in February, 1961, and was immediately replaced

by his son, Hassan II. King Hassan II mixed even more
intimately in politics than his father had during his last year.
He hurried the preparation of the constitution, which was
promulgated in December, 1962. He then called for Parliamentary elections in the spring of 1963.

At the beginning of 1963, Reda Guedira formed the Front
pour la Défense des Institutions Constitutionnelles (FDIC), a
coalition of the MP, the Parti Démocratique Constitutionnel
(PDC), the Liberal Independents (Guedira's own party), and
some independents. Many observers feel that this was done
at the request of the King and that the FDIC was to support
the monarchy, serving a purpose similar to that of the
Gaullist party in France.

Unfortunately, in the parliamentary elections of May,
1963, the FDIC failed to get a majority of the seats. Out of
144 seats, the FDIC got 69, Istiqlal received 41, UNFP 28,
and Independents six. In addition, seven out of 11 ministers
of the King's government, who were members of the FDIC,
failed to be elected to the Parliament. The King remained
as Prime Minister for six months after the elections.

Just prior to the elections, in April, 1963, al-Fassi, the
leader of the Istiqlal, gave a speech in which he blasted the
King for not pressing Morocco's claim to Mauritania. In
July, 1963, the Istiqlal newspaper called for nationalization
of all foreign-owned farmland and stated that no, or only
token, compensation should be paid for the land.[61] It called
for cooperatives and self-management, as in Algeria. For
these and other reasons the Istiqlal gradually lost face, and
the King has not appointed any Istiqlal ministers since late
1963.

Late in 1962, the UNFP and the UMT both came out
against the constitution. They accused the palace of plotting
to perpetuate the regime and said that the constitution had
been drafted by foreign enemies of the people.

In July, 1963, the King banned meetings of the Istiqlal
party and banned publication of the UNFP newspaper. The
police arrested 130 leaders of the UNFP, who were accused
of plotting to overthrow the King. Medhi Ben Barka, head
of the party, and some of the other leaders escaped into exile,
but the party was emasculated and essentially ceased to
function. There have been no UNFP ministers appointed
since that time, but the party does exist on the official list of
parties, with Abdelahmim Bouabid as its recognized leader.

King Hassan II stayed on as Prime Minister until November, 1963, when he appointed Ahmed Bahnini to that office

and attempted to run a constitutional-parliamentary monarchy.
However, the FDIC, which did not have a majority to begin
with, soon split, and Reda Guedira formed the Parti Socialiste
Démocratique (PSD), which grouped all of the elements of the
FDIC except the MP. Very little was accomplished by the
Parliament or by the government during the following year,
and a deteriorating economic situation led to popular dissension.

In March, 1965, very serious riots in Casablanca were
quelled by the riot squads at the cost of many deaths. This
led the King to try to form a new government, including
ministers from all parties, but he was unable to do so. As a
result, he decided to dispense with democratic government.
In June, 1965, he dismissed the Parliament and the government, became his own Prime Minister, and formed a new
government. He said that the incapacity of Parliament had
demonstrated the need to revise the constitution, and he
promised to make such revisions.

Since that time the political situation has remained static.
The King appoints ministers as individuals, with little regard to former party label. There have been no elections, and
consequently little party activity. As a result, while the
UNFP, the Istiqlal, the MP and the PSD exist officially as
political parties, there is little life in any, except perhaps
the MP. The Communist party exists and is active, with
perhaps 500 to 1,000 members, but it is illegal.[62]

Meanwhile, the UMT, still under the leadership of Ben
Seddik, is dabbling very little in politics. In 1961, the UNFP
had attempted to get the UMT to call several general strikes
in support of the UNFP political activities. The workers had
little taste for this, however, and the attempted strikes were
abortive. In December, 1961, Reda Guedira, who was then
a close confidant of the King, reached an agreement with UMT
officials that the UMT would be free to strike in support of
demands for higher wages and better working conditions, but
would keep its nose out of politics.[63] Although the UMT newspaper, L'Avant Garde, editorializes and prints many speeches
criticizing the government's policies, insofar as strike action
is concerned this agreement was honored until July, 1967,
when Ben Seddik sent a telegram to the King protesting the
government's policies vis-à-vis the Middle East crisis and
calling for a more anti-Zionist position; at the same time, the
UMT leader called a general strike. As a result, Ben Seddik
was arrested, very quickly brought to trial, and sentenced
to 18 months in prison. The government, meanwhile, had
taken a very strong position against the strike, threatening

striking workers with possible loss of jobs. As a result, the strike was only 20 percent effective the first day and almost non-existent the second.

As indicated earlier, the King selects his ministers to give the government the "tone" that he feels it should have at any given time. The ministers are often shifted from one ministry to another, and the responsibilities of given ministries vary quite frequently. The general tone of the government during the past several years, however, has been that the ministers are felt by the King to be personally loyal to him and to the monarchic regime. As a consequence, the King has surrounded himself with conservatives, many of whom worked for the French protectorate government. The nationalists who fought for independence have been shunted aside, arrested, or, like Ben Barka, exiled.

One aspect of the leaders of Morocco's government today is that whereas most of Tunisia's leaders had studied in Paris and had formed friendships with each other there, many Moroccan leaders studied either at their own Islamic college or in Cairo--and consequently are far more Arabic in their outlook. Whereas Bourguiba was unmoved by the creation of Israel, al-Fassi, the head of the Istiqlal and a former professor of Arabic literature, was incensed. It is interesting to note, in the light of the 1967 Middle East war, that as early as 1952 al-Fassi had asked the Sultan to send Egypt $50,000 to be used in its struggle against Israel.[64] This explains the strong anti-Jewish undercurrent in Morocco in mid-1967, even though the King was following a restrained policy and made every attempt to draw a distinction between the international Zionist movement and the Jewish community in Morocco.

NOTES

1. Jacques Bonjean, L'Unité de l'Empire Chérifien, pp. 145-164.

2. Albert Ayache, Le Maroc, p. 60.

3. Camille Fidel, Les Intérêts Économiques de la France au Maroc, p. 166.

4. Ibid., p. 199.

5. Guy Evin, L'Industrie au Maroc et ses Problèmes, p. 82.

6. Ayache, op. cit., pp. 106, 107.

7. Evin, op. cit., pp. 81, 82.

8. Ayache, op. cit., pp. 77, 78.

9. Jean d'Esme, Le Maroc Que Nous Avons Fait, p. 298.

10. Fidel, op. cit., p. 22.

11. Augustine Bernard, Le Maroc, p. 184.

12. Henri Dugard, Le Maroc de 1919, p. 83.

13. Evin, op. cit., p. 181.

14. Ibid., p. 2.

15. Ibid., p. 76.

16. Ayache, op. cit., p. 117.

17. Evin, op. cit., p. 77.

18. d'Esme, op. cit., p. 299.

19. Ayache, op. cit., p. 117.

20. Banque du Maroc, Études Financières (November, 1952).

21. d'Esme, op. cit., p. 286.

22. Fidel, op. cit., pp. 194, 195.

23. Henri Terrasse, Histoire du Maroc, p. 368.

24. René Hoffrerr and Roger Moris, Revenues et Niveaux de Vie Indigènes au Maroc, p. 177.

25. Ibid., p. 203.

26. Charles F. Stewart, The Economy of Morocco, 1912-1962, p. 121.

27. Ibid., pp. 153, 154.

28. Government of Morocco, Annuaire Statistique du Maroc. 1926.

29. Hoffrerr and Moris, op. cit., p. 22.

30. Government of Morocco, Annuaire Statistique du Maroc, 1952, p. 12.

31. Ayache, op. cit., p. 252.

32. Ibid., pp. 149, 154.

33. Steward, op. cit., p. 77.

34. Government of France, L'Enseignement dans les Territoire Français d'Outre-Mer, p. 7.

35. "L'Enseignement Publique au Maroc," La Vie Marocaine (January, 1954), 7-10.

36. Ayache, op. cit., p. 323.

37. Ibid., pp. 138-141.

38. Lorna Hahn, North Africa: Nationalism to Nationhood.

39. J. J. Boissard, "La Place de la Communauté Française dans l'Économie Marocaine," Confluent, No. 15 (October 1957), 317.

40. The Plan Quinquennal, 1960-1964, p. 61, also indicated that in subsequent years the flight capital probably amounted to the following amounts: 1957, $11 million; 1958, $3 million; 1959, $6 million; and 1960, $1 million.

41. French Embassy of Morocco, "Les Investissements Français dans l'Industrie Marocaine" (unpublished).

42. Abdelwahab Benkirane, "Échanges et Coopération Entre le Maroc et les Pays Socialistes de l'Europe," Bulletin Économique et Social du Maroc (October-December, 1966), 54.

43. Albert Waterston, Planning in Morocco, p. 13.

44. International Bank for Reconstruction and Development, The Economic Development of Morocco, pp. 81, 82.

45. Government of Morocco, Plan Quinquennal, 1968-1972.

46. "Efforts Importants dans le Domaine de l'Enseignement," Maroc '66, No. 6 (March, 1966), 44-46.

47. André Tiano, La Politique Économique et Financière du Maroc Indépendent, p. 86.

48. From discussions with government officials in the Moroccan Ministry of Finance (July, 1967).

49. GNP figures for 1952-60 were taken from the Plan Quinquennal, 1960-64; the remainder came from La Situation Économique du Maroc en 1965.

50. International Bank for Reconstruction and Development, op. cit., p. 181.

51. CEDIES Information No. 444 (March 20, 1965).

52. From discussions with the Director of the Moroccan Investment Commission.

53. International Bank for Reconstruction and Development, op. cit., p. 177.

54. Ibid., p. 314. The figures are compared on the basis of 1960 prices.

55. The data for 1951-64 are from International Bank for Reconstruction and Development, op. cit., p. 314. The figure for 1967 was taken from data furnished by the U.S. Embassy, Rabat. The growth rates, in real terms, were derived from La Situation Économique du Maroc en 1965.

56. L'Avant Garde (March 28, 1964).

57. From unpublished reports of the U.S. Embassy, Rabat.

58. Douglas E. Ashford, Political Change in Morocco, p. 327.

59. Ibid., p. 312.

60. Ibid., p. 378.

61. Al Istiqlal (July 21, 1963).

62. From an informed source in Rabat (July, 1967).

63. Ibid.

64. Hahn, op. cit., p. 111.

12

POLICY STATEMENTS OF
MOROCCAN POLITICAL
LEADERS AND GOVERNMENT

As seen in Chapter 11, Morocco is now being run as a
monarchy, pure and simple. The former constitution (of
1962) is not operative. King Hassan II has promised to provide a new constitution, but he has not announced a deadline
for doing so. Thus, the opinion of the King is the one which
counts on any problem. This chapter begins, therefore, with
several statements by King Hassan II regarding the role of
private investment in the Moroccan economy.

The most important governmental documents dealing with
this question are the economic development plans. Pertinent
excerpts have therefore been taken from them. The five-
year plan (1960-64) and the three-year plan (1965-67) have
both appeared since King Hassan II ascended the throne and
therefore reflect his opinion.

Although the King is the King, his policies reflect the
pressures which he feels from various interest groups and
political parties in the country. The political parties, as
such, are now inactive, but the leaders still control some
public opinion. Also, although the UMT is not capable of con-
fronting the army, it is a potentially disruptive force. Consequently, the views of some leaders of the UMT, and of Reda
Guedira, the leader of the PSD, are presented.

Finally, statements of several of the top governmental
officials are included. Although these men are not political
leaders, they are in positions where their views and policies
can greatly affect the political climate for private investment.

KING HASSAN II

On December 13, 1962, after the constitution had been
approved (and the day before it was officially promulgated),
King Hassan II gave a speech in his chambers to his top

officials and political leaders. It was taped and broadcast on
the following day. He spoke of his joy that Morocco finally
had a constitution and went on to say:

> The constitution's primary aim is to facilitate and
> accelerate the economic and social development of the
> country . . . . The constitution forces the orientation
> of our policies; a planned development, but one which is
> open to initiatives of everyone . . . . In liberty and
> through liberty, we must accept the sacrifices and sub-
> mit to the inevitable structural reforms so that our agri-
> culture and industry progress. [1]

Several months later, on March 3, 1963, at the celebration
of the second anniversary of his accession to the throne, the
King gave a speech similar to the "State of the Nation" speeches
given before Congress by U.S. Presidents. It touched on most
aspects of the politics, society, and economy of Morocco.
Speaking of economic independence, of policies for industrialization, and of agrarian reform, he had the following to
say:

> Faithful to the policy followed with perseverance since
> independence, we plan that the economy of Morocco shall
> become a Moroccan economy and that our citizens shall
> become capable of taking control. We plan also that the
> state can, each time that it is necessary, intervene in
> the economic life of the country where it is possible to
> have an influence and provide, within the desired time
> period, the impulse needed for development.
>
> For example, the take-over by the state of the con-
> cessions of the EEM and the CFM [EEM, the electric
> power complex, and CFM, the railroad company, were
> controlled by the Banque de Paris et des Pays Bas] ,
> which has already been done, will permit the government
> to orient the evolution of these two key sectors, energy
> and transportation, so as to aid the general economic ex-
> pansion of the nation.
>
> We must follow a realistic policy of industrialization,
> which, while devoting an important effort toward the es-
> tablishment of heavy industries (a measure of our future),
> shall be oriented primarily toward increasing the number
> of manufacturing industries which employ many workers
> and can be distributed throughout our territory.
>
> This policy of industrial expansion requires a coordi-
> nation of the efforts of the state and the private sector
> and the indispensable harmonization of their interventions.
> To the state belongs the role of guide and initiator, which,

meanwhile, permits flexible planning. It is also up to
the state to be directly in control of the key sectors of
the economy: heavy industry, transportation, and energy.
The private sector must orient itself resolutely toward
productive investments and abandon the sterile policy of
utilizing its capital in speculative real estate and commercial operations.

Agrarian reform, whose principle has already been
established, must henceforth be conducted with vigor. . . .
It will result in a complete remaking of agrarian structures by a limitation on the size of property and by a
redistribution of the land, for the well-being of our people,
the growth of our economy, and in conformity with the
disposition of our constitution. This reform, essential
to our development, will be carried out in such a fashion
as to injure no one, through the procedures which will be
followed and by the fact that equitable compensation will
be paid to those whose property is affected. [2]

The King was interviewed on June 3, 1964, by a reporter
from the French newspaper Le Figaro. One of the questions
posed to him was:

Of the three North African countries, it is in Morocco
that the most Frenchmen have stayed and the most
Frenchmen have come to live since independence. To
what do you attribute this favorable spot which Morocco
occupies the mind of the French?

To which the King responded:

Without doubt, it is because they feel at ease here. Their
lives and those of their children are assured. Their goods
and their work are protected from capriciousness and
changes in the direction of the wind. It is because Morocco
has always been a hospitable land; the people are warm
and tolerant . . . .

In the private sector, many possibilities are open to
the activity of the French. There are no barriers to their
establishing themselves here and to their free enterprise;
in fact, every effort is made to incite them to invest and
to contribute, by their work and capital, to the general
prosperity. Our liberal democracy, of the Western type,
assures and encourages them.

Of course, our policy in the area is within the framework of the general development of the country and takes
into account the need to achieve an eventual Moroccanization, especially in certain sectors. But, notwithstanding
the imperatives of our development and of Moroccanization,

I remain convinced that the favorable place which our
country occupies in the hearts of so many of your compatriots is not near to being eliminated.[3]

On another occasion, King Hassan II was interviewed by
the Belgian television station one month before he dismissed
the parliament. He was asked whether, in his current battle,
he was covered on both the left and the right. He responded:

We are not in a battle of swordsmen where one says,
"Sir, guard your left and guard your right." We are not
at all in such a situation: there is no left or right in the
country when it comes to ideals and goals. To be sure,
the geography of the 20th century necessitates that, in
a semi-circle, some people are seated on the left and
others on the right and others in the center. I feel,
however, that for the common people, for whom we must
do everything, for those who are neither civil servants
nor have any certain income, who are not sure where
they will get some bread to eat tomorrow, there is no
right or left. The problem is to be able to improve their
lot and increase their living standard. The exercise of
being to the left or to the right is a luxury, a luxury of
political or philosophical speculation. I feel, personally,
that if we exercise such a luxury, we will be political
dilettantes, for we are a country which must work and
struggle, which cannot afford luxury, either as an end
or as a means, from material luxuries to intellectual
luxuries.[4]

When King Hassan II addressed the opening session of the
High Commission for Planning and National Promotion, which
was to review the final draft of the three-year plan (1965-67),
he noted first that the economic situation was serious, that
in preceding years the growth of GNP had averaged 1.6 percent while the population was growing at 3 percent. Because
of financial and other limitations, the priorities of the plan
would, he said, be placed on agriculture, tourism, and education. He then went on to say:

Our option for increasing agricultural production, and
for touristic development and education to receive the
priority in our objectives, does not at all mean that the
state is forgetting about other tasks which are within its
responsibility, for the state is always disposed, in regard
to industrialization, to assume its obligations, either
directly or indirectly, or in collaboration with those who
desire to cooperate with the state in this direction. It
should be emphasized that the field is open for the private

sector; we do not plan, at all, to deprive this active
sector of the necessary means of action. It suffices that
the private companies are healthy and working within a
framework which conforms with our aspirations and takes
into account the interests of the nation in order for them
to benefit from the encouragement and best wishes of the
state.

As to the primary infrastructure, which constitutes
the base of the economy, which is to say the roads, ports,
railroads, communications, and energy, the state will
continue its activities to improve these facilities, taking
into consideration that the projects are really useful and
have an assured return. [5]

Several weeks later, in January, 1965, when its review
of the three-year plan was completed, the High Commission
for Planning and National Promotion was again addressed by
the King. After reviewing the priority sectors of agriculture,
tourism, and education, he stated:

Industrialization is certainly an undeniable and lasting
necessity in our economic effort, but this effort necessarily presupposes a division of labor, and if it is normal
that the state take charge directly and completely of the
investments in certain sectors, the industrial sector must
constitute the example of a concerted effort, of an active
participation of the private sector within the framework
of a quasi contract which defines its obligations and re-
ciprocal advantages. [6]

ECONOMIC DEVELOPMENT PLANS

King Hassan II had not yet ascended the throne when the
first development plan, the two-year investment plan (1958-
59), went into effect. This plan was the first to allocate
some capital expenditures to industrial investment by the state.
It also contained an initial enunciation of the role which the
state would play in the area of industrialization:

The State can play an important role in accelerating the
process of industrialization: on one hand, by developing
the conditions which favor the birth of new industries
. . . ; on the other hand, by direct investment in industrial
companies, especially in the sector of basic industries.
Within the framework of the two-year plan, two actions
will be undertaken: (a) encouragement of private investors

by tax and other advantages, within the framework of a
law which will define the policy for encouraging private
investment; (b) by establishing a Bureau d'Études et de
Participations Industrielles, which will intervene in all
those cases where direct action by the state must supplement private initiative . . . . The goal of the direct investment by the state is to stimulate the movement of
capital toward the industrial sector. These investments
will provide security and profitability. They are to encourage domestic and foreign private capital to take an
active interest in industry. At the same time they will
serve as an efficient means of orienting industrial investments toward the priority sectors, so as to achieve the
industrial development of the country in a balanced fashion.[7]

There was, however, no indication of how much private
investors were expected to invest nor the industries in which
such investments were to be made.

When the Minister of Economics and Finance, M'Hamed
Douiri, presented the five-year plan (1960-64) to the King for
signature, he noted that one of the imperatives of the plan
was the "establishment of basic industries and the intervention
of the government into the industrial domain."[8]

The extent to which the government planned to intervene
can be seen only by the table of investments and their sources.[9]
In the mining sector, the government, primarily through its
semi-autonomous bodies, such as the BRPM and the OCP,
planned to invest about $39 million, leaving the private sector
to invest approximately $45 million. For the remainder of
industrial investment (including such basic industries as a
steel mill, an oil refinery, and a chemical complex), however,
the plan foresaw an investment by the government (through
BEPI and the BNDE) of $50 million, along with an investment
of $240 million by the private sector, both domestic and foreign.

The plan details a number of specific investments in industry, but only in the mining sector is it indicated which
investments are expected to be made by the public and private
sectors. For the other industries there is no specific delinea-
tion. It does, however, state that the government, via BEPI:
   . . . will intervene in the following sectors: steel;
   chemical complexes; synthetic organic chemicals; oil refining; shipyards; industries which will have a monopoly
   in the market; processing industries which pose complex
   problems and necessarily call for the intervention of the
   state; and competitive sectors, where one cannot be precise as to what intervention the government might

undertake, but where BEPI has the authority to create
or invest in a company. [10]

In discussing the organization of industrial companies,
the plan notes that existing companies will continue to be
governed by company law and managed by their chosen directors. It goes on to say:

It is important, however, to note those situations where
modifications appear to be desirable. The key sectors,
such as transportation and energy, could be subject to
basic modifications, if the conditions for such changes
are present. In addition, it is desirable that Moroccan
companies which are subsidiaries of foreign firms, while
maintaining their valuable liaison with their parent companies, to assure the supply of technical know-how and
managers which this country does not yet possess, adapt
their organization by whatever means they may choose
so that their decision making and their investments take
into account the economic realities of this country.

In the new industries which are created exclusively
with private capital, there seems to be no need to anticipate a change in their organizations, which are regulated
by law. In new industries where the government is a
partner, the government often has a minority interest.
Often, therefore, the private partners will assume the
responsibility for the management and will reap the benefits. However, the government cannot be completely
passive and be content to receive annual dividends. It
will often have played a determining role in the creation
of the company and will attempt to assure the best possible
management, so that the government's investment contributes more than finances and assures that the industry
operates in the public interest, of which the government
is guardian. It should be noted, in passing, that it is in
conformity with the public interest that the government
obtain a profit from the companies in which it invests. [11]

Finally, in a section entitled "Private Initiative," the
plan states the following:

We have indicated the lines of force of direct governmental
action in the field of industrialization. All areas where
the intervention of the government [via BEPI] is not
obligatory are left to the initiative of private investors.
This means that Moroccan industry has a large field of
action for the private entrepreneur, who is called upon
to build, to produce, and to prosper. The government
will intervene to aid him and to defend him against outside

competition. It will be a grave deception for the country
if private capital, and particularly local private capital,
does not appear in an amount sufficient to play the role
which has been left to it. In that case the government
will have to broaden its interventions. We have seen that
it has reserved this possibility. [12]

Moving to the three-year plan (1965-67), we find in the
very first section a review of the goals and accomplishments
of the five-year plan. It notes that the latter had distinguished
three sectors of activity: the public, the semi-public, and
the private. It then states:

For the private sector the plan was, above all, an indicative program providing private enterprise with a forecast
of the market in different sectors of the economy and with
a list of desirable and realizable investments. The
indicative character of this program was reinforced by an
investment code which gave financial and legislative encouragement. It is, however, incontestable that although
the public sector managed to execute almost the entire
program assigned to it, a large distortion resulted because of an insufficient effort by the private sector.

The consequences of this disequilibrium were serious
for the economy: (1) the social and infrastructure investments by the state were not compensated for by a sufficient
increase in production; (2) the state of the government's
finances therefore deteriorated, and the monetary policy
which followed resulted in inflation; and (3) foreign exchange reserves decreased, expenditures having increased
more quickly than receipts.

Following this is a table showing that public investments
exceeded the provision of the five-year plan in all sectors
except in health, welfare, and education, the excess being on
the order of 8 percent. Another table shows that total investment was 30 percent below that provided for by the plan.

In the section of the three-year plan entitled "Perspectives" is a section which defines the policy of governmental
intervention and promotion of industrialization:

In spite of the incontestable success of certain institutions, the complexity of the procedures and the multiplicity of paper work developed in the preceding years
have prevented a sufficient impulse to industrial development. The action of the government during the next three
years shall be inspired by the need to arrive at a clearer
understanding and more efficient means of promoting
investments.

Intervention by the public sector is necessary to achieve development, to assure the establishment of basic industries, and to supplement private initiative in the areas where it is lacking. Still, a distinction must be made, as clearly as possible, between those limited sectors where the state reserves a monopoly position for the establishment of public companies and those sectors where the state intervenes within a competitive framework. In this last case, the intervention of the State has as its purpose either to demonstrate to the private sector the possibilities of investing in a certain industry, or to supplement private capital. In both cases, such investments will not be of a permanent nature, and the sale of such investments to the private sector shall be carried out when that becomes possible. . . .

Finally, a system of incentives has been developed to encourage investments. . . . The efficiency of this system requires that the relationship between the state and private enterprise be defined in quasi-contractual terms, the commitment of the investor, in the form of invested capital and the jobs which he creates, having as its counterpart the incentives provided by the state plus, in the case of foreign investors, the security of the invested capital and the guarantee that it can be transferred. [13]

In the section of the three-year plan relating to industrial production, there is an attempt to refine the definition of the role which the government might play and the areas in which it might invest. It states:

The government will try to obtain the confidence of private investors by clearly defining, as of now, the respective domains of the government and of private initiative. It has been decided that in the future, the state will not intervene except when the following two conditions are present: (1) the private sector is dilatory in a given branch, in which case a consultation procedure with the private sector will be undertaken. (2) A bottleneck in a given branch acts as an obstacle to the development of private initiative and this bottleneck cannot be eliminated except by government intervention.

These limits do not, however, exclude the voluntary association of the public and private sectors. [14]

With regard to the nationalization of French-owned farmland, the three-year plan states:

The present distribution of land and the deficiencies which are apparent in the methods of exploitation constitute an obstacle to the progress and the development of agricultural production and, as a result, do not permit an increase in production by the peasants.

A change in the agricultural structure will be effected by the recovery of all lands, cultivated or cultivable, which now belong to foreigners.

The total recovery of these lands will be accomplished during the period of this three-year plan and will make it possible to include such lands in the domain of the state. . . .15

Finally, we come to the five-year plan (1968-72), which was issued early in 1968. It envisages a total investment, over the five-year period, of $2.3 billion, of which $271 million is to go into manufacturing and about $240 million into the mining industry. In the manufacturing sector, the government expects to invest $60 million in public or semipublic corporations, the remainder to come from the private sector. On the other hand, most of the mining investments are to come from the public sector.

In Volume II, Chapter 7 ("Industry") of the plan, the government states its industrialization policy and spells out the role of the state in this process:

The state has a triple function in the organization of the conditions for industrialization: (i) The state will create an atmosphere for industrialization in such a way as to promote to the maximum the free play of competition. To this end, regulations and laws will be changed so as to simplify and clarify the rules of the play of the market . . . . (iii) The state will, however, intervene directly in those cases where the private sector is deficient. This will occur in those situations where the amount to be invested is too great, or where it is a question of a sector of industry which, in spite of its importance to the development of the country, does not attract . . . private entrepreneurs.

UMT

The institution in Morocco which is stronger, organically and perhaps also politically, than any of the political parties is the UMT. It is leftist (if not Marxist) oriented and has, in recent years, called for more and more radical measures on the part of the government. Its leader, Mahjoub Ben Seddik, who has been President of the union for many years, was jailed in 1966 on an 18-month sentence. Still, the union can call strikes and as such is the only organized force in the country with potentially disruptive powers. (The army serves completely as an instrument of royal power, and the peasants are totally unorganized.) As a consequence, the views of the leaders of the UMT are important.

In reviewing the May Day speeches of Ben Seddik, we find that, in 1959, there was no mention of socialism.[16] However, the second congress of the UMT, held at the end of April, 1959, passed a resolution which recommended the nationalization of electricity and transportation and of that portion of French-owned farmland which had been obtained through the protectorate government (the lots de coloni-sation).[17]

In Ben Seddik's May Day speeches of 1960 through 1963, there was no mention of nationalization. In 1964, however, he gave a speech in which he advocated socialism as one of the solutions to the problems of Morocco:

During the past year, the rulers have been unmasked; it has become more and more apparent that the government is in the service of foreign monopolies, of the reaction-aries, and of the feudalists; an unpopular government which is following the policy of the imperialists and the neo-colonialists; an oppressive, mystical, and tyrannical government.

Certainly, those in power are aware of the force of the people's desire for socialism--people who want no more of the exploitation of man by man, in all its forms. Socialism is triumphing everywhere in the world. . . . This march of the people toward socialism, its effect on our masses, frightens those in power in Morocco and pushes them again and again to use our words to sow confusion. They agree now that socialism is a necessity and declare that they are socialists, but it is a socialism of the rich, a socialism which does not exclude capitalism, a socialism which maintains the exploitation of man by man, guarantees the continuance of colonial and feudal lands, the means of production in the hands of the monopolies, credit and commerce for the bankers, and power for the reactionaries.

But the true and authentic socialism to which we aspire, and which we will obtain, excludes capitalism.

Our socialism signifies simply the land to those who work
it, the factories to the producers, and the power to the
people, with the working class and the peasants at its
head. [18]

This was a very strong speech to be made in a monarchy,
but fortunately for Ben Seddik, King Hassan II was at that
moment trying to make a parliamentary monarchy operate.
By May, 1965, after using the troops to repress the riots in
Casablanca, the King was on the point of dismissing the
Parliament and re-establishing personal rule. Neither in
1965 nor in 1966 did Ben Seddik's May Day speeches mention
socialism.

From time to time there have been strikes by the UMT
against some company, and when the company delayed responding to the demands of the union, the union newspaper,
L'Avant Garde, would sometimes call for the expropriation
of the company, asking that it be put under worker-management.
This was the case with a large, French-owned sugar refinery
called COSUMA. An editorial in L'Avant Garde stated:

Since 1957 the workers have called for the nationalization
of imports of tea and sugar. The nationalization of tea
has been achieved, but for sugar nothing has been done.
This would be easier to understand if sugar were processed
by Moroccan capitalists, but it is done by foreign groups
whose power is demonstrated by the pressure which they
can put on the government. Thus, COSUMA has for
years continued to exploit the Moroccan people, contrary
to the practice in other countries, such as Algeria.

The workers are determined to put an end to this
situation and obtain the nationalization of COSUMA, the
management of this company by the workers. [19]

Soon thereafter an editorial in L'Avant Garde made the
following significant observations with regard to socialism in
Morocco vis-à-vis her sister Maghreb countries:

It is eight years after independence, and yet the best land
in Morocco, as well as the mines, remain in the hands
of colonialists and foreign capitalists. Our commerce,
our industry, our banks, and our insurance companies
are still in the hands of neo-colonialists. . . .

Meanwhile, in Algeria the land has been given to the
peasants and a portion of the industry is already in the
hands of the working class. . . .

While the colonialists and reactionary press are
still all-powerful in Morocco, our Algerian, Tunisian,
and Egyptian brothers have thrown them out and, in

Tunisia, publicity, which is the nerve center of the press, has been put in the hands of a government office. . . .

We are certain that our brother countries will continue to progress on the road to democracy and socialism . . . . On the other hand, Morocco is regressing and will continue to regress as long as the government is in the service of the reactionaries and neo-colonialists-- as long as the working class and the peasants remain oppressed and exploited.

It serves no purpose to go against the march of history, for the future belongs to the workers and the success of our brothers beyond our borders constitutes a demonstration of the triumph of the revolution which, in Morocco, still remains to be accomplished.[20]

Finally, between December 14 and 17, 1966, there was an international congress of labor unions in Budapest, Hungary. The UMT was represented by one of its top officials, Abdelaziz Balal. His speech, which purported to represent the viewpoint of the UMT, contained the following remarks:

The possibility of true economic development based on foreign private capital, according to the experience in Morocco, is a myth, and a dangerous one. What we must do, above all, is to create the conditions necessary for development and undertake the measures necessary to organize the internal sources for the mobilization of capital. . . . Only after the task is achieved--which implies profound internal transformations--can one hope, as a subsidiary measure, in case of real necessity, to call upon foreign investments.

This means that these foreign investments--given the powers that they can exercise--cannot be utilized in a positive manner except by those countries which have freed their economies from the grip of the imperialists and the parasitic social strata, those countries which seriously manage, control, and plan their economic development and which, thus, can impose a true control over action of the foreign private investors. . . .[21]

POLITICAL FIGURES AND
TOP ADMINISTRATORS

Reda Guedira has been one of the leading political figures in Morocco since independence. He had been a confidant of the Sultan prior to independence and continued to have a fairly close working relationship, not only with King Mohammed V but also with King Hassan II. Should political parties have an increased significance in the future, Guedira will have a leading role. In the meantime, his opinions are heard in the inner circles.

When he first formed the PSD early in 1964, Guedira and his second in command, M'Hammed Bahnini, issued a statement outlining their program: "Economic development will take place under socialism or not at all."[22] They declared that the objectives of the party were planning, agrarian reform, direct ownership by the state of basic sectors of the economy, redistribution of revenues, and reform of the channels of distribution, including the Moroccanization of the internal trade structure.

Later the same year, Guedira gave the following as his views on political economics: ". . . socialism is liberal in the political sphere and an organizer in the social field." He stated that his goal was ". . . the installation of a socialist society within the framework of the constitution and in support of the King." He went on to say:

> . . . liberal economics, as we conceive of it, calls for a control of the key sectors of the economy; I said control, but this does not mean nationalization. The intervention of the government is necessary in the form of orientation, within limits, submitting the citizens to a somewhat strict discipline while leaving private initiative its place and its share. The idea is to conciliate liberalism and dirigisme. Morocco does not have an administration which is competent and strong enough, or enough civil servants to permit the government to intervene everywhere. Our experiments with governmental intervention have put some very important sectors in the hands of men without competence, without an idea of public service, without an administrative tradition. These civil servants have had too much power given to them prematurely; this is one of the reasons for our corruption, and this corruption increases the cost of goods and the cost of living. But the intervention of the government, and private initiative, are both necessary.[23]

Although Ahmed Alaoui, Minister of Commerce, Industry, and Mines, is not a politician per se (he was not a leader of one of the political parties), he is a cousin of the King and has been a member of the in-group since the King assumed personal powers in 1965. His responsibility, as Minister of Commerce, Industry, and Mines, puts him in a special position

to influence the political economy of Morocco. Unfortunately,
he has not been at all verbose, publicly, on this topic. In
his speech of April 27, 1967, inaugurating the International
Fair of Casablanca, in the presence of the King, he did make
several remarks on this subject:

> The International Fair of Casablanca . . . has a special
> aspect this year, for it is organized within a framework
> which received its inspiration directly from the enlightened
> policies of Your Majesty, whose objective is to lead the
> country toward a situation where it will enjoy a consider-
> able degree of economic independence. Such a goal will
> be achieved only to the extent that the policies applied
> take into account the actual needs and possibilities of
> Morocco.
>
> Your Majesty has defined, with realism, the role
> which industrialization must play in this effort, and the
> directives of Your Majesty, preparing the framework
> for the industrial renaissance of our country, constitute
> the basis of a policy which tends to create a better
> equilibrium between the requirements of consumption
> and the conditions of production.
>
> If we wish to pursue the course of industrialization,
> and that is one of the objectives of the economic policies
> of Your Majesty, we must advance the manufacturing
> process so as to produce, in this country, the entire line
> of intermediate products, semi-manufactures and basic
> materials which until now we have imported to transform
> into finished products. In a word, the time has now come
> to achieve the vertical integration of our industry by in-
> corporating the intermediate processes and, where poss-
> ible, the manufacture of basic products.
>
> This is why the government . . . elaborated the
> various sectoral plans and, in this same framework, the
> individual projects which must be achieved.
>
> The ensemble of all of the anticipated projects . . .
> represents an investment of about $360 million.
>
> The state can better assist in the achievement of the
> larger projects to the extent that the private sector takes
> more and more responsibility in the manufacture of
> finished products, as demonstrated by the applications
> submitted to the Investment Commission and the invest-
> ment permits accorded by that Commission since 1966.
> This makes possible the allocation of larger public re-
> sources, which often exceed the capabilities of private
> investors, to the more important projects for basic in-
> dustries.

The task which we are undertaking is not at all
passive. To the action of your government there must
be a reaction, namely, the spread of creative initiative
among the government officials and among the businessmen, combined with that of foreign investors, whose
realism must be inculcated with faith in the future of
our country. [24]

The final quotation is from Amine Bengeloun, President
of the BNDE during the early years of its operation. The
BNDE is the most powerful instrument of the government in
industrial investment. Now that the BEPI has been disbanded,
the BNDE is essentially the only organization for governmental
investment in productive industry outside the mining sector.
While Bengeloun is no longer President of BNDE, his policies
shaped the institution and tend to be followed today. Also,
he has since become a minister in the King's government and
a member of the in-group.

On April 9, 1963, he gave a long talk before the Moroccan
chapter of the International Chamber of Commerce on the
problem of industrial investment in Morocco. It is an important speech, for in it Bengeloun enunciates, in detail, the
view which seems to be pervasive among the top officials of
the current government, as well held by the King himself,
with regard to the reliance to be placed on private enterprise.

He began with a discussion of the difficulties which the
Moroccan economy had encountered in the preceding years
and went on to say:

The plan forecast, for 1962, a total investment of DH
1,527 million [$305 million], which is roughly 50 percent
more than actually obtained. Whereas the plan provided
for an increase by 50 percent in 1962 over 1960, the increase was only about 10 percent. . . .

Our plan does not belong in the category of documents,
found in many countries, which seem to be pure exercises in writing style. Our plan, if I may remind you, is
a very reasonable plan. It provides only for an increase
in living standard of about 1 percent per year and even
permits the present 40 percent unemployment rate to increase slightly.

To appreciate the investment situation in our country,
one must take into account these many factors which are
not satisfactory but are, perhaps, hopeful. The effort
necessary cannot be accomplished without paying the price
of a growing budgetary deficit, which today poses problems with which we are all familiar. Roughly, one can

say that Morocco is in a situation where the annual increase of public expenditures is on the order of 10 percent while the rate of increase of fiscal receipts will
not pass 5 percent. It is clear that the ratio of two to
one between these two figures poses grave problems,
particularly problems of prices, salaries, and the distribution of national income.

With regard to this subject, allow me to observe
that peasants constitute 70 percent of our population and
that half of them, if one believes the results of the excellent consumer survey recently published by the
Ministry of Economics, have no more than DH 1,500
[$300] per household per year to live on, which repre-
sents less than DH 250 [$50] per year per person. . . .
That, gentlemen, is a figure which we must all know and
on which none of us, I feel, can cease to meditate.

The Causes of This Situation

It appears that the causes of this situation have no relationship to the question of doctrinal choices but, rather,
[are related] to psychological and economic factors.

Vanity of Doctrinal Opposition

Even though most observers agree, today, on the diag-
nosis of the investment situation in Morocco, two schools
of thought exist with regard to the doctrinal analysis of
this situation. For one side, all of the evils are a result
of an excess of liberalism; for the other, the contrary
is true--the governmental actions and controls are the
cause.

The Thesis of Statism. For the first, the low investment
level is a result of our economic system's leaving too
much responsibility to the private sector. The doctrine
which constitutes the basis of this thesis postulates a
system of governmental ownership of industry and commerce.

Allow me, apropos this subject, to make two observations. First, the government can play a determining
role in investments even in a non-socialist system. In
most of the countries of Western Europe, for example,
the government controls 40-60 percent of the investments
without, however, putting the liberal foundations of the

economy in jeopardy. On the contrary, study of these
countries shows that the modern liberal state, drawing
its lesson from the large investment banks, ends up controlling numerous companies without subscribing to a
very large fraction of their capital. Usually, 10-30 percent suffices for the government to be the master.

Nothing would be more wrong than to interpret the
above remarks as the nostalgic thoughts of outdated
liberalism. No one doubts, today, the need for economic
planning, particularly in the underdeveloped countries,
to assure . . . optimum growth. Nor can anyone contest
that the government, which is responsible for the general
interest, must take direct charge of a certain number of
productive activities, particularly in such sectors as
energy, certain basic industries, and certain investments
beyond the means of the private sector, such as ocean
shipping and airlines; the government can and, in certain
cases, such as that of Morocco, must go further.

But, and this is my second observation, one should
not conclude from this that state ownership and control
are the panacea for the development of the backward
economies. To remain attached to such a thesis, as are
certain individuals in Morocco, is to be one generation
behind and to refuse to see certain realities.

Our experience these last several years shows that
while it is easy for a new state to assume the traditional
tasks of the public authority, it is difficult to interfere
in the economic sphere and, above all, to transform itself
into an entrepreneur. This is not to say that the state
cannot do it. But one must measure the price one pays
for this policy and appreciate the limits, taking into
account, above all, the human factors.

After 35 years of experience with socialism, the
evolution of thought in the Soviet Union is, in this regard,
significant. One could not recommend too highly, to
certain of our compatriots, the reading of the program of
the Communist party of the Soviet Union, published on
July 30, 1961, and approved by the 22nd Congress of
October, 1961, as well as the minutes of the debates
which took place last year during the 16th and 17th
sessions of COMECON and a number of articles in Pravda,
such as those published on September 9 and October 5
of last year, under the signatures, respectively, of Professor Liberman of the Economic and Technical Institute
of Karkov and of Monsieur Borovitski, Director of the
tire factory of Omsk.

One finds now, in the Soviet Union, a true rehabilitation of the notions of profit, interest rate, and efficiency.

This entire evolution of thought moves in the opposite direction from the principles which have been in effect until now. They are based on the dangers of waste which accompany a system of publicly owned enterprises tied too closely to a centrally planned economy. Before bringing any peremptory judgment on our present situation, Moroccans who would like to be enlightened would do well to study the good authors of <u>Pravda.</u>

<u>The Liberal Thesis</u>. With regard to these statist doctrines, there, are, in this country, a number of people who, while freely asking the government for help to cover their losses, defend, just as obstinately, liberalism with regard to profits. For them, the solution to the problem of investments depends on three types of measures: (1) reduced interest rates; (2) reduced taxes; and (3) more aid for foreign investors. This second theory does not appear to me to be less contestable than the first.

. . . There remains the problem of aid for foreign private investors. . . . Although the investment code has been applied in a very liberal manner for the past three years, the amount invested in equipment (less amortization) has remained obstinately constant. Perhaps even that is a positive result, but how insufficient! Under these conditions it is unrealistic, and even ridiculous, to demand that the government give more incentives to the private investor. Actually, the problem of foreign private investment is much less a problem of governmental assistance than it is a problem of guarantees.

As a result, the problem of the level of investment in our country appears, in large measure, to be unrelated to doctrinal considerations of any type.

Psychological Aspects

It is certain, on the contrary, that psychological problems determine, in a large measure, the current situation.

Ten years ago . . . Morocco appeared to be a sort of California of Africa. But its growth, on the one hand, affected only a few isolated islands of development and, on the other hand, resulted from foreign entrepreneurship, capital, and know-how. During the period which followed, it was expected that the foreign investors would assume a wait-and-see attitude. But, after seven years of independence, during which period neither public order nor social order was threatened, one still waits for a reappearance of the fallen spirit.

It is true that during this period a new elite of Moroccan industries has arisen, to which I pay homage. . . . In the many sectors of the economy, I see the young Moroccan industrialists, who are efficient and dynamic, and who are one of the best assurances of our future as a country.

But it is an elite which is too small, which too often encounters what is perhaps the gravest problem in the development of our industry--the insufficiency of our domestic market.

If it is true that the insufficient number of investments can be explained essentially by a complex combination of psychological factors (by this I mean insufficient spirit of initiative), I cannot do better than to refer to the principles of our constitution in order to analyze more closely that which, today, must represent the basis for our hope.

In the first place, the preamble of our constitution says that "Morocco . . . constitutes a part of the Grand Maghreb." That is our hope for the long term, for an extension of our national economic sphere, whose importance we should not underestimate and in relation to which we should already base our projects.

In addition, the constitution of December 7, 1963, is written within a framework of political liberalism which is undoubtedly the most appropriate for the development of private enterprise. Moroccan democracy should be available and equal for everyone.

Finally, each of you should draw his own conclusions from Article 15, which reads as follows: "The right of property rests guaranteed. . . . It cannot be expropriated except by due process of law."

In other words, our constitution, adopted by an immense majority . . . strictly guarantees the right of property in all those cases where its use does not constitute an insurmountable obstacle to the social and economic development of the country.

There are, thus, a group of principles which constitute a framework which is both necessary and sufficient for the blossoming and success of any private initiatives.

The Dynamism of the Entrepreneur

It is thus clear that the industrial future of our country and the growth of investment depend upon this entrepreneurial spirit. . . . I arrive, then, at the heart of the problem of investments in Morocco . . . . Permit me to recall how often history demonstrates the importance of nationalism as a motor for economic development. There are examples as different as Germany, Russia, Japan, and Yugoslavia. But once foreign victory has been obtained, a twin path is available to nationalism.

The first consists of consolidating the economic progress achieved during the struggle, to have a basis for true development, which is seen as increased living standards. The second path, or rather, the second temptation which appears to former victims of colonialism, consists of assuming a type of internal neo-colonialism, which results in a repression of the middle class.

To avoid this latter path, to show that we are worthy of our great national hopes: such, I believe, is our present task, confronted by the problem of investments in Morocco, to which our duty to our country calls us.[25]

NOTES

1.   Le Maroc en Marche: Discours de Sa Majesté Hassan II, pp. 202-210.

2.   Ibid., pp. 232-249.

3.   Ibid., pp. 407-408.

4.   Ibid., pp. 500-506.

5.   Ibid., pp. 452-457.

6.   Ibid., p. 463.

7.   Plan Biennal d'Équipement, 1958-1959.

8.   Plan Quinquennal, 1960-1964, p. 2.

9. Ibid., p. 30.

10. Ibid., p. 182.

11. Ibid., pp. 180-81.

12. Plan Triennal, 1965-1967, pp. 4-5.

13. Ibid., pp. 27-28.

14. Ibid., pp. 430-31.

15. Ibid., p. 123.

16. L'Avant Garde (May 2, 1959).

17. Ibid., (May 1, 1959).

18. Ibid., (May 1, 1964).

19. Ibid., (March 21, 1964).

20. Ibid., (April 4, 1964).

21. Ibid., (December 31, 1966).

22. Le Monde (May 12, 1964).

23. Jeune Afrique (December 13, 1964), 18-19.

24. Government of Morocco, Note de Documentations, special edition on the 22nd International Fair of Casablanca, pp. 7-12.

25. Le Petit Casablancais (April 19, 1963).

CHAPTER **13** MOROCCAN GOVERNMENT
ACTIONS AFFECTING THE
POLITICAL CLIMATE FOR
PRIVATE INVESTMENT

As indicated in Chapter 12, the political leaders and the government of Morocco are generally quite favorable to a dependence on private investment for the achievement of industrialization. However, they have also stated that there are certain industries which should be in the public sector and that the government will step in to provide guidance and an impetus to private investment in all other sectors of the economy. These types of measures will often be interpreted by private investors as excessive dirigisme and a step toward socialism. In addition, of course, a number of governmental actions vis-à-vis private investment are politically motivated and arise from the colonial heritage of the country.

ACTIONS THAT DISCOURAGE PRIVATE INVESTORS

Nationalization of Farmland

(Information on land nationalization was obtained from files of and discussions with officials of the French Embassy, Rabat.)

At the time of independence, about 2 million acres of farmland belonged to about 5,800 French farmers. The land plus buildings and equipment represented an investment of about $350 million. During the year following independence, only about 200 of these farmers left Morocco, most of them renting their land to neighbors. But the farmers who remained slowly sold off some of their holdings to Moroccans. Also, in 1959 the Moroccan government seized about 50,000 acres of land which the protectorate had taken from some tribes, and returned it to the tribes. This was land which

had never been sold to the French owners, but had been
rented to them in perpetuity.

By 1963, Frenchmen still owned 1.45 million acres.
This land produced two-thirds of Morocco's agricultural exports, representing foreign exchange earnings of $52 million
per year. This land was divided into two types, lots de colonisation and melk. The former was land which had been taken
over by the protectorate government and distributed to French
owners, while the melk land was bought in a more or less
usual manner by the French owner from a Moroccan owner.

On September 23, 1963, a law was passed nationalizing
556,000 acres of land, which included all of the lots de
colonisation and about 25,000 acres of melk land. The government said that this acquisition of melk land was not a
matter of policy but occurred because it was land which had
been bought by owners of lots de colonisation and had been
attached to the lots.

The government did not immediately take actual possession of all of the nationalized land. It took only 125,000
acres and said that it would take possession of the remainder,
part by part, over a three-year period, and that meanwhile
the former owners should continue to operate the farms. A
decree was issued in December, 1963, stating that crops
growing at the time of government take-over would belong to
the former owner. The last of this land was taken over by
the government in July, 1966.

The 556,000 acres which were nationalized had been
planted as follows: grains, 340,000 acres; citrus fruits,
20,000; olive trees, 12,500; vineyards, 25,000; truck gar-
dens, 12,500; eucalyptus trees, 32,000; meadows, 6,000;
sugar beets, 9,000; miscellaneous and grazing land, 99,000.
This land was put under either the Office National d'Irrigation
or the Office National de la Modernisation Rurale, depending
upon whether or not it was irrigated. The original intention
of the government was to distribute the land, in small parcels,
to the peasants who had worked on it as farm laborers. This
was tried on some of the land, but it was found that they did
not have the know-how and that production and exports decreased. Instead, the land was divided into large parcels
(1,000 acres), each under the direction of a government
agricultural expert who worked for one of the government
bureaus.

The nationalization law had said nothing about indemnifying
the former owners, but discussions between the French and
Moroccan governments brought about a solution of reimbursing

the former owners for the buildings, equipment, and livestock which went with the land. In 1963, out of the $16 million
in foreign aid which the French had planned to give Morocco,
$6 million was deducted and used to indemnify the French
farmers. Of the $6 million, $2.2 million was for buildings,
equipment, and livestock; the other remainder was a loan to
the Moroccan government, in French francs, to make possible
the transfer of the savings of the farmers who moved back to
France. A similar formula was applied during the following
years. Nothing has been paid for the land, and there does
not appear to be any plan to indemnify for that loss.

Meanwhile, approximately 800,000 acres of melk land
still belongs to Frenchmen. In addition, about 200,000 acres
belong to Spanish, Italian, English, and other nationalities.
Early in 1965 there were talks between the Moroccan and
French governments regarding the possible nationalization of
this land. Moroccan officials said that they did not wish to
discuss their rights to nationalize, but wished to discuss
timing and compensation so as not to present the French with
a fait accompli. During the succeeding years, however, there
has been little indication that the government plans to nationalize these lands. It does not fit in with the liberal policy of
the King since he closed the parliament and took over the government.

Nationalization of Industry

There has been no nationalization nor expropriation of
industry in Morocco since independence. There have been a
number of negotiated purchases of part or all of a company
by the government, usually a governmental institution. (Most
of these are discussed under "Public Investment in Existing
and New Companies.") There has, however, been one situation widely talked about as a nationalization--the government
take-over of electric power companies and railroads. This
was not, however, a nationalization.

One of the institutions in Morocco which ideologists would
label as the outstanding example of imperialistic capitalism
was the Banque de Paris et des Pays Bas. Its entry into
Morocco occurred in 1910 with a loan to the Sultan. It later
helped to establish the Banque d'État, which, as noted in
Chapter 9, served as Morocco's central bank during the
protectorate. The Banque de Paris et des Pays Bas was in
a position to control the major decisions of that central bank.

The Banque de Paris et des Pays Bas then set up two major holding companies, Omnium Nord Africain and Compagnie Générale du Maroc. The former made widespread investments in mining, industry, commerce, and real estate, and the latter concentrated on the operation of public service concessions in the fields of water, electricity, urban transportation, railroads, and tobacco. In the management of Omnium Nord Africain, the Banque de Paris et des Pays Bas acted as an investment bank, promoting investment opportunities, finding French companies to provide the technical know-how and the management, enlisting the financial support of other banks, retaining 20-30 percent of the stock for itself, and providing long-term credits sufficient to be in a controlling position.

Through the Compagnie Générale du Maroc, the bank operated most of the public services of the country. These public service companies were owned, in most cases, by the Moroccan government, which financed the investments and guaranteed the loans, but the bank, through its holding company, which in turn set up subsidiary companies to operate each concession, had very long-term concessions to operate the public services and reap the profits.

Following independence, the Banque de Paris et des Pays Bas was a natural target for anti-imperialist and decolonizing forces. The treatment of this bank and its holdings by the Moroccan government is highly significant, for it is indicative of the government's general attitude vis-à-vis pre-independence investments and toward private investment in general.

The government has not touched the holdings of Omnium Nord Africain. Its only action vis-à-vis the concessions of the Compagnie Générale du Maroc has been to negotiate a settlement for an early termination to several long-term concessions, the details of which follow.

Most of the electricity in Morocco was provided by Société d'Énergie Électrique du Maroc, which was a subsidiary of Compagnie Générale du Maroc and had a concession to operate the installations and distribute electricity until December 31, 1999. This concession was signed on May 9, 1923, and gave the government the right to buy the concession rights as early as 1980, with a two-year notice.

Another subsidiary of the Compagnie Générale du Maroc was the CFM, which had concessions to operate the major railroads of the country. These concessions were signed in 1914, 1920, and 1927 and were to run until 1999, 1999, and 1997, respectively.

In 1962, the government began negotiations with the Banque de Paris et des Pays Bas for an early termination of the above-mentioned concessions. An agreement was signed on April 30, 1963, whereby the government would indemnify the operating companies for an immediate end of the concessions. These take-overs became law on August 8, 1963. [1]

According to the terms of this settlement, the government was to pay a total of $12 million, of which $5 million could be transferred abroad in five equal annual installments. The remaining $7 million would have to be reinvested in Morocco, within a period of 10 years, in productive industries, such investments to be approved by the government. [2] These investments could not be in existing companies--they must start new ventures. If all or part of the $7 million was not invested within the 10 year period, the government could decide where to invest the money without the approval of the bank, although the resulting investments would still belong to it.

The government has since approved the transfer of the entire $5 million. Meanwhile, the Banque de Paris et des Pays Bas has established a Société d'Étude et de Création Industrielle du Maroc to determine how and where to invest the other $7 million. By mid-1967, only about $1.6 million had been invested, but another $2.4 million was planned for 1968.

Most of this capital is being invested in hotels. One innovating investment, however, was the establishment of Maroc Leasing, the first leasing company in the country. For this venture, the bank put up 40 percent of the capital, brought in a U.S. leasing company for 20 percent, the BNDE for another 20 percent, and obtained the remaining 20 percent from some of the bank's subsidiary companies. About one-third of this $1.6 million has gone into two textile companies and a small amount has been invested in a starch (and other corn products) factory, combining with an investment by a Belgian company and a local company owned by French interests

Meanwhile, the tobacco concession held by a subsidiary of the Compagnie Générale du Maroc died a natural death in 1963 and was taken over by the government. The concessions to operate the water companies in Casablanca, Rabat, and Fez expired in 1965 and were taken over by the municipal governments. (However, the pipes which bring the water from the reservoirs to the cities are still owned by the Compagnie Générale du Maroc, which receives a rental payment from the cities.) Finally, the concessions to operate urban bus lines are gradually (and quietly) expiring and being assumed by the various cities.

We see, therefore, that the Moroccan government contrary to the publicity at the time, did not nationalize the electricity and railroad companies. It only negotiated a settlement (quite acceptable to the Banque de Paris et des Pays Bas) for an early termination of several concessions. In addition, the government has let other concessions reach their legal termination dates, rather than make a clean sweep in 1963. Finally, the government has made no attempt to take over the industrial, mining, and real estate interests of the Banque de Paris et des Pays Bas.

Public Investment in Existing and New Companies

The government owns the Office Chérifien de Phosphates, which has a monopoly on the mining, sale, and export of phosphates. The government monopoly dates from 1921, when the exploitation of phosphates began, and does not reflect any policy decision since independence. Its investments are a part of the national budget and its profits (which have been considerable) are an important part of government revenues.

Other than the phosphate industry, there are very few instances where the government has entered directly into the purchase or the establishment of productive enterprise. It has tended to operate through one of five different organizations: BRPM, BEPI, BNDE, Caisse de Dépôt et de Gestion (CDG), and Société Nationale d'Investissement (SNI).

BRPM

The BRPM was created in 1928 as a government-owned public corporation to carry out exploration for and production of coal and oil. Its scope of action was expanded in 1938 to include all minerals. It carried out research and joined with private companies for the production of minerals after they had been found. Prior to independence, BRPM never took more than a 49 percent interest in a company. Since 1956, however, the policy is to own at least 50 percent of new firms which it helps to create. In addition, through negotiations with existing companies, BRPM has increased its share in a a number of companies in which it previously had a small minority interest.

By 1965, BRPM had shares in over 36 mining companies and mineral research companies, the capital of which was equivalent to about $40 million. BRPM's share was $13.6 million, its share in several large companies being as small as 3 percent. By 1967, however, BRPM held the following percentages of stock in the following mining sectors: coal, 55 percent; oil, 50 percent; manganese, 46 percent; iron, 26 percent; zinc, 25 percent; and lead, 25 percent.

One of the companies in which the BRPM has a majority interest is the Société des Charbonnages Nord Africains, which exploits the only major coal mine in Morocco, in Jerada. The company was, at the time of independence, owned 50.5 percent by French and Belgian interests and 49.5 percent by BRPM. It was, however, having difficulty in selling its fines and was experiencing financial difficulties. In 1957, BRPM signed an agreement guaranteeing an annual dividend of 6 percent to the private shareholders for a period of five years. When the agreement came up for renewal in 1962, BRPM (having paid over $1 million to its partners) agreed to renew the arrangement, but asked for an increase of its share to 55 percent. The private shareholders agreed, and have continued to receive their 6 percent dividends, and BRPM is making efforts to find utilization for the excess fines. Unfortunately, some conservatives called this BRPM action, which gave it a majority interest, a nationalization.

The other major action of BRPM since independence, relates to the country's only iron ore mines, the Minas del Rif, located in the former Spanish zone and owned, prior to independence, by Spanish interests. In the early 1960's, the company had to increase its investment in order to maintain production but was hesitant about putting its own money into the venture. As a result, it sold 26 percent of its shares to BRPM to raise the necessary capital. The mine had been exploited by "open-mining" methods, but by 1966 it became apparent that this would not be possible after several more years of production. Subsurface mining would be necessary, requiring very costly investments. The government was eager to have this done to assure a domestic supply of iron ore for a steel mill which it planned to build. The Spanish interests did not want to be involved, so the government announced in April, 1967, that it was going to take over the mines. It did not do so immediately, however, but began negotiations with the Spanish interests to arrive at an agreeable indemnity. The result will be a negotiated purchase rather than a nationalization.

It is highly possible that the BRPM will find it necessary to increase its interest in or to buy out other mining companies. A number of the various ore deposits which are now being exploited are near exhaustion; new deposits are being found and will have to be opened up, requiring considerable fresh investment. If the private companies do not do so, the BRPM will.

BEPI

BEPI was created in 1957 as an organism of the government to carry out feasibility studies of industrial projects and to promote these projects, using its own capital as necessary.[3] It was also authorized to invest in any existing companies whose continued operation was of general interest to the country's economy. The capital of BEPI came directly from the government's investment budget.

In its first several years of operation, BEPI entered into a number of projects, some in association with foreign investors, some with Moroccan investors, some a combination of both, and some 100 percent government-financed. The major investments of BEPI in those early years were the following:

1. Berliet-Maroc. This company was organized in 1958, with a capital of $1.5 million, to assemble trucks. Berliet, a French truck manufacturer, owned 60 percent of the shares and BEPI had 40 percent. It started operation in 1962.

2. Société Marocaine de Construction Automobile (SOMACA). SOMACA was organized in 1959, with a capital of $2 million, to assemble Simca and Fiat automobiles. Its share distribution was as follows: Simca, 20 percent; Fiat, 20 percent; BEPI, 46 percent; private Moroccan investors, 14 percent. Production started in 1962.

3. Pneu Général. This company was organized in 1958, with a capital of $2.5 million, to manufacture automobile tires and to have a monopoly position in this field for 10 years. General Tire, a U.S. company, holds 51 percent of the shares, BEPI has 42 percent, and private Moroccan investors hold the remaining 7 percent. It started production in 1961.

4. Société Anonyme Marocaine Italienne de Raffinage (SAMIR). Organized in 1959, with a capital of $7 million, as an oil refinery, SAMIR had its capital evenly divided between BEPI and ENI, the Italian holding company. It started operation in 1961.

     5.   Compagnie de Filature et de Textiles (COFITEX). It was organized in 1959, with a capital of $1.6 million, to weave cotton fibers. BEPI holds 38.8 percent of the capital and the remainder is held by private Moroccan investors. It began operation in 1962.

     6.   Arsenal de Fez. Although this company was organized by BEPI in 1960, it is owned 100 percent by the Moroccan government. It began production of small arms in 1965.

     7.   Maroc-Chimie, S.A. (also known as the Safi chemical complex). It was organized by BEPI in 1960 to produce super-triple phosphate and other high-grade fertilizers. BEPI initially attempted to interest foreign chemical companies in investing in this plant, but failed to reach an agreement. As a result, it helped to create Maroc Chimie, S.A., a public corporation whose capital is held entirely and directly by the government (rather than through BEPI). With an investment of approximately $13 million, it started operation in 1965.

     8.   TARIK. This company was set up in 1959 as a joint venture of BEPI and a French manufacturer of tractors to assemble tractors for the Moroccan market. Unfortunately, the company was unable to sell its product and had to close after two years of operation.

     9.   MAFITEX. It was created in 1953 to exploit the cork forests of northern Morocco (the Spanish zone), as a joint venture between Spanish and Moroccan interests. Immediately after independence the Spanish partners ceded their interest to the Moroccan stockholders, and the company soon found itself in difficulty. In 1958 BEPI attempted to come to the company's rescue and bought 34 percent of the stock for $170,000, hoping to continue to provide jobs for the 650-2,000 workers (depending upon the season). The company continued to experience financial difficulties and, in 1960, BEPI bought out the private interests in an attempt to improve the management. The company went bankrupt soon thereafter.

     The above projects constitute the main investments of BEPI. Its activity was greatly reduced after 1963. After that year it participated in the establishment of a small company which produces fish meal and of another for the manufacture of pharmaceutical products. Other than these, it made a number of studies but hesitated to create the new companies. Thus, its rate of investment was considerably reduced. There was a realization in government circles, and in the new management of BEPI, that many of its investments had been made on non-economic bases and that they were costing the government, and the consumers, a lot of money.

Although BEPI was organized on the principle of selling its shares to private investors when such becomes possible, it did not wish to sell to foreign investors, since this would result in a de-Moroccanization of industry. At the same time, BEPI officials stated that they had been unable to find private Moroccan investors who were interested in buying any of BEPI's holdings. There are, however, mixed reports on this matter. There is some indication that Moroccan investors had offered to buy BEPI's shares of Pneu Général (one of its few profitable holdings) but that BEPI was unwilling to sell its one big "winner."

BNDE

The BNDE was created in July, 1959, with a capital of $4 million. The government originally contributed a controlling percentage of the capital, the remainder being distributed among Moroccan and foreign banks and financial institutions. According to its operating procedures, it was to make no loans with a duration of less than two years nor more than 15 years, nor of an amount less than $10,000. In addition, the bank could invest directly in the creation or expansion of any company. Finally, it could guarantee loans in which it did not itself participate, and it could rediscount its medium-term loans with the Banque du Maroc, the country's central bank.

During the first two years of its operation, BNDE's loan activity was very high, but by the end of 1961, it had made equity investments totaling only $225,510 in five different organizations, of which three were banks and financial institutions and two were companies which were to do studies and make investments in tourism. However, in the 1961 annual report we find the comment that "during the year 1961, the BNDE decided that it would adopt a more active role in direct investments of two types. First, it will make investments of a symbolic nature in semi-public corporations which are of general interest. The bank will, by its presence on the boards of directors of these companies, be in a position to follow their financial management and give them the benefit of the bank's experience. Second, the BNDE will, in certain cases, take a minority position in private industrial companies. [Author's italics.] We hope, thus, to help Moroccanize some industries, or to improve the capital structure of some companies, or to precipitate the creation of new companies."

In following years, the direct investments of the BNDE increased rapidly, as shown in Appendix C, Table 9.

Following the policy expressed in 1961, some of the BNDE's investments have been in new companies and some represent a purchase of a part of existing companies. Some examples of the latter are the following:

1.   In 1962, the Société Marocaine de Tannerie et de Mégisserie, a French-owned tannery which employed 500 workers and was the largest in Morocco, was in financial difficulty. To avoid having to close, the company formed a joint venture with the BNDE. The bank received 38.5 percent of the shares for $270,000.

2.   In 1963, the Société des Ets. J.J. Carnoud et Forges de Basse Indre, a subsidiary of a French company by the same name which manufactures tin cans, wished to expand, but the parent company did not wish to put more money into Morocco. The BNDE purchased a minority share of the capital.

3.   In 1963, the Manufacture Marocaine d'Aluminium, a subsidiary of the French Pechiney group, which makes aluminum sheet, bars, pipes, and utensils, wished to expand and to construct a foundry. It asked the BNDE to participate in the capital expansion.

4.   Also in 1963, Cellulose du Maroc, a French-owned company which exports its entire production of wood pulp, wished to increase its capacity. The BNDE bought a minority position with an investment of $200,000.

The direct investment activity of the BNDE has, however, been a small part of its total activity. Its medium-term loans have generally maintained a level about equal to its direct investments, and its long-term loans are about 10 times greater.

At the end of 1966, the bank's capital was distributed as follows: Moroccan government, 43 percent; Moroccan banks, 9 percent; International Finance Corporation, 25 percent; foreign banks (including six French, one Belgian, three Italian, four German, and one American, the Morgan Guaranty Bank and Trust Company), 20 percent; and various insurance companies and individuals, 3 percent.[4] (Morgan Guaranty became a shareholder in 1961; International Finance Corporation, in December, 1962.)

Although the government now holds a minority position, it does control the BNDE, which thus serves as a major channel of Moroccanization of industry. Also, the BNDE avoids taking a majority position and avoids taking over management control of industrial companies in which it invests.

Although there is an expressed policy of selling its shares to
private (Moroccan) persons, this has not yet been implemented.

CDG

This financial organization was established to utilize
funds which had been paid in to the government, such as re-
tirement funds of government employees. Most of its resources are invested in government securities, but it has
recently served as a source of capital for the tourist industry,
primarily as a provider of medium- and long-term loans
but also, in a few cases, through direct investment.

It has, for example, 50 percent of the capital of Société
Africaine de Tourisme (the other half of which represents
one of the recent investments of the Banque de Paris et des
Pays Bas), which is building a series of hotel resorts along
the Mediterranean coast. It also has a 50 percent interest
in the Société Chellah Immobilière (the other half of which
is held by Ramada Hotels, Inc., a U.S. company), which has
bought the Tour Hassan Hotel and is planning a string of
hotels in the south.

The above activity of the CDG, plus four or five smaller
affairs, represented a total investment, by the middle of
1967, of only about $3 million.

SNI

As indicated earlier, there was some concern in the
period 1962-66, among some government officials, over the
operation of BEPI. One analysis of the situation was that
some of BEPI's problems stemmed from the fact that it combined the function of study with that of investment. One of
the answers to this problem was the creation of SNI.[5] The
creation of this investment company caused the dissolution of
BEPI, its investment function going to the SNI and its study
function going to another new organization.

The capital of SNI is provided by the government, and its
major purpose is to manage the portfolio of shares held by the
government in various government-owned companies or mixed
companies. It is, thus, somewhat of an investment banker
for the government. Interestingly enough, the law creating
this organization states expressly that the publicly held shares
which are turned over to it may be offered for public sale or
sold through the Office de Cotation des Valeurs Mobilières,
in Casablanca.

It was hoped that the creation of this public investment bank would result in sale of some of the government-owned shares in industry and also would give more life to the Office de Cotation. It was also expected that it would buy shares in private companies, which are offered through the Office de Cotation in Casablanca. This would achieve the goal of Moroccanizing French-owned companies; it would also, in-cidentally, serve as a means of shifting private investment into the public sector.

The SNI will, in addition, serve as a source of capital for other industrial investments which the government may wish to make.

Government-Controlled Banks

The government, as noted in Chapter 11, has made very little intrusion into the banking field. It has, of course, created a central bank. It also created the BNDE, which does not provide short-term credits in competition with the private banks. It also organized the Banque Centrale Popu-laire, but this is primarily to aid the privately held banques populaires. Thus, only with the establishment of the BMCE in 1958 did the government create a banking institution in direct competition with the private banks. Although it is government-controlled, it has among its shareholders a num-ber of private foreign banks.

Direct Government Investments

As indicated earlier, the government has made very few direct investments in industry, having chosen, rather, to invest through one of the government-owned or -controlled institutions mentioned above. The government does, of course, have a direct controlling interest in the Compagnie Maro-caine de Navigation (52.9 percent) and Royal Air Maroc (51 percent), and it owns the other public service companies pro-viding water, electricity, gas, and public transportation. But only rarely has it made a direct investment in industry. One of the very few examples to date is in the sugar industry: A sugar refinery was built and is owned 100 percent by the government.

Nationalization of Commerce

Morocco was in a situation, at the time of independence, similar to that of Tunisia, in that most of the imports and exports were handled by non-Moroccans. The major exception to this rule was phosphate exports, which were handled by the same government bureau which had a monopoly on mining phosphates. This situation continued until 1963.

Office National du Thé et du Sucre

Moroccans have become very large per capita consumers of both tea and sugar. This was brought about by the protectorate. In 1912, consumption of tea was 2,620 tons and of sugar was 54,000 tons; by 1965 it was 12,000 tons and 341,000 tons, respectively, although the population had only quadrupled. The cost and distribution of these products make them available to a very high percentage of the population, even those who are living at a subsistence level in the non-monetary economy. All of the tea is imported, as is most of the sugar, some raw and some refined. Since 1960, the government has been making an effort to increase the production of sugar beets. In 1963, a government-owned refinery started operation, to handle the local production of sugar beets. By 1963, imports of sugar were valued at $40 million, which was equivalent to 9 percent of total imports. There was, consequently, considerable political agitation, particularly by the UMT and the UNFP, for the nationalization of commerce in these products. This was done in September, 1963, with the establishment of the Office National du Thé et du Sucre. [6] It was given a monopoly on the importing and wholesaling of tea and sugar. These are, however, the only products for which the government has assumed a monopoly position on imports.

Office de Commercialisation et d'Exportation

Meanwhile, with the exception of phosphates, exports of Moroccan goods remained entirely in the private sector. But since this private sector was made up almost entirely of French citizens or companies, considerable political pressure was put on the government, particularly by the UMT and the UNFP. Articles calling for the nationalization of exports appeared frequently in their newspapers. In addition, the government felt that the French were under-invoicing exports and using this channel as an illegal means of getting capital out of the country.

The conservative bent of the government in 1965 was such that the political pressure was of less significance than the flight of capital in the decision to nationalize certain sectors of exports.

In July, 1965, a law created the Office de Commercialisation et d'Exportation (OCE), which was given a monopoly on the exportation of the following products: citrus fruits; fresh fruits and vegetables, artisan goods; canned and fresh fish; canned fruits, vegetables, and fruit juices. These products constituted about 35 percent of total exports. The text of the law began with an explanation of the motives behind the law, a rare occurrence, showing that the government realized that it was treading on ground which could affect its image as a private enterprise-oriented administration. It stated:

> The importance of exports in our economic and social life requires that the export channels for the country's main products be reviewed and reorganized. The solution which conforms most closely to the national interests is the concentration of market studies and marketing in one organization, closely controlled by the government. Since our economic development is closely tied with the growth of the producers, it is necessary to provide them with a marketing organization which is honest and in close liaison with the production. This objective will be fully achieved by giving a specialized government organization exclusive rights for these operations, thus eliminating any interventions which might be prejudicial to the economy of the country. The repatriation of the entire proceeds of the exports can thereby be achieved and will result in an improvement of the balance of payments. The expected increase in export receipts will be utilized for the needs of economic development.[7]

The OCE did not immediately attempt to assume responsibility for the export of all products for which it was given responsibility. By early 1966, it had taken over only citrus fruits, canned fish, artisan products, and fresh vegetables. It made a fiasco of the marketing of artisan products, did poorly with canned fish, about average with fresh vegetables, and an excellent job of handling the citrus fruits. In the latter case, it exported 7 percent less tonnage of citrus fruits than the preceding year (when the sector was still in private hands) but earned 50 percent more foreign exchange.[8]

Al Alam, the newspaper of the Istiqlal party, criticized this nationalization of exports as having been too hasty, and stated that the OCE was incapable of handling the job and that it was still relying on French middlemen while adding its own incompetence to the delays and costs of the operations.[9] The paper later noted that the middlemen had previously helped to finance the artisans, but the OCE was not doing so.[10] Also, the OCE was not paying the artisans a higher price than before, was buying less, and had introduced dishonesty and corruption to victimize the artisans.

The OCE has since relinquished responsibility for the export of artisan products but, on November 10, 1966, a royal decree extended the responsibility of the OCE, giving it also a monopoly position in the exportation of wine and cotton. The export of wine had previously been assumed by about 20 French-owned export houses. The government stated that since the recent nationalization of the 556,000 acres of French-owned farmland had put a large proportion of the vineyards in the hands of the government, it seemed anachronistic to leave the marketing of wine in private hands.[11]

Government Control of Investments

Contrary to the situation in Tunisia and Algeria, the Moroccan government does not require that every investment be approved by it. In principle, any individual may make an investment in commerce or industry, or may form a company to make such an investment, without the approval of the central government. It is merely necessary to register the creation of the enterprise in the register of commerce and with the tax authorities.

There are four exceptions to the above principle. Investments for the manufacture or assembly of cars, trucks, tractors, or tires require the approval of the Investment Commission. This special situation exists because the current manufacturers of these products obtained from the government, at the time of their investment, an agreement that investments in these fields would be restricted. In addition, investments in mining, tobacco, pharmaceuticals, weapons, and explosives are restricted or require special permission from a government ministry.

On the other hand, nearly all investments in productive industry (including tourism) pass through the Investment Commission, for only after examination and approval by the

Investment Commission can an investment project receive the
various economic, financial, and fiscal advantages available.
(The operation of this Investment Commission is discussed
below.)

ACTIONS DESIGNED TO ENCOURAGE
PRIVATE INVESTMENT

The Investment Code

During the last years of the protectorate, in conjunction
with the four-year equipment plans, the French regime had
passed a number of laws (as in Tunisia and Algeria) to encourage private investment. In Morocco, the most important
of these were laws dating from June, 1948, and December,
1954, offering certain tax advantages to new investments or
reinvestments.

Following independence, the Moroccan government soon
attempted to improve this regime of encouragement of private
investment and, on September 13, 1958, promulgated an investment code. At the time this code appeared, the Prime
Minister's office issued the following statement:

> The policy of His Majesty's government in regard to
> private enterprise in this country is based on the prin-
> ciple that while all sound investment is welcome, en-
> couragement should be afforded to enterprises which
> promise to bring a steady support and rapid expansion
> to those sectors of the economy which could particularly
> benefit from such capital contributions and which, con-
> sequently, further the objectives of the general economic
> plans. . . .

This 1958 code replaced the previous laws, including
their provisions and adding some new advantages: the elimination of import duties on equipment necessary for the investment, the elimination of registration taxes, accelerated
depreciation, and an interesting guarantee on the transfer
of profits by foreign investors. (The Investment Commission
was given the power to require the Exchange Control Office
to make automatic transfers of profits if, in return, the foreign
investor would agree to refrain from asking for permission
to transfer part or all of his invested capital for a period of
time, as agreed between the investor and the Investment Commission but not to exceed 15 years.)

It soon became apparent that the provisions of the 1958 code were insufficient incentives to attract the amount of private investment that was needed. As a result, on December 31, 1960, another law was promulgated. [12] It provided a new investment code to replace that of 1958. This new code contained most of the provisions of the 1958 code, plus some new ones: the availability of equipment subsidies and the statement of the absolute right of foreign investors to repatriate their invested capital.

As a result, the advantages now available to investors are as follows:

1. Partial or full exemption from duties on imported equipment.

2. Partial or full exemption from company registration and license taxes.

3. Accelerated depreciation, up to twice the normal rate.

4. The right to put up to 50 percent of annual net profits into a tax-free reserve which can be used to buy new equipment, up to 40 percent of the value of the new investment.

5. Equipment subsidy from the government: up to 20 percent of cost if location is in the province of Tangier, none if location is in Casablanca or Mohammedia, and up to 15 percent elsewhere.

6. Guarantee of retransfer of all or part of the proceeds of the liquidation of a foreign investment which was formally registered as such.

7. The transfer of dividends and interest from foreign investments is considered as "normal and current payments."

Any one or more of the above advantages are available to investors in "productive" industry (which includes tourism), but only those industries defined as basic industries (steel, heavy chemicals, oil refineries, and any industry located in Tangier province) may benefit from the whole range of incentives.

To obtain the benefit of the above incentives, investors must submit an application to the Investment Commission, which was established by the code. The decision of the Commission is given within two to 12 months, but averages three to four months. It should be noted that except for investments in motor vehicles, tires, firearms, and explosives, the Investment Commission does not decide whether the investment may or may not be made, but merely which incentives, if any, will be awarded to the investor.

The Commission accords an exemption from duties on imported equipment for nearly all approved projects. The percentage of investors who are granted the other advantages varies greatly from year to year, but about 20 percent appear to have received a reduction of income tax and one out of six have received an equipment subsidy.

Investment Guarantee Treaties and
Arbitration Convention

The Moroccan government has been much less active than the Tunisian government in negotiating investment guarantee treaties. Only three are in effect: with the United States, West Germany, and Belgium.

The treaty with the United States was the first, dating from July 3, 1958. It is the standard "agreement on the guarantee of private investment," (See Chapter 5.)

The treaty with West Germany was signed on August 31, 1961, and became effective on July 10, 1962; the treaty with Belgium was signed on April 28, 1965, and became effective on October 18, 1965. These are the same as the treaties which West Germany and Belgium signed with Tunisia. (See Chapter 5.)

Like Tunisia, Morocco was one of the original signatories of the World Bank-sponsored international arbitration convention, which went into effect on October 14, 1966.

Fonds National d'Investissement

The Fonds National d'Investissement, a national investment fund, was instituted on December 31, 1961, as a means of encouraging private investment.[13] All companies had to pay annual contributions in to the fund, based on their profits: 3 percent of that portion of profits less than $7,200; 8 percent of the portion between $7,200 and $10,000; and 15 percent of all above $10,000. At the time of the contribution, the companies received provisional shares in the fund. These contributions then became forced savings, or a tax, or a government borrowing, depending upon the final use and upon one's attitude.

There were four possibilities once provisional shares had been received from the FNI: (a) They could be left there for three years, during which time the shareholder received no interest and at the end of which time they were converted into permanent, non-transferable shares paying 3 percent interest. They became "permanent" government bonds with no terminal date. (b) They could be converted into permanent shares, at the request of the shareholder, at any time before the end of the three-year period. (c) They could be sold to another company, with the approval of the government, if that company was going to make a productive investment. That other company would then turn them in to the FNI for cash, but would have to invest at least as much of its own capital as it received from the FNI. (Thus the holder of the shares could, if he himself had no plans to invest, sell them at a discount to another company, providing that other company with cheap money and at the same time increasing his own liquidity. (d) The shareholder could sell his shares back to the FNI if he would use the capital to make a productive investment and would invest at least an equivalent sum of his own funds. He could, in fact, obtain more capital from the FNI than he had paid in during the past three years, the excess to be deducted from the amount that he would otherwise have had to pay in during the following two years.[14]

It can be seen that the FNI was conceived as a two-pointed weapon. It would either provide an incentive to the private sector to invest (as a way of recouping what they had paid in), or it would be an additional tax on profits, providing the government with additional funds to invest in the public sector.

Unfortunately, it incited very little private investment which would not otherwise have occurred. The government was not pleased with the results and in April, 1966, decided to liquidate the FNI, the interest on outstanding shares to be paid by the treasury.[15]

Sociétés d'Investissement

The same law which created the SNI also authorized the creation of various sociétés d'investissement by private individuals. These are, in effect, open-end mutual funds. Such a fund must have a minimum capital of $1 million, cannot own more than 20 percent of the shares of any given company or invest more than 15 percent of its capital in any one company, and must invest at least 25 percent of its capital either in government bonds or in stocks listed by the Office de Cotation in Casablanca. In addition, these investment funds are not permitted to participate in the management of any company or to buy shares of any company which is not at least three years old. The dividends distributed by these funds are not taxed.

It is thus apparent that these sociétés d'investissement
were devised as a means of increasing and channeling savings. To the extent that they succeed, their operation will
result in a healthier private sector.

Free Trade Zone of Tangier

In April, 1960, Tangier lost all of the special advantages
which had protected it from Moroccan taxes, import duties,
and exchange controls. By the end of the year, 567 companies,
representing a capital of $6 million, were dissolved; most of
the others were simply abandoned. [16]   The result was catas-
trophic to the economy of the city and its surrounding areas.
It had accomplished a political purpose--integration into the
Moroccan system--but resulted in an economic problem. By
the end of 1961, therefore, a law appeared which created a
semi-free trade zone in the port area of the city of Tangier.
However, although this law existed, it was not implemented.

During the following years, there was an active search
for ways of revitalizing the city, and a number of commissions
and international missions studied the problem and made
recommendations. The gist of these was that Tangier's main
asset was its tourist possibilities, but that port activity should
be developed and free trade zones established--one for commercial activity and one for industrial activity. [17] The consensus, however, was that because of a lack of raw materials,
the distance from large markets, the high cost of power, the
lack of trained workers, and the incompatibility of heavy industry with tourism, any effort to industrialize Tangier should
be restricted to light industry.

On August 4, 1965, a royal decree canceled the 1961 decree and created a commercial free trade zone. This was
implemented by a decree of November 8, 1965, which provided the operating regulations of the free trade zone.
Finally, on June 30, 1967, this zone was officially opened
and began operation with 25 companies. [18]

Meanwhile, although a site had been selected and site
preparation begun for an "industrial" free trade zone in
Tangier, no law was written nor signed, by mid-1969, to
authorize its establishment or provide its operating regulations.

Freeing of Blocked Accounts

As in Tunisia following independence, many French citizens who were residents of Morocco transferred their capital and savings out of the country, resulting in a large flight of capital, until the flow was stemmed by the institution of exchange controls in 1959. Subsequently, large sums of capital which belonged to Frenchmen who returned to France were placed in "blocked accounts, " which could not be transferred out of the country and whose use in the country was severely restricted.

In February, 1966, however, the government instituted a program which offered the owners of these blocked accounts a way out. A total of $2 million in Moroccan government bonds was made available for purchase with the funds in these blocked accounts. Upon maturity, the cash from these government bonds would be freely convertible to any foreign currency.

The sale of this first issue started very slowly, but confidence built up, and by the end of 1966 it had been sold out. The government then offered an additional $6 million in bonds under similar conditions.

Official Creation of an American Chamber of Commerce

There have long existed in Morocco a French Chamber of Commerce, an Italian Chamber of Commerce, and a Spanish Chamber of Commerce; and a Moroccan Chamber of Commerce, representing primarily Moroccan citizens, was created soon after independence. However, none of these has been officially recognized by the government. It was, therefore, an innovation and an expression of the government's desire to promote interest in Morocco by U.S. businessmen when the King issued a royal decree on October 12, 1966, which recognized and authorized the creation of the American Chamber of Commerce of Morocco.

Creation of a National Investment Promotion Center

The government had declared its intention to create an investment promotion center for a number of years, and this was officially accomplished by royal decree in December, 1967. [19] It was created as a semi-autonomous organization attached to the royal Cabinet. Its appearance earlier was announced by the King, who stated:

> Morocco wishes to make available, to all those who desire to invest in Morocco, maximum help and facilities in making contacts with private organizations and in the preparation of necessary studies and projects oriented toward those sectors of the economy which are considered the most useful and economically viable. In other words, in establishing this center, Morocco wishes to make available to the foreign investor an efficient organization which can aid him in all of the necessary investigations and studies which will permit him to plan and implement his projects without getting lost in the usual administration routine and red tape. [20]

NOTES

1.   Dahir No. 1-63-182 and Dahir No. 1-63-184 (August 8, 1963); Bulletin Officiel No. 2650 (August 9, 1963).

2.   Maroc Information (May 2, 1963); discussion with officials of the Banque de Paris et des Pays Bas.

3.   Dahir of 31 December 1957; Bulletin Officiel (January 10, 1958).

4.   From unpublished papers of the BNDE.

5.   Royal Decree No. 194-66 (October 22, 1966); Bulletin Officiel No. 2818 (November 2, 1966).

6.   Dahir No. 1-63-214 (September 7, 1963); Bulletin Officiel (September 20, 1963).

7.   Royal Decree No. 223-65 (July 9, 1965); Bulletin Officiel No. 2750 (July 14, 1965).

8.   "L'Office de Commercialisation et d'Exportation et sa Nouvelle Mission," Note de Documentation, Special No. (April 27-May 14, 1967), 20.

9.   Al Alam (August 30, 1965; September 2, 1965).

10.   Ibid. (January 17, 1966).

11.   Le Monde (July 29, 1966).

12.   Dahir 1-60-383 (December 31, 1960); Bulletin Officiel No. 2520 (February 10, 1961).

13.   Dahir No. 1-61-445; Bulletin Officiel (December 30, 1961).

14.   Arrêté du Ministre de l'Économie Nationale et des Finances (April 4, 1962); Bulletin Officiel (April 6, 1962).

15.   Arrêté du Vice Premier Ministre (April 25, 1966); Bulletin Officiel (May 11, 1966).

16.   Vie Économique (March 17, 1961).

17.   Maroc Informations (November, 1964).

18.   Le Petit Marocain (July 1, 1967).

19.   Royal Decree No. 420-67 (December 29, 1967).

20.   Le Petit Marocain (August 1, 1967).

CHAPTER **14** APPLICATION OF THE
MODEL TO MOROCCO

The post-independence experience of private enterprise in Morocco has not been all roses and sunshine. First of all, some foreign-owned farmland was nationalized without compensation. In addition, the government has followed a policy of increasing its ownership in the mining industry through the BRPM, attempting thereby to obtain a majority interest in the many joint mining ventures. Sometimes directly, but usually through such public organizations as BEPI, BNDE, and CDG, the government has created or purchased part ownership in a fairly large number of industrial companies. Also, the government has created, besides the BNDE, the BMCE, which competes directly with the private commercial banks. Finally, the government has a monopoly on the importation of sugar and tea and on the exportation of artisan goods and of fresh and processed food products, which constitute about 35 percent of Morocco's exports.

All of these actions represent a considerable encroachment of government into the private sector. To evaluate their significance, however, one must examine the circumstances under which they took place.

The nationalization of foreign-owned farmland did not apply to all such land--only to about one-third of the total. This land had never been sold to the owners but, to circumvent the religious laws existing during the protectorate, had been "leased in perpetuity." Such an operation had been highly suspect in legal terms, at its origin, and was possible only because the French protectorate government had exercised its power in a questionable manner. Hence, the Moroccan government, in recovering these properties, did not feel obligated to compensate the owners for the land. The government did, however, pay compensation for equipment and crops which went with the land. It is, in this same context, noteworthy that the Moroccan government resisted pressures to nationalize all foreign-owned farmland in 1963 and 1964, at a time when this policy was followed in the neighboring countries of Algeria and Tunisia.

The production of phosphate, which is by far the largest
mining industry, has been in the public sector since its inception in 1921. Only through an inconsistent policy did the
French permit most of the remainder of Morocco's mining
industry to be developed by private investors. One might
have expected the Moroccan government, in keeping with its
French heritage, to nationalize the remainder of the mining
industry. It has shown restraint in not doing so, and the
purchase of additional shares in the existing companies since
independence has not been so much a matter of policy as a
question of pragmatism. The purchases have usually resulted
when a private company is reluctant to provide additional
capital needed for modernization or expansion and hence
utilizes, for this purpose, the funds provided by the government's purchase of additional shares.

The investments of the BNDE have grown at an increasing
pace, but only a small percentage of its operations have consisted of creating public corporations. The emphasis has
been on providing additional capital for private firms which
need help, always following the policy of taking only a minority
interest and leaving the management of the company to the
private owners. Thus, it usually plays only the expected role
of a development bank. It is not a vehicle which the government established to follow a policy of increasing its ownership
or control of production.

On the other hand, the nationalization of certain areas of
foreign commerce appears to be at least partially the result
of pressures from the socialist elements in the Moroccan
power structure. The UMT, the Moroccan labor union, had
pressed for the nationalization of the importing and processing
of tea and sugar. The large consumption of these products
by all levels of the population makes them very sensitive
products. They are, thus, "basic industry." Hence, the
government take-over of this sector is an ideological act.

Returning briefly to the BEPI, we find that a large portion
of its invested capital went into the creation of an oil refinery,
which is also "basic industry." In addition, the government
has invested directly, and owns 100 percent of a number of
companies. These are for the manufacture of matches and
cigarettes, the production of super-triple phosphate, the
manufacture of small arms, and the refining of sugar. Also,
the government negotiated the purchase of a 51 percent interest
in the only French-owned sugar refinery. Thus, the government has not escaped entirely from a policy of public control
of basic industries. On the other hand, the government

monopoly on exports of artisan products and on certain agricultural products was based partially on ideology and partially on practicality. The export of these products by French businessmen, many of whom followed a policy of under-invoicing, constituted a channel for the illegal repatriation of capital, and hence led to a considerable decrease in Morocco's foreign exchange earnings.

The major aspect of the government's actions to date, however, is that it has avoided nationalization or expropriation of industry. The temptation to nationalize undoubtedly arose as frequently as it did in Tunisia, but in each case the government chose to enter into negotiations for the purchase of the property in question, or to wait for the expiration of leases and concessions before taking over the operation of the industry concerned.

The number of actions of the government to encourage private investors exceeds those which have had a discouraging aspect. These favorable actions began with the promulgation of an investment code in 1958 and an improved code in 1960. This illustrates that the government decided at an early date to encourage private investors, both domestic and foreign. This attitude toward foreign investors is reinforced by the early signature of an investment guarantee treaty with the United States, followed by similar treaties with Germany and Belgium, and adherence to the World Bank's international arbitration convention. It should be noted that Morocco has not signed an investment guarantee treaty with France, which indicates a desire not to increase greatly the already predominant position of the French in Moroccan industry.

The creation of the FNI and the decree authorizing the formation of sociétés d'investissement are both interesting attempts to encourage private investment. The first failed and the latter has had minimal results, but these poor results reflect the attitude of the private investor rather than that of the government.

A review of all of the government's actions to date, both discouraging and encouraging, gives a picture which is quite favorable to private enterprise. The analysis would therefore be very simple if the past were always a forecast of the future. But the important part of applying the model is to attempt to forecast the future climate for private investment. What is the likelihood that past governmental attitudes vis-à-vis public versus private investment will continue into the foreseeable future?

Utilizing this approach, the attitude of the King is of greatest importance. What does he have to say on this matter? A review of his remarks reveals, first of all, that he places full reliance on private enterprise to carry out the industrialization of Morocco. He feels that the economic infrastructure (railroads, communications, and electric power) should be the responsibility of the government, as should basic industry. For the rest, the state will engage only in flexible planning. He never says directly that if the private sector fails to invest to the extent expected, the state will do so. He came closest to saying this when he noted the failure of the private sector to invest sufficiently during the five-year plan (1960-64): " . . . the state is always disposed, in regard to industrialization, to assume its obligations, either in a direct or an indirect manner. . . ." Similarly, in his March, 1963, speech, the King stated, "We plan also that the state can, each time that it is necessary, intervene in the economic life of the country, where it is possible to have an influence, and provide, within the desired time period, the impulse needed for development." It is possible, but difficult, to interpret these statements as threats of state intervention in industrial investment.

If the King is not disposed toward public investments in industry, what is the possibility of his reacting against the predominance of French investment in the economy? We find that nowhere does he utilize the term "decolonization." He has no burning desire to transfer the industrial and commercial sectors of the economy into the hands of Moroccans. If the King (or his father) had been so inclined, there were two occasions when diplomatic relations between Morocco and France were ruptured, in 1956 and in 1966, at which times French financial aid was stopped, which would have provided the Moroccan government with opportunities to nationalize some or all French investments. These opportunities were not seized. But the King recognized, in 1964, that the French predominance cannot continue indefinitely. He stated that his development policy, while leaving "many possibilities open to the activity of the French . . . takes into account the need to achieve an eventual Moroccanization."

Finally, we find that the King has avoided publicly embracing an ideology. When pressed to state his position (the reporter assuming that the King was in the center), the King said, "The exercise of being to the left or to the right is a luxury of political and philosophical speculation . . . a luxury [which Morocco] cannot afford. . . ." The King thus allowed himself maneuverability for pragmatic solutions to the country's economic woes.

The development plans have, however, been much more specific as to possible intervention by the state in industrial investment. The two-year plan (1958-59) noted that the BEPI would "intervene in all cases where direct action by the state must supplement private initiative." The five-year plan (1960-64) noted that the state, through BEPI, would intervene in the steel, chemical, oil refinery, and shipyard sectors, as well as in other industries which would have a monopoly in the market, or in processing industries which pose complex problems, or in other sectors "where one cannot be precise as to what intervention the government might undertake."

During the late 1950's, the political forces with socialist tendencies were at the peak of their power. It was during 1958 and 1959 that the farthest-left government was in office, that BEPI was created to channel government intervention, and that most of such investment took place. Also, the five-year plan was drawn up by this government. However, the leftist forces were on the way down. As a consequence, the language of the three-year plan (1965-67) and of the five-year plan (1968-72) is much softer on this question, and the government's actions are much more specific. It was during the three-year plan period that the government dissolved the BEPI, thus eliminating its main channel of intervention in industrial investment. This action best illustrates the tendency of the present government.

The statements of some of the leading political figures, men who play a role in today's government and who will probably be prominent in the future, follow the same line. Guedira notes that Morocco's "experiments with government intervention have put some very important sectors into the hands of men without competence. . .," and the long speech by Amine Bengeloun emphasizes the error which he feels Morocco would make if it were to attempt to place too much reliance on state intervention in industry.

Thus, the King and the ministers whom he has chosen to run the government represent the conservative school of economics, which will attempt to avoid direct government investment in productive industry, will not press for decolonization measures, will not nationalize industry, and probably will not carry out any further agrarian reform. As a monarchy, the government will, when possible, opt for the status quo. The question then arises as to what forces might cause it to budge from this policy.

With the political parties in disarray, the only organized, non-governmental force with socialist tendencies is the UMT. The second congress of the UMT called for the nationalization of electricity and transportation. and of the lots de colonisation portion of the foreign-owned farmland. These were, soon thereafter, taken over by the government. In his May Day speech of 1964, Ben Seddik, the President of the UMT, called for the nationalization of imports of sugar and tea and of the one large sugar refinery. The government has since taken over this import sector and has purchased a majority interest in the sugar refinery. Thus, the government has, in the past, reacted to the demands of the UMT. The labor union has, more recently, called for broad measures of decolonization, referring to continued French dominance in commerce, industry, and finance as "neo-colonialism." It also has taken a position against encouraging additional foreign investment.

However, even though the UMT has been urging measures which would darken the political climate for private invest- ment, it appears that the government has ceased to react to these pressures. The strongest indications of this are the 18-month jail sentence given to Ben Seddik in 1966 and the subsequent, demonstrated willingness of the government to use the army to keep the union members in line.

Are there other forces which threaten the status quo? The three-year plan (1965-67), which was written prior to the dissolution of Parliament and therefore reflects a broader political spectrum, called for the total recovery by the state of foreign-owned farmland and for a redistribution of large landholdings to the peasants. This was to be accomplished during the term of the plan. The Parliament was dissolved in June, 1965, and neither of these steps has been taken. Meanwhile, the population growth rate of 3-3.5 percent per year is resulting in lower and lower living standards for the large peasant class. They are, however, disorganized, and in any case there is no political party activity permitting the furthering of their cause.

Meanwhile, the economy is performing very badly; in- vestment remains at a low rate, and unemployment of the urban population, which was at 40 percent in 1966, is growing at a rate even more rapid than that in the rural areas, where in 1966 the unemployment rate was already 50 percent. In addition, the development plans, which are modest in their growth and investment forecasts, go unfulfilled, partly as a result of insufficient private investment.

As a result, pressures for change will increase but will, under the present political organization, have to remain underground. These pressures will demand agrarian reform and nationalization of foreign-owned land. If the government decides to bow to them, nationalization with compensation will be costly to the governmental budget and to the foreign exchange reserves. These pressures will demand more government investment in industry, which will further add to the budgetary and balance of payments deficits. There will also be more and more sensitivity to the predominance of the French in industry and commerce, and there will be pressure for decolonization measures (sooner or later these French businessmen will become a handy whipping boy). Again, the government cannot afford to buy out these large investments, and the Moroccan businessmen have demonstrated their inability or lack of desire to invest in these companies, which leaves nationalization without compensation as the only alternative.

Added to the above pressures is the spirit of Arab nationalism, which is radiating out of the Middle East and Algeria, leading to an increased distrust of foreign influence and hence of foreign investment.

Since 1965, the government has resisted all of these pressures and, as a result, has followed policies which appear favorable to private investors. But what of the future? If the government bows to any of these pressures, private investors will react negatively. If it maintains a status quo, the investment rate will probably remain at low levels, and the economy will remain relatively stagnant.

There are, however, several bright spots on the horizon. One of these is the gradual modernization of agriculture, utilizing new hybrid grains and greatly increasing the use of fertilizer rather than agrarian reform. This should greatly increase agricultural production, although it will not satisfy the desire of most peasants to own more land. The other is the future of tourism, which is attracting domestic as well as foreign private investment and could, over a medium term, transform the economy. The King apparently is relying greatly on these two factors to gain time.

The prognosis, therefore, is that the government will not change its policies and that, with the faithful support of the army, it will be able to contain the pressures for change during the foreseeable future. Hence, the political climate for private investment is favorable.

PART   V   CONCLUSION

15

GENERAL APPLICABILITY
OF THE MODEL

THE THREE NORTH AFRICAN COUNTRIES

This study of Tunisia, Algeria, and Morocco has provided an interesting contrast in the political climate for
private investment. All three came from a common Berber
heritage; all had been occupied and ruled by the Phoenicians,
the Romans, the Arabs, the Turks (except for Morocco), and
finally the French, and all three have an Islamic culture.
Yet even with this high degree of commonality in their history,
they have developed in widely separate directions since their
independence.

Algeria has nationalized a broad spectrum of industry,
plus banking, insurance, and foreign-owned farmland; has
instituted a system of worker-management; and several key
officials have stated that the government is determined to
establish a socialist economy in which private investment
will eventually wither away.

The Moroccan government has avoided the use of the term
"socialism" and has avoided nationalizing any industry. It
is attempting to reduce the rate of public investment in industry and is following policies designed to encourage private
investment, both domestic and foreign. At the same time,
however, the economic situation is deteriorating in such a
way that if conditions do not change, the political situation
may become unstable.

In the middle of the road is Tunisia, which has nationalized some industry and all foreign-owned farmland and has
continued to increase the amount of public investment in industry at a greater rate than the private sector has, but still
is making strong efforts to attract foreign and domestic
private investment. Although Tunisia has adopted a type of
socialism to identify its politico-economic policies, it does

not, even in the long run, exclude a large private sector. In
addition, its economic and political situation's are quite stable.

Thus, in North Africa there is one country which appears
to be Marxist socialist, wherein the state is rapidly taking
over the entire private sector of industry and commerce and
has a major portion of the good agricultural lands. (Algeria
represents an extreme which is quite rare among the underdeveloped countries.) There is another country, sharing a
similar history and geography, which has avoided nationalization and is frankly private-enterprise oriented, a policy
which is equally rare in Africa and Asia. And a third country
is following the more typical policy of a mixed economy, with
a good probability of a long-term co-existence of the public
and private sectors.

SOME OTHER EX-COLONIES

As indicated in Chapters 1 and 25, an investor should
make every effort to apply this model to <u>any</u> newly independent
country as one of the inputs into the investment decision-
making process. Such a study is, in fact, one of the critical
inputs, although in many cases its weight can be lessened by
government investment guarantee programs in the investor's
country. It will be useful to look briefly at several other
countries in order to highlight the usefulness of the application
of the model.

Three countries which are particularly interesting from
this point of view are Guinea, the Ivory Coast, and Senegal.
Like North Africa, these three countries have the common
heritage of French colonization, are adjacent to each other,
and have somewhat similar economies. The fascinating
similarity, however, is that Guinea appears to have chosen
a system which approaches the Marxist socialist route (like
Algeria); the Ivory Coast is private enterprise-oriented (like
Morocco); and Senegal (like Tunisia) has its special brand of
socialism and is following a pragmatic policy of encouraging
private investment while building up the public sector. Let's
look in a bit more detail at each of these three countries, for
while these broad similarities with the North African countries
do exist, there are great differences.

<u>Guinea</u> did not have to fight a long and terrible war to
achieve its independence, but it did suffer an economic and
psychological jolt immediately thereafter. When President

De Gaulle gave Guinea (and other colonies of the French Community) the right of self-determination, Guinea chose immediate independence without interdependence with France. As a result, France withdrew her army, her government administrators, her teachers, her technicians, and all movable capital equipment. The economy was dealt a crippling blow overnight, and there were very few qualified people left in the country to work for its rejuvenation. The President, Sékou Touré, consequently turned to the Soviet Union and China for help. The government took over the electricity and water companies, transportation, banking, insurance, and foreign trade. However, the major mining company, Fria, which was foreign-owned, was left untouched, as were some of the other industries. The strong and very effective President has tended to avoid the use of the term "socialism", because he does not believe that the Marxist theories of the class struggle are applicable to Guinea. He states, rather, that Guinea has chosen the "non-capitalist route of development." However, in 1962 Sékou Touré, in conjunction with the National Assembly, issued an investment code designed to attract foreign investment, and in 1963 he denationalized the diamond industry. Thus, there apparently is a role to be played by private investment, but in which sectors, under what conditions, and for how long? What is the actual political climate for private investment? Obviously, a much more detailed study is required.

The Ivory Coast has followed, since independence in 1960, a constant policy of encouraging private enterprise and avoiding, when possible, actions which might discourage it. In 1961 the government passed a liberal investment code and in 1962 signed an investment guarantee treaty with the United States. At the time of independence there were only about 80 industrial companies in the country, with total annual sales of about $40 million. The government has not nationalized any of this existing industrial sector. A 1962 law, however, does permit the government to engage in business, and subsequent development plans have resulted in some public investment in industry, although the government continues to place primary reliance on private investment to achieve its industrialization goals. Still, the government finds that the youth and the intellectuals of the country want a more revolutionary (socialistic and nationalistic) policy, so the pressure is in that direction. However, President Houphouët-Boigny does not labor under the same handicap as does King Hassan of Morocco, for the economy of the Ivory Coast is one of the

most buoyant and rapidly growing in all of Africa. So, unlike
Morocco, in the Ivory Coast economic growth acts as a
foundation for political stability.

Senegal finds itself on a middle ground between the "non-
capitalist" ideological tendency of Guinea and the private
enterprise orientation of the Ivory Coast. At the time of
independence (1960), Senegal was far more industrialized
than either Guinea or the Ivory Coast because it had been the
administrative and commercial capital of French West Africa.
Consequently, most of the industrial investment had been
scaled to fit this much larger market. Between 1948 and
1960, new private investment (almost entirely by French
nationals or companies) totaled about $120 million, and by
1960 there were some 320 firms with annual sales totaling
about $300 million. Within a year after independence, the
government issued a development plan which gave the private
sector the predominant role in industrial investment.

However, the two leaders, Mamadou Dia and Léopold
Senghor, both loudly proclaimed the need for socialism in
Senegal. They both agreed that they were not speaking of
the socialism of Marx and Engels, but that Senegal would
choose from the various Western techniques and institutions
those ideas which would be most useful and applicable to the
country. Partly as a result of this, little private investment
appeared--less than 15 percent of that foreseen by the
development plan. Prime Minister Mamadou Dia was probably
more ideologically oriented than President Senghor and more
concerned about the predominance of the French in Senegal's
industry. Mamadou Dia was removed from the government
late in 1962, however, after he had led an abortive coup
d'état, and since then President Senghor has tried to encourage
private investment. An investment code which had been
issued in 1962 was subsequently liberalized, and the government signed an investment guarantee treaty with the United
States. On the other hand, the government nationalized the
exportation of peanuts (which constituted over 80 percent of
the country's exports), nationalized the importation of some
basic food products, and began to invest in new industry through
a newly created development bank. What direction will the
government follow in the future? There is a larger question
mark than the one in the Ivory Coast, though this is not so
much a result of the government's actions as it is the reaction
of private investors to the government's continued use of the
term "socialism" to describe its orientation and the government's insistence that it will quickly step in to invest in industry if the private sector does not do its full share.

Shifting to another part of Africa, it is useful in the context of this study to take a quick look at Tanzania, a British colony which obtained independence late in 1961. The struggle for independence was led by Julius Nyerere, who has been President and chief ideological leader since independence. The basis of his ideology has been the term ujamaa, which, in Swahili, means something like "family" or "brotherhood." When speaking in English, however, President Nyerere utilizes the term "socialism," but with a meaning as vague as that of ujamaa in Swahili. Although he had stated the need for some form of socialism since independence, President Nyerere had taken no actions which were directed against the private enterprise sector. As late as February, 1967, he could point only to a state-owned insurance company and a few state-owned factories here and there. Private investors were hesitant, however, because of his use of the term "socialism," because Zanzibar (which depends primarily upon East European countries and China for foreign aid) joined Tanganyika to form Tanzania, and because some Chinese and Soviet delegations were occasionally seen.

In February, 1967, ideology was converted to policy. The important document, the Arusha Declaration, was pronounced on February 5. In this speech, President Nyerere outlined (among other things) his government's credo on socialism and economic development.

> How about the enterprises of foreign investors? It is true we need these enterprises. We have even passed an act of Parliament protecting foreign investment in this country. Our aim is to make foreign investors feel that Tanzania is a good place in which to invest because investments will be safe and profitable, and the profits can be taken out of the country without difficulty. We expect to get money through this method. But we cannot get enough. And even if we were able to convince foreign investors and foreign firms to undertake all the projects and programs of economic development that we need, is that what we actually want to happen? . . . How can we depend upon gifts, loans, and investments from foreign countries and foreign companies without endangering our independence? ... The policy of inviting a chain of capitalists to come and establish industries in our country might succeed in giving us all the industries we need, but it would also succeed in preventing the establishment of socialism, unless we believe that without first building capitalism we cannot build socialism.

On the day following the Arusha Declaration, the government nationalized the 10 commercial banks, all of which were
foreign-owned, then operating in Tanzania. By the end of
that week, the government had also nationalized the flour
mills, the export and import houses, and the private insurance
companies. In addition, the government took a controlling
interest in seven of the leading firms, including a shoe company and a tobacco company, and stated that it would soon take
a controlling interest in the sisal industry, the country's third
largest earner of foreign exchange.

Then, as swiftly as the nationalizations had begun, they
ended. President Nyerere promised full and fair compensation to those affected and assured the remainder of the private
sector that he would go no further. He has since stated his
wish to invite additional private investment, both domestic
and foreign, to come into those sectors not earmarked for
public ownership.

The political climate for private investment in Tanzania
has been badly marred, but what of the future? What are the
underlying political, economic, and social forces? How does
one evaluate the risk of investing there today? Obviously a
more detailed study is required.

The last country to be considered in this section is India,
another former British colony, but in a non-African setting.
She obtained her independence in August, 1947, with Nehru
as Prime Minister. He was sensitive to the high percentage
of British investment in the country. In addition, he had long
been sympathetic to socialistic ideas. However, he realized
that it would be economically unwise to upset the business
community. Consequently, in April, 1948, he had the Parliament pass the Industrial Policy Resolution, according to which,
instead of following a policy of nationalization, industry was
divided into four broad categories. In the first category, to
be a government monopoly, were munitions, railroads, and
atomic energy (this was a continuation of pre-independence
policy). The second category consisted of such basic industries
as coal, steel, aircraft, shipbuilding, and petroleum, in which
the state would be exclusively responsible for all new under-
takings unless, in the national interest, the state were to find
it necessary to secure the help of the private sector. Existing
private companies in these industries were to be left free for
10 years. A third category of "important industries" was to
be subject to close government control and regulation. All the
remaining industries constituted a fourth category which was
to be left to private enterprise and the free play of market
forces.

But Nehru did not forget his original goals. Under his influence, the Parliament formally accepted, in December, 1954, a "socialist pattern of society as the objective of social and economic policy." In 1955, the Imperial Bank of India was nationalized and renamed the State Bank of India. It opened over 400 branches and soon had about one-third of the commercial banking activity in India. Private airlines and gold mines also were nationalized. Early in 1956, life insurance companies were nationalized and combined into the Life Insurance Corporation of India. It should be noted, however, that the shareholders in all of these nationalized enterprises were given a fair and equitable compensation.

This was followed, in April, 1956, by a new Industrial Policy Resolution, which greatly increased the number of industries in the first category, whose future development was to be the exclusive responsibility of the state. A second category consisted of industries "which will be progressively state-owned and in which the state will therefore generally take the initiative in establishing new ventures." A third category contained the remaining industries, whose future development generally would be left to the private sector. The 1948 and 1956 resolutions were effectively translated into development plans. The first five-year plan (1951-55) projected industrial investment which was split 50-50 between the public and private sectors, while the second five-year plan (1956-60), which followed the second Industrial Policy Resolution, allotted the public sector 61 percent, leaving only 39 percent of total industrial investment to the private sector.

It is noteworthy that the private sector did not, as a result of these policies, cease to risk its capital for industrial investment. In fact, although the private sector failed to meet the projected investment during the first five-year plan (1951-55), during the period 1956-60 industrial production rose 55 percent and approximately 45 percent of new industrial investment (6 percent more than called for by the plan) was made by the private sector.

By 1960 only about 10 percent of total industrial output was in the public sector, which is less than in many countries of Western Europe. But, as plan follows plan, if the public sector continues to contribute about 50 percent of new investment in industry, the relative importance of the public sector will grow.

Foreign investment has been welcome officially since the "Policy Statement on Foreign Capital" was issued by the Prime Minister on April 6, 1949. This statement was elaborated by the first five-year plan in 1950. The general philosophy has been that such investment should be allowed only in high-priority fields where special types of experience and technology are needed; that it should be in the form of joint ventures with Indian firms (or with the government); that such joint venture agreements are subject to the approval of the government; and that all details are to be judged on a case-by-case basis.

As a result of the government's positive policy, foreign investment has grown at an increasing rate. Although little foreign investment arrived during the first decade following independence (investors apparently adopted a wait-and-see attitude), between 1957 and 1966 over 2,000 new foreign collaborations (licensing agreements as well as equity investments) were initiated. The majority of foreign investment continues to come from Great Britain, followed by the United States, Germany, Switzerland, Japan, and Italy. Thus, total existing foreign investment rose from $790 million in 1948 to $2.0 billion in 1965. Of the $2.0 billion, British investments totaled $1.1 billion, and the U.S. portion was $400 million. This foreign investment was an important supplement to India's three five-year plans, amounting to 25 percent of total private industrial investment during that 15-year period. Most of it, however, has appeared since 1960.

Thus, India appears to have passed an important landmark in her post-independence history. Although an important percentage of India's industry was British-owned or -controlled at the time of independence, the government avoided widespread or indiscriminate nationalization. Still, it took about 10 years before the indigenous private sector found the courage to invest in industry, in the face of the government's insistence that India was going to follow "a socialist pattern of society." Within several years after the Indian businessmen gained confidence, foreign investment also increased in volume.

Yet many businessmen hesitate to invest in India. Not only does the term "socialism" scare them, but the political climate for private investment varies greatly from one industry to another. A more detailed study than usual is required in such a situation.

CONCLUSIONS

The brief review, in this chapter, of the political climate for private investment in several other countries is sufficient to demonstrate that the current situation in the three North African countries and the process by which it developed are not unique. Newly independent countries react to their continued economic colonialism in different ways, but in ways which follow a pattern. The amount and the speed of the reaction are functions of seven major determinants.

The first determinant is the type of colonization to which the country had been subjected. This includes such aspects as the number of colonists who settled in the country; whether they settled on the land or in the cities; the portion of good land owned by the colonists; the amount of industrialization which took place; the portion of total industry and commerce owned by companies or citizens of the colonizing country; and the dependence of the economy on trade with the colonizing country.

The second determinant is the social and economic policies followed by the former colonial power. To what extent did education permit the formation of an indigenous entrepreneurial class? To what extent could an indigenous elite accumulate elite accumulate capital and therefore be in a position to invest in industry after independence?

A third determinant is the process by which the country achieved its political independence. If there was active resistance to the colonizing power, how severe were the repressive measures? If there was armed conflict, how violent and how prolonged was it?

A fourth determinant is the reaction of the colonizing power to the independence. Did most of the colonists leave suddenly, causing a collapse of the economy? Did the former colonial power stop all financial aid and technical assistance? Did it eliminate prior trade preferences, thereby closing its markets to the new government and causing a disruption of the former colony's economy?

A fifth determinant is the ideological orientation of those who achieved power and assumed leadership positions in the new government. Were they ideologically committed prior to independence, or are they non-ideological, pragmatic reformists?

The sixth determinant is the existence of a strong minority force in the country which pressures the new government in either a socialistic or a capitalistic direction.

The seventh determinant is the degree of probability of armed intervention by the former colonial power or by any of the major powers, should the new policies be Marxist socialist in nature.

In reviewing the above determinants, it is obvious which prior conditions and which reactions would tend to foster a more socialistic policy or would lead the government rapidly to increase the importance of the public sector on non-ideological bases. One of the major forces would be a strong, popular nationalistic desire to "decolonize" the economy. In addition, pragmatic solutions to the problems of development will lead the government to participate directly in the industrialization process. In almost all cases the government identifies a role to be played by private enterprise, both domestic and foreign. This role may initially be very small, or it may be large, but it is there. The problem is that in any given country, the government will have taken certain measures, employed certain slogans, and announced certain policies which obfuscate the political climate for private investment--which adds to the level of uncertainty in the decision-making process and causes the potential investor to over-estimate the political risk.

This uncertainty can be reduced, however, by the application of the model described in Chapter 2. The potential investor must study all of the actions of the government vis-à-vis the private sector, both favorable and unfavorable. He must study the policy statements promounced by government officials and contained in government documents which relate to the expected relative roles of the public and private sectors. And he must become familiar with the political, economic, and social past of the country to understand the historical context within which the actions and policy statements took place, so that they can be correctly evaluated.

APPENDIX A

TUNISIA: SELECTED STATISTICS

APPENDIX FIGURE 1

Comparative Growth of Population and Production in Tunisia, 1936-54

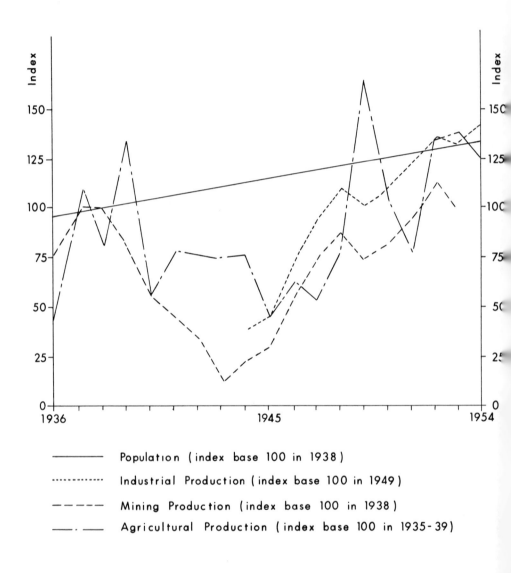

Population (index base 100 in 1938)

Industrial Production (index base 100 in 1949)

Mining Production (index base 100 in 1938)

Agricultural Production (index base 100 in 1935-39)

Source: Jules Lépidi, L'Économie Tunisienne, p. 72

TABLE 1

Foreign Aid Received By Tunisia, 1957-June 30, 1967

United States		(millions)
Financial		$249.7
Technical Assistance		22.6
Agricultural (PL480)		261.6
	TOTAL	$533.9
France		
Financial		$22.6
Technical Assistance		?
Other		?
	TOTAL	
Germany		
Financial		$50.0
Other		25.0
	TOTAL	$75.0
Soviet Union		$33.3
Kuwait		$29.6
Italy		$22.0
Czechoslovakia		$10.0
Poland		$10.0
Yugoslavia		$ 5.0
Netherlands		$ 2.7
Sweden		$ 2.3
Denmark		$ 1.4

Source: Unpublished records of the Secrétaire d'État aux Affaires Étrangères, Tunis.

TABLE 2

Private Investment In Tunisia, 1947-63

| | New Companies | | | | Existing Companies | | | | Total | |
| | SA's | | SARL's | | | | | | | |
	Number	Capital ($ million)	Number	Capital ($ million)	Number	New Capital ($ million)	Incorporation of Revenues ($ million)	Total ($ million)	Number	Capital Invested ($ million)
1947	41	3.8	362	1.5	121	5.4	6.1	11.5	524	16.8
1948	31	0.9	371	1.9	399	10.0	14.2	24.2	801	27.0
1949	29	9.2	270	1.0	391	6.0	9.1	15.1	690	25.3
1950	20	0.5	286	1.2	194	10.6	3.7	14.3	500	16.0
1951	26	2.2	289	1.5	115	8.3	7.2	15.5	430	19.2
1952	26	1.2	205	1.7	109	13.1	1.6	14.7	340	17.6
1953	18	3.3	232	1.4	116	18.2	3.4	21.6	366	26.3
1954	12	0.4	158	1.1	86	7.2	5.7	12.9	256	14.4
1955	11	0.8	120	1.6	80	8.6	3.5	12.1	211	14.5
1956	18	0.7	108	0.7	131	10.4	7.4	17.8	257	19.2
1957	18	0.5	86	0.6	109	3.6	3.0	6.6	213	7.7
1958	28	1.3	113	0.6	152	7.4	2.1	9.5	293	11.4
1959	30	3.0	117	1.1	46	12.2	1.3	13.5	193	17.6
1960	58	3.5	147	1.4	58	8.6	2.9	11.5	263	16.4
1961	48	5.6	113	1.3	55	6.2	1.7	7.9	216	14.8
1962	32	3.4	122	1.6	54	4.6	6.8	11.4	208	16.4
1963	35	9.0	150	2.2	64	9.6	14.7	24.3	249	35.5

Note: SA=Société Anonyme; SARL=Société à Responsibilité Limitée

Sources: Government of Tunisia, Données Statistiques de Base, 1960-1963 (Tunis, 1964); and Annuaire Statistique de la Tunisie, 1957-1958.
Banque Centrale de la Tunisie; Rapport Annuel; Jules Lépidi, L'Économie Tunisienne, p. 117.

TABLE 3

Companies With More Than 50 Employees in Tunisia, 1953

Type of Industry	Number of Companies	Salaried Employees Men	Salaried Employees Women	Unskilled Workers	Semi-Skilled Workers	Skilled Workers	Highly Skilled Workers	Apprentices	Total
Fishing, Forest, Agriculture	6	110	9	1012	605	121	5	26	1,888
Water, Gas, Electricity	5	347	33	265	421	263	123	13	1,465
Fuels	3	214	31	293	71	107	41	3	760
Mining	30	596	95	9041	2460	1152	207	318	13,869
Metallurgy	5	67	2	556	120	68	36	55	904
Metal Transformation	18	292	56	522	396	354	106	152	1,878
Glass	1	18	2	81	7	9	-	-	117
Ceramics, Construction Material	20	325	44	3082	376	266	93	87	4,273
Construction	50	864	93	8671	2159	1337	625	187	13,936
Chemicals, Rubber	7	110	21	725	87	56	9	2	1,010
Food	32	283	18	2798	802	162	29	47	4,139
Textiles	2	15	18	43	19	59	2	-	156
Clothing	3	41	27	25	79	65	17	5	259
Leather, Skins	5	43	9	125	97	67	22	78	441
Wood, Furniture	4	23	8	178	43	89	14	14	369
Paper, Cartons	3	38	7	90	24	15	3	39	219
Printing	4	100	19	32	23	132	25	4	335
Transportation	18	1294	134	6048	2881	1096	483	228	12,164
Commerce	25	976	403	1034	184	305	58	13	2,973
Hotels	1	30	13	8	4	-	-	1	56
Real Estate, Banking, Insurance	12	1294	418	79	-	-	-	-	1,791
TOTAL	254	7080	1460	34708	10858	5723	1898	1272	62,999
French-Owned	213	4147	1104	1555	2234	1823	939	445	12,247
Tunisian-Owned	24	1737	191	31342	6460	1862	230	525	42,347
Foreign-Owned	17	1196	165	1811	2164	2038	729	302	8,405

Source: Royaume de Tunis, Annuaire Statistique de la Tunisie, 1951-1952 (Tunis, 1952).

TABLE 4

Principal Sectors of Industrial Production in Tunisia; 1946-54

(tons)

Industrial Sector	1946	1949	1950	1951	1952	1953	1954
Fish Canning	1,194	3,576	3,057	3,933	5,000	4,820	5,380
Fruit, Vegetable Canning	3,220	2,613	1,885	2,575	2,598	4,184	3,341
Vegetable Oils	3,700	13,000	6,000	7,020	4,000	5,150	12,456
Refined Vegetable Oils	-	-	-	1,322	-	1,520	3,846
Soap	-	-	-	5,100	5,050	4,480	5,977
Beer	-	70,000	65,000	85,000	88,000	75,000	95,000
Cement	81,830	167,600	169,300	186,600	208,000	226,600	282,958
Gypsum	65,059	87,900	96,200	93,200	78,600	90,800	91,813
Plaster	12,466	12,718	12,946	12,490	10,800	11,800	11,990
Bricks (thousands)	44,795	43,300	40,400	45,600	32,200	41,200	39,239
Superphosphate Fertilizer	24,800	43,600	49,600	54,000	52,700	52,100	99,710
Salt	97,000	98,000	94,000	160,000	94,000	139,000	165,000
Glassware	-	-	-	1,241	1,350	1,441	1,145
Refined Lead	7,482	19,498	23,536	22,906	25,506	27,280	27,190

Source: Jules Lépidi, L'Économie Tunisienne, p. 58.

TABLE 5

Division Of Taxpayers,
By Level Of Income And By Profession
in Tunisia, 1956

By Income (dollars)	Tunisian Taxpayers	European Taxpayers
515-1,030	8,550	17,091
1,030-1,425	2,358	6,933
1,425-2,850	2,311	10,671
2,850-5,700	756	3,934
5,700-14,300	230	937
over 14,300	34	136
	14,239	39,702
By Profession		
Merchant	845	2,692
Farmer	393	1,315
Employee	12,776	33,027
Law, Medicine, etc.	225	2,668
	14,239	39,702

Source: Government of Tunisia, Annuaire Statistique de la
Tunisie, 1956.

TABLE 6

Industry	Establishments in Tunis and Suburbs			Establishments Outside Tunis Area			Total for All Tunisia
	Under 50 Employees	Over 50 Employees	Total	Under 50 Employees	Over 50 Employees	Total	
Number Of Industrial Establishments In Tunisia, 1954							
Fishing, Agriculture, Forestry	74	5	79	113	2	115	194
Electricity, Gas, Water	73	3	6	7	2	9	15
Petroleum Research	0	3	3	1	0	1	4
Solid Fuel Research	2	0	2	0	0	0	2
Mining	39	13	52	21	11	32	84
Metal Production	5	3	8	1	0	1	9
Mechanical, Electrical	718	5	723	694	4	698	1,421
Glass	10	1	11	3	0	3	14
Building Materials	45	15	60	126	1	127	187
Construction, Public Works	823	64	887	625	18	643	1,530
Chemical, Rubber	66	4	70	29	3	32	102
Food Products	630	23	653	1,406	18	1,424	2,077
Textiles	175	2	177	101	0	101	278
Clothing	610	4	614	267	0	267	881
Leather, Hides	401	5	406	283	0	283	689
Wood	180	3	183	70	0	70	253
Paper, Cartons	9	3	12	0	0	0	12
Mixed	117	5	122	79	1	80	202
Miscellaneous	246	0	246	192	0	192	438
TOTAL	4,153	161	4,314	4,018	60	4,078	8,392

Source: Jules Lépidi, L'Économie Tunisienne, p. 57.

TABLE 7

Gross Domestic Product of Tunisia; 1964-67

(in $ million at constant 1960 prices)

Sector	1964	1965	1966	1967*
Agriculture	157.0	162.0	115.0	102.8
Food Industries	48.8	50.3	48.8	47.5
Petroleum	6.1	5.7	11.0	17.1
Electricity	6.6	7.2	10.1	7.2
Other Energy Sources	6.6	6.8	7.0	7.4
Construction Materials	8.2	8.0	8.3	8.5
Mining	13.3	14.6	15.6	17.3
Mechanical, Electrical	3.2	3.4	6.5	10.0
Chemical	2.1	2.9	2.9	3.2
Textiles, Clothing, Leather	14.5	16.1	19.0	20.2
Furniture	5.5	6.3	6.6	6.6
Paper	6.5	6.8	8.6	8.7
Construction, Public Works	59.0	64.3	62.8	52.4
Transportation, Communication	53.1	59.3	63.7	67.4
Rents	29.7	32.1	33.6	36.2
Commercial Services	52.0	64.7	80.0	89.3
Commerce	98.7	102.5	95.0	101.1
Government Services	94.7	100.0	108.0	115.3
Domestic Services	4.4	4.4	4.4	4.4
Indirect Taxes	110.0	114.1	115.1	112.2
GROSS DOMESTIC PRODUCT	780.0	831.5	822.0	834.8

*The figures for 1967 were estimates, which have been adjusted by the author, based on a wide variety of sources.

Source: Government of Tunisia, Rapport sur le Budget Economique de l'Année 1967 (Tunis, 1967), p. 49.

TABLE 8

Public vs. Private Investment
in Business Enterprises in Tunisia, 1960-67

(millions of current dollars)

	Public [1]	Private
1960	12.5	16.4
1961	36.8	14.8
1962	45.7	16.4
1963	65.0	35.5
1964	71.0	32.9
1965	115.0	28.8
1966	100.0	38.0
1967 [2]	79.3	55.8

Notes: [1] An enterprise is considered public if it is controlled directly by the government, or indirectly by government-controlled banks, i.e., STB, BNA, and, before 1966, the SNI.

[2] The 1967 figures are estimates made by the World Bank, based on actual expenditures as of November, 1967.

Sources: Unpublished data from World Bank, "Memorandum on Private Investment in Tunisia" (1968); Government of Tunisia, Données Statistiques de Base, 1960-1963 (Tunis, 1964)

LIST 1

Electricity, Gas, Water, and Transportation Companies
Nationalized by the Tunisian Government

This list was compiled from information in the files of the French Embassy, Tunis.

1. The Compagnie Tunisienne d'Électricité et Transport produced and distributed electricity, and provided public transportation (electric railway and buses), in Tunis and within a radius of about 60 miles from Tunis. That portion of the company which produced and distributed electricity was placed under government management on August 4, 1958, and nationalized on April 3, 1962. The nationalization decree indicated that a later law would deal with methods of indemnification, but this has not taken place to date. The former owners claim a loss of $1.3 million.

2. The Compagnie du Gas et Régie et Eaux de Tunis distributed gas, electricity, and water in the region of Tunis. It was placed under government management by a decree of November 25, 1959, and nationalized April 3, 1962. The former owners claim a loss of $30 million.

3. The Société Nord Africaine d'Électricité, Gas et Eaux distributed electricity in the city of Sfax. It was placed under government management on July 19, 1960, and nationalized on April 3, 1962. The former owners claim a loss of $8.4 million.

4. The Union Électrique Tunisienne distributed electricity in several cities in southern Tunisia. It was put under government management on July 19, 1960, and nationalized on April 3, 1962. The former owners claim a loss of $6.7 million.

5. The Omnium Tunisien d'Électricité distributed electricity in several cities and regions in southern Tunisia. It was placed under government management on July 19, 1960, and nationalized on April 3, 1962. The former owners claim a loss of $2.4 million.

6. The Société d'Énergie Électrique de la Ville de Bizerte distributed electricity in the city of Bizerte. It was placed under government management on July 19, 1960, and nationalized on April 3, 1962. The former owners claim a loss of $580,000.

7. The <u>Union Électrique d'Outre-Mer</u> produced and distributed electricity in the west-central part of Tunisia. It was placed under government management on July 19, 1960, and nationalized on April 3, 1962. The former owners claim a loss of $733,000.

8. The <u>Compagnie Tunisienne d'Électricité et Transports</u> had that portion of the company which provided public transportation (electric railway and buses) in and around Tunis placed under government management on June 30, 1960, and nationalized on March 14, 1963. This law also indicated that a future law would provide indemnification. The former owners claim a loss of $6.2 million.

9. The <u>Transport Automobile Tunisienne</u> provided transportation for individuals and for merchandise. It was placed under government management on July 11, 1960, and nationalized on March 14, 1963. The former owners claim a loss of $2.2 million.

10. The <u>Société Tunisienne des Transports Automobiles du Sahel</u> provided transportation for individuals and merchandise. It was placed under government management on July 11, 1960, and nationalized on March 14, 1963. The former owners claim a loss of $610,000.

LIST 2

Companies Subjected to Management Take-Overs
by the Tunisian Government

This list was compiled from information in the files of
the French Embassy, Tunis.

1. The Compagnie des Eaux Thermales et du
Domaine de Korbous exploited a source of mineral
water and hot springs in the region of Korbous. It was
put under government management by a decree dated
August 22, 1959, such management later taking over
control of the property. The owners claim a loss of
$440,000.

2. The Société des Magasins Généraux et Entrepôt
Réel de Tunis operated a warehouse and a number of
department stores. It was put under government management by decree of August 11, 1958, such management
later taking over control of the property. The owners
claim a loss of $276,000.

3. The Société Tunisienne des Établissements
SIGG & Cie. cured and exported olives. The facilities
of the company were requisitioned by order of the
governor of Sousse on November 8, 1962, at a time when
the factory was not in operation. The company claims
a loss of $422,000.

4. Ripoll Montero et Garcia manufactured boats
and sport shoes. The government issued a decree on
September 23, 1961, following the Bizerte crisis, taking
over the management of the company. The reason given
at the time was that "...the company said it had stopped
operating because of financial difficulties, but this was
found to be incorrect. By this work stoppage the company
purposefully tried to harm the economic and social
situation by leaving its workers without income." The
owners claim a loss of $780,000.

LIST 3

Companies Placed Under Control of a Tunisian Government
Committee and Later Returned to the Rightful Owners

This list was compiled from information in files of the
French Embassy, Tunis, and from the Journal Officiel de la
République Tunisienne.

1. Société Tunisienne de l'Accumulateur. On
December 30, 1061, the government canceled the decree
of April 11, 1961, whereby it had taken over the management of this company.

2. La Dépêche Tunisienne. By decree dated October
4, 1961, the government took over the management of
this company "because of a state of emergency." On
February 14, 1962, another decree canceled the government committee.

3. Société Tunisienne du Liège. This company
manufactured and exported cork products. The governor
of Souk-el-Arba sequestered it by decree dated August 24,
1961, but canceled the decree on October 29, 1962.

LIST 4

Companies Which Were Sequestered and Later Purchased
by the Tunisian Government

This list was compiled from information in the files of
El Bouniane and the French Embassy, Tunis, and from
Journal Officiel de la République Tunisienne.

      1. Ets. Schwich et Baizeau (El Bouniane). Follow-
ing the Bizerte crisis, the government, by decree of
August 11, 1961, seized the major operating companies
of Ets. Schwich et Baizeau, giving "a state of emergency"
as the reason for seizure. The subsidiaries of this
industrial complex were the following:
      a. Société Les Ciments Artificiels Tunisiens
      b. Société La Tunisoise Industrielle
      c. Société Les Carrières Tunisiennes
      d. Société La Céramique Tunisienne
      e. Société Les Plâtrières Tunisiennes
      f. Société Briqueterie de l'Oued Drajia
      g. Société Raffinerie Tunisienne de Soufre
      h. Société Les Carrelages Tunisiens.
These companies were placed under a government-
appointed board of directors. The government entered
into negotiations with Ets. Schwich et Baizeau to attempt
to normalize the arrangement. A protocol was signed
in November, 1962, and resulted in a convention dated
August 16, 1963. By this convention, Ets. Schwich et
Baizeau agreed to divest itself of all holdings outside
of Tunisia, such holdings to be retained by the shareholders, intact. Also, financial interests inside Tunisia
were transferred out of the country and retained by the
shareholders. What remained was the eight companies
which had been subjected to the prise de gestion, plus
several smaller manufacturing companies, plus considerable real estate holdings. These were valued at a
total of $7.2 million. A new company, Société Tunisienne
d'Economie Mixte--El Bouniane--was then formed, with
a capital of $6 million. The former shareholders of
Ets. Schwich et Baizeau, who numbered about 350 and about
90 percent of whom lived in France, were given 49 percent
of the shares in El Bouniane; the government bought the
other 51 percent. The government agreed to pay, for

the 51 percent, a total of $1.92 million, of which $1.2 million would be paid in transferable dinars and $720,000 paid in cement, the delivery to be made in France and the proceeds paid to the shareholders of Ets. Schwich et Baizeau.

2. Les Pêcheries Tunisiennes operated fishing boats and a fishery. The company's license was revoked on May 20, 1957, and the property was requisitioned. The owners originally claimed a loss of $375,000. The amount of settlement was not announced.

3. The Société Tunisienne d'Équipements et de Modernisation Industriels et Agricoles operated a dairy, a refrigerated warehouse, and a fresh fruit and vegetable packaging plant. It was placed under government management on March 31, 1961. The capitalization of the company was $446,000. The amount of settlement was not announced.

4. The Usines à Tuyaux de Ben Arous manufactured pipes and tubes. These factories belonged to two companies, the Société des Tuyaux Bonna and the Société Commerciale et Minière d'Afrique du Nord. They were placed under the management of a board of directors appointed by the government by a decree dated July 25, 1961, "because of a state of emergency. . . ."

5. The Société des Mines de Douaria mined iron ore. A government decision of November 16, 1961, gave SOREMIT (a government-owned mining company) the responsibility of assuring the exploitation of the mines, amounting, in effect, to a sequestration. The company originally claimed a loss of $1.78 million. The amount of settlement was not announced.

LIST 5

Companies Subjected to Negotiated Purchase
by the Tunisian Government

This list was compiled from information in the files of
the Compagnie des Phospates et du Chemin der Fer de
Gafsa and of the Belgian Embassy, Tunis, and from the
Journal Officiel de la République Tunisienne.

1. Compagnie des Phosphates et du Chemin de Fer
de Gafsa. From 1950 to 1955 this company maintained
a constant level of production and each year made a
very small profit. Near the end of this period there
were increasing problems with the labor force. The
world price for phosphates fell about 20 percent during
the late 1950's, and profits disappeared. There was
no attempt to modernize equipment to achieve greater
and more efficient operations. There was some question
about the continuation of operations.

On October 30, 1959, President Bourguiba gave a
speech in which he indicated a desire that this company
maintain full production, and he asked that, by the end
of the year, there be found "a reasonable solution which
would guarantee the continuity of the activities of the
company.... We must do this even if, to do so, we must
take charge of the activities and manage them ourselves,
as we have already done in numerous areas."

The President of the company subsequently noted
that "the speech indicated the desired solution, the
conditions of which narrowly limited the margin of discussion by the company." An exchange of three letters
between the company and the government achieved an
agreement on the method by which the government could
become a part owner. It was decided that there would
be a reduction of capital from $9.35 million to $5.61
million by reducing the nominal value of each share from
$9.80 to $6.00. Then the capital would be increased to
$12 million by issuing 1.06 million new shares. The
government then reserved the right to purchase 1 million
of the new shares 50 percent of total shares outstanding.
The government would pay immediately for 25 percent
of the shares it bought, which would provide the company

with the liquidity needed for implementation of an investment program. The government would pay the remaining 75 percent over a five-year period. Finally, it was agreed that the place of incorporation would be moved from France to Tunis and that the president of the re-organized company would be appointed from among the government representatives on the board of directors.

The president of the old company submitted the above proposal to the shareholders on May 23, 1960, indicating that there could be no discussion of individual points. The program would have to be approved or disapproved in its entirety. He noted that if they were to vote negatively, it still would not be possible to maintain the former structure of the company. On the other hand, an affirmative vote would give effective control to the government because of the concentration of their 50 percent of the shares and because the president of the board of directors would be a government official.

The shareholders approved the proposed reorganization. The liquidity obtained from the government participation was used for increased investment in equipment. Output has increased. In 1962 the company showed a profit of $38,000, and in 1963 a profit of $960,000.

2. Cie. Royale Asturienne des Mines, S.A. This Belgian firm has mining activities in several countries. In Tunisia its branch had land concessions and all the mining equipment required for mining and transporting lead and zinc ore. Its net value was appreciably above $2.4 million. According to Belgian officials, the government offered, in 1962, to buy 50 percent of the Tunisian operations for $1.2 million. This was agreed to, reluctantly, by the stockholders, and the Tunisian branch was changed to a société anonyme. The 50 percent of this new company which remained in the hands of the parent company in Belgium was later ceded to the government with no reimbursement. Nor has the $1.2 million for the original 50 percent actually been paid.

3. Cie. Nouvelle de Phosphates du Djebel M'Dilla. By decree dated August 10, 1962, the government announced that it had reached agreement with the company to buy 100 percent of the outstanding shares for a total of $800,000. The payment was to be made in the form of phosphates, in 10 equal annual installments. These installments have been paid each year without undue delay.

LIST 6

Industrial and Commercial Enterprises Owned or Controlled
Directly By The Government of Tunisia

This list was compiled from papers of the Secrétariat
d'État au Plan et à l'Économie Nationale, Tunis.

A. Government "Offices"
1. Office National de l'Artisanat
2. Office National de l'Huile
3. Office National des Mines
4. Office National des Pêches
5. Office des Ports Nationaux
6. Office National des Textiles
7. Office National du Vin

B. Electricity, Transportation, Communications
1. Société Tunisienne d'Électricité et de Gaz
2. Compagnie Tunisienne de Navigation
3. Société Nationale des Chemins de Fer Tunisiens
4. Société Nationale des Transports
5. Société Tunisienne de l'Air
6. Société de Transport des Marchandises
7. Agence Tunis-Afrique Presse
8. Maison Tunisienne de l'Édition
9. Société Anonyme Tunisienne de Production et
d'Exploitation Cinématographiques
10. Société Tunisienne de Diffusion
11. Société Tunisienne de Publicité

C. Mining, Petroleum
1. Compagnie Nouvelle des Phosphates du Djebel
M'Dilla
2. Compagnie des Phosphates et du Chemin de Fer
de Gafsa
3. Société du Djebel Djerissa
4. Société Tunisienne d'Exploitations Phosphatières
5. Société Anonyme AGIP
6. Société d'Études et de Recherches Pétrolières
7. Société Italo-Tunisienne d'Exploitation Pétrolière
8. Société Tuniso-Italienne de Raffinage

D. Steel, Shipyards
1. Société Tunisienne de Sidérurgie "El Fouladh"
2. Société de Constructions et de Réparations
Mécaniques et Navales

E. Tourism, Housing
   1. Société Hôtèliere et Touristique de Tunisie
   2. Société Immobilière et Hôtèliers de Kasserine
   3. Société Nationale Immobilière de Tunisie
F. Banking, Insurance
   1. Banque Nationale Agricole
   2. Société Nationale d'Investissement
   3. Société Tunisienne de Banque
   4. Société Tunisienne d'Assurance et de Réassurance
G. Manufacturing
   1. Compagnie des Eaux Thermales et du Domaine de Korbous
   2. Industries Chimiques Maghrebines
   3. Les Ciments Artificiels Tunisiens
   4. Régie Nationale des Tabacs et Allumettes
   5. Société des Ciments Portland de Bizerte
   6. Société "El Bouniane"
   7. Société des Engrais Pulverisés
   8. Société de la Fonderie Fathalla
   9. Société des Fonderies Mécaniques
  10. Société Générale des Industries Cotonières
  11. Société Générale des Industries Lainières
  12. Société Industrielle d'Acide Phosphorique et d'Engrais
  13. Société Nationale du Liège
  14. Société Nationale Tunisienne de Cellulose
  15. Société de la Raffinerie Tunisienne de Soufre
  16. Société "La Tunisie Industrielle"
  17. Société Tunisienne du Sucre

Private Foreign Investments in Tunisia

At the time of independence nearly all foreign investment had been by French companies or by Frenchmen living in Tunisia. The exceptions to this were the following:

1. The British firm Fisons, Ltd., had a small percentage ownership in the Cie. des Phosphates et du Chemin de Fer de Gafsa,

2. The Shell Oil Company had investments in the distribution of petroleum products,

3. The Belgian firm Purfina owned a company for the distribution of petroleum products,

4. The Belgian firm Cie. Royale Asturienne des Mines owned a lead and zinc mine,

5. Belgium interests owned Chimie Couleur, a manufacturer and distributor of paints and varnishes.

Following independence, foreign investors were very hesitant. For the first five or six years almost no new investors arrived. By 1963, however, not only had confidence in the regime increased, but the economy, following institution of the first three-year plan, was growing at a rapid rate. Nearly all of the following foreign investments have been made since 1963, with a significant increase in the rate of investment each year.

The following list was compiled by the author from a wide variety of sources between 1966 and 1968.

Denmark

1. SOTUMO--A minority investment by a Danish company for the manufacture of diesel engines.

France

2. Société Tunisienne d'Électronique--Manufactures radios. The French firm, Cie. Téléphonique sans Fils, has a 34 percent interest. It invested $240,000 in 1963.

3. SICOAC--Manufactures asbestos cement, pipes, roofing, etc. The French company ETERNIT invested in 49 percent of the capital in 1963.

4. Union Internationale des Banques--The French bank Crédit Lyonnais invested $238,000 in 1963.

5. Berliet--Assembles trucks. Investment by the French Company Berliet in 1964.

6. SALMAN--Manufactures textiles. The French company Unité de Tissage invested $200,000 in 60 percent of the capital in 1965.

7. SOTACER--Manufactures stoves. The French company ACER has 30 percent interest, invested in 1966.

8. Bernadaud--Manufactures kitchen ceramics and dinnerware. A 50 percent joint-venture investment by the French company Bernadaud in 1967.

9. DMC--Manufactures thread. A 50 percent joint venture of $76,000 by the French company Dolfus Mieg et Cie. in 1967.

10. A tourist hotel. An investment of $500,000 by the Cie. de Navigation Mixte Française in 1967.

Germany

11. Union Internationale des Banques--The Commerzbank invested $67,000 in 1963.

12. SOTALCO--Manufactures clothing exclusively for export. An investment by Enders A.G. in 1964.

13. Strand Hotel--Individual investment in 1964.

Great Britain

14. British Bank of the Middle East--Opened subsidiary in Tunisia in 1957 with an investment of $264,000.

15. Société Tunisienne d'Assurances et de Réassurances-- Several British insurance companies invested $24,000 in a small percentage of the capital in 1963.

16. Union Internationale des Banques--Several British banks invested in a small percentage in 1963.

Italy

17. Union Internationale des Banques--The Banca Commerciale Italiana invested $134,000 in 1963.

18. Société Tuniso-Italienne de Raffinage--An oil refinery. An investment of $3.8 million by ENI for 50 percent of a joint venture in 1963.

19. STAG-SACEM--Manufactures small electric motors. A joint-venture investment by the Italian company SACEM in 1966.

20. Pozzi--Manufactures ceramic bathroom fixtures. A joint-venture investment by the Italian firm Pozzi, S.A., in 1967.

Netherlands

21. STIET--Assembles radios. A joint-venture investment with majority ownership by Phillips N.V. in 1964.

Sweden
22.   NPK Engrais--Manufactures superphosphate
      fertilizer.   An investment of $3.6 million by the
      Swedish firm NPK for 60 percent ownership, in 1961.
United States
23.   NPK Engrais--Manufactures superphosphate
      fertilizer.   An investment of $1.2 million by Freeport
      Sulphur International Corp., for 20 percent ownership,
      in 1961.
24.   Union Internationale des Banques--The Bank of
      America International invested $65,000 in 1963.
25.   IMAL--Fabricates aluminum door and window frames.
      Investment by Alcoa, in 1963, in 50 percent of a
      joint venture.
26.   Banque de Tunisie--The Bankers International Corp.
      invested $50,000 in 1964.
27.   Banque d'Escompte et de Crédit à l'Industrie en
      Tunisie--The Morgan International Banking Corp.
      invested $140,000 in 1964.
28.   International Harvester, S.A.--Assembles tractors.
      An investment in a joint venture, owned 70 percent
      by the parent company, in 1964.
29.   Mendustrie--Fabricates wooden window and door
      frames.   Investment of $20,000 by Marshall Erdman
      & Assoc. in 1966.
30.   Firestone, S.A.--Fabricates automobile and truck
      tires.   An investment in 60 percent of a joint venture
      in 1967.

APPENDIX B

ALGERIA: SELECTED STATISTICS

TABLE 1

Active Algerian Population by Socio-Professional Category,
October 31, 1954

| | Male | | Female | | |
	European	Algerian	European	Algerian	Total
1. Agricultural					
Owner-Managers	17,000	554,300	1,400	10,000	582,700
Housewives, Servants	3,900	478,000	1,800	960,300	1,444,000
Workers	8,300	564,000	100	7,000	579,400
	29,200	1,596,300	3,300	977,300	2,606,100
2. Non-Agricultural					
a. Independents, Managers					
Artisans	16,600	27,500	2,600	2,600	49,300
Fishermen-Owners	700	300	-	-	1,000
Commerce	23,300	78,100	6,900	1,000	109,300
Industrialists	5,200	1,500	200	-	6,900
Liberal Professions	9,200	2,100	1,800	100	13,200
	55,000	109,500	11,500	3,700	179,700
b. Supervisors, Workers					
Intellectuals,					
Top Supervisors	15,100	1,300	1,600	-	18,000
Technicians	26,600	7,900	13,000	500	48,000
Office Workers	26,300	9,000	21,000	400	56,700
Commerce Clerks	5,100	5,600	3,700	200	14,600
Unskilled Workers	6,500	139,400	700	1,900	148,500
Skilled Workers	25,200	58,900	2,900	2,000	89,000
Highly Skilled Workers	44,400	38,300	5,300	1,200	89,200
Miners	300	8,600	-	-	8,900
Fishermen-Workers	2,000	2,400	-	-	4,400
Servants	400	1,000	8,600	23,500	33,500
Services	4,000	16,300	4,300	1,200	25,800
Army, Police	16,500	5,600	200	-	22,300
	172,400	294,300	61,300	30,900	558,900
Urban Unemployed	12,900	130,500	1,200	2,600	147,200
TOTALS	269,500	2,130,600	77,300	1,014,500	3,491,900

Source: Government of Algeria, Tableau de l'Economie Algérienne, 1960 (Algiers, 1961)

TABLE 2

Algerian Oil Production, by Company, 1964-65
(1,000 tons)

Company	1964	1965
CREPS	10,346	9,076
SN REPAL	6,152	6,350
C.F.P. (Algeria)	6,116	6,342
C.P.A.	672	819
C.E.P.	346	454
EURAFREP	425	448
SAFREP	430	413
MOBIL	228	299
S.N.P.A.	364	296
SINCLAIR	283	272
COPEFA	92	255
COPAREX	261	253
FRANCAREP	218	237
OMNIREX	69	191
PHILLIPS	58	159
VEEDOL	116	112
AMIF	36	48
SOFRAPEL	20	24
PETROPAR	10	12
CAREP	4	4
SEHR	240	417
TOTAL	26,486	26,481

Source: French Government, "La Situation Économique de
l'Algérie," Notes et Études Documentaires, No. 3406-
3407 (July 6, 1967), 53.

TABLE 3

Mineral Production in Algeria, Selected Years, 1953-65
(thousand tons)

	1953	1958	1961	1962	1963	1964	1965
Iron Ore	3388	2335	2867	2062	1976	2746	3147
Phosphates	619	561	426	390	348	73	86
Coal	295	153	66	53	30	n.a.	n.a.
Lead Ore	12	15	13	13	12	14	15
Zinc Ore	34	55	71	70	56	64	64
Iron Pyrites	30	25	49	43	38	61	57
Copper Ores	1	2	2	3	4	4	4

Note: n.a. = not available.

Sources: Government of Algeria, Annuaire Statistique de
l'Algérie--1961, p. 98; and Bulletin Mensuel de
Statistique Général (January, 1964); Government of
France, "La Situation Économique de l'Algérie,"
Notes et Études Documentaries, No. 3406-3407
(July 6, 1967), 61-63.

TABLE 4

Value of Algerian Agricultural Production, 1957 and 1964
($ million)

Product	1957	1964
Cereals	111	135
Dried Vegetables	4	3
Wine	224	108
Fruits	44	48
Fresh Vegetables	42	30
Cotton, Tobacco, Sugar Beets, etc.	10	6
	435	330
Meat	49	38
Dairy Products	38	14
Wool	4	4
Eggs, Chickens	20	10
	111	66
TOTAL	546	396

Source: Government of France, "La Situation Économique de l'Algérie," Notes et Études Documentaires, No. 3406-3407, (July 6, 1967), 43.

TABLE 5

Companies in Algeria Under Self-Management,
December 31, 1965

Industrial Sector	Number of Companies	Number of Workers
Mechanical, Electrical	41	1520
Chemical	13	1345
Textiles	10	615
Food	87	3120
Wood	220	1710
Construction, Construction Materials	106	6260
Miscellaneous	30	365
TOTALS	507	14,935

Source: Government of France, "La Situation Économique de l'Algérie," Notes et Études Documentaires, No. 3406-3407 (July 6, 1967), 46.

APPENDIX C

MOROCCO: SELECTED STATISTICS

TABLE 1

Industrial Investment in Morocco, 1926

Industry	Number of Factories	Number of Workers
Food	275	2,881
Construction	163	1,411
Wood	115	1,869
Metalworking, Foundries	67	587
Textiles	3	266
Miscellaneous	177	3,976
TOTAL	800	10,990

Source: Gouvernement Chérifien, Annuaire Statistique Générale du Maroc, 1926 (Rabat, 1927).

TABLE 2

Investments in Morocco, 1949-57

Sector	Moroccan Long-Term Investment Program (1949-53)		Moroccan Second Investment Plan (1954-57)	
	Investment ($ Million)	Percent	Investment ($ Million)	Percent
Transportation	93	22	78	12.1
Communications	28	6.9	28	4.3
Irrigation	79	18.9	116	18.1
Fuel, Power	61	14.6	56	8.7
Agriculture, Forestry	18	4.3	91	14.2
Fishing	--	---	4	0.6
Mining	6	1.5	36	5.7
Education	50	12.0	45	7.0
Housing	28	6.8	83	13.0
Public Health	26	6.2	23	3.6
Public Construction	18	4.3	81	12.5
Miscellaneous	10	2.3	1	0.2
TOTALS	417	100.0	642	100.0

Note: This is a tabulation of actual expenditures rather than the projected expenditures. It provides for no public investment in industry, hoping that private initiative would take care of this sector. Growth under this plan was fairly rapid, but unbalanced. Gross domestic product increased 22 percent during the plan period, but an appreciable portion of this increase came about because of the demand generated by the Korean War on mining and part of the modern industrial sector. Also, the stagnation of the traditional agricultural sector prevented any long-term growth of internal demand.

Source: Government of France, Deuxième Plan de Modernisation et d'Équipement (Paris, 1954), pp. 289-97, 335.

TABLE 3

Growth of Industrial Production in Morocco, 1938-53

	Unit	1938	1948	1953
Nonferrous Metal				
Lead Products	tons	-	1,000	2,000
Soft Lead	tons	-	2,800	28,000
Lead Pipe	tons	-	-	600
Metal Transformation				
Wire	tons	-	-	3,000
Metal bars	tons	-	-	1,600
Foundries, Metallic Fabrication				
Steel	tons	200	1,000	2,000
Cast Iron	tons	6,500	5,500	6,500
Fabricated Steel Products	tons	6,000	19,000	32,000
Agricultural Equipment	tons	-	-	750
Household Equipment	tons	-	1,500	3,500
Metal Packaging	tons	5,500	14,700	12,300
Electrical Products				
Batteries	each	-	2,000	24,500
Cables, Wire	tons	-	-	1,900
Precision, Optical Equipment				
Glass Lenses	each	-	10,000	50,000
Meters	each	-	-	6,000
Cameras	each	-	-	6,000
Clocks	each	-	-	150,000
Glass				
Bottles, Goblets	tons	-	1,200	7,800
Ceramic Products				
Tiles	tons	8,000	9,000	13,000
Bricks	tons	60,000	80,000	144,000
Pottery	tons	40,000	50,000	69,000

(Continued)

TABLE 3 (Continued)

	Unit	1938	1948	1953
Construction Materials				
Plaster	tons	3,000	4,500	25,000
Limestone	tons	3,500	5,000	9,000
Cement	tons	157,000	260,000	610,000
Cement Pipe	each	-	42,000	100,000
Asbestos Cement Pipe	each	-	11,200	18,000
Chemical Industry				
Sulphuric Acid	tons	18,000	20,000	28,000
Superphosphates	tons	40,000	55,000	77,000
Hydrochloric Acid	tons	-	100	50
Oxygen	cubic meters	-	650,000	1,210,000
Acetylene	cubic meters	-	70,000	230,000
Explosives	tons	700	1,100	2,750
Paints, Varnish	tons	500	3,000	8,800
Rubber	tons	-	550	900
Plastics	tons	-	30	200
Matches	million boxes	-	69	98
Fat Products				
Vegetable Oils (treated)	tons	8,500	46,600	19,000
Olive Oil (raw)	tons	11,500	7,500	12,000
Margarine	tons	-	600	1,000
Soap	tons	12,000	11,500	19,000
Flour Products				
Flour	tons	150,000	177,900	235,000
Food Starches	tons	3,500	7,000	15,000
Sugar, Drinks				
Refined Sugar	tons	125,000	123,000	190,000
Beer, Soft Drinks	hectoliters	144,000	250,000	300,000
Fruit Juices	tons	-	2,000	1,400
Canning				
Fish	1,000 cases	600	1,260	1,600
Vegetables	1,000 cases	50	120	96
Fruits	tons	2,300	3,800	4,000
Textiles				
Wool Cloth	tons	110	650	500
Cotton Cloth	tons	100	250	1,800

	Unit	1938	1948	1953
Textiles (Continued)				
Wool Thread	tons	-	700	865
Cotton Thread	tons	-	290	2,100
Rayon Cloth	tons	-	500	480
Cloth Sacks	tons	-	900	1,236
Rayon Fiber	tons	-	-	220
Vegetable Fiber	tons	66,000	57,000	75,000
Leather Industry				
Leather	cubic meters	470,000	1,200,000	1,820,000
Shoes	pairs	120,000	533,000	720,000
Paper, Cartons				
Cartons	tons	500	4,000	17,300
Bags	tons	-	2,500	4,250
Miscellaneous				
Fish Flour	tons	400	6,500	12,700
Fish Oil	tons	800	450	5,800

Source: Gouvernement Chérifien, Maroc: Cinq Ans de Réalisation du Programme d'Équipment, 1949-1953 (Casablanca, 1954).

TABLE 4

Distribution of Working Population in Morocco, by Occupation, 1951

Occupation	Moslems Number	Percent	Jews Number	Percent	Europeans Number	Percent	Total Number	Percent
Fishing, Forestry	8,445	0.3	113	0.2	1,150	0.8	9,708	0.3
Agriculture	2,055,155	70.8	476	0.9	8,382	6.2	2,064,013	66.8
Mining	18,795	0.6	47	0.1	2,366	1.7	21,208	0.7
Handicraft, Manufacturing	286,275	10.0	25,693	47.9	36,517	26.9	348,485	11.3
Transportation	241,330	8.3	2,347	4.4	10,745	7.9	254,422	8.2
Commerce	106,560	3.7	12,400	23.1	15,261	11.2	134,221	4.3
Personal, Health Services	68,685	2.4	4,506	8.4	8,958	6.6	82,149	2.7
Government, Liberal Professions	60,900	2.1	4,143	7.7	35,412	26.1	100,455	3.3
Police	26,320	0.9	55	0.1	10,251	7.6	36,626	1.2
Unclassified	26,990	0.9	3,905	7.2	6,714	5.0	37,609	1.2
TOTALS	2,899,455	100.0	53,685	100.0	135,756	100.0	3,088,896	100.0

Source: Charles Stewart, The Economy of Morocco, 1912-1962, p. 65.

TABLE 5

Projected Investments for Morocco's Three-Year Plan, 1965-67
($ million)

Sector	Public Investments	Semi-Public Investments	Private Investments	Total Investments
Agriculture	170		?	170
Tourism	27		18	45
Technical Education	23		?	23
Economic Infrastructure	78		-	78
Energy	24	24	-	48
Industry	107	70	92	269
Education, Social Affairs	30		-	30
Administrative Infra-structure	25		?	25
Miscellaneous	8		?	8
TOTALS	492	94	110	706

Source: Government of Morocco, Plan Triennal, 1965-1967, p. 46.

371

TABLE 6

Moroccan Government Investment Expenditures,
Percentage Distribution by Selected Sectors

Sector	Average, 1954-57	1959	1964
Education	7	11	9
Public Health	3	2	3
Housing	13	17	8
Agriculture	32	34	25
Transportation	12	20	19
Manufacturing - (Industry)	0	2	18

Sources: The 1954-57 average was taken from Government of France, Deuxième Plan de Modernisation et d'Équipement (Paris, 1954), pp. 289-297; the data for 1959 and 1964 come from World Bank, The Economic Development of Morocco, p. 26.

TABLE 7

Foreign Private Investment in Morocco Since 1956

Moroccan Firm	Foreign Investor	Industry
ITALY		
1. SAMOCA	Fiat	Automobile Assembly
2. SAMIR	ENI	Oil Refinery
3. SOMIP	ENI	Oil Research
4. LEPETITPHARMAGHREB		Pharmaceuticals
5. ALGERAS-MAROC	Simmenthal	Dehydrated Seaweed
6.	Lancellotte	Women's Hose
7.	Bertuzzi	Fruit Juice
8.		Refrigerator Assembly
9.	ENI	Motels
10. BNDE	Three Banks	Banking
FRANCE		
1. SAMOCA	Simca	Automobile Assembly
2. BERLIET-MAROC	Berliet	Truck Assembly
3. TARIK	Tarik	Tractor Assembly
4. BNDE	Six Banks	Banking
GERMANY		
1. BNDE	Four Banks	Banking
U.K.		
1. Unilever	Unilever	Detergents
2. British Bank of the Middle East	British Bank of the Middle East	Banking
U.S.		
1. COLGATE-PALMOLIVE	Colgate-Palmolive	Soap
2. PROCTER & GAMBLE	Procter & Gamble	Detergents
3. PUNE GENERAL	General Tire	Automobile Tires
4. INTERNATIONAL HARVESTER-FRANCE	International Harvester	Tractor Assembly
5. MALCO	Alcoa	Aluminum Products
6. OCCIDENTAL PETROLEUM	Occidental Petroleum	Oil Research
7. RAMADA, MAROC	Ramada Inns	Hotels
8. HOTEL CORP. OF AMERICA	Hotel Corp. of America	Hotels
9. HOLIDAY INN	Holiday Inn	Motels

(Continued)

373

TABLE 7 (Continued)

Moroccan Firm	Foreign Investor	Industry
10. Banque Americaine- Franco-Suisse Pour le Maroc	Continental Illinois	Banking
11. FIRST NATIONAL CITY BANK	First National City Bank	Banking
12. BARDOL	Bardol	Petroleum Products
13. MOBIL OIL	Mobil Oil	Petroleum Distribution
14. ESSO	Esso	Petroleum Distribution
15. TEXACO	Texaco	Petroleum Distribution
16. BNDE	Morgan Guaranty	Development Banking
17. BMCE	Bank.of America	Development Banking
18.	Newmont Mining Corp.	Lead, Zinc Mines
19.	St. Joseph's Lead Co.	Lead, Zinc Mines

TABLE 8

Morocco's Industrial Production Index, 1959-66

Sector	Weight Factor	1959	1960	1961	1962	1963	1964	1965	1966
Energy	110	98	101	105	129	139	147	153	162
Mining	375	108	114	119	116	111	125	126	123
Industry	515	97	111	115	121	128	130	128	136
Metal Transformation	75	87	105	106	104	103	107	103	102
Building Materials	30	97	110	118	123	137	143	139	145
Chemicals	35	95	97	111	106	111	117	134	152
Oils, Fats	20	86	113	124	145	145	121	125	130
Food	215	96	110	115	122	121	127	127	138
Textiles	55	105	119	124	147	183	184	181	190
Leather	25	111	125	124	113	121	102	100	104
Paper	15	98	121	122	128	134	138	133	143
Miscellaneous	45	103	116	108	116	138	129	117	122
General Index	1000	101	111	115	120	123	130	130	134

Note: 1958 = 100

Source: Government of Morocco, La Situation Économique du Maroc en 1966, p. 118.

375

TABLE 9

Direct Investments of Morocco's BNDE, 1960-1966

Year	Amount Invested During Year ($ thousand)	Total Amount Invested as of December 31 ($ thousand)	Total Number of Companies Involved
1960	105	105	3
1961	121	226	5
1962	371	597	8
1963	437	1,034	10
1964	235	1,269	14
1965	1,075	2,344	17
1966	1,637	3,981	24

Source: Annual reports of the BNDE.

SELECTED BIBLIOGRAPHY

SELECTED BIBLIOGRAPHY

BOOKS

Ahroni, Yair. The Foreign Investment Decision Process. Boston: Harvard University, Graduate School of Business Administration, 1966.

Amin, Samir. L'Économie du Maghreb. Paris: Éditions de Minuit, 1966.

d'Arcy, Francois, Annie Krieger, and Alain Marill. Essais sur l'Economie de l'Algérie Nouvelle. Paris: Presses Universitaires de France, 1965.

Ashford, Douglas. Morocco-Tunisia: Politics and Planning. Syracuse; New York: Syracuse University Press, 1965.

_____. National Development & Local Reform: Political Participation in Morocco, Tunisia and Pakistan. Princeton: Princeton University Press, 1967.

_____. Political Change in Morocco. Princeton: Princeton University Press, 1961.

Ayache, Albert. Le Maroc. Paris: Editions Sociales, 1956.

Barlow, E. R., and Ira T. Wender. Foreign Investment and Taxation. Cambridge; Massachusetts: Harvard Law School, 1955.

Behr, Edward. The Algerian Problem. London: Hodder and Stoughton, 1961.

Beling, Willard A. Modernization and African Labor: A Tunisian Case Study. New York: Frederick A. Praeger, 1965.

Bernard, Augustine. L'Algérie. Paris: Librarie Felix Alcan, 1929.

_____. Le Maroc. Paris: Librarie Felix Alcan, 1913.

379

Bernard, Stephane. Maroc 1943-1956: Le Conflit Franco-Marocaine. Brussels: Institut de Sociologie de l'Université Libre de Bruxelles, 1963.

Bertrand, Pierre. Dix Ans d'Économie Marocaine (1945-1955). Paris: Institut National de la Statistique et des Études Économiques, 1957.

Blough, Roy. International Business: Environment and Adaptation. New York: McGraw-Hill, 1966.

Bonjean, Jacques. L'Unité de l'Empire Chérifien. Paris: Librarie Générale de Droit et de Jurisprudence, 1955.

Boualam, Bachaga. L'Algerie sans la France. Paris: Éditions France-Empire, 1964.

Brace, Richard. Morocco, Algeria, Tunisia. Englewood Cliffs, New Jersey: Prentice-Hall, 1964.

Brown, Leon Carl, ed. State and Society in Independent North Africa. Washington, D.C.: The Middle East Institute, 1966.

Brugnes-Romieu, M. P. Investissements Industriels et Développement en Tunisie. Tunis: Centre d'Études et de Recherches Économiques et Sociales, 1966.

Bryce, Murray. Industrial Development. New York: McGraw-Hill, 1960.

Chaliand, Gerard. L'Algérie Est-Elle Socialiste? Paris: François Maspero, 1964.

Cowan, L. Gray. The Economic Development of Morocco. Santa Monica, California: Rand Corporation, 1958.

Debbasch, Charles. La République Tunisienne. Paris: Pichon et Durand-Auzias, 1962.

Dresch, Jean, et al. Industrialisation au Maghreb. Paris: François Maspero, 1963.

Dugard, Henri. Le Maroc de 1919. Paris: E. Durand, 1920.

Dumoulin, Roger. Les Structures Asymetriques de l'Économie Algérienne. Paris: Presses Universitaires de France, 1959.

Duwaji, Ghazi. Economic Development in Tunisia. New York: Frederick A. Praeger, 1967.

d'Esme, Jean. Le Maroc Que Nous Avons Fait. Paris: Hachette, 1955.

Estier, Claude. Pour l'Algérie. Paris: François Maspero, 1964.

Evin, Guy. L'Industrie au Maroc et ses Problèmes. Paris: Librairie du Recueil Sirey, 1933.

Fatouros, A. A. Government Guarantees to Foreign Investors. New York: Columbia University Press, 1962.

Fayerweather, John. Facts and Fallacies in International Business. New York: Rinehart & Winston, 1962.

_____. Management of International Operations. New York: McGraw-Hill, 1960.

Fidel, Camille. Les Intérêts Économiques de la France au Maroc. Paris: Challamel, 1903.

Galissot, René. L'Économie de l'Afrique du Nord. "Que-sais-je?" Series. Paris: Presses Universitaires de France, 1962.

Gallagher, Charles F. The United States and North Africa. Cambridge; Massachusetts: Harvard University Press, 1963.

Garas, Felix. Bourguiba et la Naissance d'une Nation. Paris: René Julliard, 1956.

Gordon, David C. North Africa's French Legacy. Cambridge; Massachusetts: Harvard University Press, 1962.

_____. The Passing of French Algeria. London: Oxford University Press, 1966.

Goutor, Jacques R. Algeria and France. Muncie, Indiana: Ball State University Press, 1965.

Guen, Moncef. La Tunisie Indépendente Face à Son Économie. Tunis: Circle d'Études Économiques, 1961.

Guillot, J. Le Développement Économique de l'Algérie. Paris: Cahiers de l'Institut de Science Économique Appliquée, 1960.

Hahn, Lorna. North Africa: Nationalism to Nationhood. Washington, D.C: Public Affairs Press, 1966.

————. and Mark I. Cohen. Morocco: Old Land, New Nation. New York: Frederick A. Praeger, 1966.

Halpern, Manfred. The Politics of Social Change in the Middle East & North Africa. Princeton: Princeton University Press, 1963.

Hoffrerr, René, and Roger Moris. Revenues et Niveaux de Vie Indigènes au Maroc. Paris: Librairie du Recueil Sirey, 1934.

L'Industrie Tunisienne en l'An X de l'Indépendence. Tunis: Union Tunisienne de l'Industrie, du Commerce et de l'Artisanat, 1966.

International Bank for Reconstruction and Development. The Economic Development of Morocco. Baltimore: Johns Hopkins Press, 1966.

Joesten, Joachim. The New Algeria. Chicago: Follett Publishing Co., 1964.

Johnson, Rossall, Dale McKeen, and Leon Mears. Business Environment in an Emerging Nation. Evanston, Illinois: Northwestern University Press, 1966.

Julien, Charles-André. L'Afrique du Nord en Marche. Paris: René Julliard, 1952.

————. Histoire de l'Afriqui du Nord. Paris: Payot, 1956.

Katzarov, Konstantin. The Theory of Nationalization. The Hague: Martinus Nijhoff, 1964.

Klein, Jacques. La Tunisie. Paris: Presses Universitaires de France, 1949.

Knight, Melvin M. Morocco as a French Economic Venture. New York: Appleton-Century, 1937.

Krassowski, Andrzej. The Aid Relationship: American Experience in Tunisia. London: Overseas Development Institute, 1968.

Lachéraf, Mostefa. L'Algérie: Nation et Société. Paris: François Maspero, 1965.

Lahaye, Remy. Les Entreprises Publiques au Maroc. Rabat: La Porte, 1961.

Laitman, Leon. Tunisia Today: Crisis in North Africa. New York: The Citadel Press, 1954.

Lamunière, Marc. Histoire de l'Algérie. Paris: Éditions Gauthier, 1962.

Landau, Rom. Invitation to Morocco. London: Faber & Faber, 1950.

_____. Morocco Independent Under Mohammed the Fifth. London: Allen and Unwin, 1961.

Lépidi, Jules. L'Économie Tunisienne Depuis la Fin de la Guerre. Tunis: Imprimerie Officielle, 1955.

Ling, Dwight L. Tunisia: From Protectorate to Republique. Bloomington: University of Indiana Press, 1967.

Maridalyn, Henri. Présence Française au Maroc: 1912-1952. Monte Carlo: Regain, 1952.

Martin, Claude. Histoire de l'Algérie Française: 1830-1962. Paris: Éditions des Quartre Fils Aymon, 1963.

Micaud, Charles A., Leon Carl Brown, and Clement Henry Moore. Tunisia: The Politics of Modernization. New York: Frederick A. Praeger, 1964.

Mitterrand, François. Présence Française et Abandon.
Paris: Librairie Plon, 1957.

Moore, Clement. Tunisia Since Independence. Berkeley:
University of California Press, 1965.

Negandhi, Anant R. Private Foreign Investment Climate in
India. East Lansing; Michigan: State University, Institute
for International Business Management Studies, 1965.

Obstacles and Incentives to Private Foreign Investment,
1962-1964. New York: National Industrial Conference
Board, 1965.

Oppermann, Thomas. Le Problème Algérien. Paris:
François Maspero, 1961.

Pawera, John C. Algeria's Infrastructure. New York:
Frederick A. Praeger, 1964.

Perroux, François. L'Algérie de Demain. Paris: Presses
Universitaires de France, 1962.

Pickles, Dorothy. Algeria and France: From Colonialism
to Cooperation. London: Methuen, 1963.

Polk, William. The Developmental Revolution: North Africa,
the Middle East and South Asia. Washington, D.C.: The
Middle East Institute, 1963.

Rouze, Michel. Maroc. Lausanne: Éditions Recontre, 1962.

Roy, Claude, and Paul Sebag. Tunisie: De Carthage à Demain.
Paris: Delpire, 1961.

Rudebeck, Lars. Party and People: A Study of Political
Change in Tunisia. Stockholm: Almquist & Wiksell, 1967.

Sachs, Ignacy. Patterns of Public Sector in Underdeveloped
Economies. New York: Asia Publishing House, 1964.

Saint-Germes, J. Économie Algérienne. Algiers: La Maison
de Livres, 1950.

Sebag, Paul. La Tunisie. Paris: Éditions Sociales, 1951.

Le Séminaire National sur la Coordination des Secteurs
Économiques. Tunis: La Commission Économique et
Sociale du Parti Socialiste Destourian, 1965.

Steel, Ronald, ed. North Africa. New York: The H. W.
Wilson Co. , 1967.

Stewart, Charles F. The Economy of Morocco, 1912-1962.
Cambridge; Massachusetts: Harvard University Press,
1964.

Une Stratégie Économique pour le Maroc. Washington, D. C. :
Continental Allied Co. , 1960.

Teillac, Jean. Autogestion en Algérie. Paris: Peyronnet
& Cie. , 1965.

Terrasse, Henri. Histoire du Maroc. Casablanca: Éditions
Atlantides, 1950.

Thèses, Résolutions et Déclarations se Rapportant à
l'Autogestion. Algiers: Front de la Libération Nationale,
1966.

Tiano, André. La Politique Économique et Financière du
Maroc Indépendent. Paris: Presses Universitaires de
France, 1963.

Tlatli, Salah, Tunisie Nouvelle. Tunis: Sefan, 1957.

Vernon, Raymond. The Dilemma of Mexico's Development.
Cambridge; Massachusetts: Harvard University Press,
1963.

Waterston, Albert. Planning in Morocco. Baltimore: Johns
Hopkins Press, 1962.

Whitman, Marina. Government Risk-Sharing in Foreign
Investment. Princeton: Princeton University Press, 1965.

Wurfel, Seymour. Foreign Enterprise in Colombia: Laws
and Policies. Chapel Hill: University of North Carolina
Press, 1965.

Zartman, I. William Government & Politics in Northern
Africa. New York: Frederick A. Praeger, 1963.

_____. Morocco: Problems of New Power. New York:
Atherton Press, 1964.

Ziadeh, Nicola. Nationalism in Tunisia. Beirut: American
University Press, 1962.

NEWSPAPERS

Al Alam (Casablanca). August 30, 1965; September 2, 1965;
January 17, 1966.

Alger Ce Soir (Algiers). January 24, 1965; August 22, 1965.

L'Avant Garde (Casablanca). May 1, 1959; May 2, 1959;
March 21, 1964; March 28, 1964; April 4, 1964; May 2, 1964;
December 31, 1966.

La Dépêche Quotidienne d'Algérie (Algiers). March 11, 1960.

La Dépêche Tunisienne (Tunis). September 25, 1956;
October 9, 1956.

Les Échos (Algiers). July 16, 1964.

Al Istiqlal (Casablanca). July 21, 1963.

Maroc Information (Casablanca). May 2, 1963; November
3, 1964.

Le Monde (Paris). July 14, 1957; May 12, 1964; October
9, 1964; January 2, 1965; May 4, 1965; October 10, 1965;
January 1, 1966; January 24, 1966; May 17, 1966; May
30-31, 1966; July 29, 1966; December 12, 1966; December
24-26, 1966; March 18, 1967; September 6, 1967; May
16, 1968; May 28, 1968; June 16, 1968.

El Moudjahid (Algiers). June 20, 1965; October 22, 1965;
March 26, 1966; May 21, 1966; July 2-4, 1966; August 6,
1966; August 31-September 1, 1966; October 8, 1966;
October 22, 1966; December 29, 1966; May 23, 1967;
May 30, 1967; August 30-31, 1967; September 16, 1967.

New York Times. July 23, 1961; January 22, 1963; August
    31, 1967.

Le Petit Casablancais (Casablanca). April 19, 1963; July
    1, 1967; August 1, 1967.

Le Peuple (Algiers). March 8, 1965.

La Presse (Tunis). June 20, 1964; February 1, 1967;
    April 15, 1967.

Révolution et Travail (Algiers). May 28, 1964.

Vie Économique (Casablanca). March 17, 1961.

Wall Street Journal. May 31, 1966.

OFFICIAL DOCUMENTS

ALGERIAN GOVERNMENT (Algiers)

Actualité et Documents. Ministère de l'Information.

L'Algérie, Cinq Ans Après. Ministère de l'Information, 1968.

Bulletin de Statistique Générale: 1961-1965. Ministère des
    Finances et du Plan, 1966.

La Charte d'Alger. Ministère de l'Information, 1964.

Discours de Ben Bella--1963. Ministère de l'Information,
    1964.

Journal Officiel.

FRENCH GOVERNMENT (Paris)

L'Enseignement dans les Territories Français d'Outre-Mer.
    Ministère de l'Éducation Nationale, 1946.

Études et Programmes. La Caisse d'Équipement pour le
    Développement de l'Algérie, 1961.

Guide de l'Industriel en Algérie. La Caisse d'Équipement pour le Développement de l'Algérie, 1961.

La Micro-Industrie. Secrétariat Social d'Alger, 1959.

Plan de Constantine, 1959-1963. Direction du Plan et des Études Économiques, 1960.

Plan de Constantine: 2 Ans de Rélisation. La Caisse d'Équipement pour le Développement de l'Algérie, 1961.

"La Situation Économique de l'Algérie, " Notes et Études Documentairies, No. 34063407. Direction de la Documentation, 1967.

Tableaux de l'Économie Algérienne, 1960. Statistiques Générales de l'Algérie, 1961.

MOROCCAN GOVERNMENT (Rabat)

Annuaire Statistique du Maroc. Service Central des Statistiques.

Bulletin Officiel.

Le Maroc en Marche: Discours de Sa Majesté Hassan II. Ministère de l'Information, 1965.

Note de Documentation. Ministère du Commere, de l'Artisanat, de l'Industrie et des Mines.

Plan Biennal d'Équipment, 1958-1959. Ministère de l'Économie Nationale, 1957.

Plan Quinquennal, 1960-1964. Ministère de l'Économie Nationale, 1960.

Plan Quinquennal, 1968-1972. Secrétariat d'État au Plan et à la Formation des Cadres, 1968.

Plan Triennal, 1965-1967. Cabinet Royal, Délégation Générale à la Promotion Nationale et au Plan, 1965.

La Situation Économique du Maroc en 1965. Ministère du Développement, 1966.

TUNISIAN GOVERNMENT (Tunis)

Annuaire Statistique de la Tunisie. Secrétariat d'État au
Plan et aux Finances, 1956-60.

Les Discours du Président Bourguiba. Secrétariat d'État à
l'Information et à l'Orientation, 1955-68. (Not bound.)

Perspectives Décennales de Développement: 1962-1971.
Secrétariat d'État au Plan et aux Finances, 1961.

Plan Quadriennal: 1965-1968. Secrétariat d'État au Plan
et à l'Économie Nationale, 1964.

Plan Triennal: 1962-1964. Secrétariat d'État au Plan et
aux Finances, 1961.

Soixante-Dix Ans de Protectorat Français en Tunisie.
Imprimerie Officiel, 1952.

ARTICLES AND OTHER PUBLICATIONS

"Algeria Changes Course," Africa Report (November, 1965).

"L'Algérie." Unpublished report by the French Resident
Minister, Algiers, 1957.

Banque Centrale de la Tunisie. Rapport Annuel. Tunis,
1959-67.

Banque Industrielle de l'Afrique du Nord. Rapports Trime-
striels. Paris: October, 1963.

Banque du Maroc. Études Financières. Rabat, 1952.

Barbe, Raymond. "Les Classes Sociales en Algérie,"
Économie et Politique (Paris, September-October, 1959).

Benkirane, Abdelwahab. "Échanges et Coopération Entre
le Maroc et les Pays Socialistes de l'Europe," Bulletin
Économique et Social du Maroc (Rabat, October-December,
1966).

Bernis, Gerard Destanne. "Les Investissements en Tunisie,"
Cahiers de l'Institut de Science Économique Appliquée,
No. 109, (January, 1961), 31-53.

Boissard, J. J. "La Place de la Communauté Française
dans l'Économie Marocaine," Confluent, No. 15, (Rabat),
October, 1957.

CEDIES Information, (Casablanca, May 13, 1967), March 20,
1965.

Chambre de Commerce et de l'Industrie d'Alger, Flush, No.
1, (1964); No. 11, (1967); No. 12, (1967).

"Efforts Importants dans le Domaine de l'Enseignement,"
Maroc '66, No. 6 (Rabat, March, 1966).

"L'Enseignement Publique au Maroc," La Vie Marocaine
(Casablanca, January, 1954), 7-10.

Gallagher, Charles F. "North Africa Series," American
Universities Field Staff Reports, I-XII, (1967).

Hahn, Lorna. "North Africa; A New Pragmatism," Orbis
(Spring, 1964), 125-40.

Hamzaoui, Abdelaziz. "Independent Tunisia: Economic
Planning and Growth." Unpublished dissertation, Medford
Massachusetts: Tufts University, Fletcher School of Law
and Diplomacy, 1964.

"Les Investissements Français dans l'Industrie Marocaine."
Manuscript. Rabat, French Embassy.

Robock, Stefan. "It's Good for Growth but Who's Swallowing,"
Columbia Journal of World Business, (November-December,
1967), 13-23.

Root, Franklin R. "Attitudes of American Executives To-
wards Foreign Governments and Investment Opportunities,"
Economic and Business Bulletin (Temple University,
Philadelphia, January, 1968), 14-23.

Schaar, Stuart H. "North Africa Series," American
Universities Field Staff Reports, XIV (1968).

"Secteur Privé dans le Plan Quadriennal," La Tunisie Économique, No. 14 (Tunis, September-October, 1965).

Société Tunisienne de Banque. Exercises. Tunis, 1959-67.

Stoleru, Lionel. "A Quantitive Model of Growth of the Algerian Economy." Unpublished dissertation. Stanford, California: Stanford University.

"Tunisie 1956," Le Monde Économique, Numéro Spéciale, (Tunis, 1957).

ABOUT THE AUTHOR

Lee Charles Nehrt, Professor of International Business at the University of Indiana, has been professionally involved in the field of foreign investment since the mid-1950's. He is currently Chief of Party for an Indiana University-Ford Foundation project in Dacca, East Pakistan.

From 1965 to 1967, while on leave from Indiana University, Professor Nehrt served with the Ford Foundation as Adviser to the Minister of Planning and Economics of Tunisia. During the period 1956-60, he worked for North American Aviation as a foreign operations supervisor in the Atomics International Division. The author of several books in the fields of international marketing, international finance, and international business research, he has also been a consultant to the World Bank and to various private companies. As a result, he has traveled extensively throughout Europe, Africa, and Asia.

Professor Nehrt did post-graduate work in political science at the Institut d'Etudes Politiques of the University of Paris and in economics at the University of Southern California. He received a Ph. D. in international business from Columbia University.